HISTORY OF WORLD ARCHITECTURE

Pier Luigi Nervi, General Editor

BYZANTINE ARCHITECTURE

Cyril Mango

Harry N. Abrams, Inc., Publishers, New York

Editor: Carlo Pirovano

Design: Diego Birelli

Photographs: Bruno Balestrini

Drawings: Enzo Di Grazia

Library of Congress Cataloging in Publication Data

Mango, Cyril A.
  Byzantine architecture.
  (History of world architecture)
  Bibliography: p.
  Includes index.
  1. Architecture, Byzantine—History. I. Title.
NA370.M36 1975   723'.2   75-4805
ISBN 0-8109-1004-7

Library of Congress Catalogue Card Number: 75-4805
Copyright © 1974 in Italy by Electa Editrice, Milan
Published by Harry N. Abrams, Incorporated, New York, 1976
Printed and bound in Japan

PREFACE

Architectural criticism has nearly always been concerned with the visible aspect of individual buildings, taking this to be the decisive factor in the formulation of value judgments and in the classification of those "styles" which appear in textbooks, and which have thus become common knowledge. But once it is recognized that every building is, by definition, a work subject to the limitations imposed by the materials and building techniques at hand, and that every building must prove its stability, as well as its capacity to endure and serve the needs it was built for, it becomes clear that the aesthetic aspect alone is inadequate when we come to appraise a creative activity, difficult enough to judge in the past, rapidly becoming more complex in our own day, and destined to become more so in the foreseeable future.

Nevertheless, what has struck me most, on studying the architecture of the past and present, is the fact that the works which are generally regarded by the critics and the general public as examples of pure beauty are also the fruit of exemplary building techniques, once one has taken into account the quality of the materials and the technical knowledge available. And it is natural to suspect that such a coincidence is not entirely casual.

Building in the past was wholly a matter of following static intuitions, which were, in turn, the result of meditation, experience, and above all of an understanding of the capacity of certain structures and materials to resist external forces. Meditation upon structural patterns and the characteristics of various materials, together with the appraisal of one's own experiences and those of others, is an act of love toward the process of construction for its own sake, both on the part of the architect and his collaborators and assistants. Indeed, we may wonder whether this is not the hidden bond which unites the appearance and substance of the finest buildings of the past, distant though that past may be, into a single "thing of beauty."

One might even think that the quality of the materials available not only determined architectural patterns but also the decorative detail with which the first simple construction was gradually enriched.

One might find a justification for the difference in refinement and elegance between Greek architecture, with its basic use of marble—a highly resistant material, upon which the most delicate carvings can be carried out—and the majestic concrete structures of Roman architecture, built out of a mixture of lime and pozzolana, and supported by massive walls, to compensate for their intrinsic weaknesses.

Would it be too rash to connect these objective architectural characteristics with the different artistic sensibilities of the two peoples?

One must recognize, therefore, the importance of completing the description of the examples illustrated with an interpretation of their constructional and aesthetic characteristics, so that the connection between the twin aspects of building emerges as a natural, logical consequence.

This consequence, if understood and accepted in good faith by certain avant-garde circles, could put an end to the disastrous haste with which our architecture is rushing toward an empty, costly, and at times impractical formalism. It might also recall architects and men of culture to a more serene appraisal of the objective elements of building and to the respect that is due to a morality of architecture. For this is just as important for the future of our cities as is morality, understood as a rule of life, for an orderly civil existence.

PIER LUIGI NERVI

TABLE OF CONTENTS

In this book I have attempted to present the development of Byzantine architecture in relation to the men who created it and the historical and material conditions that prevailed at the time. Given the limited length of the text, it should be regarded as an extended essay rather than as a handbook. I have not discussed a great number of pertinent monuments and have even left out of consideration whole geographical areas, such as Italy (with the exception of Ravenna and Venice), North Africa, Cyprus, Cappadocia, Georgia, the Crimea, and the region of Novgorod. Nor have I tried to be exhaustive in the annotations: the existence of elaborate bibliographic aids (see the Bibliography under "References") has made this task redundant.

I should like to thank the institutions and individuals that have kindly supplied photographs and have helped me in other ways: the Dumbarton Oaks Byzantine Center, Washington, D.C., the Michigan-Princeton-Alexandria Expedition to Mount Sinai, and Yale University; Mr. R. Anderson, Mr. N. V. Artamonoff, Dr. R. Cormack, Professor G. H. Forsyth, Mr. M. Jeremić, Professor J. Morganstern, Miss M. C. Mundell, Professor I. Ševčenko, Mr. R. L. Van Nice. I am particularly grateful to Miss Mundell for her invaluable help in assembling the illustrations and compiling the Chronological Table; and to Mrs. N. Levine and Mrs. M. L. Masey for editing and typing my manuscript.

When we speak of the Byzantine Empire we are using a convention of modern historiography. In reality, there never existed a state that called itself the Byzantine Empire; there was instead the Roman Empire centered on Constantinople, the New Rome. The inhabitants of this Empire identified themselves as Romans or simply as Christians, and the better educated among them thought that their Empire had been instituted by Augustus. We are, therefore, posing an academic question when we ask, "When did the Byzantine Empire begin and when did it end?" The only answer that can be given is that historians, in their need to carve up the past into manageable and reasonably coherent periods, have decided that the Byzantine Empire began with the foundation of Constantinople in A.D. 324 and ended with its capture by the Ottoman Turks in 1453. It is an arbitrary but convenient division.

Under this definition, Byzantine architecture was the architecture of the Byzantine Empire and had a life-span of eleven centuries, discounting its prolongation in lands of the Orthodox faith well beyond the boundary date of 1453. This, however, leads us to a further question: "Granted that this chronological division is acceptable to historians, is it also a meaningful one in terms of architecture?" Or, to put it differently: "Do the monuments erected within the Byzantine Empire between 324 and 1453 share certain traits that identify them as Byzantine and distinguish them from those of other cultures and styles, such as the Roman, the Romanesque, the Gothic, or the Islamic?" It is difficult to give an unqualified answer. One may be inclined to say that after the seventh, and surely after the ninth, century Byzantine architecture did acquire a distinctive physiognomy which it retained until the end, whereas in the early period (the fourth to sixth centuries) one is still dealing with an architecture that is essentially antique, though in the process of transformation.

Thus there is considerable justification for drawing a line somewhere in the seventh century and applying the term Early Christian (or Late Roman) to the architecture that precedes this line, and Byzantine to that which follows it; the more so as such a line would correspond to a very real division, not to say a chasm, in the history of the Empire. If one adopted this expedient, however, one would be robbing Byzantine architecture of what is generally regarded as its first golden age, namely, the age of Justinian; and Byzantine architecture without St. Sophia is somewhat like a body without its head. But if we take in the age of Justinian, where are we to set the limit? Between the foundation of Constantinople and the accession of Justinian in 527 there was no dramatic break in the fortunes of the Eastern Empire; and so we are inevitably brought back to a starting point in the early fourth century.

More than a hundred years have passed since European antiquarians began showing a systematic interest in monuments of Byzantine architecture. The first book bearing the general title *Byzantine Architecture* was, if I am not mistaken, that published in 1864 by Charles Texier, the indefatigable explorer of Asia Minor, and by a certain R. Popplewell Pullan.[1] It still retains some value for the record it contains of several buildings that have since disappeared or been altered; in other respects, however, it is a hodgepodge of undigested and often irrelevant information. Nor could it have been otherwise: for in 1864 there did not exist a sufficient corpus of material upon which to base a general account of Byzantine architecture.

In the following decades the accumulation of material proceeded apace. The Christian monuments of Syria were recorded by the Marquis de Vogüé and by H. C. Butler; those of Asia Minor by H. Rott and Gertrude Bell, among others; those of Armenia by N. Marr, T. Toramanian, and J. Strzygowski; those of Constantinople by A. van Millingen, W. S. George, and J. Ebersolt; those of Greece by G. Lampakis and G. Millet. Thanks to the intensive exploration carried out by these and many other scholars, a vast body of material was built up. How was it to be classified and interpreted?

The approach that commended itself at the beginning of this century may be termed *typological*. This means that buildings were classified by genera and species. Thus we obtain the group "basilica," which is divided into subgroups: basilicas with or without a transept; with three or five aisles; with or without a gallery; with timber or masonry roof; with one or more apses. Or we have the so-called centralized building, which may be square, circular, polygonal, or cruciform; it may be timber-roofed, vaulted, or domed; if it has a dome, this element may be supported on squinches or pendentives. Once the classification had been established, the next step was to determine the "origin" of each group and distinctive feature, meaning usually their geographical origin. So the question was posed, "What is the origin of the dome?" and was answered, for example, by the statement "The dome comes from Mesopotamia," as if one were saying, "The kangaroo comes from Australia." As in the biological sciences, this approach further assumed that types of buildings underwent a gradual evolution like independent organisms.

The typological method is that of the historian of art, whose primary concern is with forms. Its main weakness, it seems to me, lies in its abstraction from reality, whereas buildings are by definition concrete; indeed, they are, in the first instance, utilitarian. This deficiency was clearly seen by Jean Lassus, whose *Sanctuaires chrétiens de Syrie* (1947) represents the first serious attempt to apply to the study of Byzantine architecture a new method, namely, the *functional*. This is the approach of the archaeologist, who wants to know what a building was used for and who believes that its form was largely dictated by its function.

At first sight the functional approach appears very attractive. It teaches us to pay little attention to those disembodied forms that were supposed to have floated from one end of the ancient world to another without much regard to historical probability or the means of their transmission. It tells us, for example, that the church was designed for the celebration of the liturgy, and as liturgical usage changed so did its architectural setting; that a martyrium, that is, a shrine enclosing an object of Christian "testimony"—whether this was a martyr's tomb or a place sanctified by Christ's life on earth—was planned differently from an ordinary congregational church;[2] that a monastery was intended to be inhabited by a group of monks who, in addition to their devotions, also practiced agriculture.

The functional method is refreshingly concrete where the typological one is abstract. Yet, when we attempt to apply it to specific cases, it often fails to produce the results it promises. A note of warning is sounded by one of the best living authorities on Roman architecture. "Under the early Empire," he writes, "each aspect of daily life still had its own clearly defined architectural setting. You could not possibly mistake a temple for a market, or a law-court for a bathing establishment. By the third century these distinctions were rapidly disappearing . . . and by the time of Constantine it was becoming increasingly difficult to tell at a glance the sort of building with which one was dealing."[3]

If this is true of the age of Constantine, it is equally true of the subsequent Byzantine period. Leaving aside the controversial problem of martyria, we may cite two examples. The first concerns monasteries. There was certainly a difference of function between the monastic church and the parochial church, if only for the reason that the former excluded members of the opposite sex. Whatever architectural provisions were made in a parochial church for segregating men from women (if, indeed, any were made), these were not needed in a monastic church. In reality, however, no difference existed between these two types of churches, and the only way of telling them apart is by the presence of subsidiary buildings. The second example is more specific. In the courtyard of Hadrian's Library at Athens a large quatrefoil building was constructed at the beginning of the fifth century. In ground plan it resembles a group of important churches of the fifth and sixth centuries found in many parts of the Empire, especially in Syria. It was, in fact, considered for a long time to have been a church, until it was shown with the help of an inscription that it was probably a reading room or lecture hall.[4] In other words, the architectural form of the building was not dictated by its function.

These examples (and many more could be cited) are not intended to show that the functional method is invalid. On the contrary, every student of Byzantine architecture should pay the closest attention to the destination of the buildings he is considering. In so doing, however, he will often discover that function and form do not necessarily go hand in hand.

The study of ancient and medieval architecture is not the exclusive preserve of the art historian and the archaeologist, however important their contributions may be. Buildings provide the most tangible and concrete legacy of a past civilization. They are historical "documents," no less so than written documents; in some cases they even speak with a clearer voice than the written word. This, I believe, is true of every period, but it is particularly applicable to the Byzantine. The reason for this is that the written records of Byzantine civilization, plentiful as they are, exhibit a curious opacity. They speak in clichés and seldom come down to the particular. They tell us a great deal about the nature of Christ and very little about the facts of everyday life. If we ask a simple question such as, "What was the nature of a provincial Byzantine town in the tenth century?" it is almost impossible to obtain an adequate answer from written records. It is here that the study of architecture comes to our aid. it can show us what kinds of buildings were erected and what kinds were not (the negative aspect is, I think, as revealing as the positive); how big they were; what materials were available and what was the level of technology; finally, by paying attention to the forms, we can detect the presence or absence of innovative trends and of foreign influences.

This *historical* approach is the one I have attempted to follow in this book. I realize that its application to a general treatment of the subject may be premature, and that it lends itself better to limited investigations of given areas than to a synthesis encompassing many centuries and many lands. The results which an approach of this kind can yield are illustrated by the admirable work of G. Tchalenko, *Villages antiques de la Syrie du nord* (1953–58). In it he examines the monuments of a particular area—the Limestone Massif of northern Syria—within a broad framework of economic history, thereby succeeding in bringing to life an entire culture and in illuminating the monuments themselves in a manner which no amount of art history could have achieved. The case of the Limestone Massif is, of course, exceptional: its monuments, built of large squared stones, have never been subjected to deliberate devastation, and so have survived nearly intact—whole villages with their houses, farms, churches and monasteries, and their "industrial" installations (oil presses), which provide the key to the economic development of the region. In most other parts of the Byzantine Empire an investigation of this kind would yield much poorer results, but there are areas other than the Limestone Massif in which it could be successfully applied.

Until a number of such regional studies have been undertaken, a survey of the eleven centuries of Byzantine architecture cannot attain the kind of contact with the historical, geographical, social, and economic realities of the Middle Ages that would be desirable. If I have attempted this task, it was with a view to posing some questions that appeared to be interesting rather than in the hope of solving them. The reader, on his part, will require some familiarity with Byzantine history and culture, which he can gain from any one of several excellent handbooks.[5]

A final word of warning. In spite of the vast amount of material at our disposal, we still have very fragmentary and unbalanced knowledge of Byzantine architecture. Consider the following facts. Constantinople, which we know much better than most other Byzantine cities, had in the course of the Middle Ages more than five hundred churches and monasteries. Of these, about thirty have survived in varying degrees of ruination, that is, less than ten percent. There is almost no trace of the two imperial palaces—the Great Palace and the palace of Blachernae—and of the hundreds of great mansions of the capital only two or three are represented by some insignificant remains. The second most populous city of the Empire—I am speaking of the Early Byzantine period—was Alexandria, yet we know nothing of its Christian architecture. The third largest city, Antioch, has been partially excavated, but none of its more important buildings has been recovered.

So much for the fragmentary character of our documentation. Another serious limitation is that the documentation is not representative. The casual observer may be excused for thinking that the Byzantines built nothing but churches; in fact, they built many other categories of structures, such as houses, palaces, baths, cisterns, fortifications, and bridges. A considerable volume of secular architecture has survived from the Early Byzantine period, much less from the Middle and Late; it has received, however, very little attention, as compared with ecclesiastical architecture. I have attempted, whenever possible, to rectify the balance, but have been obliged, like my predecessors, to speak mostly of churches. A great deal of preparatory work will have to be done before we can make any general statements concerning secular Byzantine architecture.

In the Byzantine period, building techniques remained remarkably stable on a regional basis from century to century—a stability that is easily explainable because the techniques in question depended first, on the local availability of building materials, and, second, on certain established workshop traditions that often persisted regardless of such upheavals as foreign occupation. A general understanding of these techniques is essential, since they determined, to an appreciable extent, what could or could not be done architecturally—given, of course, the technological possibilities of the times.

Very broadly speaking, Byzantine construction falls into two categories. The first is ashlar masonry, characteristic of Syria-Palestine, much of Asia Minor, as well as the border regions of Armenia and Georgia; the second is brick and rubble, typical of Constantinople, the western coast of Asia Minor, the Balkans, and Italy—hence representing the central tradition of Byzantine architecture.[1] Ashlar masonry lent itself admirably to the construction of vertical surfaces that could be enlivened by carving, but was less suitable for roofing. Small spans could be covered in stone, either in slabs laid down flat or in blocks forming vaults, but this could not be done for large areas, which had to be roofed in timber or some other comparatively lightweight material, such as brick or scoriae.[2] The comments that follow will be largely confined to the second kind of construction, which we may call, for convenience, Constantinopolitan.[3]

The normal way of building a wall was, first, to put up its two faces consisting of squared, oblong stones. This was done course by course, and the intervening space was filled with a core of rubble set in a great quantity of mortar. When the construction reached the height of a few feet, there followed a band of brick, often five courses high, which went right through the wall, from one side to the other. Then the process was repeated.

In a sense, brick was the basic element of construction. Apart from binding walls together, it determined their thickness and hence served as a module. In Constantinople bricks were made square, the sides being about 14 to 15 inches and the thickness 1 1/2 to 2 1/2 inches—somewhat larger than normal Roman bricks. A wall 2 bricks thick would thus measure (allowing for 1 mortar joint) 29 1/2 to 31 1/2 inches. The manufacture of bricks seems to have been subject to some kind of control, and, between the fourth and sixth centuries, they were often stamped, although the exact meaning of these stamps has not yet been determined. Arches, vaults, and domes were built exclusively of brick, which, in arches of great span, was occasionally of double size, like the Roman *bipedales*.

During certain periods we encounter buildings that are made

1. *Constantinople, city walls. Coursed construction of brick and stone.*

2. *Constantinople, city walls. Brick-and-stone construction in cross section.*
3, 4. *Yalova (Turkey), cruciform secular building. All-brick construction.*

entirely or predominantly of brick. Confining ourselves to Constantinople, we may mention the ruined basilica of St. Mary Chalkoprateia (c. A.D. 450), which is all of brick, although the contemporary basilica of St. John of Studius has three courses of stone alternating with five of brick. During the period of Justinian we find a characteristic type of masonry: the lowest part of the walls, roughly up to the springing of the arches of the first story, is built of stone; from there upward it is brick, except that at intervals of about six feet we find a single course of stone. All-brick construction appears again in the tenth century at Bodrum Camii.

As for the normal system of rubble and brick, it persisted throughout the Byzantine period, at any rate until the fourteenth century, when all-rubble construction appeared because bricks were no longer available. Such was the conservatism of Byzantine builders that no clear method has yet been found of distinguishing the work of one period from that of another. Only in the eleventh and twelfth centuries do we find a distinctive variation, which consisted in slightly recessing every second course of brick and concealing it beneath the mortar joint, which, as a result, appears disproportionately thick. Some observers have seen a gradual diminution through the centuries in the size of the bricks, others a slight thickening of the mortar joints, but these factors are subject to so much variation, even within the same building, that no criterion of practical applicability can be drawn from them.

The methods I have described were directly descended, as was only natural, from those used in western Asia Minor and the Balkans in the second and third centuries A.D. Superficially, Byzantine construction looks like Roman construction of the Imperial period in Italy, yet there is a fundamental difference between the two: Italian Roman construction is predicated on a core of cement, which, thanks to the unique properties of *pozzolana*, is homogeneous and (once it has set) monolithic; the facing is skin-deep and can be removed without doing any damage to the structure.[4] In Byzantine construction the rubble core does not achieve a homogeneous mass and is kept together by the facing; without the latter it tends to disintegrate. This explains the importance of the bonding courses of brick and the relative thickness of these courses. To put it differently, Byzantine architects inherited a repertory of Roman forms, but lacked the technical means of translating them fully into practice.

Byzantine mortar was of lime and sand and contained an admixture of inert matter, namely, crushed brick or, occasionally, pebbles. It was applied very liberally. While in Roman buildings of the Imperial period the mortar joints are thinner than the bricks, in Byzantine buildings the reverse is true. The ratio between the thick-

9. *Dara, city walls. Cellular stone masonry with rubble fill (6th century).*
10. *Resafa, cistern, barrel vault (6th century).*

11. *Constantinople, St. Irene, construction of cross-groined vault (6th century) (after W. S. George, 1912).*
12. *Zenobia (Halabiye), praetorium, cross-groined vault (6th century).*
13. *Constantinople, St. Mary Pammakaristos (Fethiye Camii), cistern, uncentered barrel vault (12th century).* ▷

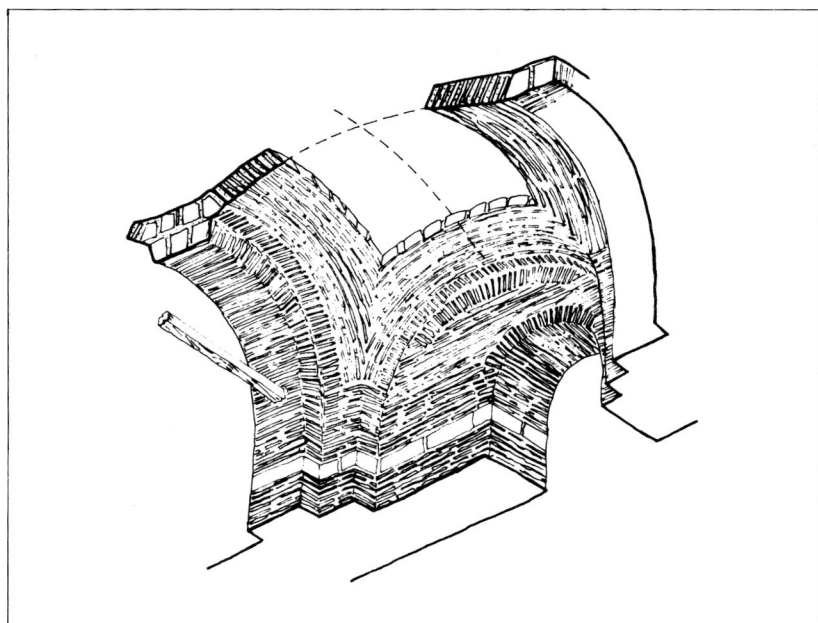

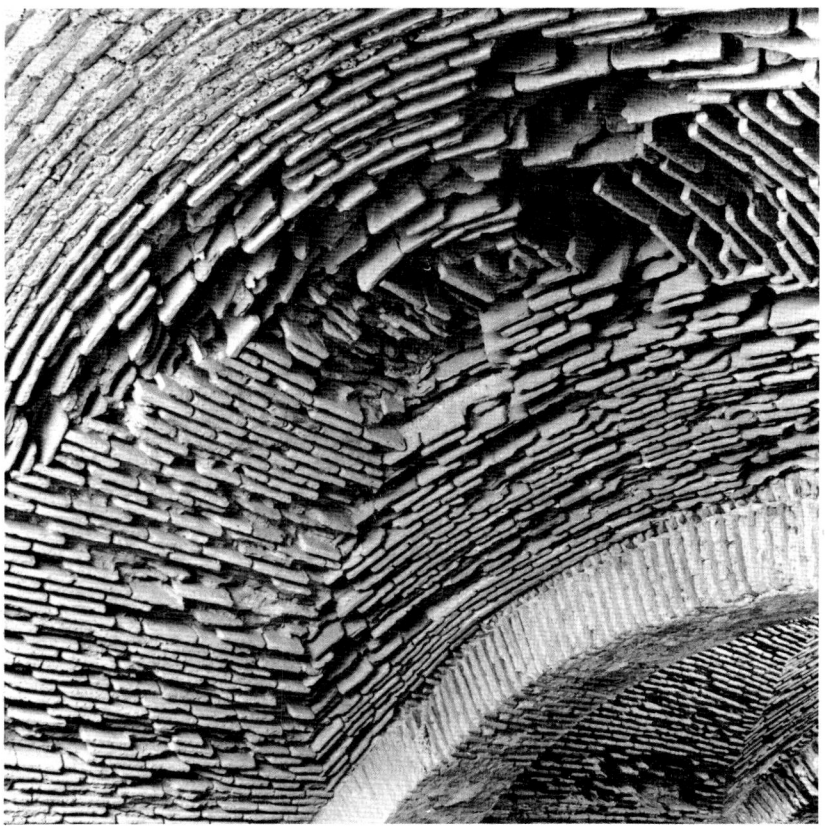

14. *Constantinople, Christ Pantocrator (Zeyrek Kilise Camii), cross-groined vault (12th century).*

15. *Resafa, Audience Hall of al-Mundhir, stone domical vault without pendentives (6th century).*

16. *Constantinople, substructure of martyrium of Sts. Carpos and Papylos, apse (half of domical vault, 4th or 5th century).*

17. *Constantinople, Karagümrük cistern, domical vaults (11th or 12th century).*

18. *Selymbria (Silivri), substructure of Apokaukos church, domical vault (14th century).*

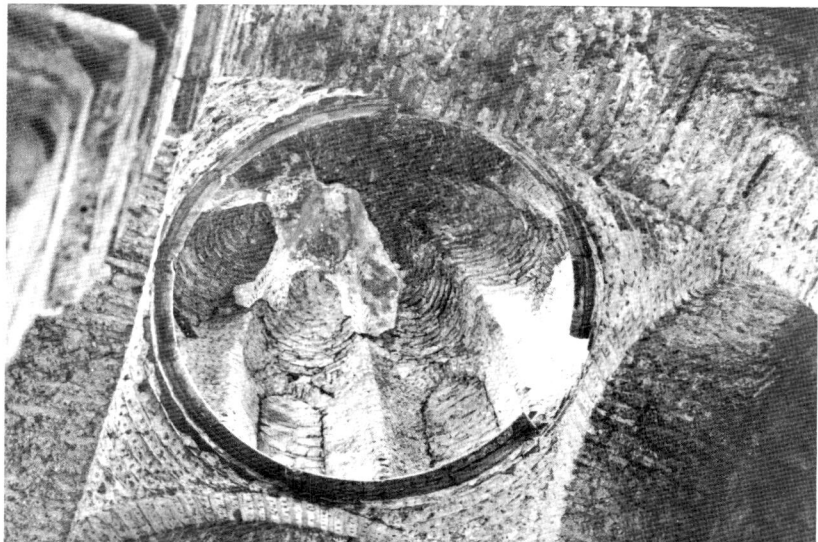

ness of brick and mortar joint was about 1:1 in the fourth century and nearly 2:3 in the sixth. This practice is probably to be explained by a desire to economize on bricks. Whether this was so or not, the excessive use of mortar had an unavoidable result: buildings tended to settle and warp as the mortar dried out, and this process must have begun already during construction. In large buildings this was especially serious, as we shall observe in the case of St. Sophia; but nearly all Byzantine buildings show irregularities and deformations that are connected with the large quantity of mortar they contain.

Byzantine vaulting is basically of three kinds: the barrel vault, the domical vault, and the cross-groined vault. All of these could be built with or without centering, depending on their span. The method of building an uncentered barrel vault was the following. First, the four walls had to be brought to their full height. Then the workmen started at both ends of the space to be covered, placing the bricks radially, but at a slight inclination away from the center to prevent them from slipping down. They must have worked quickly and used a fast-drying mortar. When the two ends of the construction came together in the middle, the intervening wedge-shaped space was filled with a "plug" of brick, thus locking the entire vault into position. Domical and cross-groined vaults were built over spaces delimited by four arches. In the former case the bricks were laid at a gradually increasing inclination from the horizontal, first to form pendentives and thus provide a circular base for the vault, and then proceeding upward until the crown was reached. In the groin vault the bricks were laid parallel to the extrados of the arches: where they met at the corners of the space to be covered, they naturally formed a ridge, but this gradually disappeared nearer to the crown. The dead spaces above the springing of vaults were often filled with earthenware jars so as to reduce the load. In vaulted construction we normally find a great deal of irregularity and improvisation: the geometrically accurate diagrams found in modern publications are rather misleading in this respect.

The dome, which usually formed the crowning element of Byzantine churches as well as other types of buildings, was constructed on the same general principle as the domical vault, that is, it rested on pendentives. The difference between the two is that whereas in the domical vault the pendentives and the calotte form a continuous spherical surface, this is not the case in the dome, which is built on a smaller radius than that of the pendentives beneath it. This distinction in no way affects the nature of the pendentives, which are the same in both cases.[5] The shell of the dome was often ribbed or gored on the inside so as to produce a number of tapering segments that could be either flat or concave. These ribs or ridges contributed to the strength

21. *Mount Sinai, St. Catherine's Monastery, timber roof (6th century).*

22. *Constantinople, St. Sophia, west facade, external marble revetment (6th century).*

of the dome, but they were not constructive in the sense that, unlike Gothic ribs, they were integral with the web between them.

We are less well informed on the use of timber, which was employed for the roofs of basilicas and houses, for scaffolding, centering, and for tie beams. The supply of long, straight timbers must have been generally scarce, except in certain heavily wooded areas, such as the Lebanon range, Cyprus, and Lycia. A couple of examples may serve to illustrate this point. The sixth-century saint Nicholas of Sion, later confused with the more familiar St. Nicholas of Myra, is said to have felled a huge cypress tree that was inhabited by a demon. After the tree had been trimmed, it was decided to use it as a beam in the church he was building, but as it was being transported, three cubits were broken off its length. This was considered a great disaster, because the trunk was now too short for its intended purpose. But St. Nicholas miraculously restored it to its full length, and it took its place in the roof of the church.[6] This story is set in Lycia, hence in a densely wooded area, and shows how much importance was attached even there to a tall, straight tree. Several centuries later, and under Arab rule, the patriarch Thomas I of Jerusalem (807–20) restored the roof of the Anastasis, the circular church erected over Christ's tomb. For this purpose he had to import at great expense fifty trunks of pine and cedar from Cyprus.[7] He would doubtless have had far less trouble had the roof been of masonry.

A unique example of a timber truss roof of the sixth century is preserved in the monastery of St. Catherine on Mount Sinai.[8] After this period fewer and fewer basilicas were built, and one reason for the adoption of the masonry-roofed church may have been precisely the difficulty of obtaining suitable timber.

The exterior of buildings was occasionally plastered, but more often appears to have been left plain. The joints between the courses of brick and stone were pointed up with a thin layer of fine mortar, which was pressed with a blunt implement so as to form a slight groove. Often incised lines were added. Ornamental patterns of brick are quite exceptional before the tenth century. Exterior marble revetments are even rarer (for example, the western facade of St. Sophia). The treatment of the interior stands in sharp contrast to that of the exterior: here (except in buildings of ashlar masonry) every inch of the walls was covered with marble placage, stucco, painting, and mosaic.

This brings us to the important topic of marble. In terms of structural elements, the use of marble was confined to columns, cornices, and architraves, but it was also applied to a great number of subsidiary features such as door jambs and lintels, window grilles, parapet slabs, pulpits, and, of course, pavements and mural revetment.

Ever since exotic colored marbles were introduced to Rome in the Late Republican period, they became, so to speak, a status symbol, and their production was enormously expanded in the first and second centuries A.D.[9] No building of any pretension could do without them, and it is noteworthy that the Byzantine *ekphrasis* usually devotes more space to marble than to any other feature of a building. The total effect of a Late Roman or Early Byzantine interior was to a large extent predicated on a lavish use of marble.

To achieve the multicolored effect that was so greatly prized, a great number of quarries, situated all around the Mediterranean, had to be exploited. Red porphyry, the most prestigious and expensive of all stones, came only from Egypt; green porphyry from Laconia; verd antique from Thessaly; fiery yellow marble *(giallo antico)* from Tunisia; ivory-colored onyx from Hierapolis in Phrygia.[10] The supply of these materials depended on a combination of factors: the existence of a servile labor force to work the quarries, ease of communication and, in particular, of navigation in the Mediterranean, and the ability to lift up and transport very heavy blocks of stone for which special ships had to be built. Since transport by sea was much easier and cheaper than transport by land, quarries situated close to the seashore enjoyed a natural advantage. This, no doubt, explains in part the extraordinary diffusion of Proconnesian marble (from the island of Proconnesus in the Sea of Marmara), which, already in the first century A.D., was being widely exported, and which became the standard marble of Byzantine architecture. While not particularly fine-grained or striking in appearance (it is nearly white with a blue-gray vein), it had the advantage of being an all-purpose marble, equally suitable for ornamental carving as for large elements such as column shafts.[11]

While our knowledge of ancient marbles is constantly growing, we are still unable, in most cases, to answer a question of particular interest to the historian of Byzantine architecture, namely, "When did the various quarries cease production?" The supply of red porphyry seems to have ended about A.D. 450, if one may judge by the descriptions of imperial sarcophagi, which, until that date, were normally made of porphyry. The green marble of Carystus, in Euboea, extensively used for columns in the Roman Imperial period, was still quarried in the early fifth century A.D. The Thessalian quarries of verd antique were certainly in operation at the time of Justinian. I suspect that the majority of marble quarries were abandoned in the sixth or seventh century because of the deteriorating situation of the Empire and the dwindling of the servile labor force. I am not even sure that the quarries of Proconnesus continued to be worked after that date. This was, doubtless, an important factor in shaping the development of Middle Byzantine architecture.

We now come to the men who erected the buildings. In the Early Byzantine period the architectural profession was represented by two kinds of specialist, the *mêchanikos* or *mêchanopoios* (*mechanicus* in Latin) and the *architektôn*, the former category being by far the more exalted.[12] The term *mêchanikos* is often translated as engineer, but this is somewhat misleading: he could more properly be described as an architect having a grounding in mathematics. His social position was quite high. The architects of St. Sophia, Anthemius and Isidore, were both *mêchanikoi*, and Anthemius was a prominent mathematician. In his far-flung building operations, Justinian relied on the services of such men. The reconstruction and fortification of the frontier city of Dara was supervised by the *mêchanikos* Chryses of Alexandria. When this city was damaged by a sudden flooding of the stream that flows through it, the emperor called in Anthemius and Isidore for consultation. The problem was solved by building a dam, whose design was revealed to Chryses in a vision. The building of the city of Zenobia on the Euphrates was carried out by two young *mêchanikoi*, John of Constantinople and another Isidore (nephew of the first).[13] The latter subsequently supervised the reconstruction of St. Sophia at Constantinople after its original dome had collapsed in 558.

The *mêchanikos* was, however, a fairly rare individual. The *architektones*, or master builders, ranked decidedly lower. In the fourth century they were still supposed to have a liberal education, and they gave professional instruction, for which, however, they received rather modest wages: a little more than teachers of elementary mathematics and shorthand, but exactly half of what surveyors and teachers of literature were allowed to charge. We may imagine that, as time went on, the *architektones* sank to the level of craftsmen. The majority of Early Byzantine structures were probably put up by such master builders or even by foremen. It is worthy of notice that after the sixth century hardly any Byzantine architects are recorded by name.[14]

Below the *architektones* came the skilled craftsmen who belonged to the plebeian class. Their relative status is revealed by the salaries specified in Diocletian's Tariff of A.D. 301 (their absolute worth is almost impossible to calculate): figure painters got 150 *denarii* per day plus their food; wall painters, 75; mosaicists, 60; ordinary masons and carpenters, 50.[15] Theoretically all such craftsmen belonged to hereditary guilds *(collegia)*, which, unlike modern trade unions, were organized not for the protection of workers but for their coercion. As such, the craftsmen were liable to all kinds of compulsory services, such as cleaning out drains.

23. *Dara, stone quarry (6th century).*

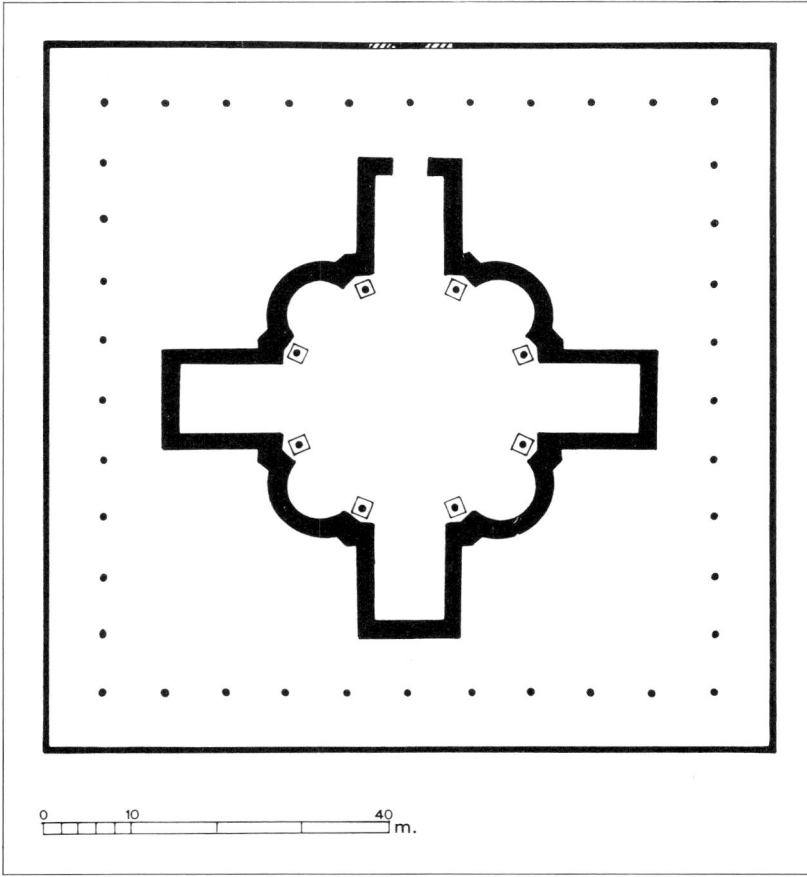

0 10   40
m.

the materials were obtained, and what the role of the architect was.

Our first text is the well-known letter of the emperor Constantine to Macarius, bishop of Jerusalem, concerning the erection of the church of the Holy Sepulcher in 326. It may be summarized as follows: "We wish this church to be the most beautiful in the world. We have issued instructions to this effect to the *Vicarius Orientis* and the governor of Palestine. After consulting with you, these officials will provide the necessary craftsmen and materials, and defray the expense. You are, however, to communicate directly with us in regard to the following two points: 1. The nature and quantity of the marble to be supplied; 2. Whether the ceiling is to be coffered, for in that case it should also be gilded."[18]

A perusal of this bureaucratic document prompts the following observations. First, Constantine himself does not seem to have been particularly concerned about the architectural form of the church as long as it was the most beautiful in the world. Second, the church was to be built entirely at government expense—understandably so, since it was a "propaganda monument." Third, whereas the provincial administrators had been instructed to furnish the necessary labor (by the system of the forced corvée) and materials, it was the bishop who acted, as it were, as the chairman of the planning commission. No mention whatever was made of the architect (we happen to know from another source that it was a certain Zenobius). Fourth, the bishop was to communicate directly with the emperor with regard to the marbles and the gilding, probably because these were the most expensive items on the agenda. Besides, marble was not produced in either Palestine or Syria and would have to have been imported from provinces lying outside the jurisdiction of the two officials mentioned in the letter.

The second document, dating from about A.D. 380, is a letter of St. Gregory of Nyssa to Amphilochius, bishop of Iconium.[19] Gregory was in the process of constructing a martyrium. First, he explained its form and gave the dimensions: it consisted of a central space, in the shape of an octagon with a conical roof, and four radiating arms so as to give a cruciform plan; something like Qal'at Saman, only much smaller, since the arms were eight cubits wide and twelve long, and the walls three feet thick. Gregory trusted that his correspondent, who was skilled in such matters, would be able, on the basis of the measurements he had supplied, to make a rough reckoning of the volume of work involved and dispatch to Nyssa as many workers as were needed. The structure was to be built of brick (since no stone was available locally), but it would comprise certain elements of stone or marble, namely, eight columns together with their capitals and pedestals for the octagon, a carved doorframe, and

It is no wonder that they sought to escape the tentacles of the central government by fleeing to the countryside. A decree of the emperor Honorius of A.D. 400 complains that the cities were losing their splendor because the *collegiati* had abandoned their upkeep and hidden themselves in the country. By the fifth century the system of compulsory services in the building profession seems to have broken down, and we may imagine that the number of independent, floating workmen increased correspondingly.[16] In the tenth century, at Constantinople, construction workers were once again organized in guilds and subject to regulation by the city prefect.[17] It is unlikely that the same situation existed in the provinces.

Such, in brief, were the materials and techniques used, and such were the men that carried out construction. A number of contemporary texts may help us to understand how, in different parts of the Empire and at different times, a building (usually a church) was put up, how a peristyle of at least forty columns. Gregory had been offered local labor—thirty masons for one *solidus* (gold piece) per day plus food—but he considered these terms to be exorbitant. The workers from the region of Iconium, he thought, would be less demanding; furthermore, he wanted to have a clear contract of how much each workman was to do per day. Financial necessity compelled him to be exacting in this respect.

Here we are dealing not with a government project, but with a small building that was put up at the expense of the local church or bishop, whose limited funds obliged him to cut corners whenever possible. Once again, there was no mention of an architect. St. Gregory was in possession of a plan or some type of drawing of a fairly rudimentary kind: he was rather vague about the elevation of the building, saying that the height of the arms was to be proportionate to their length and width, and about the peristyle, which was to consist of about forty columns. Evidently, such matters could be improvised on the spot. He also assumed that his colleague, the bishop of Iconium, was sufficiently expert in matters of construction to be able to calculate the necessary number of masons. As for the wages, the terms that had been offered to St. Gregory were indeed rather exorbitant: a daily wage of 1/30 of a *solidus* per man would have amounted, assuming fairly steady employment, to a yearly income of about 10 *solidi,* whereas the average rate for the fourth to sixth centuries, as we know from other sources, was about 5 to 7 *solidi.* Gregory assumed that the masons of Iconium would not only be more reasonable, but would also be willing to travel a distance of about one hundred miles, which presupposed the existence of a floating labor force.

Our third text concerns the construction of the cathedral of Gaza from 402 to 407.[20] Here, as at Jerusalem, the project was state financed, but it appears that the labor was supplied voluntarily by the Christian community rather than by forced levy. Gaza at the time was still predominantly pagan, having a Christian flock of only 280 persons, while its total population certainly numbered several tens of thousands. Yet, armed with imperial support, Bishop Porphyry did not hesitate to burn down the pagan temple of Zeus Marnas. Upon its site the new Christian cathedral was to be built. A dispute then arose among the faithful. The Marneion had been a circular building having some kind of a dome and two concentric porticoes. Some thought that the church should be built according to the same formula, while others urged that it should not be in any way reminiscent of the pagan temple. The bishop decided to wait. Soon thereafter he received a letter from the empress Eudoxia containing a plan *(skariphos)* of the church drawn on a sheet: the plan was cruciform. Porphyry engaged the services of an architect *(architektôn)* from Antioch, a certain Rufinus, who marked the outline of the plan on the ground by means of chalk. The foundation trenches were then dug, the bishop himself taking part in the work. Stone was obtained from a local quarry. The following year the empress sent thirty-two columns of Carystus marble (veined green marble from Euboea). Five years later the enormous cathedral was completed.

Some interesting observations may be made on the basis of this text. We are here dealing with an ordinary episcopal church, not a martyrium; yet some persons suggested a circular domed plan, and the church that was eventually built was cruciform. Secondly, the plan was sent ready-made from Constantinople. The honest architect Rufinus had no part in designing it; he was called upon to realize it, and he had no control over the dimensions of the thirty-two columns that were shipped from Euboea on orders of the empress, after the lower part of the walls had already been built.

The three texts we have quoted reflect very different historical and local circumstances, yet they have some points of similarity. In each case the dominant role was played by the bishop. The architect, or master builder, if he was mentioned at all, did not appear as the originator of the plan but merely as its executor, and he seemed to be working on the basis of fairly sketchy drawings. The marble columns received particular mention, and they were provided directly by the imperial government. The laborers might be raised by forced corvée; they might be provided voluntarily by the Christian community; or they might be hired by the bishop.

If these conditions were typical (and I think they were), we need not be surprised by the uniformity of Early Christian architecture. The task of the master builder was not so much to design and invent as to improvise on the basis of accepted formulas; and he had to work fairly quickly. Unlike Gothic cathedrals, Early Christian churches were put up with remarkable speed. If the cathedral of Gaza took five years to complete, this may have been due to the smallness of the Christian community; St. Sophia at Constantinople also took five years.

We may now take one fairly untypical example, the monastery of St. Simeon Stylites the Younger (to distinguish him from his more famous namesake of Qal'at Saman) on the "Wondrous Mountain," a short distance southwest of Antioch. Its ruins are still standing and cover a considerable area: a walled precinct measuring about 400 by 550 feet with a complex of churches forming a rectangle 200 by 280 feet.[21] The monastery was built roughly between the years 541 and 565 and is clearly modeled on Qal'at Saman: an octagonal court in the middle enclosing the saint's pillar, and four radiating arms, except that here three churches were placed side by side to the east of the octagon—a central basilica, a smaller basilica to the north, and a martyrium with a trefoil chevet to the south.

The *Lives* of Simeon and of his mother Martha describe in some detail how this complex was built. The plan was allegedly traced by an angel, and then a multitude of Isaurian masons appeared bringing their sick, so that the saint would cure them. These Isaurians must have been migrant workers who sought employment at Antioch, probably on a seasonal basis. Year after year they kept coming to the Wondrous Mountain and, in return for being healed of various diseases, put in periods of work. They even brought their own tools and provisions. The capitals of the main basilica were carved by a monk who had had no previous training in this craft, but was miraculously granted a "spirit of wisdom."

Particularly curious is the account of the construction of the martyrium of St. Martha. Its plan, too, was revealed supernaturally by the deceased saint, who particularly insisted on having the trefoil chevet covered by a barrel vault. The builder had other ideas (we are not told what they were), but he was quickly disposed of. Thereupon another Isaurian builder turned up, and he, without being instructed, put up exactly the kind of vault that St. Martha had wanted.[22]

Here, then, we have a "do it yourself" operation which shows the remarkable resources that could be mobilized by a holy man who set up a popular center of pilgrimage. Important architectural features, such as the roofing of the trefoil, were, if we are to trust the text, improvised on the spot. What is particularly interesting, however, is that the entire work appears to have been done without any money changing hands. We may wonder how many of the rural churches of the Early Byzantine period were put up by voluntary labor and with the help of the contributions in kind made by the faithful.

This brings us to the final point of finance and patronage. The erection of public buildings was entirely in the hands of the state, which in the fourth and fifth centuries repeatedly attempted to discourage such activity in favor of the restoration of existing buildings.[23] The problem arises, therefore, only with regard to churches, and here three kinds of patronage were involved that cannot always be distinguished: the state, the local church, and private benefactors. As we have seen from the above examples, the government and the Church often acted in concert, the former providing either the total cost or part of it. The same kind of overlap existed between ecclesiastical and private patronage. Without wishing to minimize the amount of disinterested piety that found an outlet in the construction of churches, we should nevertheless indicate some of the complex economic interests that were involved in this domain.

The Church was immensely rich in the Early Byzantine period or, to put it more accurately, an immense amount of money passed through its hands. This came mainly from two sources: the offerings of the faithful, in principle voluntary (but in practice not always so), and rents from the properties, which accrued by way of bequest. On the debit side were the salaries paid to the clergy, the maintenance of buildings, and the distribution of charity. It was the bishop's task to encourage donations; a substantial donor, however, often wished to see his liberality immortalized by a monument. A new church meant new jobs for the clergy and a new source of offerings: indeed, laymen often built churches as a commercial speculation and then drew a share of the proceeds. At the same time a new church, if not sufficiently endowed, meant an added drain on the resources of the bishopric.

There are indications that by the sixth century the system was beginning to break down. Too many churches had been built, too many clergymen appointed under pressure from patrons. The field was "saturated," and expenditures were exceeding receipts. Even the Great Church of Constantinople (meaning a group of four churches, including St. Sophia, that were served by the same clergy) was in desperate financial trouble: Justinian was forced to decree that no further ordinations be made.[24]

There is no doubt in my mind that a more thorough examination of these economic factors would shed a great deal of light on the pattern of ecclesiastical architecture in the Early Byzantine period; conversely, the archaeological evidence could be used to supplement that of the written sources. It may be possible in this way to find an explanation of certain puzzling architectural phenomena, such as the high incidence of multiple churches, that is, two or three churches built side by side. Was not the intention, perhaps, to satisfy the wishes of individual donors and at the same time cut down on overhead by having a single body of clergy and of custodians for the whole group? In a broader sense we may gain a better understanding of the extraordinary wave of church building, especially in the fifth century, and of its subsidence in the reign of Justinian. This subsidence was caused not only by the deteriorating condition of the Empire, but also by the sclerosis of the mechanism of church finance.

As to the cost of erecting a church, perhaps the only reliable figure we have is that relating to S. Vitale at Ravenna: 26,000 *solidi,* an enormous sum for those days.[25] The patron was the banker *(argentarius)* Julianus, who was also concerned with the construction of several other churches at Ravenna. We have no means of determining, however, whether Julianus expended so much money out of his own pocket or whether he was financed by the imperial treasury. The figures we are given for the erection of St. Sophia at Constantinople are clearly fantastic.

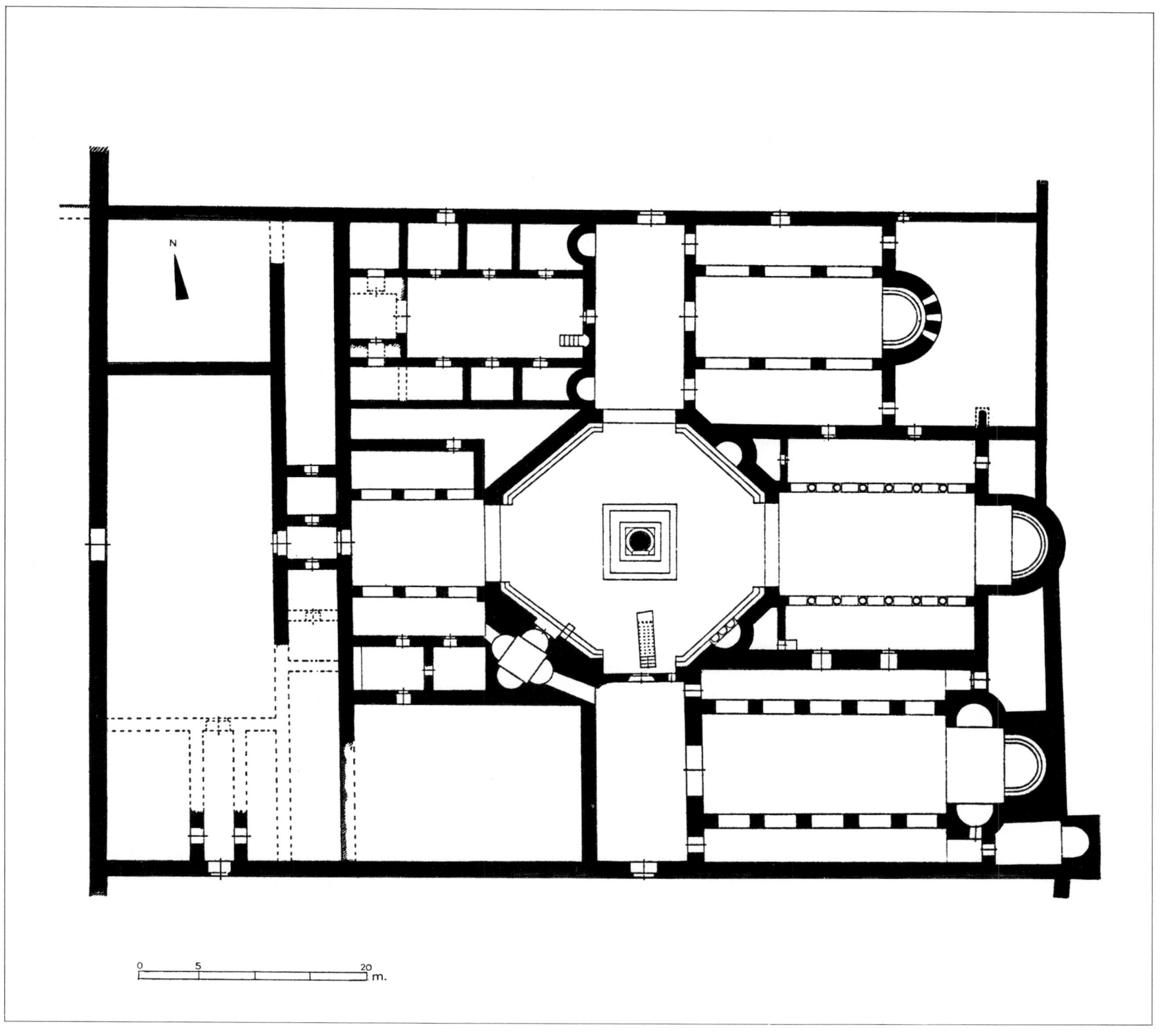

25. *Monastery of St. Simeon Stylites the Younger, near Antioch, ground plan (after W. Djobadze, 1965).*

26. *Gerasa, city plan (after C. H. Kraeling, 1938).*
1. Temple of Artemis | 2. Cathedral | 3. St. Theodore | 4. Synagogue | 5. Church of Bishop Genesius | 6. Sts. Cosmas and Damian | 7. St. John the Baptist | 8. St. George | 9. Sts. Peter and Paul | 10. Temple of Zeus | 11. Forum | 12. South tetrapylon | 13. Procopius church | 14. Church of the Prophets, Apostles, and Martyrs | 15. Propylaea church | 16. Public baths.

The question may well be asked whether it is possible to speak of the Byzantine city as a distinct architectural complex. In the vast majority of cases a Byzantine city (I am speaking now of the period down to the sixth or seventh century) was merely the continuation of a Roman city, which, in turn, may have been founded in the Hellenistic period or even earlier. Usually the cities in question had reached their peak during the second century A.D. In the second half of the third century there was widespread urban decline, which in many instances extended into the fourth century. The fifth and sixth centuries were marked by an upsurge of building activity in the eastern provinces. Then, in the seventh, came a catastrophic crash, often amounting to a cessation of urban life. The Byzantine period in the life of such cities was not marked by any radical change in the layout of the streets, the system of fortification, of burial, or of the water supply. The most obvious alterations were the erection of churches and the abandonment of the pagan temples; there were also less noticeable developments connected with civic administration, marketing, and public entertainments.

A second, much smaller, category is represented by cities that were founded *de novo* during the Early Byzantine period. The case of Constantinople, which is that of an antique city enlarged into a huge metropolis in the fourth and fifth centuries A.D., is exceptional.

As an example of the first category of cities we may take Gerasa (Jerash) in Jordan, not because it was a place of particular importance in the ancient world, but for the rather more prosaic reason that it has been quite thoroughly investigated[1] and is not encumbered by later settlements. Gerasa was a Hellenistic foundation, but its development occurred during the Roman period. In the first century A.D. it was laid out on a grid pattern with a straight colonnaded *cardo* 1,000 yards long and with 2 *decumani*. The entire city, covering an area of 210 acres, was at the same time enclosed by a wall. In the reign of Hadrian a plan was formed of extending the city walls to the south so as to enlarge the enclosed area by about one third, but this was never carried out. The most spectacular public buildings were put up at the end of the first century and in the second century. Gerasa was endowed with 2 theaters, the south theater with a seating capacity of 3,000 and a smaller north theater; 2 monumental temples, that of Zeus in the south section of the city (c. A.D. 163) and that of Artemis (c. A.D. 150–80) fronting on the *cardo* and covering, with its *temenos* and dependencies, an area of 8.4 acres; several bathing establishments; an elegant nymphaeum (A.D. 191), and an extramural hippodrome (date uncertain; perhaps Severan period), seating about 15,000 spectators. In Diocletian's time a circular plaza was laid out around the south tetrapylon to serve as a commercial center or bazaar.

Gerasa naturally became a bishopric in the fourth century, but, in fact, nothing definite is known of its monumental history until the middle of the fifth. The two major temples appear to have ceased functioning at about this time, but were not demolished. Instead, a vast ecclesiastic complex arose directly to the south of the temple of Artemis, replacing a pagan sanctuary that may have fallen into disuse at an earlier period. Including its later accretions, this complex measured 600 feet from east to west and, like the adjacent temple, it fronted on the *cardo*. A monumental entrance of the second century A.D. was used to give access to the complex, which was built on several successive terraces. After mounting a staircase, the visitor found himself facing the rear wall of the cathedral, a rectangular basilica measuring about 140 by 75 feet. This was erected perhaps in the second half of the fourth century (it is, unfortunately, undated), largely out of reused building material. Farther west lay an open colonnaded courtyard, at the center of which was a fountain whose water miraculously turned to wine on the day of Epiphany. A second basilica, nearly as large as the first, was added in 494–96; this was a martyrium dedicated to St. Theodore. It had an atrium of its own and various dependent structures, one of which was used as a baptistery. To the north of St. Theodore's lay a maze of rooms that must have housed the clergy, and next to them a bath (presumably for the use of the clergy) that was built by Bishop Placcus in 454–55 and renovated in 584.

This great episcopal complex, the result of accretions extending over two centuries, prompts a number of observations. Comparison with the adjacent temple of Artemis is particularly instructive. The latter, placed in the middle of a vast open courtyard, was intended to be seen from all directions. In the case of the Christian complex, on the other hand, it would have been practically impossible to obtain an exterior view of the basilicas, so hemmed in were they on all sides. This observation applies to the majority of Early Christian churches. Some attempt at monumentality was indeed made here: I am referring to the broad staircase leading up from the *cardo*. Yet the custom of orienting the apse of the cathedral all but negated this attempt, for, after mounting the stairs, the worshiper found himself facing a blank wall. He then had to walk through a narrow passage along the side wall of the cathedral before he could reach the courtyard with its miraculous fountain. Even from the courtyard he could see only the triforium level of the facade, the rest being hidden from view by the surrounding colonnade. Before the erection of St. Theodore's there may have been a western entrance to the atrium, but we happen to know that the area in question was anything but monumental; it was used as a dump for the carcasses of animals, and the stench was

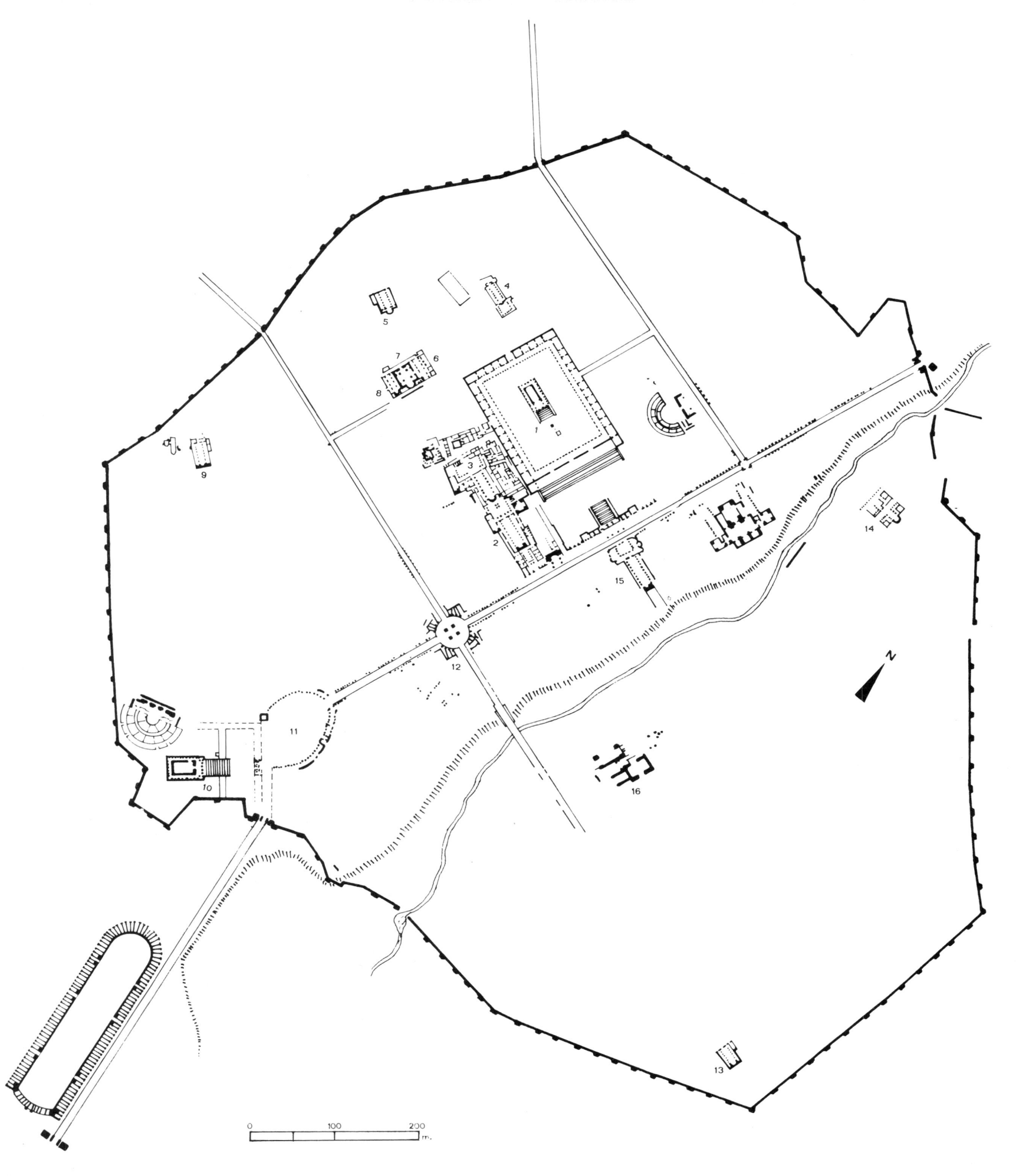

0   100   200
m.

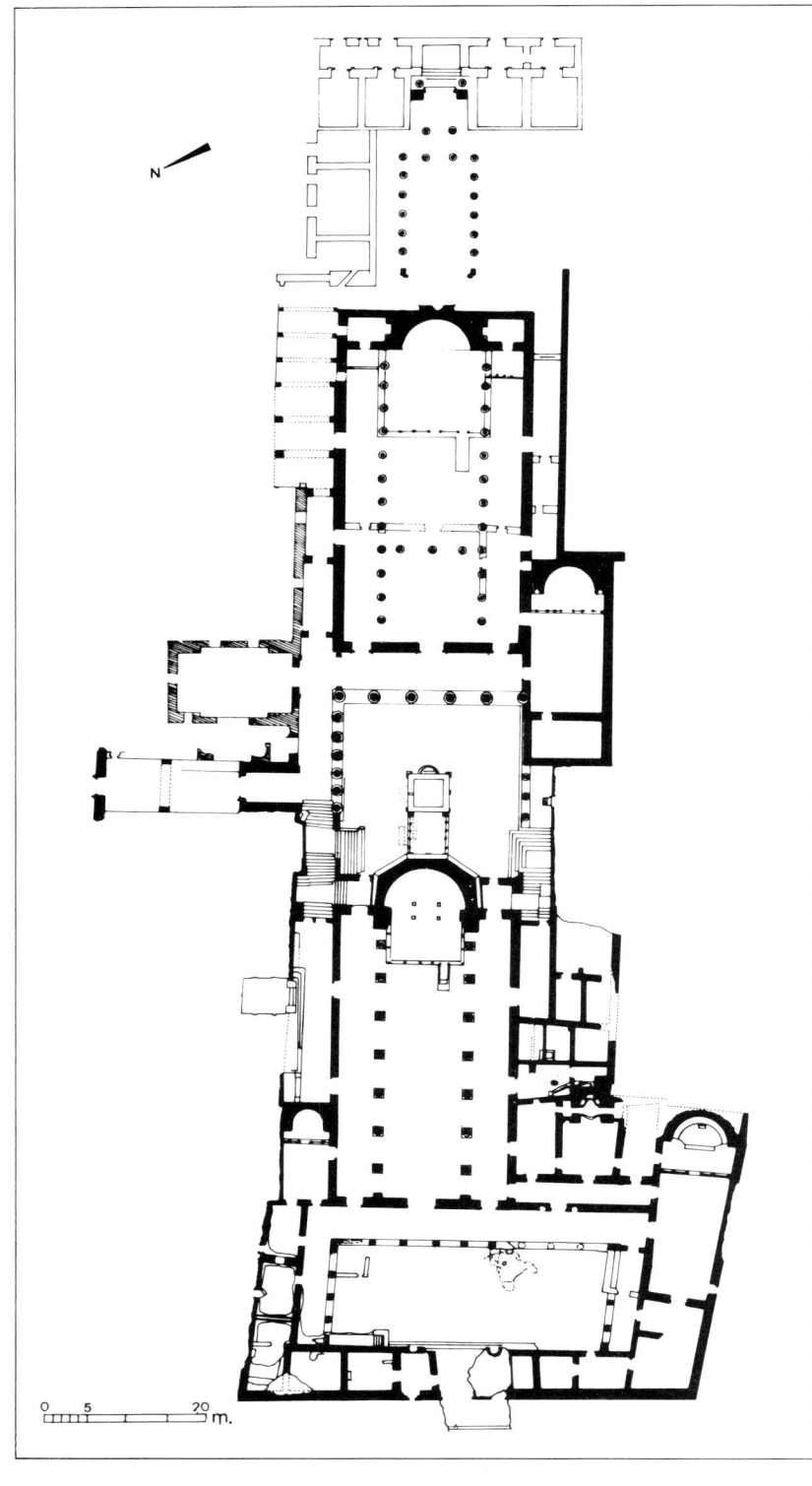

27. *Gerasa, cathedral complex, ground plan (after C. H. Kraeling, 1938).*
28. *Gerasa, cathedral complex, Fountain Court, looking southeast.* ▷

29. *Gerasa, cathedral, reconstruction of Fountain Court.*

so bad that one had to hold one's nose with the hand—a rare case where epigraphy unveils to us the realities of a Near Eastern town.[2]

A number of other churches arose in Gerasa. That of the Prophets, Apostles, and Martyrs, of cruciform plan enclosed in a square, was put up in the northern part of the city in 464–65 at the expense of a lady called Marina. A martyrium of unknown dedication, basilican in plan (referred to as the Procopius church), was built in the southeast corner of the city in 526 from the benefactions of Bishop Paul and the deacon Saul, under the direction of a clergyman called Procopius. A group of three conjoined churches sharing a common atrium was put up in 529–33 a short distance west of the cathedral complex. The central church, of circular plan with corner exedrae (531), was built in honor of St. John the Baptist at the expense of a certain Theodore; the south church (529), the gift of an anonymous donor, was dedicated to St. George and had the form of a basilica whose arcades were carried on piers instead of columns; the north church, named after the medical saints Cosmas and Damian (533), was similar in form to that of St. George. It was put up at the expense of the same Theodore with supplementary contributions from other persons, including the tribune Dagisthaeus, later to become one of Justinian's generals.

The remaining churches of Gerasa are all basilicas. They are the so-called Synagogue church, built in 530–31 on a site previously occupied by a synagogue; the church of Sts. Peter and Paul, put up by Bishop Anastasius about 540; the Propylaea church (perhaps of 565), incorporating large portions of an antique building; and finally the church of Bishop Genesius (611), whose mosaic pavement was donated by the goldsmith John and a certain Saul.

A study of the epigraphic material associated with these churches demonstrates that the local bishop had become the most important patron of the arts at Gerasa. It was he who erected churches at his own or diocesan expense; or he persuaded rich members of the congregation to do so. Nowhere is the name of an architect mentioned; and in only one case, as we have seen, does a superintendent of works appear, who happens to be a cleric.

We know much less concerning nonreligious public activities at Gerasa during the Christian period. It appears, on the basis of coin finds, that the hippodrome continued to be used until the end of the sixth century. Concerning the fate of the 2 theaters within the walls the excavators have nothing to tell us; but there is an interesting piece of evidence attached to another small theater (seating capacity 1,000), a building of the second or third century, situated next to a pool at a place now called Birketein, about half a mile north of the city. Here was found an inscription of the year 535 recording the celebration,

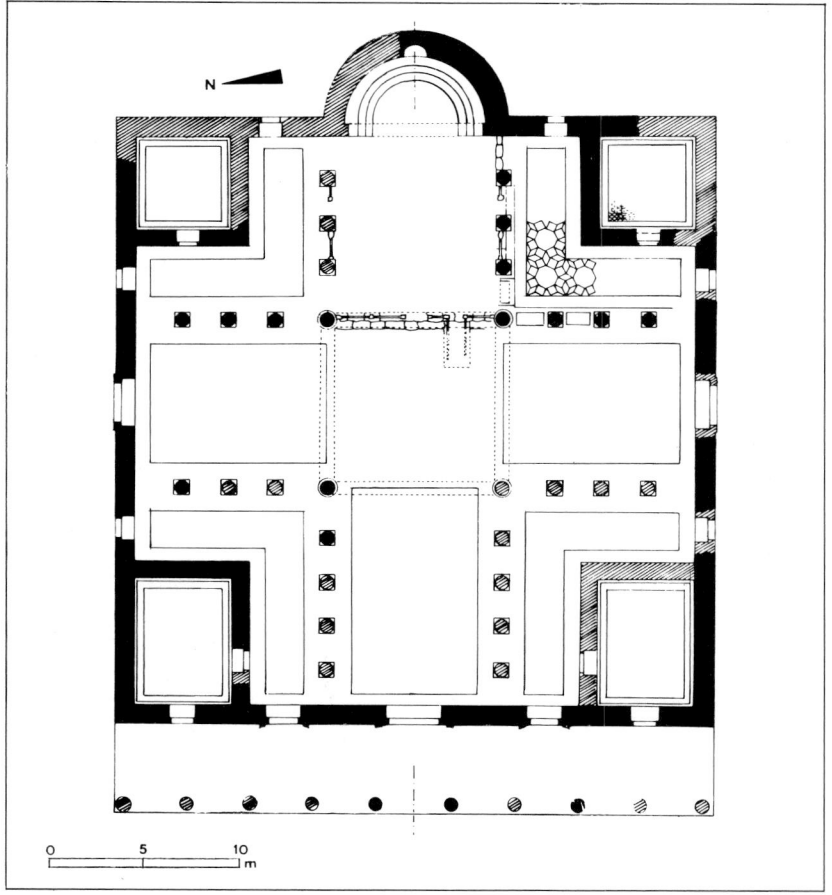

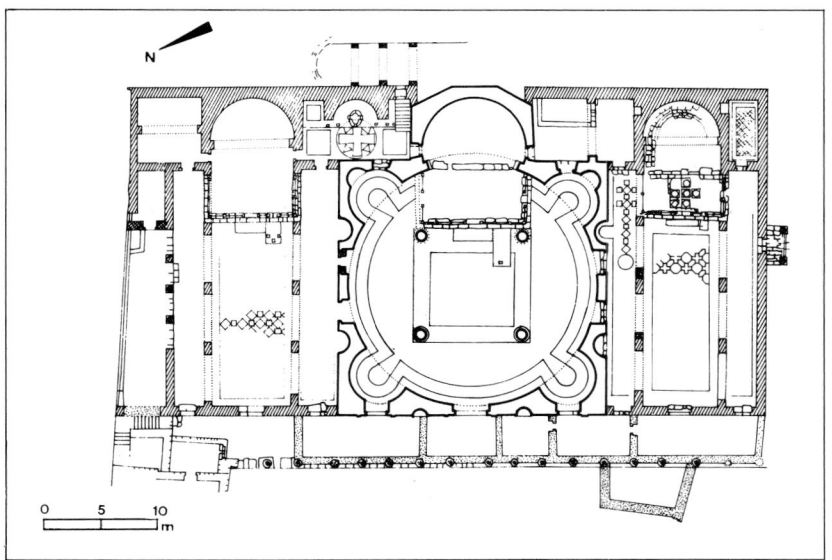

under official auspices, of a festival called Maioumas.[3] This festival was of Syrian origin but was widely diffused in the Roman world; it comprised some form of scenic representations, that is, mimes, and had a bad reputation, for which it was repeatedly banned by imperial legislation—apparently to little avail. At Constantinople it persisted until the eighth century.

The observations I have made concerning Gerasa could also be applied, *mutatis mutandis,* to the classical cities of western Asia Minor, such as Ephesus, Pergamum, Miletus, and Sardis. Most of these were fortified in the third century, at the time of the Gothic invasions, and survived without substantial diminution until the beginning of the seventh. Their temples were despoiled and used as quarries of building material; churches were built; gymnasia and bouleuteria were abandoned, while public baths and theaters were maintained. Retail marketing shifted from the agora to the colonnaded street, called *embolos,* and in some cases large avenues were laid out for this purpose, like the Arcadiane at Ephesus. In the domain of charity there was even an expansion of public services, since the Church provided poorhouses, inns, and hospitals. In other words, the texture of life gradually changed, but life went on until the great crash, which in Asia Minor was caused by the Persian invasion in the second decade of the seventh century. Thereafter the majority of cities were abandoned and replaced by mountaintop castles; among the few survivors were Ephesus and Smyrna, which, however, were greatly diminished as compared with their former size.

Our second category, that of cities founded in the Byzantine period, is represented by few examples that have been explored. All of them, moreover, have had a short life-span, hardly longer than a century. The city that has been most thoroughly studied is probably Caričin Grad in Yugoslavia, plausibly identified with Justiniana Prima.[4] This was an artificial creation of the emperor Justinian, built to honor his own birthplace. The excavated walled city is elongated in plan and quite modest in size (length 550 yards, average width not much more than 109 yards), in fact, only slightly larger than the monastic complex of Qal'at Saman, which is 440 yards long and over 109 yards wide. The acropolis is entirely occupied by the episcopal cathedral and palace—Justiniana Prima was made the seat of the archbishop of Illyricum. The lower city was traversed by a long colonnaded *cardo,* intersected by a much shorter *decumanus.* At the point of intersection was a circular piazza which, as at Gerasa, was the commercial center. To the east of the *cardo* four churches have been found and to the west, one: between them, they take up a considerable portion of the city's area. The only other large public building that has been identified was a bath. Water was supplied by an aqueduct

0   10   50   100
m.

over a distance of twelve miles. The cemetery was situated outside the walls. In short, we have here an antique plan invaded by ecclesiastical establishments. Places of entertainment are lacking, nor would they have been required by the predominantly rural population that must have lived, for the most part, outside the walls.

Other Byzantine towns of which something is known also owe their origin to exceptional circumstances. Resafa (Sergiopolis), in the Syrian desert,[5] while serving as a caravan post between Palmyra and Soura on the Euphrates, was above all a place of pilgrimage, since it contained the immensely popular shrine of St. Sergius. It was made into a city by Justinian, who built the impressive walls that are still standing as well as the cisterns. The fortified area is trapezoid, measuring roughly 600 by 440 yards; the fact that a good part of it is occupied by churches is here less surprising than at Caričin Grad. Of the street plan very little has been recovered, since the excavators have concentrated their attention on the ecclesiastical buildings and the walls.

Dara and Zenobia were strongly fortified frontier posts. The former was founded by the emperor Anastasius in 507 and made stronger by Justinian. Unfortunately, it has not been subjected to archaeological exploration, but considerable remains are still standing. The plan is irregular because of the nature of the terrain and measures about 1,100 yards from north to south and 820 yards from east to west.[6] The stone for the construction was obtained locally, and extensive quarries are still visible to the west of the city, their vertical surfaces cut stepwise. Once the stones had been extracted, the quarries were used for burial. The visible ruins of Dara testify to the engineering skill of the Justinianian age. The walls are very strong and are surrounded on the east side by a moat. The stream that flows through the city was, as we have seen, dammed; it enters and leaves the fortifications through a series of arched openings that were once provided with iron grilles. Inside the city the most notable features today are the immense cisterns; the remains of a church are also visible. The emperor Anastasius is said to have built there "two public baths, churches, colonnaded streets, storehouses for corn, and water cisterns."

The city of Zenobia (Halabiye), which guards a gorge of the Euphrates, was not entirely a Byzantine creation, since it had been founded by Zenobia, queen of Palmyra.[7] Justinian enlarged it, however, and it seems that all the constructions visible inside the walls are of the Byzantine period. The walled area, which is more or less triangular, is not very extensive (550 yards from east to west and 440 yards along the river bank), but once again the proficiency of Justinian's *mêchanikoi* arouses our admiration. The walls, which rise

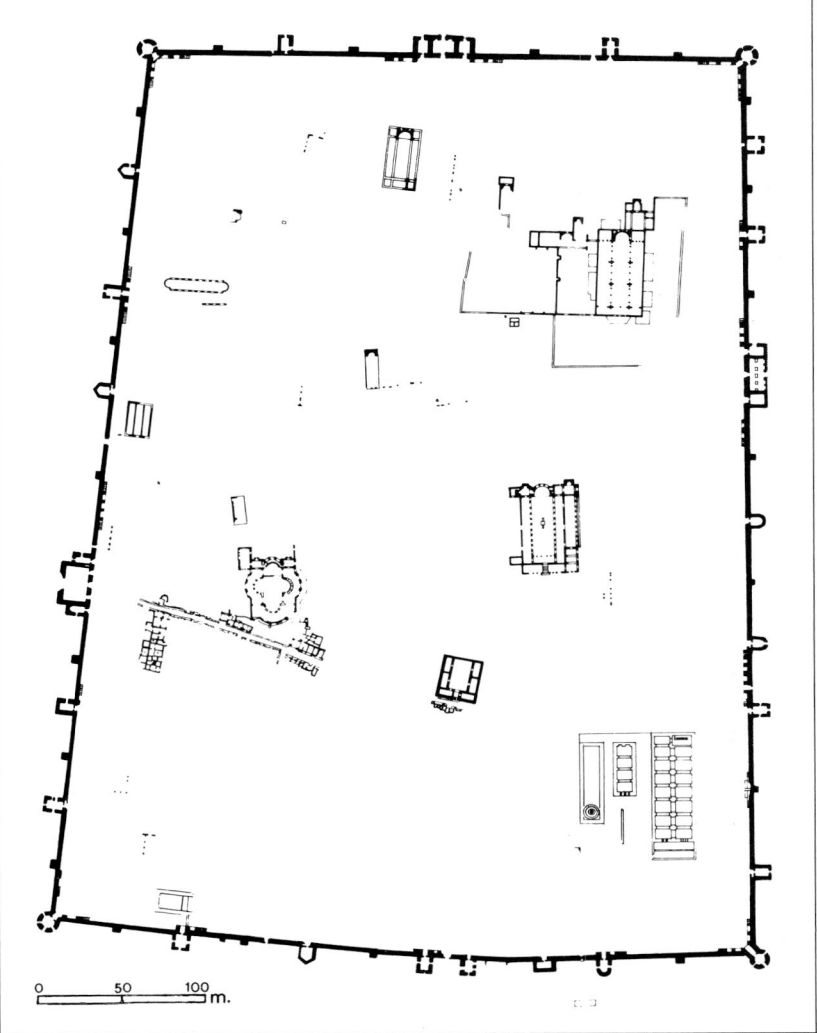

35. *Resafa, general view of city looking northeast.*

36. *Resafa, north gate.*

37. *Resafa, big cistern (detail).*
38. *Dara, city wall, south sector.*
39. *Dara, city wall, north sector, interior of tower.* ▷

40. *Dara, city wall, north sector, showing entrance of stream into city.*
41. *Dara, cisterns.* ▷

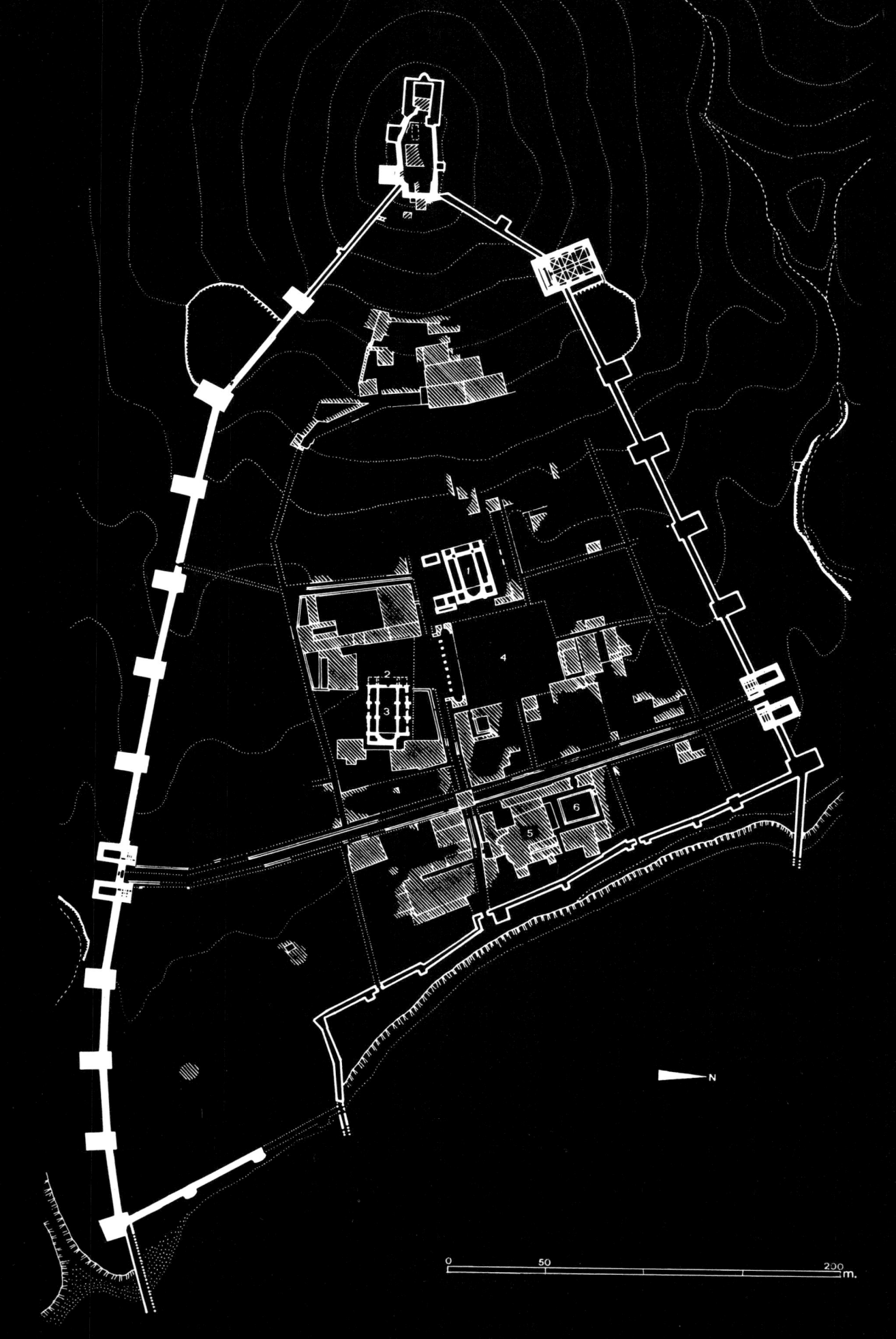

N

0   50   200
                                                               m.

◁ 42. *Zenobia (Halabiye), city plan (after F. Sarre and E. Herzfeld, 1911, and J. Lauffray, 1951).*
1. *Eastern church | 2. Atrium | 3. Western church | 4. Forum | 5. Public baths | 6. Palaestra.*

43. *Zenobia (Halabiye), general view looking south.*

steeply to an unassailable citadel, are immensely strong and comprise a three-story guardhouse or *praetorium* whose massive vaults in stone and brick are in places hardly touched by the passage of fourteen centuries. Not so the breakwater, which was ingeniously devised by John and Isidore; for the most part, it has been swept away by the Euphrates. The layout of the streets was as regular as the terrain allowed, with *cardo* and *decumanus* intersecting at right angles, and a rectangular forum. Public buildings included at least two churches and a bathing establishment. The starkness of their architecture accords well with the military character of Zenobia.

The Byzantine cities we have just described were all quite small by antique or modern standards. Dara, the largest of them (maximum diameter 1,100 yards), was considered to be a center of immense strategic importance and is called a "very big" city in contemporary sources. This gives us an interesting standard of comparison to judge the unique case of Constantinople.[8]

Of Constantine's city, inaugurated in 330, almost nothing now remains, but we can form an approximate idea of it. As I have said, it was not a creation *de novo,* but the enlargement of an earlier town going back to the seventh century B.C., and most recently rebuilt and fortified by Septimius Severus. The Severan town, with its hippodrome, its baths of Zeuxippus, and its agora, determined in large part the layout of the new capital. The hippodrome was extended to a length of nearly 550 yards to provide not only a sufficiently large "amusement center," but also a focus of imperial ceremonial. Its form was entirely standard: tiers of seats arranged in hairpin form, the arena divided by a low wall *(spina),* which supported an assortment of statues and obelisks, and an imperial box *(kathisma)* in the middle of the southeast wing. Next to the hippodrome and connected to the *kathisma,* Constantine built his palace, which, progressively added to and modified, was to remain the imperial residence until the eleventh century under the name of the Great or Sacred Palace. This was a city within a city, covering about the same area as Resafa: a law of the year 409 proclaims that the imperial authority had a right to vast spaces inaccessible to the public *(nam imperio magna ab universis secreta debentur).*[9] Constantine's palace probably had some features in common with Diocletian's at Spalato, but its exact form is unknown. In any case, it should be visualized not as a building but as a group of halls, pavilions, and churches connected by galleries and separated by gardens.[10]

The center of the Constantinian city was thus superimposed upon that of the Severan: in addition to the hippodrome, the palace, and the thermae of Zeuxippus, several other public buildings were clustered around, such as the Senate House (for Constantinople had to have a Senate of its own, even if this august assembly had become largely symbolic), a large peristyle basilica that was used for a variety of civic functions, and the first cathedral of St. Sophia, which was built by Constantine's successor, Constantius II, and dedicated in 360.

From this center, or ganglion, a wide colonnaded street, called the Regia or Mesê, led in a westerly direction to an oval forum, in the middle of which was set a porphyry pillar supporting a statue of Apollo-Helios. This pillar has survived in a disfigured condition, its pedestal covered with Turkish stonework, its shaft blackened and cracked, its capital fallen. The Mesê continued westward to the Forum Tauri, laid out in the reign of Theodosius I. Its focal point was provided by a monumental column with spiral decoration modeled after those of Trajan and Marcus Aurelius in Rome. Another feature of the Forum Tauri was a triumphal arch supported on sets of four columns each, their shafts covered with "eyes" like tree trunks whose branches have been sawed off. Proceeding farther westward, one reached a square called Philadelphion, ornamented with two porphyry columns bearing carved groups of Constantine's sons—these are the so-called Tetrarchs, now in the Piazza S. Marco, Venice.[11] At the Philadelphion the Mesê forked, one arm extending in a northwesterly direction toward the church of the Holy Apostles, where Constantine and his successors were buried, the other arm westward to the Forum Bovis and the Forum Arcadii. The latter also had a triumphal column with spiral decoration, which lasted down to the eighteenth century and whose pedestal is still preserved.

Such, in brief, was the aspect of fourth-century Constantinople. Hastily put up according to the usual formulas, it was full of "prestige" monuments rivaling those of Rome but, if possible, bigger and flashier. Hundreds of statues, looted from various cities of the Near East, further enhanced the artificially produced magnificence of the new city. It has often been said that Constantine intended to set up a specifically Christian capital, but for this I can find little evidence. On the contrary, the imitation of imperial Rome was apparent at every step, and the number of churches ascribed to Constantine on good authority is extremely small: St. Irene, the Holy Apostles, perhaps St. Acacius. Apollo-Helios, Constantine's tutelary god, surmounted the most prestigious monument of the forum. Besides, ancient Byzantium had had no Christian associations whatsoever, so that its choice as capital could not have been dictated by any motives of piety.

The urban development of Constantinople proved very rapid, so that, within a few decades of its inauguration, the populated areas were spilling beyond the walls. To protect the inhabitants from the threat of barbarian attack, a wider circuit of walls was built by Theodosius II and completed in 413. This time the enclosed space proved

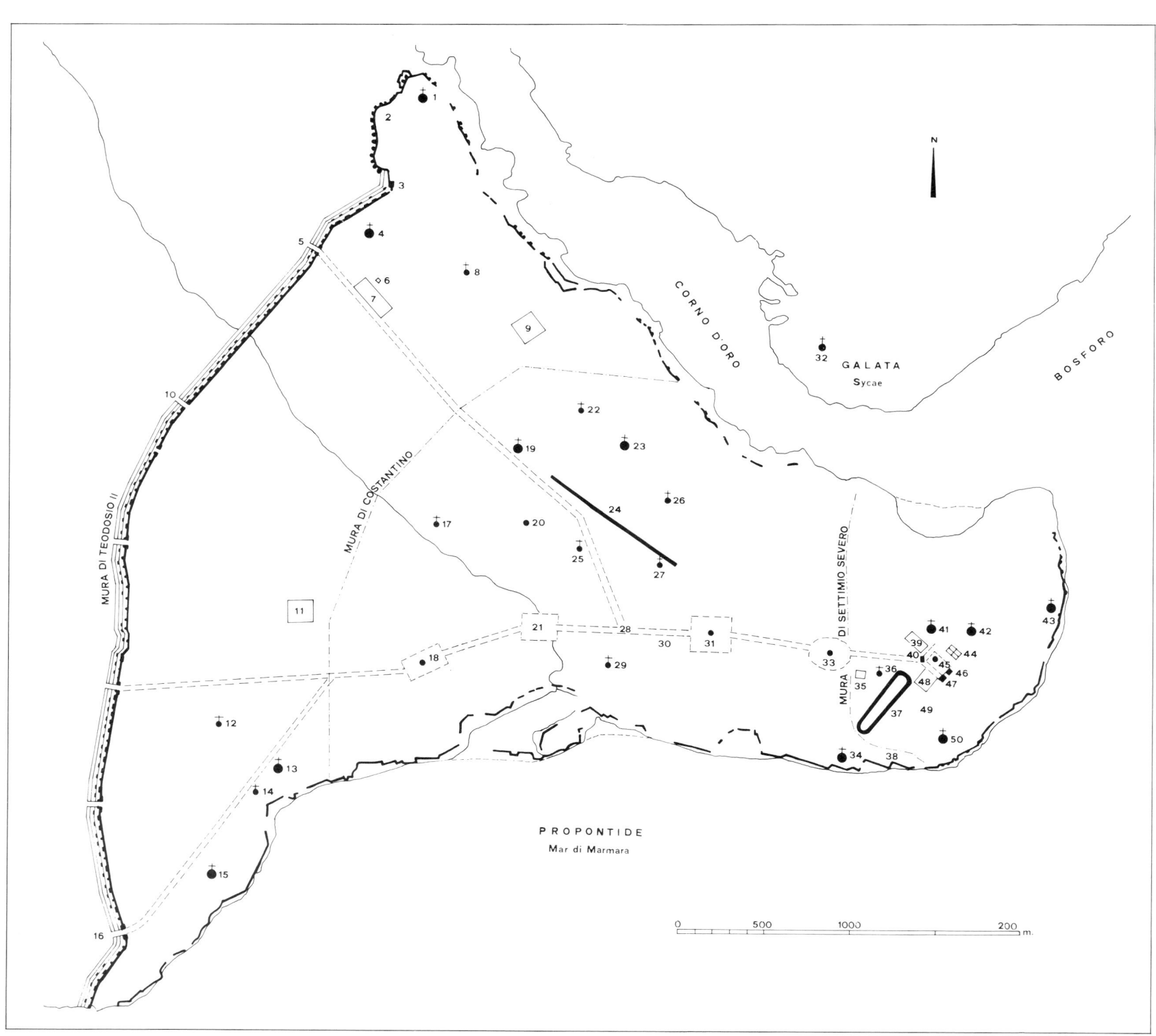

45. *Medieval Constantinople, city plan.*

1. St. Mary of Blachernae | 2. Blachernae Palace | 3. Tekfursarayı | 4. Kariye Camii | 5. Charisian gate | 6. Karagümrük cistern | 7. Aetius cistern | 8. St. Mary Pammakaristos | 9. Aspar cistern | 10. St. Romanus gate | 11. St. Mocius cistern | 12. St. Andrew in Crisei | 13. St. Mary Peribleptos | 14. Sts. Carpos and Papylos | 15. St. John of Studius | 16. Golden Gate | 17. Monastery of Lips | 18. Forum Arcadii | 19. Church of the Holy Apostles | 20. Column of Marcian | 21. Forum Bovis | 22. Christ Pantepoptes | 23. Christ Pantocrator | 24. Aqueduct of Emperor Valens | 25. St. Polyeuktos | 26. Kilise Camii | 27. Kalenderhane Camii | 28. Philadelphion | 29. Myrelaion | 30. Tetrapylon | 31. Forum Tauri | 32. Arap Camii | 33. Forum of Constantine | 34. Sts. Sergius and Bacchus | 35. Binbir Direk cistern | 36. St. Euphemia | 37. Hippodrome | 38. Bucoleon | 39. Basilica | 40. Milion | 41. St. Mary Chalkoprateia | 42. St. Irene | 43. St. George of Mangana | 44. St. Sophia | 45. Augustaion | 46. Senate House | 47. Chalkê | 48. Baths of Zeuxippus | 49. Imperial Palace | 50. Nea Ekklesia.

46. *Constantinople, Hippodrome (late 15th–century engraving).*
47. *Constantinople, curved end (sphendonê) of Hippodrome.*

48. *Constantinople, porphyry column (drawing of 1574). Library of Trinity College, Cambridge, England.*
49. *Constantinople, porphyry column as in 1957.*

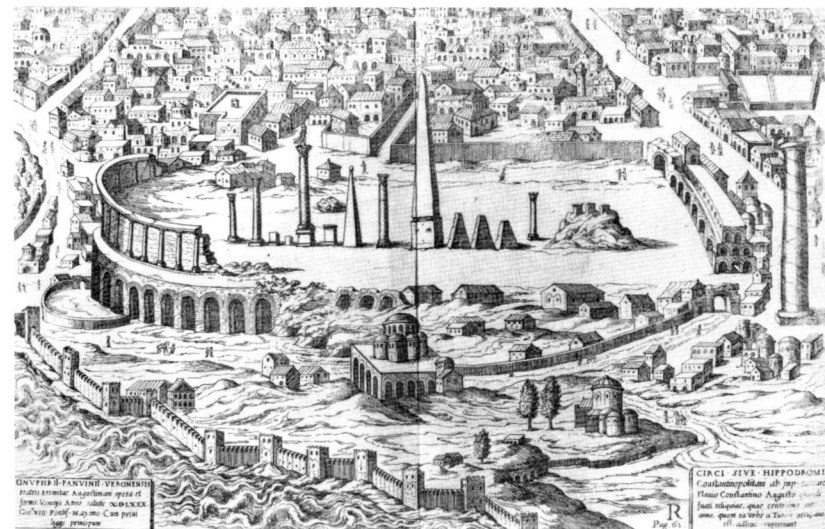

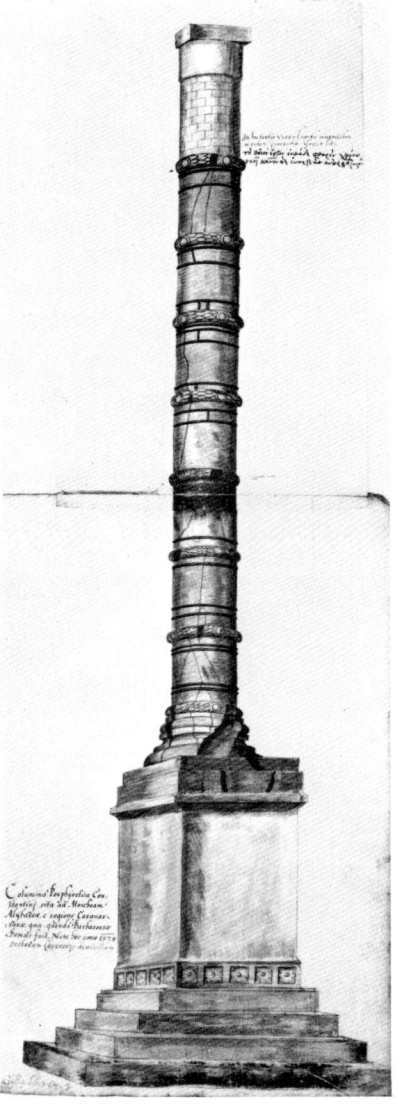

50. *Constantinople, remains of Arch of Theodosius I.*
51. *Constantinople, relief from Column of Theodosius I.*

52. *Constantinople, Column of Arcadius (late 17th-century drawing).*
Bibliothèque Nationale, Paris.

amply sufficient: no further need arose to enlarge it, except for a small extension that was added in the seventh century to protect the highly venerated church of St. Mary of Blachernae. The Theodosian walls are still extant and consist of the following elements: a moat, 65 feet wide, protected on the city side by a low parapet; then an outer walk, 46 feet wide; then the outer wall, 29 1/2 feet high, provided with towers; then an inner walk, 65 feet wide; and finally the main wall, about 36 feet high on the outside and 16 1/2 feet thick, with square and polygonal towers rising to a height of some 75 feet from the walk. This stupendous fortification described an arc some four miles long, from the Golden Horn to the Sea of Marmara. At the latter end, the Golden Gate, with its vast marble pylons and triple arcade, provided a ceremonial entrance on the main coastal road.[12]

About the year 425 a short statistical account of Constantinople was drawn up.[13] For all its brevity, it is a precious document, since it enumerates the particulars of each of the fourteen regions into which the city—like Rome—was divided, and then gives us some total figures: 5 imperial palaces, 14 churches, 8 public baths, 2 basilicas, 4 fora, 2 theaters, 4 harbors, 4 cisterns, 322 streets, 4,388 *domus* (that is, substantial private residences), 52 colonnades, and 153 private baths. In the succeeding centuries the number of churches increased at a prodigious rate. Yet, when we examine a map of medieval Constantinople, we are at once struck by the following fact: not only did the city attain its maximum extension by 413, but all the major works of public utility date from the Early Byzantine period. These include the aqueduct of the emperor Valens, the three enormous uncovered cisterns (those of Aetius, Aspar, and St. Mocius), and the vast majority of the covered cisterns, including the biggest, that of Philoxenus and the Cisterna Basilica (both from Justinian's reign). The same applies to the honorific columns and monuments of the fora: none was later than the sixth century.

A number of points emerge from the above account. First, it may be said that, setting aside the unique case of Constantinople and that of the new Byzantine foundations, which were few in number and small in size, the vast majority of the urban population of the Empire continued residing in antique cities. Second, these cities, though not actively declining in the period under review, were not expanding either, and the time of their maximum prosperity was long past. Third, there was no dramatic upheaval in the pattern of urban life in the fourth century: instead, we witness a gradual evolution. Its most obvious manifestation was the change of religion, but this, too, did not take place overnight. The suppression of paganism stretched over about two centuries, from Constantine to Justinian.

54. *Constantinople, Column of Marcian.*

55. *Constantinople, gigantic capital of honorific column (5th century) found in second court of Seraglio.*

56. *Constantinople, city walls (reconstruction by F. Krischen).*

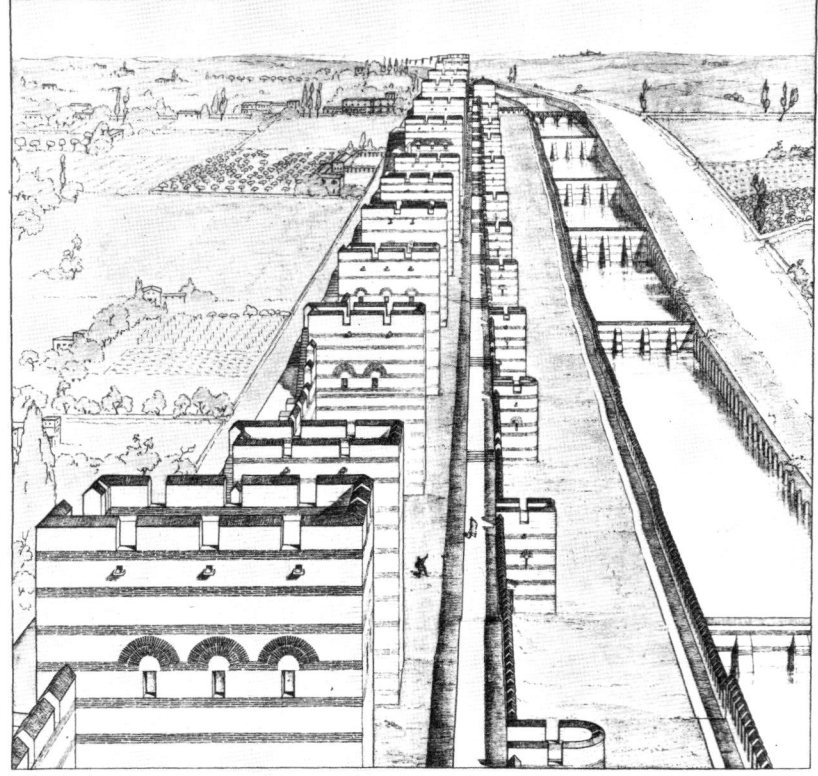

57. *Constantinople, Wall of Theodosius II.*

The law of the emperor Theodosius I of 392 prohibiting the performance of all pagan cults did not entail the immediate closing of all temples, just as the law of Theodosius II of 435 ordering their destruction was not universally obeyed. Some were destroyed, others were left derelict. The Christians, who believed these temples to be inhabited by demons, tended to set up their houses of prayer on less defiled ground. It was only toward the sixth century and even in the early seventh that pagan temples were converted into churches, as happened at Athens, Rome, and elsewhere.[14]

Other gradual changes were not connected with the religious factor. We have seen that shops tended to migrate from the agora to street porticoes, thus approximating the pattern of an Oriental bazaar. The demise of city self-government meant that buildings such as bouleuteria were no longer required. In the domain of entertainment and sports, gymnasia and stadia went out of fashion. The latter were too small to be converted to chariot racing, which was undoubtedly the most popular sport of the Early Byzantine period, but one that could be practiced only in the larger cities that possessed hippodromes. Theaters continued to be used, not, of course, for tragedies and comedies, but for mimes and pantomimes and as places of public assembly. The frequency of the disturbances that took place in them, the indecency of the shows, and the disapproval of the Church all contributed to their gradual abandonment.

The net result of these transformations was that in most cities some of the largest and most ornate public buildings became redundant. The temptation to use them as quarries, both of building blocks and carved elements, could hardly be resisted. A number of imperial constitutions prohibiting this activity (except for pagan temples) only bear witness to the prevalence of the abuse, and there is ample archaeological evidence that from the fourth century on frequent use was made of spoils. This, I believe, is a phenomenon of great importance for the understanding of Byzantine architecture. It was in the very nature of spoils that they should have been, so to speak, "given," and not tailored to the needs of the building in which they were to be reused. If, say, it was necessary to procure twelve column shafts and twelve capitals for a Christian basilica, it was not easy to find identical pieces; and there was a strong likelihood that the shafts would have been of different marble and different thickness, the capitals of different design. What may have started as an undesirable convenience created a tolerance for irregularity, which, in turn, became an aesthetic principle. By the sixth century, if not earlier, it was quite normal to introduce different capitals into the same order, even when these capitals were not reused but made specifically for the job, as in the basilica of St. Catherine on Mount Sinai. It should be noted, however,

that this phenomenon did not apply to Constantinople in the Early Byzantine period, since there the antique town was quite small, whereas the building activity of the fourth to the sixth century was prodigious; nor did it apply to new cities that did not have easy access to ancient ruins. In the following pages we shall have frequent occasion to return to the subject of spoils.

57

The reign of Constantine (307–37) is normally regarded as marking the beginning of Byzantine history, and in many respects this is a justified view; it cannot be regarded, however, as marking a turning point in the history of art and architecture. The two salient accomplishments of Constantine's administration were the adoption of Christianity as the favored (not yet the exclusive) religion of the state and the foundation of Constantinople. Neither of these exerted an immediate effect on the arts, though both exerted a delayed reaction of immense importance.

Christianity, an eschatological religion, had no artistic tradition of its own: it was indifferent and even hostile to art. Constantine's conversion meant that a "public" Christian art had to be created, using whatever formulas were current at the time. It took about a century for this art to assume its own individuality, and even longer, until about 500, before there occurred a definite change of taste. But once a distinctive Christian art had emerged, it enjoyed an enormous diffusion in space and time. The same may be said of Constantinople. The ancient city of Byzantium, as far as we know, had not been particularly noted for its art. Its sudden transformation into an imperial capital necessitated, as we saw in the last chapter, the importation and superimposition of accepted architectural formulas that must have made it resemble other capitals of the Tetrarchic period, like Sirmium or Nicomedia. But, by remaining the imperial capital, Constantinople assured over the centuries a place of primacy to the artistic traditions that flourished in its geographical area and, more generally, to Oriental influences.

"There is need of as many architects as possible; but since there are none of them, Your Sublimity shall encourage to this study those men in the African provinces who are about eighteen years old and have had a taste of the liberal arts." So runs an ordinance of Constantine of 334 addressed to the praetorian prefect posted at Carthage.[1] It may be that the shortage of architects was particularly acute in Africa; but it would be reasonable to suppose that a similar situation prevailed in most parts of the Empire, since traditions of craftsmanship must have been severely affected by the prolonged troubles of the third century, and, furthermore, Constantine's ambitious building program must have imposed too heavy a burden upon the diminished professional personnel. The historian Zosimus reports that many of the buildings put up by Constantine in his new capital soon collapsed.[2] The almost total disappearance of Constantinian architecture in the eastern provinces may lend some substance to this criticism.

How was a Christian architecture created? The Church historian Eusebius gives us a valuable clue when he tells us that in the latter part of the third century, that is, during the forty or so years of tolerance

which the Christians enjoyed before the great persecution of 303, "Christians, not content with their old buildings, erected from the ground up spacious churches in all the cities."[3] Eusebius was an eye-witness, and his testimony can hardly be doubted, at least as relating to Syria and Palestine. Can it be that these "spacious churches" provided the model for those of the fourth century? It is Eusebius again who describes the cathedral of Tyre, built sometime between 314 and 317.[4] His account of it is, unfortunately, very rhetorical, but it tells us that the cathedral was a basilica (as we use the term today) with a colonnaded atrium and a three-aisled house of prayer, timber-roofed and lit through a clerestory. Additional features were seats for the clergy and the separation of the chancel from the nave. The whole complex was enclosed by a wall. In the period 314–17 the East was ruled not by Constantine but by Licinius, and I consider it very unlikely that the bishop of Tyre would have received the plans for his cathedral by special messenger from Rome. He probably followed the formulas already adopted by the Christians in those parts before 303.

This suggestion, which is not new, cannot at present be substantiated by any physical remains and is in conflict with the commonly held view that the Christian basilica was born in Rome precisely in the year 313, which is supposed to be the foundation date of St. John Lateran. However that may be, there can be little doubt that the Christian basilica was adapted from a type of building that was widely used in the Roman world for a variety of secular purposes—as markets, courts of law, lobbies, reception halls, and audience chambers—in short, for almost any purpose that entailed the presence of a large gathering other than the celebration of pagan worship.[5] The "secular basilica" had no standard form, except that it was usually oblong, nearly always timber-roofed, and contained at the far end a tribunal that could be used by the presiding magistrate. The only preserved basilica that is firmly associated with Constantine, the basilica of Trier (built between 305 and 312), was an imperial audience hall and is an imposing single-aisled structure terminating in a semicircular apse. It is quite understandable that the Christians should have taken over a type of meeting hall that was in no way reminiscent of paganism and did not evoke any particular associations, except perhaps with the state. Other religious groups, like the Jews and the sectaries of Mithra, had adopted a similar course.

From the fourth to the sixth century inclusive, the basilica constituted in the East and the West alike the standard type of parochial, episcopal, and even monastic church. It admitted of a great number of variations which I do not intend to discuss in detail: it could have either three or five aisles, usually separated by colonnades;

a transept, the exact function of which is unclear, could be added; it had either a clerestory or a gallery; the apse normally projected on the outside, but in Syria and elsewhere in the East it was usually contained within a straight wall. Rather than listing these features, it may be more helpful to consider some concrete examples.

We may take St. John of Studius at Constantinople (c. 450) as representing the classical type of basilica in the capital.[6] Today it is a noble ruin, but most of its original features may be visualized without difficulty. The church was preceded by a square, probably colonnaded, atrium, of which the north wall is still standing. The present narthex was in fact the east wing of the atrium. It is an open structure, its middle bay divided by four columns carrying magnificent acanthus capitals and a horizontal carved entablature. The interior of the church is nearly square in plan (82 feet long, excluding the apse, and 79 feet wide). The nave was divided from the aisles by two rows of seven verd antique columns each (only the north row remains today), capped by acanthus capitals and supporting, once again, a straight entablature. Above the aisles and narthex there was originally a gallery, access to which was gained by exterior staircases or ramps. The apse, semicircular on the inside and three-sided on the outside, was lit by three large windows. There were no pastophoria.

Of the liturgical fixtures of the church, there is definite evidence of a synthronon, which had the usual annular shape, and the chancel, which projected into the nave on a stylobate of verd antique and had verd antique molded posts into which closure slabs were slotted. At the center of the chancel area a flight of steps leads down to a cruciform crypt: the altar table and ciborium must have been placed above this. No trace remains of the ambo. The fine interlace floor, of which parts may still be seen, was not original. It probably dates from the eleventh century.

The simple architectural shell of the Studius basilica contrasts with the richness of its decoration: the lavish use of verd antique, the elaborate capitals of "fine-toothed" acanthus, and the richly carved entablatures. In addition, the walls were surely covered with slabs of multicolored marble, and the apse and triumphal arch with mosaic. Two features may be worth noting: the use of the more classical, horizontal entablature, as opposed to the arcade, and the fact that the marble elements (the column shafts, capitals, and so forth) are uniform and were evidently made to order.

The contemporary basilica of the Virgin (usually called Acheiropoietos) at Thessalonica is in many respects similar to St. John of Studius, but shows some curious divergences.[7] It is larger and more elongated (118 feet long on the inside, excluding apse, and 92 feet wide), as a result of which the number of columns in each nave

62. *Constantinople, Studius basilica, ground plan (after A. van Millingen, 1912).*
63. *Constantinople, Studius basilica, narthex capital.*
64. *Constantinople, Studius basilica, exterior from the west.* ▷
65. *Constantinople, Studius basilica, interior.* ▷

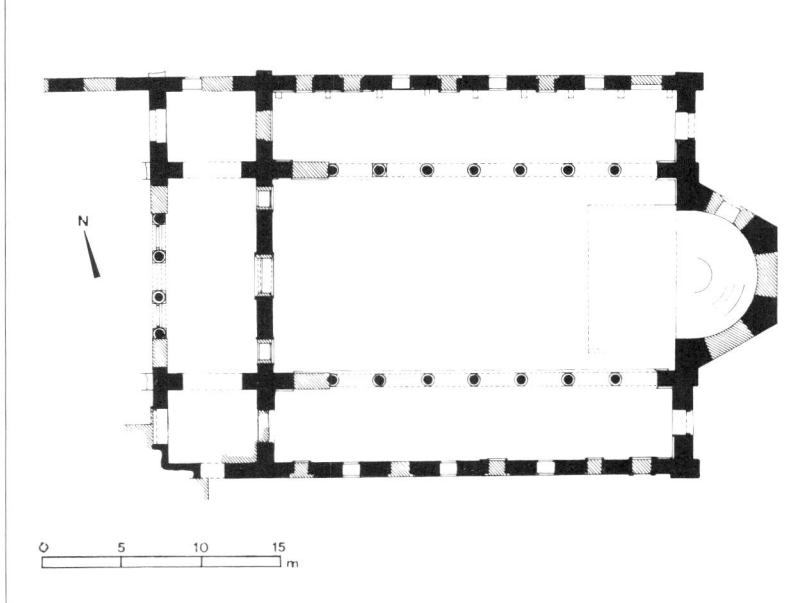

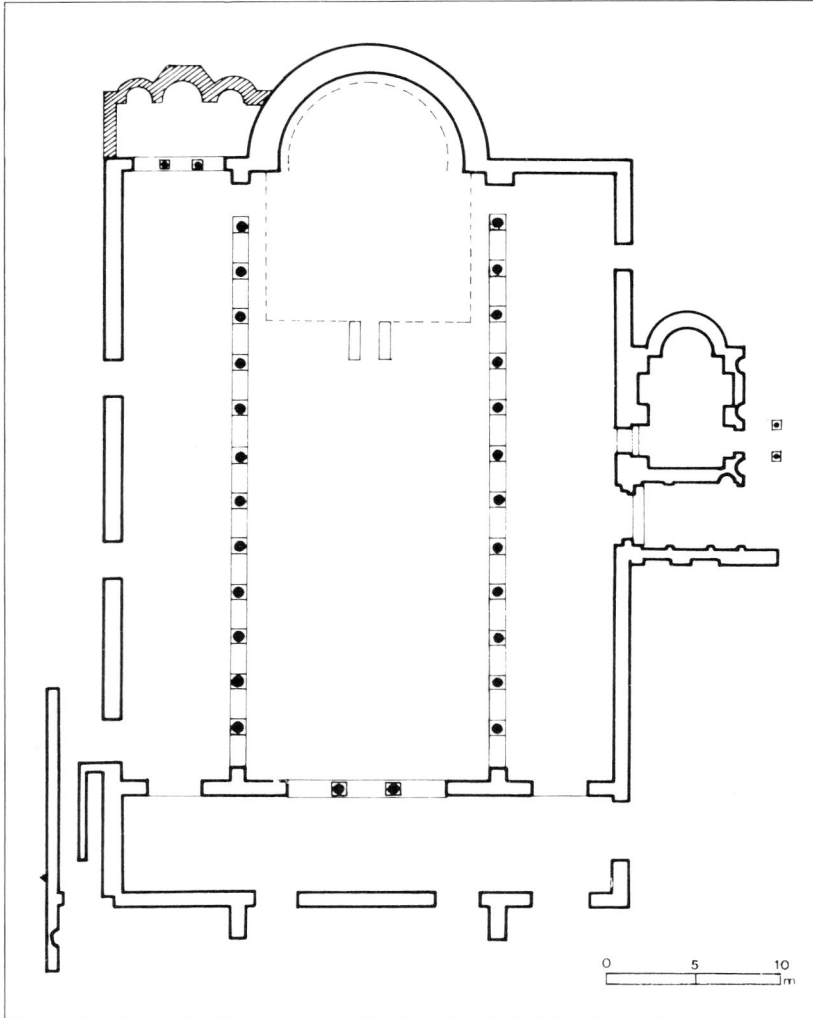

66. *Thessalonica, Acheiropoietos basilica, ground plan (after S. Pelekanides, 1949).*

colonnade has been increased to twelve. The system of galleries on a timber floor and exterior staircase is basically the same as in the Studius church. The following distinctive features may, however, be noted. First, the narthex is completely enclosed and, strangely enough, does not have a central exterior door, but only lateral doors. The reason for this arrangement (to control ingoing and outgoing circulation?) remains unclear. The opening from the narthex into the nave is, on the other hand, very wide and consists of a triple arcade or *tribelon*. The chancel arrangement, as recovered by excavation, differed from our Constantinopolitan example in that the entire interior of the apse was occupied by a low platform upon which, we may imagine, the bishop sat. Directly in front of this platform was placed the ciborium, and on either side of the latter were rectangular benches for the clergy. Further instances of this disposition may be found elsewhere in the Balkans. Another interesting feature is that the aisles were screened off from the nave by means of closure slabs inserted between the columns, whereas no such barrier existed in the Studius basilica. The marble elements were once again made to order: the acanthus capitals are all identical, as are the shafts, which are of Proconnesian marble, except for the two columns of the *tribelon,* which are of verd antique. The pavement of the nave, which appears to be original, consists of large slabs of veined marble, not of mosaic, as was so often the case in Early Byzantine basilicas.

The two examples I have quoted represent the fully evolved basilica in the central region of the Byzantine Empire. In all, several hundred basilicas are either standing or have been excavated in various provinces.[8] Some are much larger: the basilica of St. Leonidas at Lechaion (the harbor area of Corinth) was, including its narthex, nearly 360 feet long and about 99 feet wide;[9] the five-aisled basilica of Constantia, Cyprus, traditionally associated with St. Epiphanius (bishop from 368 to 403) measured 184 by 148 feet.[10] In Italy, as we know from many familiar examples in Rome and Ravenna, galleries were usually absent. This was also the case in Syria, where, under the influence of local building practice, there appeared a particularly monumental type of basilica constructed of massive stone blocks and possessing certain distinctive characteristics which we shall examine below. But whereas the Syrian basilica was timber-roofed and had a clerestory, farther north, on the Anatolian plateau and in Armenia, basilicas were often vaulted. In the latter case a continuous gable roof covered both nave and aisles, and the interior, nearly deprived of windows, was very dark.

Early Byzantine basilicas can be noble buildings, as any visitor to, say, S. Apollinare in Classe will attest. When seen in quantity, however, they produce an impression of monotony, of a ready-made

68. *Corinth–Lechaion, Basilica of St. Leonidas, ground plan (after D. Pallas, 1961).*

69. *Parenzo (Poreč), Basilica Eufrasiana, view into apse.*

70. *Parenzo (Poreč), Basilica Eufrasiana, two-zone capital in south arcade of nave.* ▷

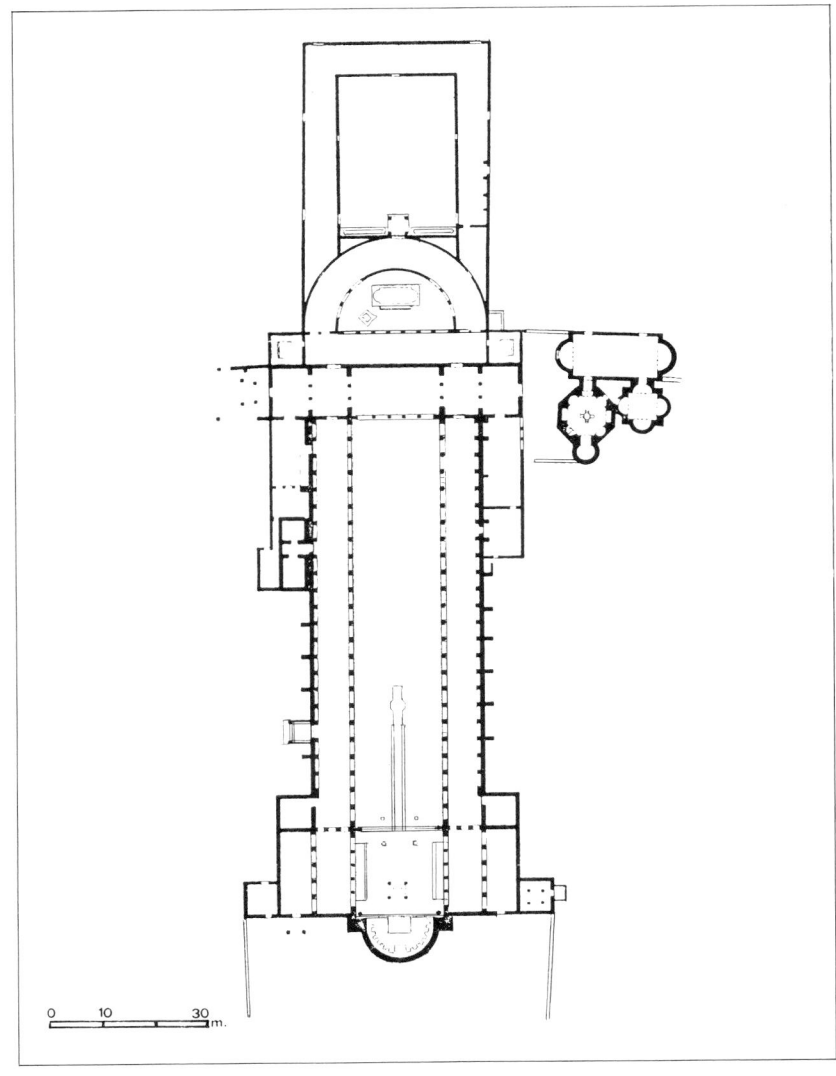

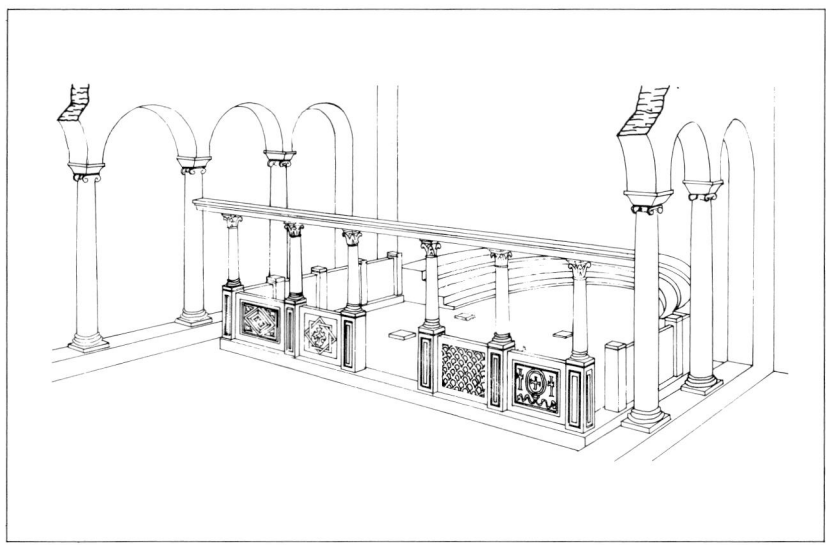

71. *Lesbos, Aphentelli basilica, reconstruction of bema (after A. Orlandos, 1935).*

uniformity. One cannot help wondering why this particular type of church building should have maintained itself so long, in so many widely scattered provinces, and, basically, with so little variation. The answer, it seems to me, is that the basilica was easy to construct and provided maximum effect for minimum effort. It could be expanded or contracted at will without creating any serious problems of engineering, the only limit being the width of the nave, which was determined by the size of the roofing timbers. Materials could be ordered in a standard size, and any moderately experienced master builder could supervise construction. In short, basilicas were mass-produced, and we all know the practical advantages of mass production.

For its effect the basilica depended not so much on its architecture as on its interior decoration: the marble columns, the carved capitals, the revetments of multicolored marble, sometimes even glass and mother of pearl (as at Parenzo), the stucco, the mosaic that was applied to the apse and triumphal arch, the tessellated or geometric pavement; also on the liturgical furniture, such as the chancel screen, the ciborium, and the ambo, which in richer basilicas were sheathed with silver. The supply of these items was dependent on the existence of a Mediterranean empire with its far-flung quarries and its network of maritime communications. For not only the raw materials, but also the finished product, were often supplied from one center. We are particularly well informed concerning the diffusion of capitals: many of these were quarried on the island of Proconnesus, shipped in a roughed-out condition, and presumably accompanied by a specialized sculptor who would finish the job on the spot. To

take a single example, in the early sixth century there came into vogue a rather ugly kind of capital known as the "two-zone" capital. It had animal protomes at the four corners (usually rams or doves), then a sharp horizontal line, and, below that, either basketwork or a grapevine, all deeply undercut. So fragile was the carving that these objects of overburdened, almost "Victorian," taste could not have been transported over any appreciable distance, nor imitated by local craftsmen. Yet we find them scattered all over the Mediterranean: in Italy, Istria, the Dalmatian coast, inland Macedonia, Greece, Asia Minor, and Egypt, in addition to Constantinople.[11] It is clear from this that, once the system of production and distribution that prevailed from the fourth to the sixth century had ceased to exist, the building of basilicas could not continue along the same lines.

The principal function of the basilica was, of course, the celebration of Christian service. Scholars have accordingly inquired whether the form of the building could not have been dictated by the requirements of the liturgy (this expresses the functional approach I mentioned in Chapter One). Stimulating as such an approach is, it seldom carries conviction. For one thing, we know far too little about the early development of the liturgy in all of its regional ramifications. Secondly, the practical requirements of Christian service in the early centuries were in themselves fairly flexible. Assuming a congregation that was being swelled by new converts, we may list the following necessities: a large meeting hall that was focused on the altar table and the officiating priest or bishop (by the fourth century it had become customary to pray in the direction of the east); a separation between clergy and laity, between the sexes, and between baptized Christians and catechumens; a pulpit for the reading of the lessons; adequate means of circulation for the procession of the First Entrance, when the clergy and congregation made their way into the church; a room with a table (the diaconicon) for the offerings of the faithful; a fountain for ablutions; and a baptistery. While these requirements were met by the basilica, they could equally well have been satisfied (and sometimes were) by a meetinghouse of entirely different form, which is equivalent to saying that the needs of the liturgy did not in themselves dictate the architectural setting.

The fluidity of usage may be illustrated with regard to the aisles and galleries. Were they used for any defined purpose? In describing the cathedral of Tyre, Eusebius appears to be saying that the aisles were reserved for catechumens. This would make good sense in terms of circulation: the aisles had their own exit doors and could be vacated without disturbing the congregation in the nave. The barrier separating the aisles from the nave (as in the Acheiropoietos at Thessalonica) could also be explained by this usage, provided it prevailed in the Balkans. But we have a contrary indication in the Byzantine use of the term *katêchoumena* (or *katêchoumeneia*) to designate the galleries, which also lent themselves to this purpose, since normally they communicated with the outside and not with the nave. To make matters more complicated, we also have evidence that men stood in the right aisle and women in the left; and, furthermore, that women were sometimes placed in the galleries.

Faced with such contradictory indications, we are tempted to conclude that there was no hard and fast rule about the utilization of these spaces, or, to put it another way, that the layout of the basilica was not specifically designed to accommodate certain definite pre-scriptions of worship. In fact, it may be suspected that in some respects the basilica was anything but functional. Take, for example, the case of predication, which was an essential component of the service. It was customary for the bishop to deliver the sermon from his throne, at the far end of the apse, whereas the ambo was used for the lections. Quite exceptionally, St. John Chrysostom preached from the ambo so as to be better heard, but he was a man of sickly physique. Even in a fairly small basilica, like St. John of Studius, the episcopal throne, placed behind the ciborium and the chancel screen, would have been at least thirty-two feet distant from the nearest members of the con-gregation, and the larger the basilica, the greater the distance. Con-sidering the fact that many sermons of the fourth and fifth centuries took as much as two hours to deliver, the demands on the preacher's vocal chords must have been almost superhuman.

Another consideration that militates against liturgical planning is that, as I have already pointed out, there appears to have been no distinction architecturally between parochial and monastic churches. The case of St. John of Studius is ambiguous since, according to one source, it was built as a parochial church, while according to another it was a monastery from the start. We have, however, many early monasteries in Syria as well as Alahan Manastīrī in Cilicia and St. Catherine's on Mount Sinai, and their churches are three-aisled basil-icas. Yet women were not normally allowed into monasteries, nor would catechumens have resorted to them. Why then was not the basilican plan altered accordingly?

Today we tend to regard the basilica as if it were an isolated building; in fact, however—especially in the case of episcopal churches—it was part of a larger complex whose function was not con-fined to religious activities.[12] We have examined one such complex at Gerasa and remarked on its lack of monumentality. Similar com-plexes have been discovered in many parts of the Byzantine Empire. Clustered around the basilica and its atrium were a great number of other buildings whose function it is not always possible to determine.

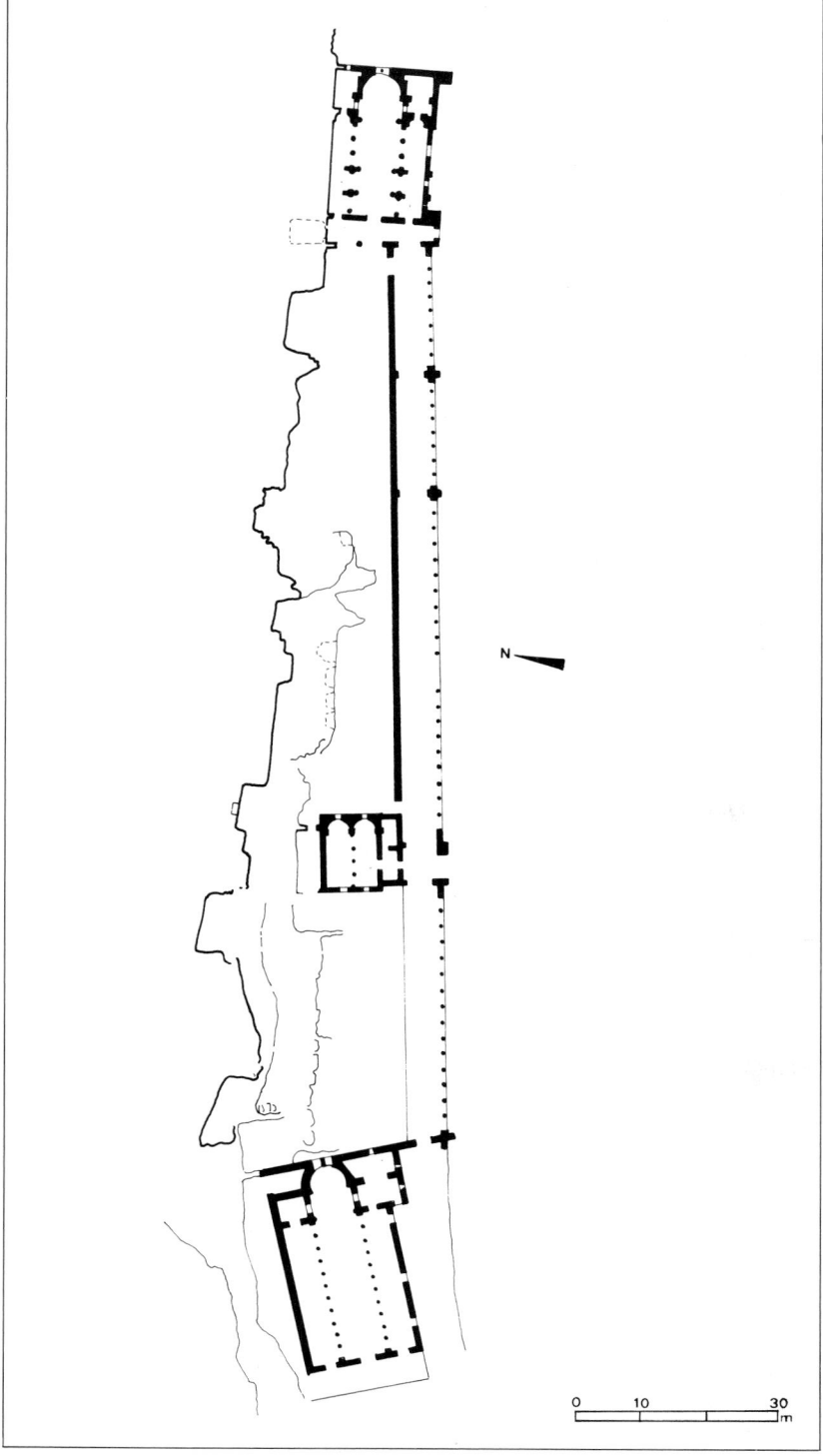

Sometimes there was a second basilica attached to the principal one. There was regularly a baptistery, whose position appears to have been random. There may have been a shrine enclosing the tomb of a saint. There were the residence of the bishop, quarters for the clergy and for visitors, and a bath. Finally, there were administrative offices and warehouses. It is only from written sources that we obtain a glimpse of the far-flung financial operations of a great see, like that of Alexandria, which even maintained a fleet of cargo ships, or the enormous administrative and judicial activity attached to the Patriarchate of Constantinople. We are still very far from knowing how these multifarious activities were translated into architecture.

Next to the basilica (episcopal or parochial), an important category of Early Byzantine architecture consisted of commemorative or pilgrimage shrines. It has become customary to refer to these as martyria, not only in the narrower sense of martyrs' sanctuaries, but also in the wider sense encompassing the Holy Places of Palestine.[13] Before inquiring whether a particular architectural type was attached to such shrines, it is well to remember that we are dealing here with a variety of commemorative arrangements. A martyrium may have perpetuated a place hallowed by Biblical history, such as the grotto of the Nativity, the Holy Sepulcher, or the Mount of Olives; or it may have housed the tomb of a martyr, or enclosed the pillar on which a famous stylite had carried out his *askesis*. Biblical sites and stylites' pillars were by definition irremovable: a shrine could be built next to them, over them, or around them. But in the case of the burials of martyrs, we face a further dichotomy. The ancient Roman custom prohibited any tampering with tombs, and this custom retained its force in the West until the sixth century. As a result, Roman martyria were built over the actual or supposed emplacement of the martyrs' tombs, that is, normally outside the walls. In the East, on the other hand, there developed the custom of transporting or "translating" holy relics from one place to another. The earliest case on record concerns the removal of the body of St. Babylas to Daphne, a suburb of Antioch, in 351–54. A couple of years later, in 356 and 357, the relics of Sts. Andrew, Timothy, and Luke were "translated" to the church of the Holy Apostles at Constantinople. Once a precedent had been set by imperial command, the migration of martyrs' relics became widespread; furthermore, it became customary to dismember them for greater distribution.[14] As time went by, nearly every church, whether commemorative or parochial, came to possess some particles of relics.

This development is important from the point of view of architectural planning. In the case of hallowed spots or monuments that were irremovable, the martyrium had to be adapted to the

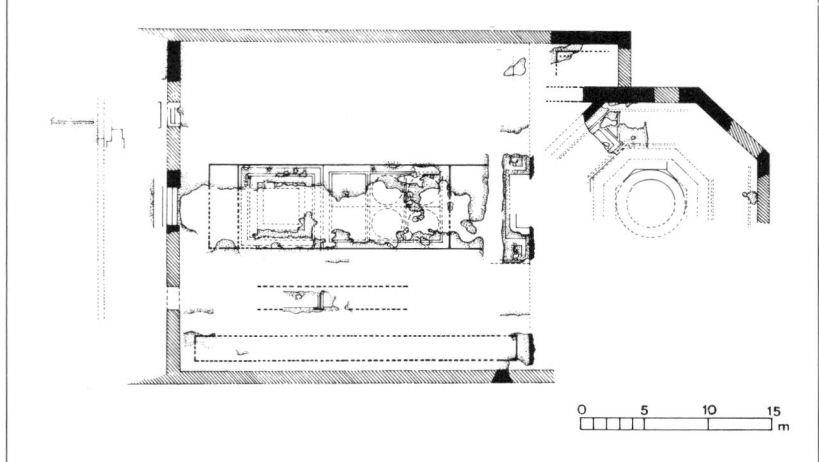

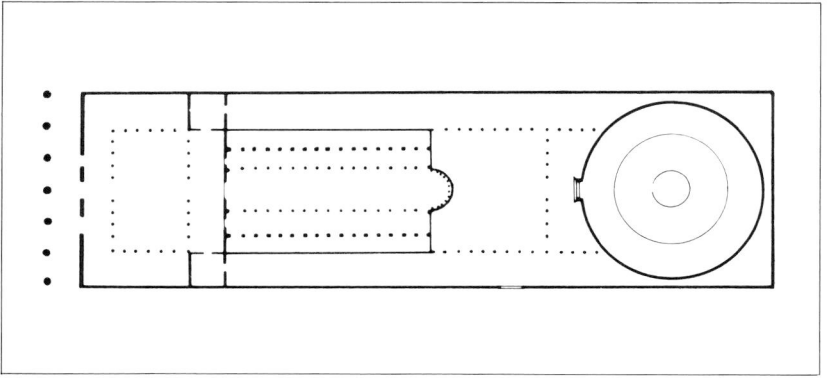

76. *Jerusalem, Holy Sepulcher, hypothetical ground plan of Constantinian complex (after H. Vincent and F.-M. Abel, 1925).*

77. *Jerusalem, Eleona church, ground plan and approximate section (after H. Vincent and F.-M. Abel, 1925).*

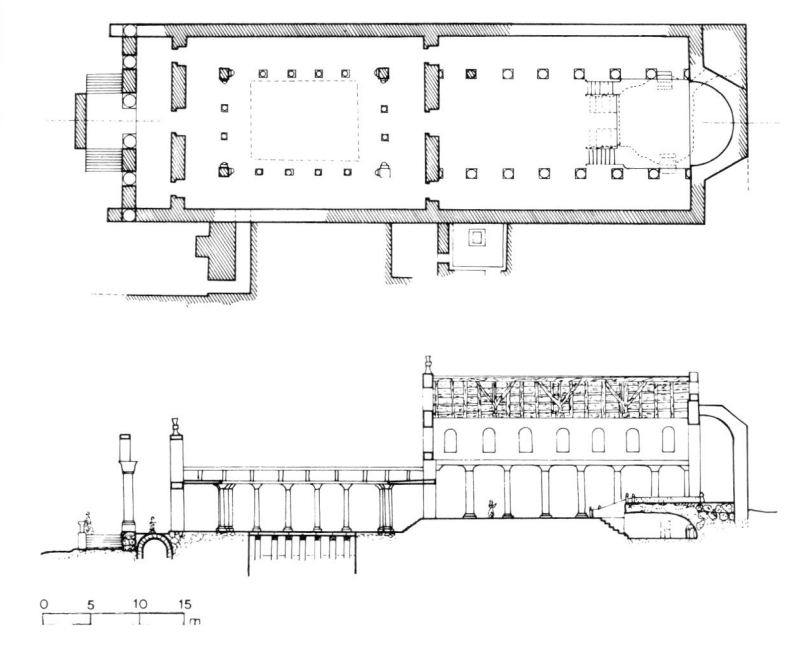

exigencies of the terrain so as to enshrine the object of veneration: the purpose of the martyrium was either purely "evidential" or both evidential and liturgical—in Rome these two aspects were combined already at the time of Constantine. When, however, the bodies of martyrs began to be moved, they no longer required a special architectural setting. They could be (and usually were) placed in churches of normal plan. Only in the case of particularly revered relics—relics that exuded a holy oil or some other effluvium that attracted a multitude of pilgrims—was a more elaborate arrangement called for.

The three principal commemorative shrines that were set up by Constantine (or St. Helena) in the Holy Land may be considered as prototypes of martyria in the East. The best-documented of the three is the church of the Nativity at Bethlehem: about half of its ground plan has been recovered beneath the present church, which was built by Justinian.[15] The Constantinian church consisted of three main parts disposed axially: an atrium, a five-aisled basilica, and an octagonal shell enclosing the cave. The basilica had a fine carpet pavement of mosaic. After traversing this, the pilgrim climbed three steps to the octagon, where a circular wellhead topped by a grille enabled him to look down into the cave, whose roof had been breached for the purpose. The octagon was surely timber-roofed. The excavations did not reveal any means of access to the cave in the fourth century nor any evidence of an altar for the celebration of the liturgy. It appears from this that the building was not primarily planned for a liturgical purpose. Furthermore, its size was quite modest and its layout not entirely symmetrical. When it was erected (before 333), the great influx of pilgrims to the Holy Places had hardly begun.

The larger and more important church of the Holy Sepulcher at Jerusalem is known to us mainly from written records.[16] It had some points of resemblance with the church of the Nativity in that it, too, was a five-aisled basilica, although it appears to have had a gallery, which was, presumably, absent at Bethlehem. The Jerusalem basilica terminated in a semicircular apse embedded in a straight outer wall, which the historian Eusebius describes as a *hemisphairion*, bordered by twelve columns which supported silver bowls. Some scholars have reconstructed the *hemisphairion* as a circle or three-quarter circle on the analogy of Bethlehem,[17] overlooking the important distinction that in the latter the octagonal appendage actually contained the object of veneration (the grotto), while at Jerusalem the Sepulcher of Christ was situated in an open courtyard to the west of the basilica and was enclosed by a separate architectural shell in the form of a baldachino. In this respect the solutions adopted were quite different. The Jerusalem basilica appears to have been intended for liturgical purposes and did not enfold the "cult object."

The third major Constantinian foundation in Palestine, the Eleona on the Mount of Olives, shows, once again, a different approach. Here, too, as at Bethlehem, there was a hallowed cave in which Christ was believed to have instructed His disciples. But instead of enclosing this *locus sanctus* within a centrally planned compartment, the architect placed it under the raised bema of an otherwise normal basilica. Of the original building hardly a stone remains in place, but its plan was established by excavation in 1910–11.[18] Placed on a declivity, the complex was terraced, rising stepwise from the outside to the atrium, from the atrium to the nave, and from the nave to the bema. The church itself (interior dimensions of rectangle 79 by 59 feet) was three-aisled and had a semicircular apse embedded in a straight exterior wall, a formula that became very common in both Palestine and Syria.

This brief survey of the Constantinian martyria of the Holy Land suggests to us that their architects improvised solutions based on the exigencies of each site rather than being guided by some general notion of "martyrial" architecture derived from Roman mausolea or Hellenistic *heroa*.

A particularly well-documented example of a great martyr's shrine is provided by the church of St. Demetrius at Thessalonica of about the middle or second half of the fifth century.[19] This almost completely burned down in 1917 and has since been rebuilt; many original elements, however, remain *in situ,* and they have been thoroughly investigated, even if a number of problems remain unresolved. St. Demetrius is a large, five-aisled transept basilica provided with a gallery. It is bigger than the Acheiropoietos and was evidently intended for a considerable concourse of people.

But what precisely were they coming to worship in the fifth century? Here lies one of the problems. It seems that originally St. Demetrius belonged to Sirmium, which was the capital of Illyricum until the seat of the prefect was moved to Thessalonica about 442. The cult of the saint may have migrated at the same time. However that may be, there arose a legend that St. Demetrius had been martyred at Thessalonica, in the heating plant of the public bath that was next to the hippodrome. This legend must have been known at the time the basilica was planned, for it was built on top of the bath and incorporated the substructure of the latter, which became a kind of crypt under the bema. The strange thing is, however, that the church did not possess any relics of the saint. The main feature of the crypt was a fountain, left over from the Roman bath, which was fenced off by means of a low marble enclosure.

The chief object of veneration in the basilica was not, however, the crypt but a hexagonal silver-sheathed ciborium, which was

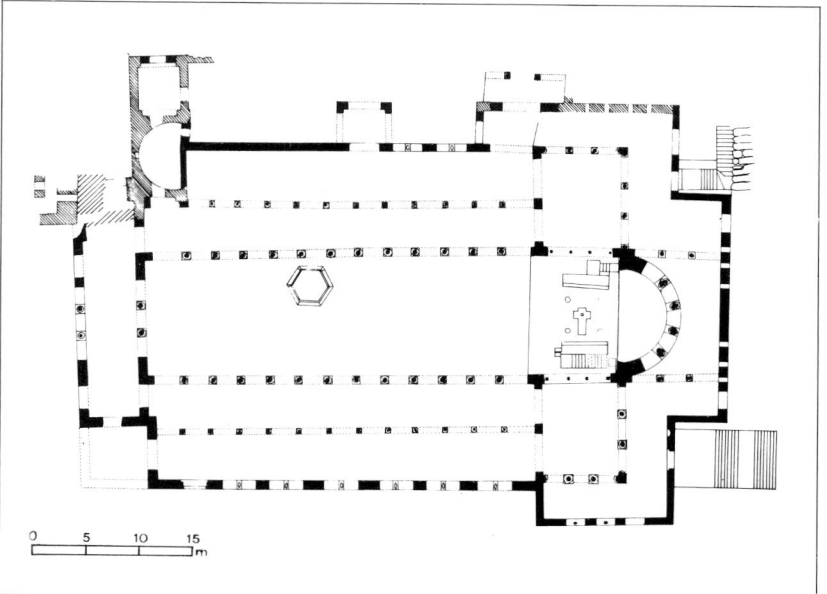

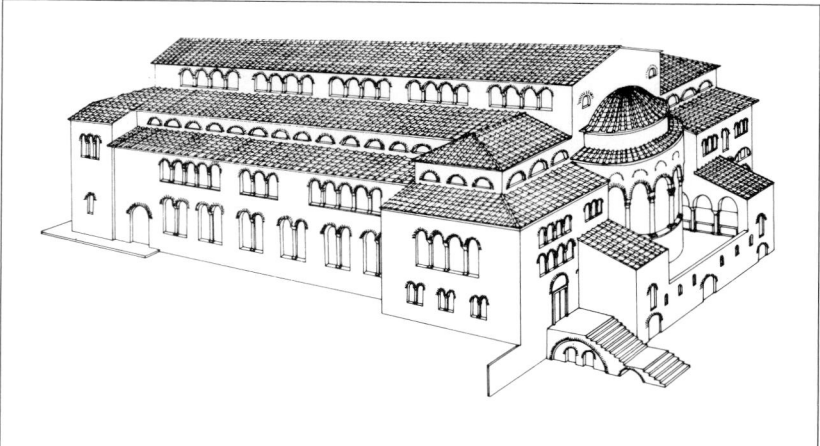

80, 81. *Thessalonica, St. Demetrius, interior before the fire of 1917.*

placed on the north side of the nave. This contained a silver object resembling a bed, on which was represented an image of the saint. But even for the ciborium no claim was made that it contained the body of Demetrius. Such were the original arrangements. At a later date, probably in the tenth century, Demetrius acquired the added distinction of exuding a miraculous oil. To satisfy the needs of the pilgrims, an elaborate and fraudulent system of concealed pipes was installed in the crypt so that the earlier water basins could be filled with oil.

We may deduce from the above that, whereas the fifth-century architect went to considerable trouble to locate the church over the spot where St. Demetrius was believed to have suffered martyrdom, he did not plan the building so as to give a central position to a cult object. The silver ciborium, which, until the seventh century was the focus of veneration, was placed off center in the nave, like a piece of liturgical furniture and no more. As for the transept, the function of this feature has not yet been ascertained: there appears, in any case, to be no reason to attach to it a martyrial significance.

Before leaving St. Demetrius, we may note that the main colonnades are assembled from reused or, at any rate, heterogeneous elements. Each colonnade is divided by two brick piers into bays of three, four, and three columns, respectively, an arrangement that is repeated at gallery level. The columns themselves are of different heights, are placed at varying intervals from one another, and are crowned by a wide variety of capitals, a few of which appear to date from the sixth century. It has been conjectured that the colonnades in question were rebuilt in the seventh century after the basilica had burned down. Some refection there certainly did occur, but I find it difficult to believe that the splendid marble revetment of the spandrels of the colonnade, including the *opus sectile* frieze representing modillions in perspective, could have been put up under the troubled conditions that prevailed at Thessalonica in the seventh century.

Almost contemporaneously with St. Demetrius there arose in northern Syria, between Aleppo and Antioch, the great complex of Qal'at Saman.[20] We know a great deal about the life of St. Simeon Stylites (c. 389–459), who stood on his pillar for more than forty years and, by this bizarre and highly public form of *askesis,* won extraordinary fame that extended, already in his lifetime, from Spain and Gaul to South Arabia. When he died, a force of 600 soldiers was sent to guard his body, which was conveyed to Antioch and deposited in the cathedral. Qal'at Saman appears to have been erected in the last quarter of the fifth century: it was not, strictly speaking, a martyrium, but a commemorative shrine centered around Simeon's pillar of forty cubits.

Strangely enough, no record exists concerning this immense architectural enterprise in which thousands of workmen must have been employed. The mountaintop which Simeon had made famous had to be partly leveled and partly built up by means of massive substructures. On this plateau was erected a huge cruciform shrine (about 310 feet from east to west and 280 feet from north to south), consisting of a central octagon enclosing the saint's pillar (its base is still preserved) and 4 radiating basilicas, the eastern one slightly longer than the others and terminating in 3 semicircular apses. Thus, only the eastern wing was used for liturgical purposes. There has been much discussion concerning the roofing of the octagon. A timber roof, probably conical, was certainly envisaged by the architect, but we do not know whether it was built. Toward the end of the sixth century the octagon was open to the sky,[21] which may mean either that it was never roofed or that the roof had already collapsed.

The concept of the cruciform church was by no means an innovation. Its prototype may have been the church of the Holy Apostles at Constantinople, built by either Constantine or his successor Constantius.[22] The martyrium at Nyssa (c. 370), tiny as it was, offered an exact antecedent of Qal'at Saman: a central octagon with corner niches in the diagonal sides, and four radiating arms.[23] Closer geographically was the cruciform church of Antioch-Kausiye, probably the martyrium of St. Babylas, erected in 381 and excavated in 1934.[24] At Qal'at Saman the builders went to much trouble to reproduce this plan on a large scale, thus indicating its symbolic importance. Originally, the saint's pillar stood very close to the western declivity of the hilltop, so that the western cross-arm had to be built almost entirely on substructures and an earth fill so as to be equal in length with the north and south arms. Traditional as the plan was, its execution must have demanded enormous resources that cannot be credited to local initiative. It has been conjectured that the enterprise was undertaken between 476 and 491 by the emperor Zeno, who is known to have encouraged large building projects in neighboring Cilicia and who sought a closer understanding with his eastern subjects. Even if this was an imperial commission, it was carried out by local craftsmen. The technique of ashlar construction and the sharp, spikelike character of the carving are unmistakably Syrian.

The cruciform church was the focus of a monumental complex that was put up either contemporaneously or in the next hundred years. To its southeast was a U-shaped monastic establishment with three-storied dormitories and a church of its own. Farther west stand a large baptistery in the shape of an octagon inscribed in a square and an adjoining basilica. Next to the baptistery there were hostels for pilgrims. At the foot of the hill the settlement of Deir Sim'an devel-

83. *Qal'at Saman, perspective view of monastic complex (after G. Tchalenko, 1953).*

84. *Qal'at Saman, ground plan of churches (after D. Krencker, 1939).*

85. *Qal'at Saman, view of churches from the northeast.* ▷

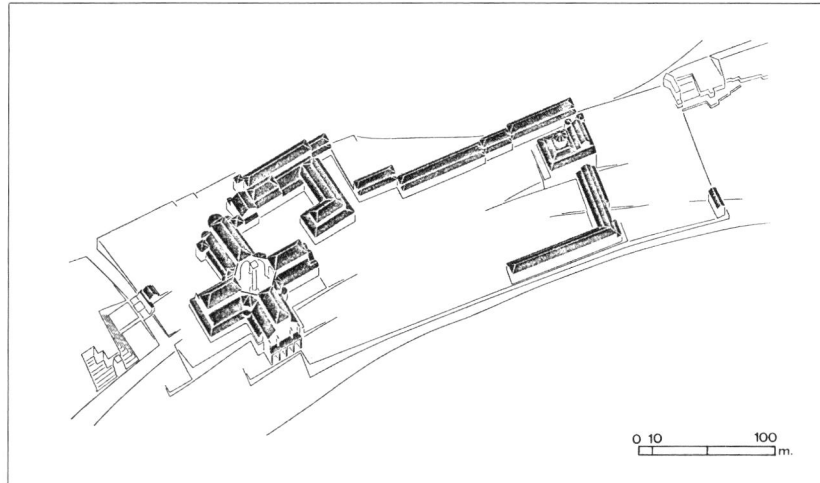

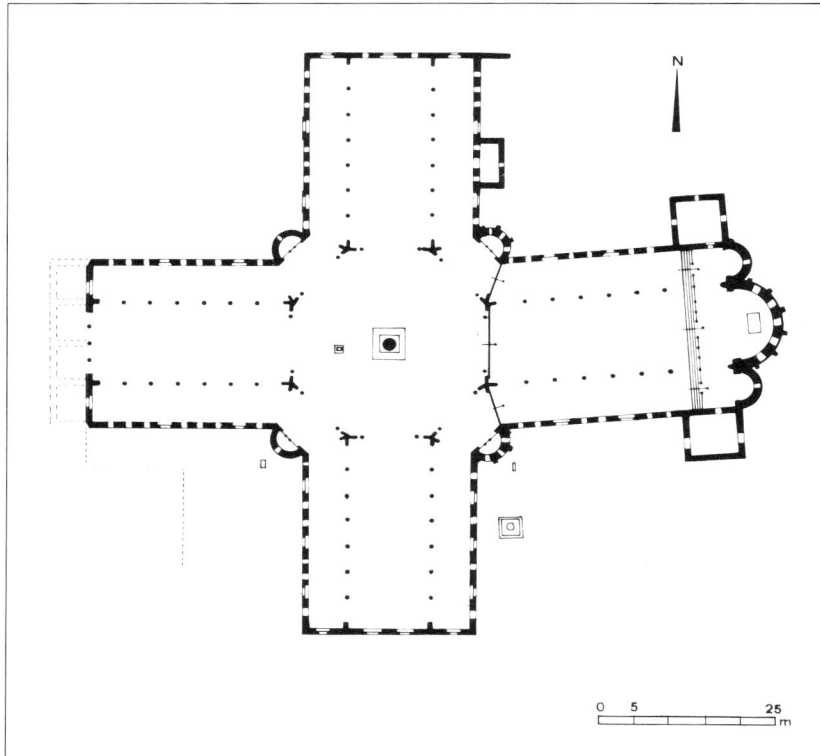

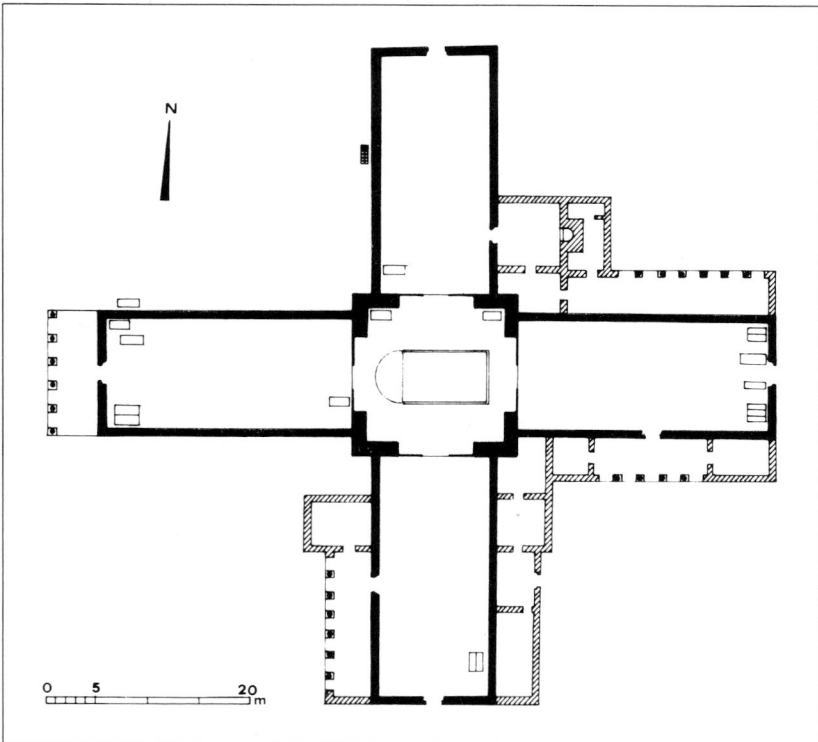

oped from a small village into a prosperous pilgrimage center with three monasteries and vast hostels. Nowhere else can we see so graphically the economic resources that could be set in motion in the Early Byzantine period by one holy man, whose supernatural gifts made him the equal, even the superior, of princes.

The above examples may have shown how difficult it is to establish a typological classification of Early Byzantine churches according to their function. While the basilican plan remained the commonest, a number of "centralized" forms were available—octagonal, cruciform, trefoil, quatrefoil, and so forth. The architect had several options, and in most cases we cannot determine why he chose one in preference to another. Thus, we are informed that the cathedral of Antioch, built by Constantine, was octagonal and had galleries, yet we have no reason to suppose that it was anything other than a cathedral. It may have served as model for the church of Nazianzus in Cappadocia, erected by Bishop Gregory (the father of St. Gregory Nazianzus) toward the middle of the fourth century: this, too, was an octagon with a gallery and was enveloped by a perambulatory. There are no grounds for thinking that it was a martyrium.

While these two churches are known to us only from brief literary descriptions, there is ample evidence that centralized plans were used for ordinary congregational purposes. A good example is provided by the cathedral of Bosra (512), a major part of which was still standing a hundred years ago.[25] This may be described as a circle, 118 feet in diameter, inscribed within a square, with projecting apse and pastophoria to the east. Concentric with the circle was an inner quatrefoil shell consisting of four columnar exedrae and four L-shaped piers which probably supported a conical wooden dome some forty feet in diameter. The resulting circular ambulatory was further diversified by four horseshoe-shaped exedrae in the corners and was amply lit by a ring of windows in the clerestory. The central space may have been occupied by an ambo, but the liturgical focus certainly lay in the exceptionally deep bema. The cathedral of Bosra is a particularly fine example of a large family of churches of the fifth and sixth centuries whose function, insofar as it can be determined, appears to have been normally episcopal. A similar quatrefoil church at Resafa was apparently attached to the bishop's palace, whereas what appears to have been the martyrium of St. Sergius (basilica B) was longitudinal in plan.[26]

Therefore, the centralized congregational church already existed in the reign of Constantine and cannot be regarded as the result of an evolution, of a gradual displacement of the basilica by the martyrium. But in that case, where did the inspiration come from?

92. *Bosra, cathedral, exterior (19th-century drawing).*

93. *Bosra, cathedral, hypothetical longitudinal section and ground plan (after A. H. Detweiler, 1937).*

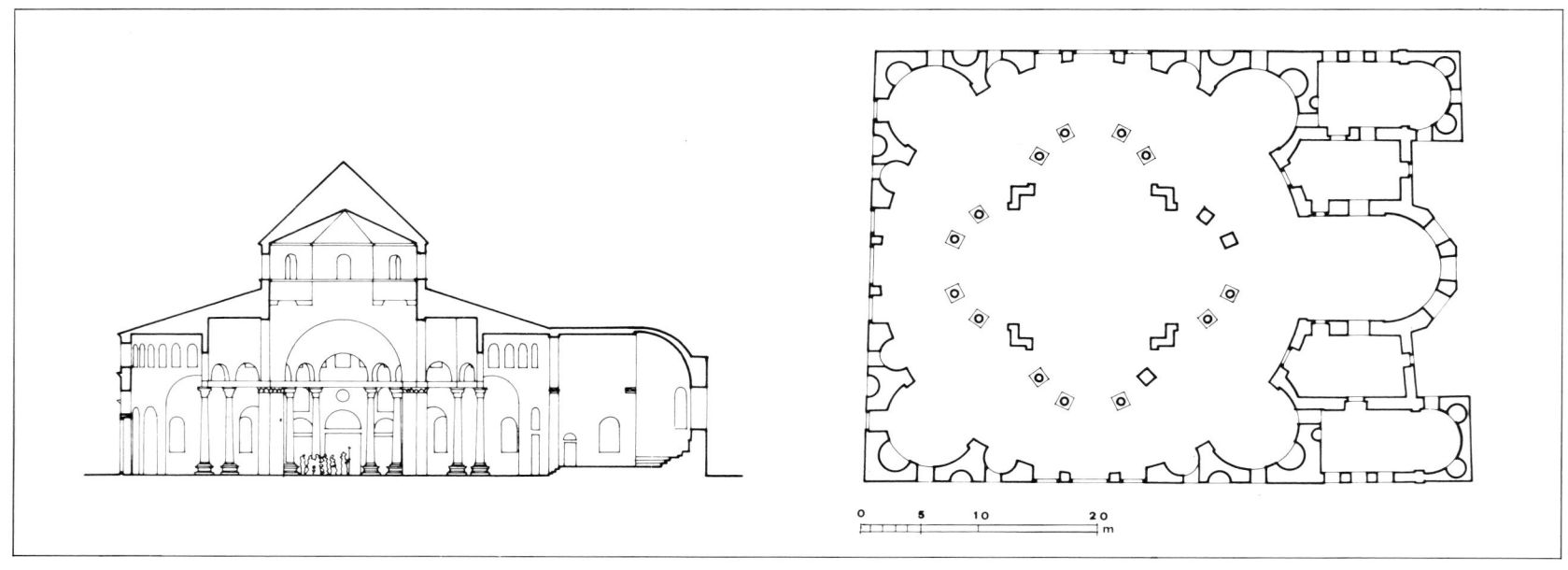

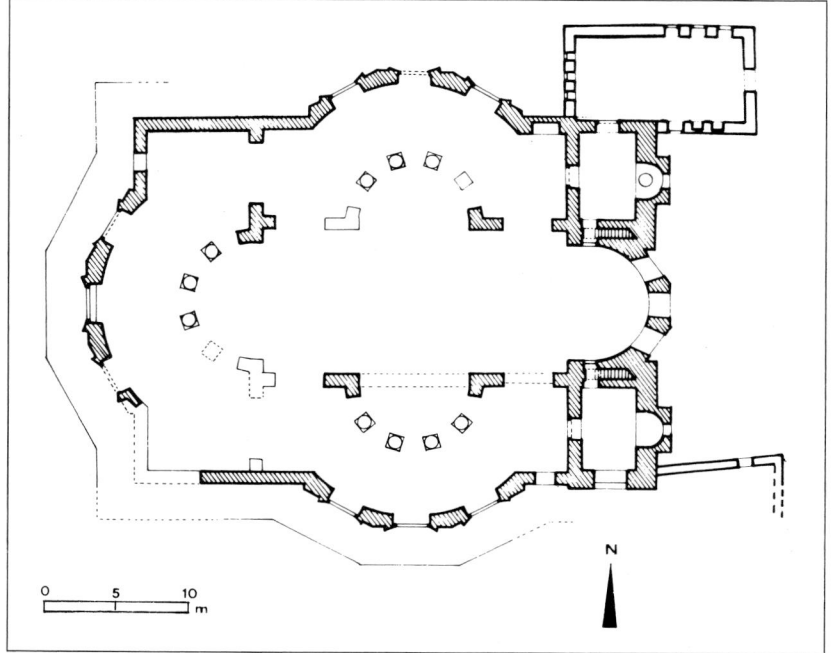

The most likely answer is that it came from the audience halls of palaces, where the earthly monarchs were surrounded by a liturgy in many ways comparable to that of the heavenly King. Indeed, what could have been more natural? Imperial art was older than Christian art, and it is generally accepted that in the realm of triumphal iconography it exerted a decisive influence on the latter.[27] The Byzantine mind imagined God's habitat as a vastly expanded and more splendid version of the emperor's Sacred Palace, so that God's house on earth could logically be cast in the same mold.

There is considerable evidence to suggest this line of derivation. The centralized *triclinium* or reception hall—circular, octagonal, or trefoil—was a regular feature of Roman palace architecture as far back as Nero's Domus Aurea. On Byzantine soil we may point, among others, to the rotunda at Thessalonica, which, whatever its original purpose, formed part of the palace of the emperor Galerius. At Constantinople we have the palace of the *praepositus* Antiochus (early fifth century), whose central hall was a hexagon with apsidal niches. It is interesting to observe that both of these were subsequently transformed into churches, the first into a shrine of unknown dedication (it is now called St. George), the second into the martyrium of St. Euphemia.[28] Constantine's palace on the other side of the hippodrome comprised an octagonal hall; and when, in the sixth century, the Imperial Palace of Constantinople acquired a new ceremonial center in the Chrysotriklinos (the Golden Hall), this, too, was a domed octagon, similar in plan, as far as we can tell, to the church of S. Vitale at Ravenna.

This deceptive identity between church and palace hall may be further illustrated by a small monument situated just outside the north city wall of Resafa. For a long time it has been considered as an extramural church and, in particular, as a cemetery church. Architecturally, the only possible objection is that the apse looks a little too small with regard to the proportions of the building. This would not have been decisive if it were not for the fact that, carved in the apse, is a Greek inscription that proclaims, "Long live Alamoundaros!" In all probability, this building was erected between 569 and 581 as the audience hall of al-Mundhir, an Arab chieftain, who was a client of the Byzantine emperor and may have held court at Resafa on the day of the saint's feast.[29] The building, put up by Syrian craftsmen, was thus a reduced version of the reception halls of greater potentates.

Some scholars, faced with the alleged anomaly of centralized congregational churches (such as that of Antioch), have tried to escape the difficulty by calling them palace churches, if they could not call them martyria. Yet there is no evidence whatever that in the Early Byzantine period there existed, either architecturally or institutionally,

95. Resafa, tetraconch, interior looking east.
96. Aleppo, Madrasa Halawiya, interior.

91

97. *Resafa, basilica A, interior looking southeast.*
98. *Thessalonica, St. George, interior looking north.*

93

99. *Constantinople, Palace of Antiochus, ground plan (after R. Naumann, 1966).*

100. *Constantinople, Martyrium of St. Euphemia, bema.*

101. *Resafa, Audience Hall of al-Mundhir, longitudinal section and ground plan (after S. Guyer, 1926).*

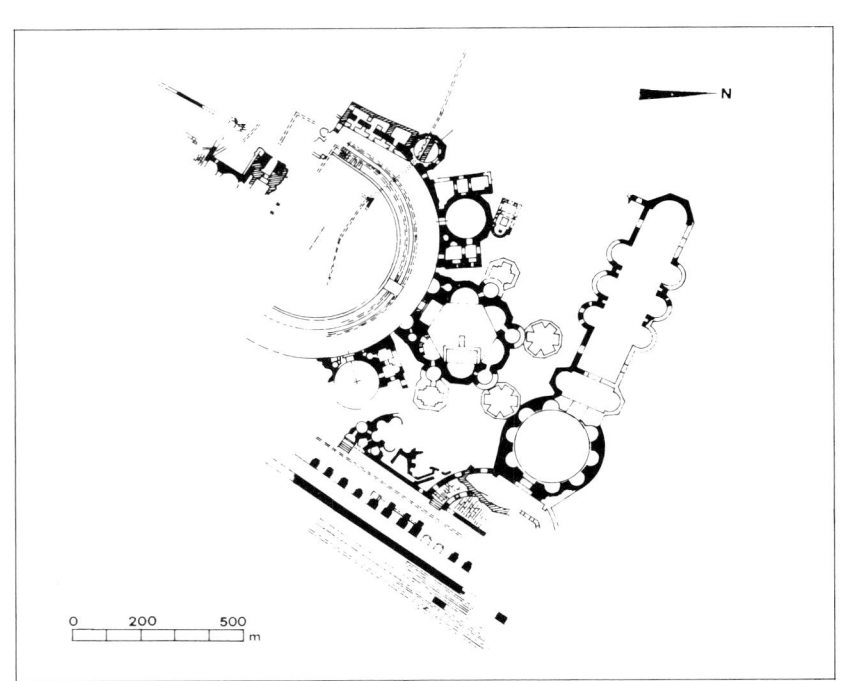

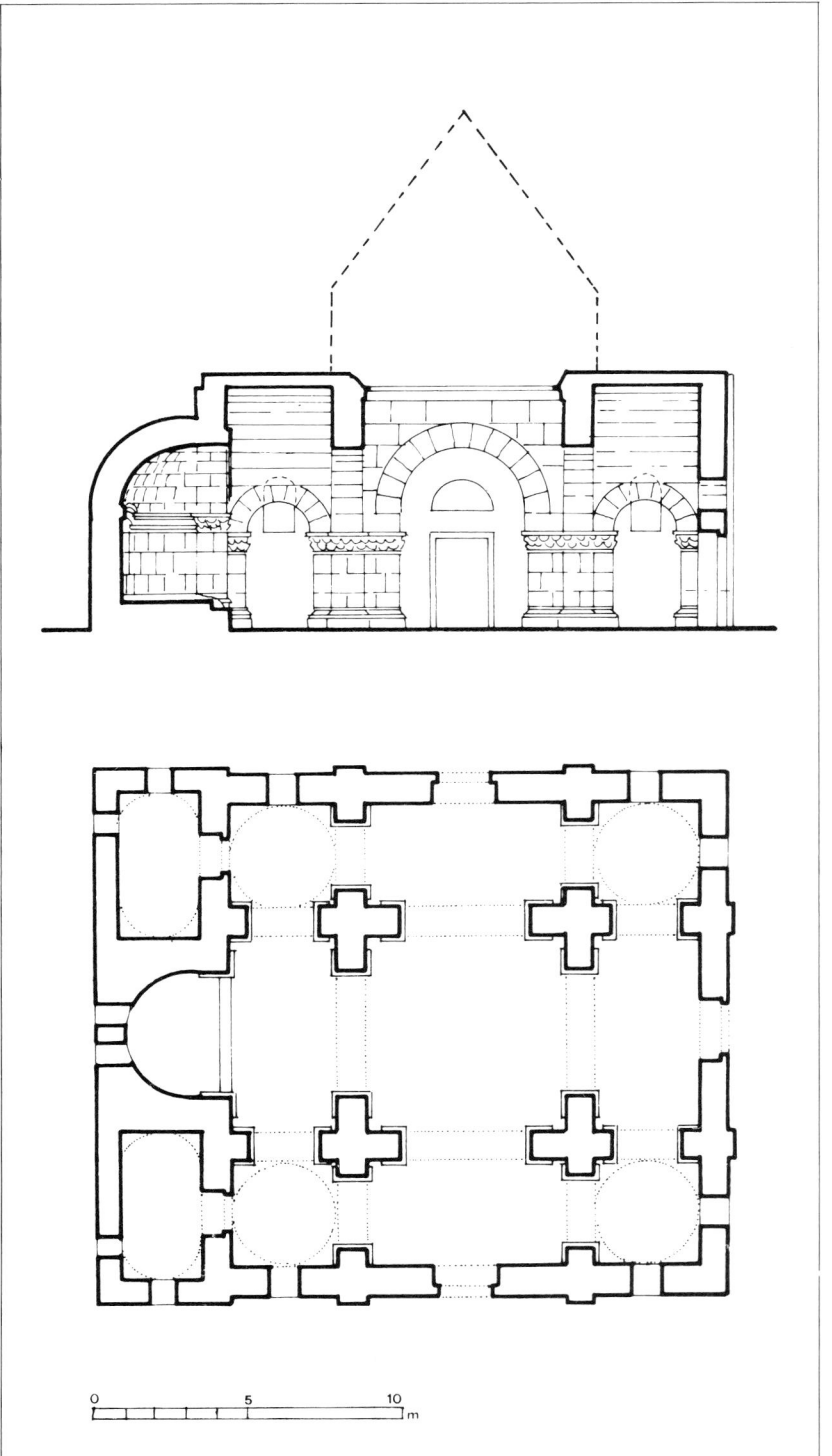

a separate category of palace churches. In the West, the palatine chapel with its own clergy was a creation of the Carolingian period; in Byzantium, too, the institution appears to have been introduced in the ninth century, but it cannot be shown to have assumed even then a distinctive architectural form. The moral seems to be that we should not invent elaborate theories with a view to fitting the diversity of Early Byzantine architecture within a preconceived formula.

When, sometime between 553 and 555, the historian Procopius wrote a laudatory work on the buildings of the emperor Justinian, a work generally known as *De aedificiis,* he included in his account the reign of Justin I (518–27) on the grounds that, already at that time, Justinian was the power behind the throne. The "Age of Justinian" covers, therefore, about half a century (518–65), even longer if we add to it the reign of Justin II (565–78), and it certainly represents the high point of Early Byzantine architecture. In many ways it is comparable to the age of Louis XIV.

Looking back, as we do, over a span of fourteen centuries, armed with the knowledge that Justinian's grandiose plans collapsed a few decades after his death, and having in mind only a few of his more famous buildings, such as St. Sophia and S. Vitale at Ravenna, we are apt to form a rather distorted view of this emperor's building activity. A perusal of the *De aedificiis* may serve as a corrective. Our initial amazement at the enormously far-flung nature of the operation soon yields to the understanding that its effort was, above all, defensive. After the initial book on Constantinople, Procopius takes us on an extended tour of the frontiers, starting at the most sensitive point, Dara in Mesopotamia, then west and south into Syria, then up the Armenian border to the Black Sea, to the Balkans and Thrace, then to Palestine and North Africa all the way to the Atlantic (Italy is not included). Everywhere Justinian strengthened the existing fortifications or built new ones, provided aqueducts and cisterns, built bridges, even diverted rivers. This great work of consolidation was begun by the emperor Anastasius; Justinian continued it on a much vaster and more comprehensive scale. He had the best engineers and the best technology in the world. By throwing a kind of Maginot Line around his reconstituted Empire, he must have thought he was making it secure for many centuries to come. The work of Procopius ends on this very note. "There can be no doubt to anyone," he says, "that the emperor Justinian has strengthened the state not only with fortifications, but also with garrisons of soldiers, from the bounds of the East to the very setting of the sun, these being the limits of the Roman dominion."[1]

The most elaborate fortifications were naturally set up on the eastern border, especially in Mesopotamia and Syria, for it was here that the Empire faced Persia, its most formidable rival and indeed the only rival that possessed a high civilization. The Persians, it appears, were not as advanced technologically as were the Byzantines. Even so, a war with Persia was a war of sieges in which every known ruse and device was used: diversion of the water supply, tunneling under the walls, artillery, and even movable wooden towers. Hence the need for a highly sophisticated defensive system, which was not

104. *Constantinople, St. Polyeuktos, pier capital.*
105. *Constantinople, St. Polyeuktos, impost capital.*

106. *Constantinople, St. Polyeuktos, niche head. Archaeological Museum, Istanbul.*

needed in the Balkans and North Africa against barbarian tribes, whose military tactics were entirely different. It was on the Persian frontier that many of Justinian's leading architects got their training, which may explain both their bold, practical approach to problems and their predilection for Eastern forms. The great pool of engineering expertise that was thus accumulated in Syria passed in the next century to the Arab conquerors, but that is another story.

Today, however, when we think of Justinianic architecture, we have in mind not the distant fortifications of Dara and Zenobia, but the churches, especially those of Constantinople. Here another word of caution is in order. The most famous monuments, the ones which, perforce, we shall have to examine in this chapter, are for the most part domed. That the domed form was more and more used for prestige monuments cannot be doubted; yet it is also true that if we had a statistical table of all the churches that were put up in the sixth century, we would find that basilicas still constituted the vast majority of them. A table of this kind that has been compiled for Palestine shows fifty-six churches and chapels of the sixth century and fourteen more that are either of the fifth or the sixth: out of the seventy, not one is of the centralized type.[2]

On the threshold of Justinian's reign stands an important if enigmatic monument, the church of St. Polyeuktos at Constantinople, erected by the wealthy princess Anicia Juliana about 524–27. Recent excavations[3] have shown that it was a very large building, 170 feet square excluding the narthex and projecting apse, and that it stood on an elevated platform to which a staircase led up from the atrium. Unfortunately, none of the superstructure has been found, so that the form of the church remains conjectural. The square plan and extraordinary thickness of the foundation walls between nave and aisles suggest that the church was domed. Furthermore, it had six curved exedrae and, as we know from documentary evidence, a gallery. The excavations have produced a mass of decorative material, such as a variety of colored marbles, columns inlaid with glass and amethysts, and floor and wall mosaics. Of particular importance, however, are the carved elements, which are of extraordinary, not to say excessive, richness. The arcade supporting the gallery had its spandrels entirely covered with a grapevine, while peacocks with outspread tails were perched in niches and faced each other across the arches. Particularly noteworthy is the presence of fully formed impost capitals with a deeply undercut ornament and a decorative repertoire that includes many Sassanian motifs. Abandoned in the eleventh century, the church of St. Polyeuktos was thoroughly looted and many of its carved elements, such as the so-called Pilastri Acritani, found their way to Venice after the Fourth Crusade. While the taste of Anicia

◁ 108. *Venice, Piazza S. Marco, Pilastri Acritani.*

109. *Constantinople, Sts. Sergius and Bacchus, ground plan (after P. Sanpaolesi, 1961).*

110. *Constantinople, Sts. Sergius and Bacchus, isometric section (after P. Sanpaolesi, 1961).*

111. *Constantinople, Sts. Sergius and Bacchus, exterior from the east.* ▷

Juliana may strike us as too gaudy for a lady of ancient lineage, her extraordinary financial resources constitute an important datum for Byzantine social and artistic history.

The other surviving Justinianic churches at Constantinople were due to imperial patronage. The church of Sts. Sergius and Bacchus has been generally regarded as a precursor of St. Sophia, but there is no evidence for this view: all we know is that it was built between 527 and 536 within the palace of Hormisdas, which the empress Theodora turned into a monastery for Monophysite monks. The palace already had one church, that of Sts. Peter and Paul, of basilican shape (erected in 518–19); this was evidently found insufficient, so a second church dedicated to the popular saint of Resafa was built alongside. Today only the second church remains.[4] While not very large, it produces a sense of noble spaciousness inside. The inner shell is octagonal, opening on the diagonals into semicircular exedrae. Two columns, capped by delicately undercut "melon" capitals, stand between each pair of piers, except on the eastern side, where the central space opens into the bema. The columns support a richly carved, horizontal entablature upon which is inscribed a long epigram in honor of the imperial couple. On gallery level the same arrangement is repeated, with the difference that the columns, capped by Ionic impost capitals, carry arches. The octagonal space rises to the dome base without the transitional element of pendentives. The dome itself is a structure of considerable sophistication, consisting of sixteen wedges, alternately flat and curved. The flat ones are pierced by windows, while the curved ones coincide with the corners of the octagon and are slightly recessed at their springing to avoid an overhang.

The ingeniousness of the design stands in contrast to the sloppiness of the execution, as can readily be seen from the ground plan. Its irregularity can hardly be explained by the fact that the church had to be squeezed into a fairly limited space determined by preexisting structures. Even if this was so, there was no reason why the internal octagonal shell should have been placed noticeably askew with regard to the outer square shell. The octagon itself is very irregular, its eastern side being much wider than the western side, and the two eastern exedrae greater in span than the western ones. It is hard to believe that these irregularities were deliberate, or that any architect having an eye for symmetry would have planned five unevenly spaced doors between the narthex and the nave, with the result that the two intermediate doors afford no view whatever of the interior except for the backs of the western piers. One can only conclude, I think, that while the basic design was conceived by a very gifted architect, its execution was entrusted to indifferent builders

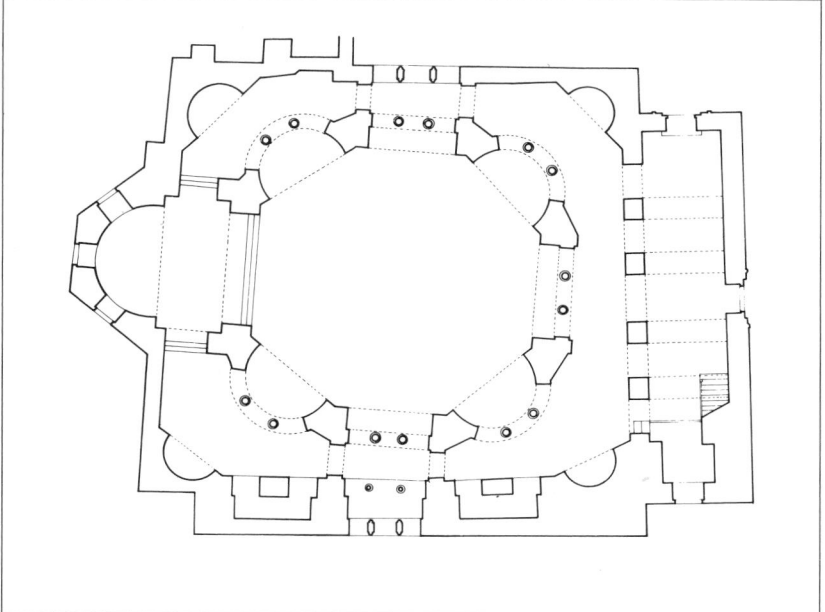

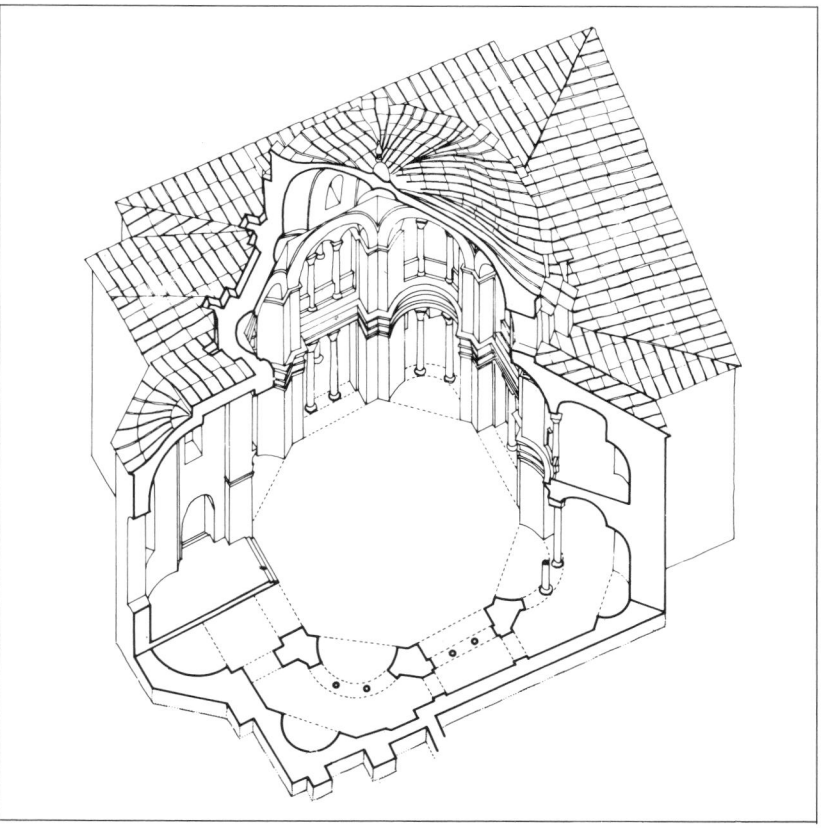

112. *Constantinople, Sts. Sergius and Bacchus, interior.*
113. *Constantinople, Sts. Sergius and Bacchus, capital.*
114. *Constantinople, Sts. Sergius and Bacchus, interior of dome.* ▷

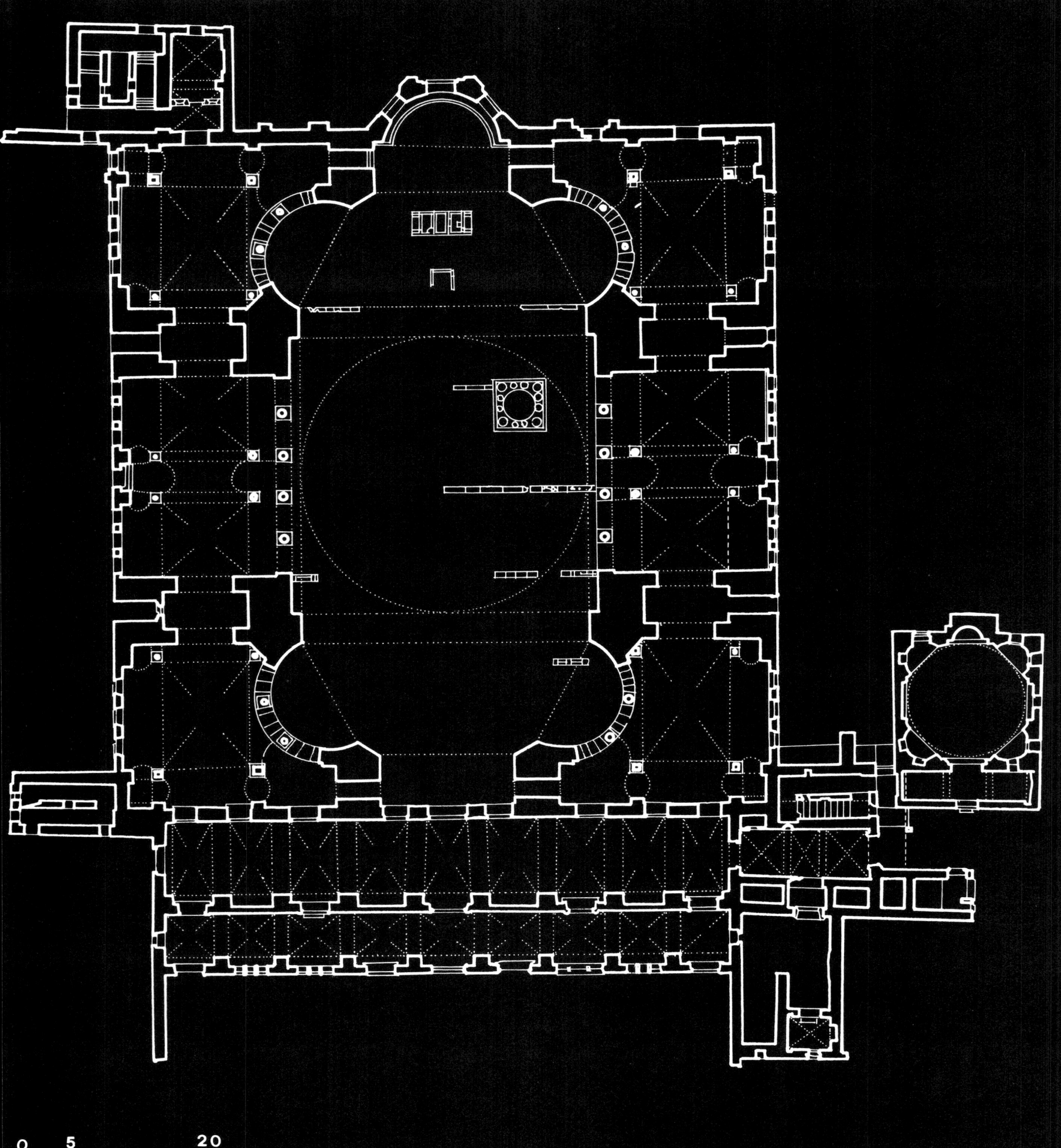

0 5 20
M

who, after marking out a lopsided plan on the ground, had to improvise as they went along.

Such "on-the-spot" compensation was possible in the case of a medium-sized building like Sts. Sergius and Bacchus (dome span 49 feet). But the larger the building—I am speaking here of vaulted construction—the graver were the problems caused by irregularity. Even if the initial layout was scrupulously carried out, it was an inherent fault of Byzantine brick-and-mortar masonry that, as the building rose into the air, considerable unevenness should occur. This consideration brings us to St. Sophia, the supreme achievement not only of Justinianic but of all Byzantine architecture.

To Justinian's contemporaries St. Sophia may have appeared a folly; to later generations it became a legend and a symbol. No building even half its size was ever erected in the Byzantine state at a subsequent period; and it is a measure of the technical and financial decline of the following centuries that the construction of St. Sophia should have seemed altogether miraculous, something that could only have been brought to completion by the intervention of heavenly forces. We may add that St. Sophia also became a white elephant—costly to maintain and repair, and altogether too vast for the diminished population of the Middle Ages.

The first St. Sophia, known simply as the Great Church (Megalê Ekklêsia), was built by Constantine or, more probably, by Constantius II, and was dedicated in 360. It was a timber-roofed basilica which burned in 404. A second church was built, and this, too, was destroyed by fire in the course of the Nika Riot in January, 532. Of the second St. Sophia (dedicated in 415) there remains part of the porch—a row of columns surmounted by a carved architrave.[5] The conflagration of 532 laid in ashes the very center of the city—not only the cathedral, but also the church of St. Irene, the baths of Zeuxippus, and part of the Imperial Palace were destroyed—and this gave Justinian the opportunity he was seeking. As soon as the rubble was cleared, construction was started on the new St. Sophia: five and a half years later, on December 27, 537, it was ceremonially dedicated. The architects were Anthemius of Tralles, a famous mathematician and eccentric,[6] and Isidore of Miletus. We may imagine that they were chosen because they combined practical experience with a high degree of theoretical knowledge, but, in fact, we do not know of any other buildings that either of them had created.

The design had no close antecedents. It is made up of elements that were current at the time, but these elements, as far as we know, had not previously been put together in the same combination. Nor was St. Sophia imitated in the following centuries—that is, not until the Ottoman mosques of the sixteenth century. This uniqueness

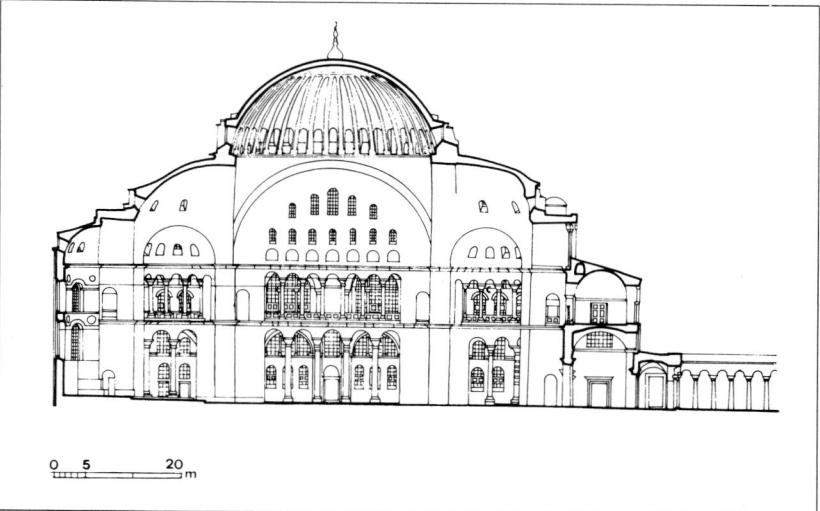

118. *Constantinople, St. Sophia, exterior from the south.*
119, 120. *Constantinople, St. Sophia, exterior from the southeast.*

makes St. Sophia difficult to classify. It has been called a domed basilica because it has a longitudinal axis and rows of columns on either side of the nave, but such a designation does not sufficiently reflect the basic structural elements. According to another analysis, the design of St. Sophia was obtained by splitting Sts. Sergius and Bacchus in half and inserting the central dome between the two halves. It may make better sense to reverse this statement. For if we compare St. Sophia with the adjacent and contemporary church of St. Irene (abstracting, of course, the elements that were introduced into St. Irene in the eighth century),[7] we can see that St. Irene has a better claim to being called a domed basilica, and that the singularity of St. Sophia lies precisely in the intercalation of the "two halves of Sts. Sergius and Bacchus."

The main problem of St. Sophia lay, however, in its scale. Byzantine architects had long experience in building domes, but a dome 100 feet in diameter that was not resting on solid walls but was "hanging in the air"—this was something that had not been done before. It is also fair to say that no architect at the time could have calculated, even approximately, the thrusts that would be generated by a masonry dome of that size. Anthemius and Isidore saw the importance of precision: the ground plan (the main rectangle measures 229 by 245 feet internally) was laid out with remarkable accuracy, and the main bearing elements—the piers—were built of stone, which, even if it was fairly soft local limestone, was not subject to the shrinkage and elasticity of brick and mortar. The outer shell, whose structural function was secondary, was built fairly thin (31 1/2 inches wide), but even here large blocks of stone were used, to a height of about 23 feet. Difficulties began once the structure reached the springing of the main arches.

Procopius has left us a vivid account of some of the unexpected crises that occurred during construction. When the main eastern arch was being built, but had not yet reached the crown, the piers on which it rested began tilting outward (today their inclination from the vertical is 23 1/2 inches). The terrified architects laid the matter before the emperor, who confidently directed them to complete the arch so that it would hold itself up. The north and south arches created a different problem, for while their masonry was still damp they exerted so much pressure on the subjacent tympana walls that the columns —either those in the tympana windows or those of the gallery—began flaking. Once again the emperor intervened and directed that the curtain walls beneath the arches be removed until the latter had thoroughly dried out.[8] Whatever truth there may be in these anecdotes, it is clear that the building began deforming while it was going up. When the dome base was reached, the space to be roofed had expanded beyond the original estimate. Even so the dome was completed, but it lasted only twenty years. Cracked by a series of earthquakes that shook Constantinople between 553 and 557, it came crashing down in 558.

The original dome of Anthemius was, according to historical sources, some 20 feet lower than the present dome and, while it must have been planned as a perfect circle, it was actually built as an ellipse, about 6 1/2 feet wider from north to south than from east to west because of the tilting of the lateral walls.[9] We must bear this in mind in trying to visualize the intended effect. Unfortunately, we are offered no further information concerning the form of the original dome. In all probability it resembled the present one in having ribs and a catwalk at its base. Another feature of the original building was the abundance of light which, in the words of Procopius, appeared not to be coming from the outside, but to be generated within. The tympana walls may originally have been pierced by huge windows, like the great west window that still exists, and the flood of light they let in was further reflected by vast expanses of gold mosaic. The mysterious penumbra that now reigns in St. Sophia, a penumbra interrupted in the early morning and late evening by oblique shafts of sunlight, is due to the progressive blocking up of windows and the loss of mosaic.

The failure of the first dome was caused by the inadequacy of lateral supports. This shortcoming may have been realized as work progressed in 532–37, and the four great exterior buttresses were heightened to nearly the level of the dome base. After the collapse of 558 a commission of experts was called in, including Isidorus the Younger, who had done work on the eastern frontier (both of the original architects had died). As a result of their recommendations, the north and south arches were progressively widened on their inward side from their haunches to the crown so as to make the central space more nearly square, and upon this slightly diminished base a steeper dome was built. This, essentially, is the dome that still exists today. Parts of it fell down and were rebuilt in later centuries— thirteen out of the forty ribs in 989, and another thirteen in 1346[10]— but the design of Isidorus the Younger was not seriously altered.

Considering the vicissitudes which St. Sophia has undergone in the course of the fourteen centuries of its existence, its state of preservation is nothing short of miraculous. The respect that the Turks have shown to this monument and its periodic repairs (the last major one carried out in 1847–49 by the Swiss architects Gaspare and Giuseppe Fossati) have contributed to this happy result. There have been, of course, many changes and losses, particularly to all the fixtures associated with Christian worship, which have to be taken into account

121. *Constantinople, St. Sophia, Theodosian porch.*

122. *Constantinople, St. Sophia, fish-eye view of vaulting.* ▷
123. *Constantinople, St. Sophia, interior looking southeast.* ▷

in trying to visualize not only how the interior looked, but also how it functioned. In the apse there was a synthronon of seven steps for the seating of the clergy—much like the preserved one in St. Irene. In front of the synthronon rose a magnificent ciborium with a pyramidal roof sheltering the altar table. The bema, fenced off by a screen of twelve columns, occupied most of the space covered by the eastern semidome. Extending westward from the door of the bema was a passage, called the *solea,* protected by a parapet of marble slabs. This led to the oval ambo, a monumental construction placed on the longitudinal axis of the church, somewhat east of center. The platform of the ambo, from which the scriptural lessons were read, was accessible by two long flights of stairs, as in the ambo at Kalabaka. A vast amount of sheet silver was liberally applied to these fixtures and added to the glitter of the interior.

The "meadows" of multicolored marbles (to use an expression beloved by medieval authors) are still there to see, and they prompt some interesting considerations. The only material that has clearly been reused is Egyptian porphyry, which was no longer quarried at the time. The eight porphyry columns in the exedrae are all of different sizes. Rather than cutting them down to the same height, the builders varied the height of their pedestals. So precious was porphyry that in some wall revetments it was sliced to a thickness of a few millimeters and given undulating edges to conceal the juncture whenever several small pieces were put together. Most, if not all, of the other marbles were produced to order, and this applies to the columns of Thessalian verd antique. The medieval tale that these were removed from the temple of Diana at Ephesus is patently absurd and deserves mention only because it reveals a facet of later Byzantine mentality: it was inconceivable that such big columns should not have been looted from an antique building. Even though made specifically for St. Sophia, the Thessalian columns also show some variation in size (by about 6 1/4 inches in diameter in the main order), and they are very imperfectly rounded—an indication of declining standards. The capitals form matching sets. The main orders have a rather heavy impost capital with vestigial volutes, entirely covered with undercut acanthus leaves, whereas in the galleries the columns that do not face the nave have Ionic impost capitals. The bases are very roughly carved and are of a piece with the plinth.

The uneven heights of the porphyry columns are but a minor example of the disregard for "classical" norms that pervades St. Sophia. In the straight colonnades of the nave, four columns on the ground floor are surmounted by six on gallery level, and in the exedrae two by six, with the result that the spacing of the upper order does not correspond to that of the lower; even from the structural

125. *Constantinople, St. Sophia, interior of dome.*
126. *Constantinople, St. Sophia, vaulting of apse.* ▷

point of view, this is unsound. In the narthex the five outer doors, except for the central one, do not directly face the nine inner doors, and the transverse arches that spring from the pilasters of the outer wall do not relate to the articulations of the inner wall. Within the broad guidelines of the overall design, there is endless variation and improvisation—at times even sloppiness. This confers on the building a feeling of life, of the unexpected; it is, on the other hand, quite disconcerting to an observer steeped in the classical tradition, and we can readily understand the disappointment of travelers in the eighteenth and early nineteenth centuries, who found St. Sophia "Gothick."

Here is a typical reaction—that of Hobhouse, the traveling companion of Lord Byron: "My general impression was, that the skill of the one hundred architects, and the labour of the ten thousand workmen, the wealth of an empire, and the ingenuity of presiding angels, had raised a stupendous monument of the heavy mediocrity which distinguished the productions of the sixth century from the perfect specimens of a happier age."[11] The Romantic movement introduced a different sensibility. Fifty years after Hobhouse, Théophile Gautier pronounced St. Sophia the most beautiful church he had ever seen: "L'architecture byzantine est à coup sûr la forme nécessaire du catholicisme. L'architecture gothique même, quelle que soit sa valeur religieuse, ne s'y approprie pas si exactement; malgré ses dégradations de toute sorte, Sainte-Sophie l'emporte encore sur toutes les églises que j'ai vues, et j'en ai visité beaucoup."[12]

So overwhelming is the interior of St. Sophia that its exterior has often been overlooked. Today it is difficult to obtain a good view of it: the heavy buttresses that lean on the building from all sides, the sultans' mausolea, the four minarets, not to mention the regrettable coat of cement, painted light yellow, that has recently been smeared over the brickwork, distract our attention from the architectural forms. The exterior is stark and heavy and was always so; and already in the sixth century the church was surrounded by subsidiary structures.

I have drawn attention to this phenomenon in the case of other Early Byzantine cathedrals: it also applied to St. Sophia. The south facade was obscured by the Patriarchal Palace—a vast complex of buildings that reached up to a considerable height and communicated directly with the gallery of the church. The north facade was also encumbered, as we can still see from a number of broken off arches that must have linked the cathedral with other buildings. Chapels and annexes were crowded against the east side. But on the west lay a colonnaded atrium, some portions of which still existed in the last century. The ground falls off steeply at this point, so that originally there may have been a staircase leading up to the atrium. After climb-

◁130. *Constantinople, St. Sophia, narthex looking south.*
131. *Constantinople, St. Sophia, panel of porphyry revetment.*

ing it, the visitor would find himself in a great court, measuring some 197 by 130 feet, with a fountain in the middle. It was from this point, and this point alone, that one could obtain an unobstructed view of the principal facade, which was reveted with slabs of Proconnesian marble. Sometime in the Middle Ages, for reasons that remain unclear, the western entrance fell into disuse and was replaced by the present south entrance, which eliminates any kind of a monumental approach.

It is difficult to imagine the organization of labor and supplies that had to be mobilized for the construction of St. Sophia within the short span of five years. Yet St. Sophia represented only a fraction of Justinian's building activity in the capital. Procopius enumerates thirty-two more churches—some of which, like those of the Holy Apostles, St. Irene, and St. Mocius, were very large indeed—six hospices, palaces, public buildings, harbors; and his list is not complete. We may briefly glance at some utilitarian constructions of Justinian's reign and, in particular, the two largest covered cisterns of Constantinople.

A short distance southwest of St. Sophia lay a large open court bordered by porticoes. This was known as the Basilica and was used for a variety of purposes, judicial, commercial, and intellectual. Justinian dug up the open court as well as the southernmost of the four porticoes and installed an underground cistern, called the Cisterna Basilica (in Turkish, Yerebatan Sarayï, that is, "Sunken Palace").[13] It forms a rectangle 453 by 213 feet and contains 28 rows of 12 columns each, a total of 366, supporting cross-groined brick vaults. The presence of ninety-eight identical acanthus capitals of fifth-century type may be explained by the supposition that this was outdated builder's stock. Various other odd pieces have been used, including a column shaft covered with a decoration of "eyes" to make it look like a tree trunk with the branches sawed off. Such utilization of materials that happened to be at hand was, of course, quite natural in a construction that was not designed for aesthetic purposes; yet the Cisterna Basilica (which still holds water) has been for centuries one of the main sights of Constantinople, and it produces a powerful impression by its forest of columns disappearing into cavernous gloom.

The so-called cistern of Philoxenus (Binbir Direk or "A Thousand and One Columns") is smaller in size (210 by 184 feet) but more daring in its construction.[14] To give the cistern greater depth, the architect has simply placed one set of column shafts upon another, 224 in each set, and connected them by means of stone drums having circular sinkings on their upper and lower surfaces. The reason for this hazardous scheme was that it was easier and cheaper to procure columns in certain standard sizes. In this way a

134. *Nicaea (Iznik), St. Sophia, interior.*
135. *Constantinople, Cisterna Basilica (Yerebatan Sarayı).* ▷

136. *Sangarius (Sakarya) River, Justinian's bridge (19th-century engraving).*

137. *Sangarius (Sakarya) River, Justinian's bridge, east end.*

depth of about fifty feet (measured to the crown of the vaults) was achieved, not fully visible today since the cistern is filled with earth to one third of its depth. To give the structure greater solidity the capitals were connected with one another by means of wooden ties. Charles Diehl may have been too enthusiastic when he compared Binbir Direk with St. Sophia by virtue of the technical skill it exhibits; and he was surely mistaken (since there is no reason to date this cistern to the year 528) in claiming that the impost capital makes its earliest appearance here.[15] Nevertheless, Binbir Direk is a remarkable feat of building, and it does represent the bold and practical spirit of Justinian's engineers.

Unfortunately, too little is known concerning the water supply of Byzantine Constantinople. It is certain, however, that the system of aqueducts in the region of the Belgrade Forest (on the European shore of the Bosphorus) is in its present state Turkish, and this includes the beautiful "Justinian's aqueduct," which has been called a masterpiece of Byzantine engineering: actually, it dates from the sixteenth century.[16] A comparable Byzantine monument is the bridge over the Sangarius (Sakarya) River, which, in all probability, is Justinian's bridge completed in 560. At the time Procopius was writing the *De aedificiis* it was still unfinished, but he does state that no previous bridge had existed across the river. The Sangarius has since changed course, and the bridge stands today in a field, deeply embedded in the ground. It is a mighty structure 469 yards long, built of massive ashlar and composed of 7 semicircular arches 75 feet in span. This must have been a major halting and control point on the Anatolian highway, for at the east end of the bridge is a large apsed building and at the west end there was (it no longer exists) a monumental doorway, thirty-three feet high, with a spiral staircase contained in one of its piers. The only survey of this monument that was ever made is the work of Charles Texier, who wrote in 1839 that if it had been better known, it would be as famous as the great structures along the Roman roads in other parts of the Empire.[17] Alas, the Sangarius Bridge has attracted no further attention, and the same may be said of other Byzantine bridges. A particularly attractive one has survived in eastern Turkey in the area of Elazığ. It is a hunchback bridge with a single arch, fifty-six feet in span and thirty-three feet high. The arch is pointed, and at first sight we are reminded of the Ottoman bridges found in Turkey and in the Balkans, but the Greek inscription that runs along the voussoirs could hardly be later than the sixth century.

A glance at Justinianic architecture in the provinces—we now revert to churches—shows that the fashionable domed forms were not adopted everywhere, and that local traditions usually pre-

143. *Ravenna, S. Vitale, ground plan (after G. Gerola, 1913).*
144. *Ravenna, S. Vitale, exterior from the north.* ▷
145. *Ravenna, S. Vitale, interior toward apse.* ▷
146. *Ravenna, S. Vitale, interior, ambulatory.* ▷

147. *Ravenna, S. Vitale, capitals.*
148. *Ravenna, S. Apollinare in Classe, interior.* ▷

vailed. In this respect the case of Ravenna is instructive, though complex. It is customary to regard the monuments of this city—those of the fifth as well as the sixth century—as Byzantine, indeed as the most perfect specimens of Early Byzantine art. But how Byzantine are they? The monumental history of Ravenna in the Early Christian period is usually divided into three periods. The first opens in 402, when the residence of the Western emperor was transferred from Milan to this obscure city surrounded by marshes and lagoons, and closes in 493, when Ravenna was captured by Theodoric after a lengthy siege. The second, that of Ostrogothic rule, extends down to 540, the date of the city's recapture by the general Belisarius. The third, which is the Byzantine period proper, features Ravenna as the capital of the Exarchate of Italy, a position it retained until 751, although no building work of any importance was done after Justinian's reign. Each of these three periods has left surviving monuments, even if they represent only a fraction of what once existed;[18] but as we survey these monuments we are struck not so much by their differentiation as by their continuity, the continuity of local tradition.

No one, I believe, would apply the epithet Byzantine to the monuments of the first period—the greatly altered basilica of S. Giovanni Evangelista, the so-called mausoleum of Galla Placidia (an annex of the cruciform basilica of Sta. Croce), and the baptistery of the Orthodox attached to the now destroyed cathedral, the Basilica Ursiana—which are Italian not only in their forms, but also in their construction techniques, the walls being built of thick bricks and the vaults of earthenware tubes. No discernible change occurs in the Ostrogothic period, for the church of S. Apollinare Nuovo of 490, originally dedicated to St. Martin and the most ambitious project of Theodoric's reign, is just another Italian basilica of perfectly standard type. The use in it of Corinthian capitals and marble columns imported from Proconnesus does not basically affect this judgment. S. Apollinare Nuovo is justly famous for its mosaics, the stately procession of martyrs on either side of the nave echoing the rhythm of the columns beneath them, and the standing prophets between the clerestory windows further accentuating the verticality of the forms. The architecture of the church is today more difficult to appreciate, since its proportions were drastically altered in the sixteenth century when the floor level was raised by four feet and the original arcade replaced by a lower one of Renaissance design. The apse, too, is modern.[19]

The advent of direct Byzantine rule may be expected to have produced a greater influx of Constantinopolitan architectural forms, and to some extent this was the case, as shown by the church of S. Vitale. But when we take stock of the entire architectural production of the sixth century, we see that S. Vitale remained an exception at Ravenna, and the native basilica the norm. The ninth-century chronicler Agnellus emphasized this singularity when he wrote: "Nulla in Italia ecclesia similis est in aedificiis et in mechanicis operibus."[20] Despite the enormous amount of investigation that has been devoted to this building, many essential problems remain. The first difficulty is provided by the fact that S. Vitale was begun under Bishop Ecclesius (521–32), whose portrait, in the guise of the founder, appears in the semidome of the apse—that is, still under Ostrogothic rule. If, as is generally accepted, this happened during the regency of Amalasuntha (526–34), when Byzantine political influence at Ravenna was growing, the question arises whether this splendid monument was meant to convey the message of Byzantine sovereignty. Another problem is posed by the identity of the patron, Julianus the banker (*argentarius*), who, as we have already noted, spent 26,000 *solidi* on S. Vitale and subsidized several other churches, namely, S. Apollinare in Classe, S. Michele in Africisco, and perhaps Sta. Maria Maggiore. All we know for certain is that he was a Greek-speaking Oriental; but the imagination of scholars, fired by his enigmatic character and his truly vast building operations, has transformed him into Justinian's secret agent at Ravenna and has even identified him with the rather corpulent official represented between Justinian and Archbishop Maximian in the famous mosaic panel at S. Vitale.[21]

Further questions have been raised. Do the presence of the imperial portraits in the presbytery and the known proximity of the church to the palace indicate that this was in some sense a palatine chapel? The answer appears to be in the negative: so far as we know, this was a martyr's shrine, replacing a previous one of the fifth century. Was the architectural plan worked out at the time of the foundation, that is, in about 526, and how much of the actual construction was done before the reconquest of 540? All we can say is that work progressed under bishops Ursicinus (534–36) and Victor (538–45), whose monograms appear on the impost blocks of the capitals, and that the church was dedicated by Bishop Maximian in 547.

While these and similar questions may never be definitively answered, the church still stands before us. Its resemblance to Sts. Sergius and Bacchus is obvious, yet it is not a derivative of the latter, not only because of the considerable differences that set them apart, but also because S. Vitale need not be the later of the two. Another Constantinopolitan building with which S. Vitale must have had a close affinity was the Chrysotriklinos (Golden Hall) of the Imperial Palace. We know from texts that this throne room had eight arches or niches, an apse to the east, and a dome pierced by sixteen windows.[22] It could not have been the model for S. Vitale, since it was

built in the reign of Justin II (565–78), but it clearly belonged to the same architectural family.

The basic design of S. Vitale is thus truly Byzantine. The same applies to most of the marble work, in particular the columns with their truncated cone capitals of diverse design and octagonal stepped bases, some of which elements even bear the marks of the Greek masons. The brickwork of the walls, too, has been brought in line with Byzantine practice: we find here, as in other sixth-century buildings at Ravenna, thin bricks separated by fairly wide mortar joints instead of short, thick bricks that were prevalent in northern Italy. Yet the execution of the building was entrusted to local craftsmen, as proved, for example, by construction of the dome, which is made not of bricks but earthenware tubes laid in horizontal courses.[23]

We may also attribute to the local architect the greater vertical emphasis, which is perhaps the most notable difference between S. Vitale and Sts. Sergius and Bacchus, even allowing for the fact that in the latter church the pavement has been somewhat raised. In Constantinople the curvature of the dome begins at the base of its windows, directly above the crowns of the eight arches, while at Ravenna there is an intermediate drum consisting of two zones, first a set of shallow squinches over the corners of the octagon, then, above and between the squinches, eight large windows; only at the crowns of the windows does the dome begin to curve inward. The visual effect is thus rather different. In Sts. Sergius and Bacchus the visitor is overwhelmed by the huge, almost perilous, overhang of the dome— an impression that must have been deliberately sought by Justinian's architects, witness the original dome of St. Sophia—while in S. Vitale the eye is led much higher up, through a zone of relative penumbra, to the light provided by the windows of the drum and so on to the dome, which does not threaten to come crashing down.

S. Vitale, as I have said, was an exceptional building at Ravenna. Its contemporary, S. Apollinare in Classe, begun by Bishop Ursicinus between 534 and 536 and consecrated by Bishop Maximian in 549, is once again a normal basilica of Italian type. It is one of the noblest surviving basilicas, with its stately rows of richly veined Proconnesian columns set upon rectangular pedestals and surmounted by identical capitals of windblown acanthus, and its broad apse dominated by the vision of the cross in a starry sky. The preponderance of local architectural traditions is further illustrated by a number of churches that have not survived, such as S. Stefano, S. Michele in Africisco, and Sta. Maria Maggiore. Ravenna absorbed the imported Byzantine influence, just as, despite its large colony of Orientals, it remained throughout its Byzantine period a city of Latin speech and culture.[24]

An even more remarkable persistence of local traditions may be seen in Syria and the neighboring regions of Mesopotamia and Palestine. Writing more than seventy years ago, Howard Crosby Butler observed that, whereas the sixth century witnessed the culmination of architecture in both northern Syria and Constantinople, "yet this architecture of northern Syria bears no closer relation to that style [the Byzantine] than it does to the Greek architecture of the time of Alexander the Great."[25]

As an example of the local tradition at its best, we may take the basilica of Qalbloseh of the fifth century. The extreme care that went into its construction, coupled with the insignificance of the surrounding village, has led to the supposition that this was a pilgrimage shrine.[26] Two features, both typical of Syrian architecture, are of particular interest here. The first is the substitution of masonry piers for columns. Syrian builders, who, since the fourth century, had used arcades instead of architraves in their churches, strove progressively to reduce the number of supports so as to integrate more fully the nave with the aisles. With columns of normal size they were reluctant (although they did so occasionally) to give the arches a span greater than about 11 1/2 feet; by using more massive piers, they could double the width of the arches. At Qalbloseh there are three arches on either side, thus unifying the interior into practically a single space. The nave was roofed with timber, the narrower aisles with flat stone slabs.

The second feature concerns the treatment of the facade, which included a central loggia flanked by towers. These towers contained staircases leading up to the western loggia (now destroyed) and also giving access to the stone roof of the aisles. There has been much discussion concerning the purpose of this feature, which is fairly common in Syria—at times we find a single tower, not always attached to the facade. In the case of isolated churches standing in the middle of an open enclosure, such as Qalbloseh, the aesthetic value of a symmetrical towered front is obvious. Yet it is hard to believe that these towers had no particular function. The most likely explanation is that they were used to call the faithful to prayer, whether through a crier, as has become customary among the Muslims, or by means of a suspended beam (the *sêmantron* of the Greek church), which was struck with a mallet. It is also possible that the open loggia was used to address the overflow of the congregation that could not be accommodated within the church.[27]

The architecture of northern Syria, as exemplified by Qalbloseh, was an architecture of cut stone. Classical in conception, it lent itself to an exuberance of carved ornament both inside and out. Particularly characteristic of the region is the use of a molding that takes the shape of a continuous ribbon that is, so to speak, draped over

154. *Qasr ibn–Wardan, general plan of monumental complex (after H. C. Butler, 1929).*

    1. Church | 2. Palace | 3. Barracks.

155. *Qasr ibn–Wardan, view of church and palace from the southeast.*

156. *Qasr ibn–Wardan, church, longitudinal section (after H. C. Butler, 1929).*

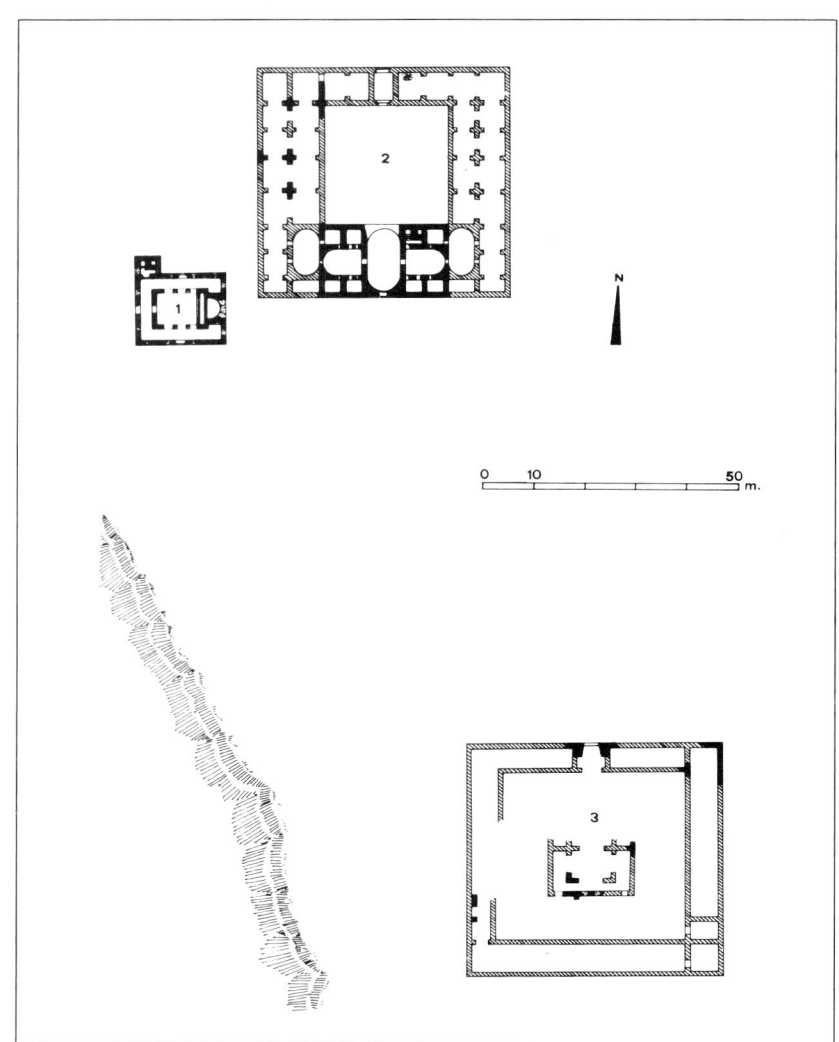

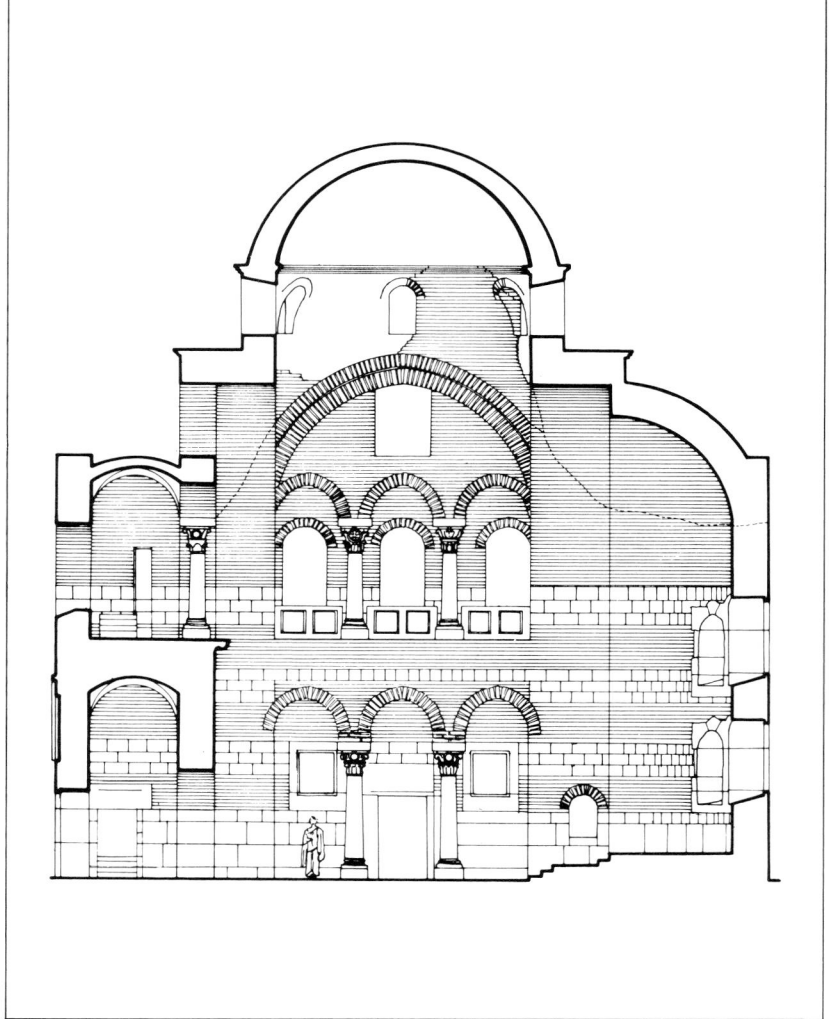

158. *Qasr ibn-Wardan, church, interior looking north.*
159. *Qasr ibn-Wardan, palace, exterior from the south.*

◁ 160. *Qasr ibn-Wardan, palace, interior looking west.*

161. *Mount Sinai, Monastery of St. Catherine, plan (courtesy of the Michigan–Princeton–Alexandria Expedition to Mount Sinai).*
162. *Mount Sinai, Monastery of St. Catherine, general view.* ▷
163. *Mount Sinai, Monastery of St. Catherine, interior of church looking east.* ▷

the windows and terminates in a kind of swirl. On the other hand, Syrian builders were not interested in the vault and its product, the impost capital.

The best-known example of the importation of Justinianic architecture into Syria—and it is practically a solitary example—is provided by the complex of Qasr ibn-Wardan, situated on the edge of the desert and dated by inscriptions to 561 and 564.[28] This monumental ensemble consisted of a palace about 165 feet square, a barracks of almost exactly the same size (now largely destroyed), and a church. It must have served as the residence of some important military commander and been built all at once. What first strikes the eye is the unusual form of the masonry: alternating bands of brick and squared basalt (in three successive courses), while the vaulting consists entirely of brick. The use of brick is not quite as unprecedented as some scholars have supposed, and we can quote several other, more or less contemporary, examples in Syria (the cisterns of Resafa, the walls of Zenobia, Sura, and Balis): but it is fair to say that the masonry of Qasr ibn-Wardan is reminiscent of sixth-century work at Constantinople, except that it contains a higher proportion of stone.

The architect of these mysterious buildings was certainly in contact with the metropolitan Byzantine style, yet there are many elements here that are not explainable in terms of Constantinople. First, consider the church. The ground plan shows us a rectangle, forty-nine by sixty-one feet, with a projecting staircase tower leading up to the gallery—what is usually, if misleadingly, termed a domed basilica. The flat east wall into which the apse is inscribed is standard in Syria but foreign to the architecture of Constantinople. It is, however, in elevation that the church exhibits its strangest features. The proportions of the inner core of the building are uncommonly tall, and the main structural arches are not semicircular but bluntly pointed. A Byzantine architect would, furthermore, have placed the dome directly upon the crowns of the great arches; this is not so at Qasr ibn-Wardan. Here a drum, octagonal on the outside, is placed upon the arches, and the pendentives, which reduce the square to a circle, spring within the drum, not below it. In addition, the four dome windows that were set on the diagonals were actually cut through the pendentives. No Constantinopolitan architect would have designed such eccentric forms. As for the carving, the door jambs and lintels are of a fairly crude, local style; the capitals, now unfortunately very battered, were elaborate Syrian imitations of Byzantine models.

The palace, too, is a highly interesting building. It is built in two stories, and today only the central part of it remains, about one half of the original frontage. Its principal feature is a large quatrefoil (possibly trefoil) hall with elongated side arms, giving a total length

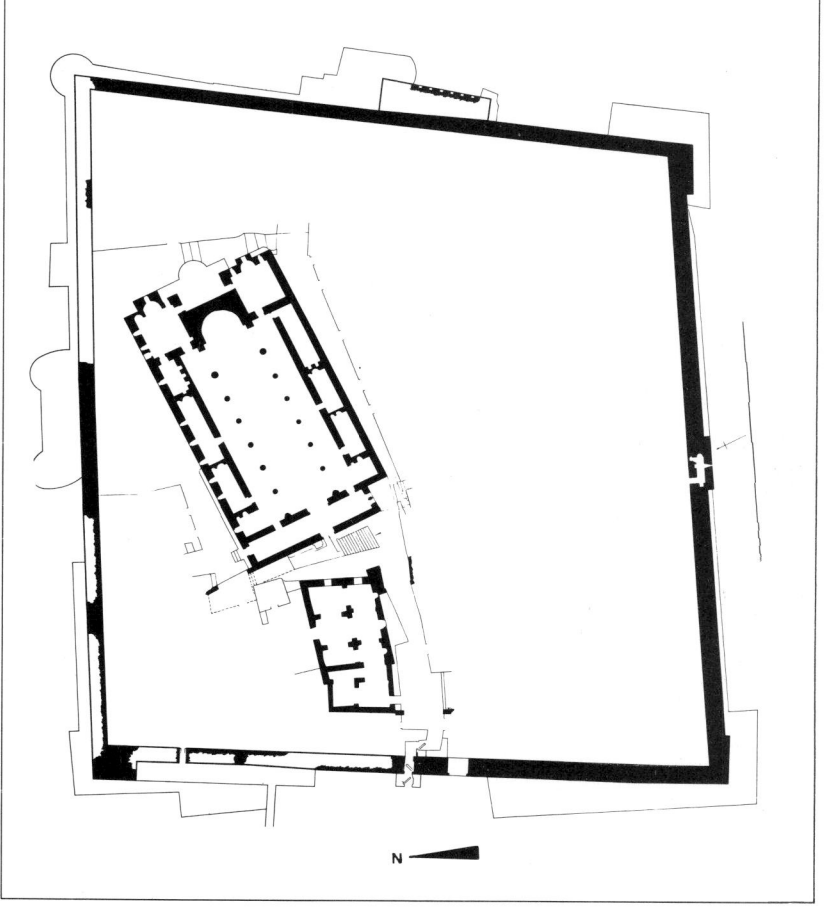

of eighty-two feet. This must have been the audience chamber. There is some indication that it was surmounted by a dome whose span (21 feet 10 inches) would have been exactly equal to that of the dome of the church. All the main vaults of the quatrefoil are pointed, more noticeably on the upper than on the lower floor.

A pertinent parallel to the palace of Qasr ibn-Wardan is provided by the remnants of the episcopal palace of Bosra, believed to be of the early sixth century; the same basic design—a square plan with a courtyard in the middle and a trefoil audience chamber placed on an axis at the far end—was later reproduced in the early Umayyad palace of Mshatta.[29] These comparisons further confirm the view that the architect of Qasr ibn-Wardan was not Constantinopolitan, but a Syrian conversant with contemporary trends of Byzantine architecture, just as the architect of S. Vitale was in all probability an Italian.

164. *Constantinople, St. Irene, ground plan (after W. S. George, 1912).*
165. *Constantinople, St. Irene, longitudinal section (after W. S. George, 1912).*

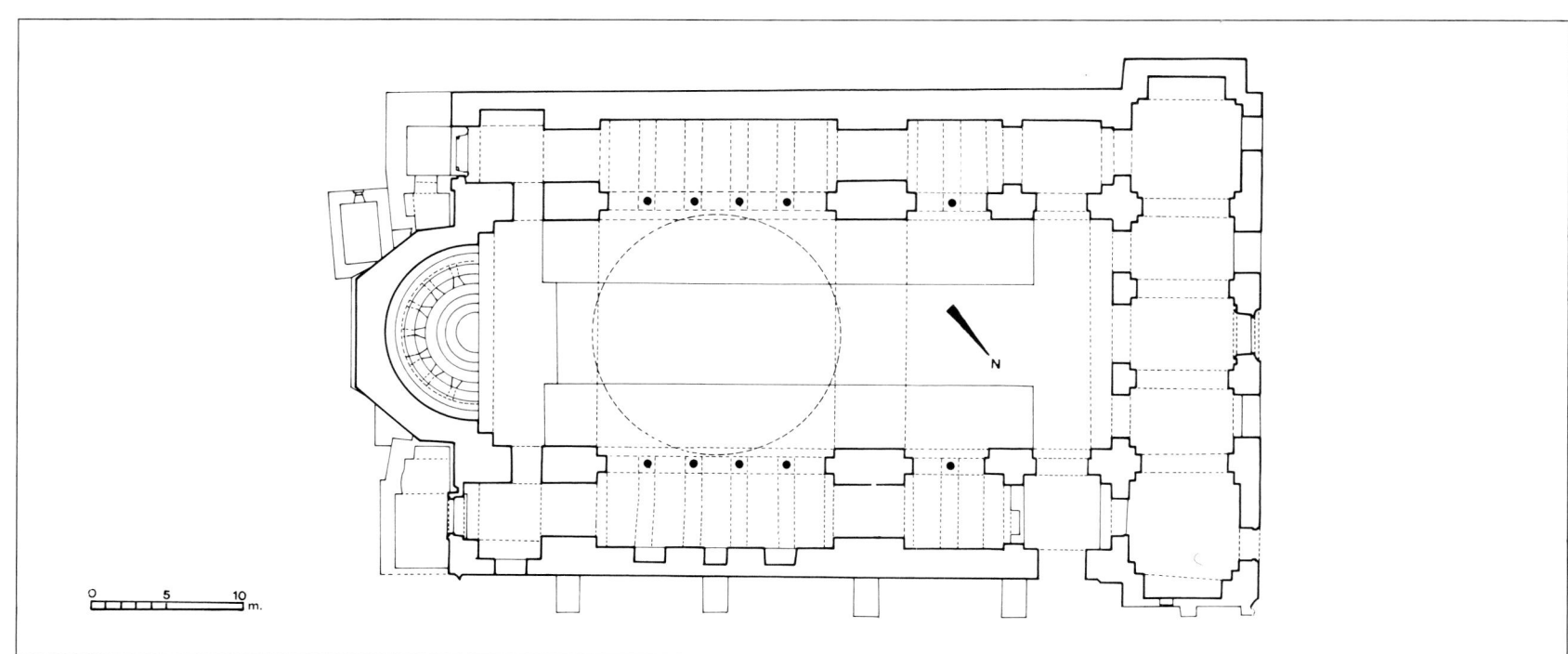

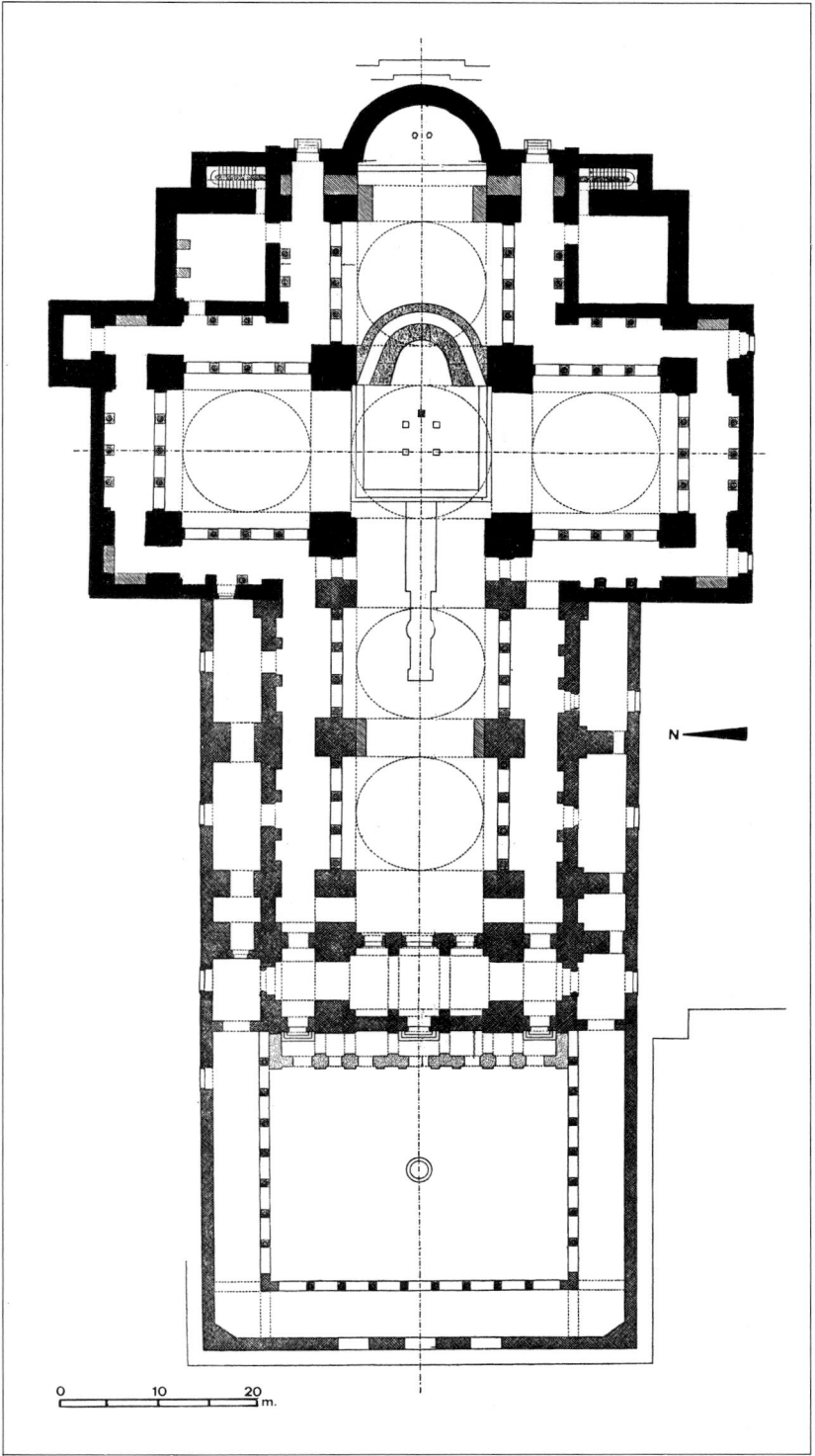

167. *Constantinople, St. Irene, interior looking east.*
168. *Ephesus, St. John the Evangelist, ground plan (after J. Keil, 1951).*

157

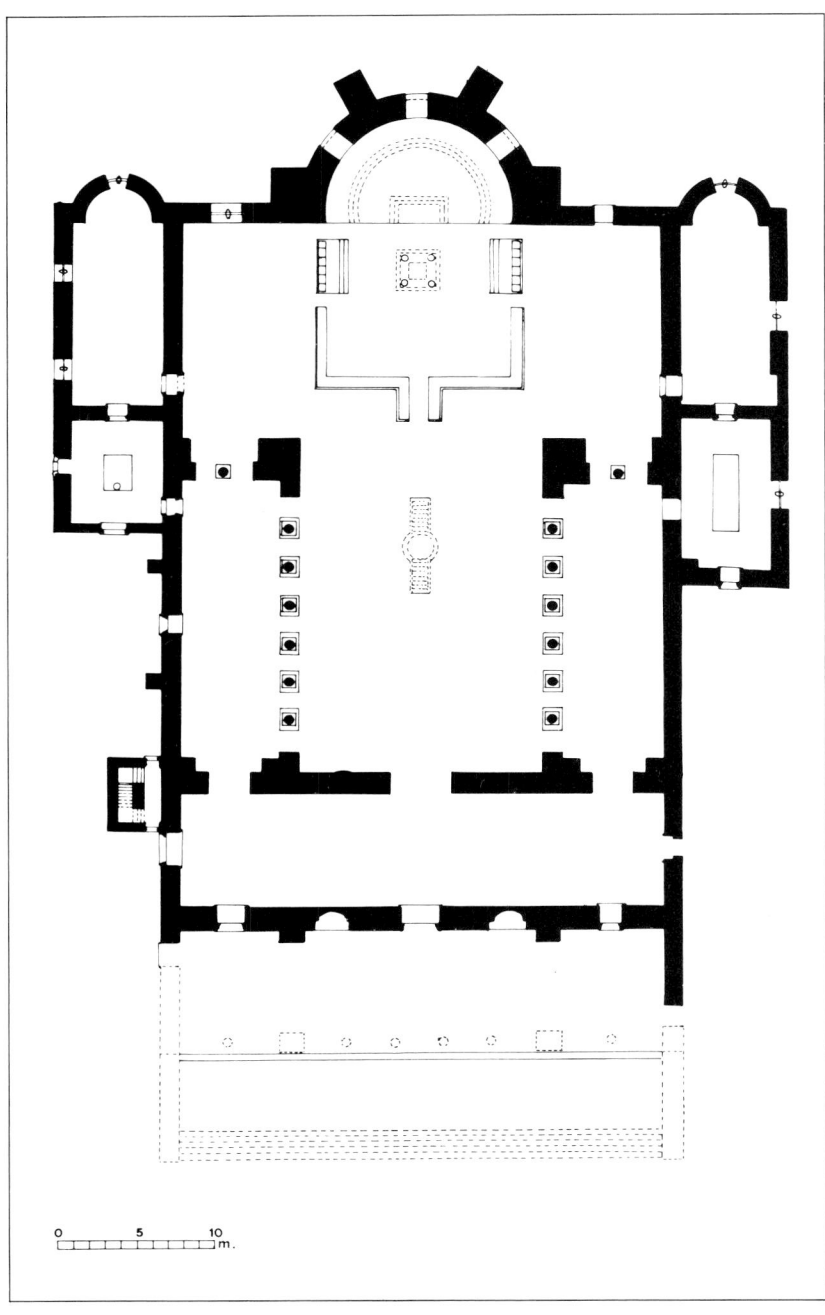

0   5   10
m.

As has been said, however, Qasr ibn-Wardan is an exceptional monument: Syrian architecture developed along its own lines until the first quarter of the seventh century, as shown by a great number of dated monuments, and then continued under the Umayyad caliphs,

who brought even larger financial resources than had been previously available in this prosperous region. The architectural forms, however, were so little affected by the conquest that scholars have long been disputing whether major monuments like Mshatta were Islamic or pre-Islamic.

Not only was Syrian architecture little affected by Constantinople; it was itself a radiating force extending northward to eastern Asia Minor and Armenia, and southward as far as the Sinai Peninsula. The monastery of Mount Sinai (later named after St. Catherine), an imperial foundation erected between 548 and 565, is interesting in this and other respects.[30] It was built as a fortified monastery, not only to give protection to the monks, but also to serve as a garrison point in an attempt to check the incursions of the Arab tribesmen into Palestine. In the sixth century fortified monasteries were a rarity, except perhaps in border areas such as the Tur 'Abdin in Mesopotamia, but they foreshadow a state of affairs that became standard in the Middle Ages.

Within the trapezoid enclosure at Mount Sinai stands a basilica built of local basalt. The architect's name is recorded—he was Stephen of Aila (on the Gulf of 'Aqaba)—but the design he used is more characteristic of Syria than of the Negev. The church has gabled ends, two towers flanking the west facade, and an apse that does not project on the outside. The capitals of the nave colonnade, which must have been carved on the spot, are of different forms, and some of them exhibit the typically Syrian broad-leaved simplification of the Corinthian order. A highly unusual feature of this church is the chapels, five on each side, which open into the aisles. What is, however, even more remarkable is that the chief cult object of Mount Sinai, namely the Burning Bush—which was attracting pilgrims already in the fourth cent   .[1] was the *raison d'être* of the whole establishment—received no architectural setting. It was left to grow behind the apse of the basilica. Had Stephen of Aila been concerned to satisfy the modern theorists of martyria, he would have enclosed it within an open-air rotunda or octagon.

Justinian's reign witnessed a belated attempt to unify a far-flung Empire that was gradually losing its cohesion. Whatever historical explanation one may wish to give of this phenomenon, the outlying provinces were going more and more their own way. The prevalence in Syria, Egypt, and, to a lesser extent, in Palestine of the Monophysite heresy, revivified in the sixth century by Jacob Baradaeus, and the emergence of Syriac and Coptic as vehicles of literary expression have often been quoted as signs of separatist, even "nationalist," tendencies, which contributed to the breakup of Justinian's Empire. The evidence of architecture is also eloquent in this respect.

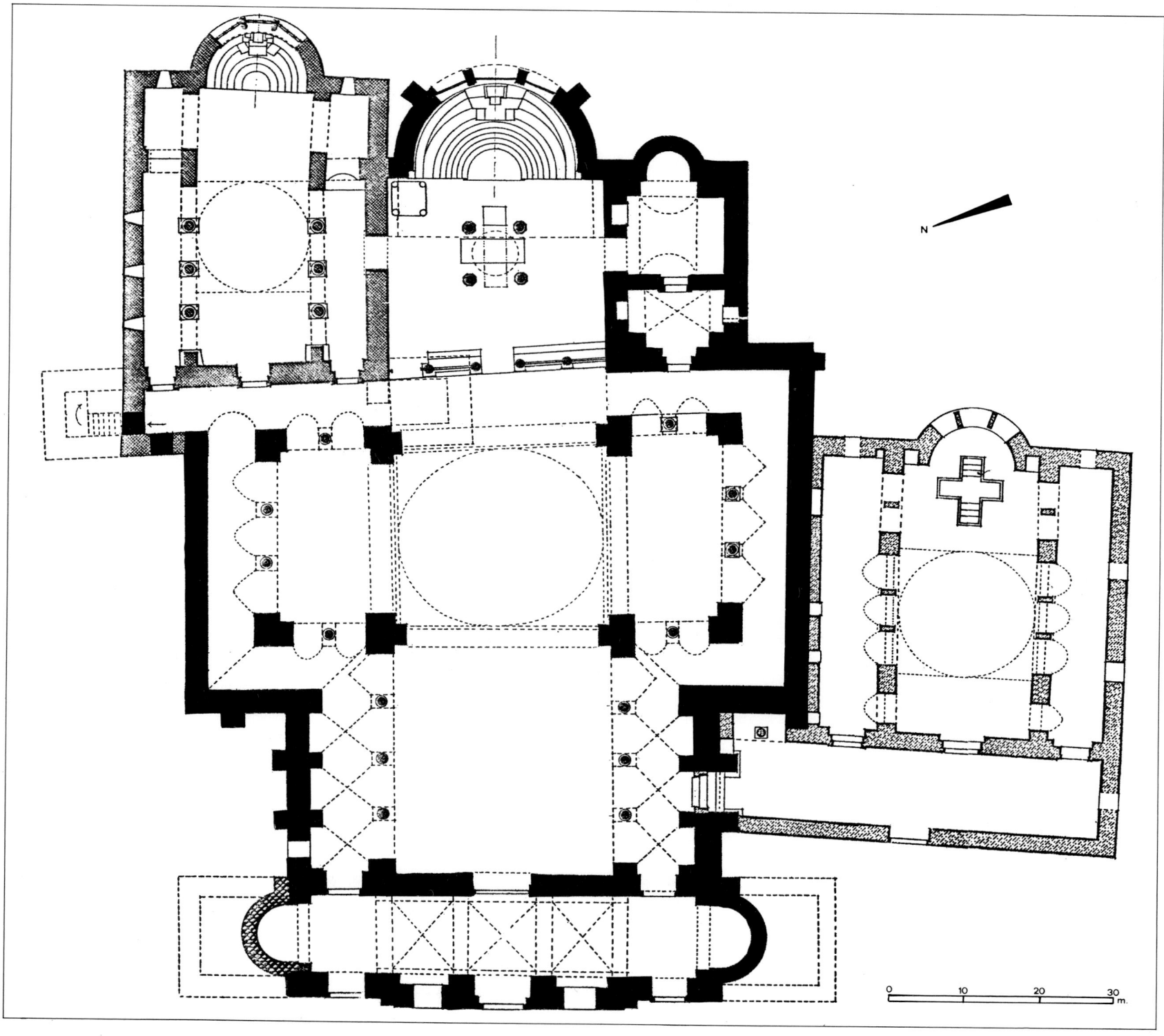

170. *Paros, Katapoliani, ground plan (after H. H. Jewell, 1920).*

171. *Gortyna, St. Titus, isometric section (after A. Orlandos, 1926).*
172. *Gortyna, St. Titus, interior looking east.*

In fact, the diffusion of the Justinianic "prestige style" was rather limited. It goes without saying that buildings as complex and sophisticated as Sts. Sergius and Bacchus and St. Sophia did not readily lend themselves to imitation. Yet there were simpler possibilities, like the one provided by St. Irene, whose essential features included a brick dome and the presence of a gallery on columnar supports. Less ambitious buildings of this kind are found in western Asia Minor and Greece and, though they exhibit great variety of form, they all bear the stamp of the period. We may mention the great cruciform church of St. John at Ephesus, begun before 548, a building imitating the lost Apostles' church at Constantinople of which S. Marco in Venice is a later reflection;[31] basilica B at Philippi and the Katapoliani on the island of Paros, both transept basilicas in plan, but covered by domes;[32] and St. Titus at Gortyna (Crete), basically cruciform in design, with a gallery over the western arm only, while the crossing and bema swell out into a triconch.[33]

Granted, therefore, that the typically Justinianic style in architecture did not have a large following, we may well ask why we consider this epoch to have been so pivotal. Our answer will take two forms. First, it may be observed that the sixth century witnessed in the metropolitan area the demise of certain antique traditions that had dominated architecture for many centuries. The classical orders went out of fashion. The Corinthian capital, which in its fanciful elaborations and perversions was still so prevalent in the fifth century, was finally displaced by the impost capital, sometimes covered by a flat lattice of acanthus leaves, but often dispensing even with this faint reminder of the past. The Ionic capital, already fused with the impost block, lost more and more its distinctive characteristics. The horizontal entablature makes its last appearance at Sts. Sergius and Bacchus. The tessellated pavement is abandoned toward the end of the century, never to appear in Byzantine architecture again. Its place is taken by a pavement of plain marble slabs and *opus sectile,* forming geometric motifs. Finally, and most important, the immemorial tradition of the "hypostyle hall," perpetuated by the basilica, fades out in Justinian's great buildings, where columns serve the subsidiary purpose of supporting the galleries, while the skeleton of the structure is of masonry.

Our second answer has to be seen in historical perspective. Byzantine architecture of the sixth century, considered as the architecture of a "universal" Empire, represents the end of a long development. Justinian's architects strained to the utmost the technical possibilities at their disposal, even, in the case of St. Sophia, overstretched them, just as Justinian himself overextended the material resources of the state to achieve his imperial dreams. Had this Empire proved viable, the subsequent history of Byzantine architecture would have been, of course, very different. But the universal Empire collapsed. And so Justinian's architectural achievement became an awesome memorial of past greatness. While it could not be equaled, it provided a lasting canon of forms to be reproduced on a much smaller scale and with greatly diminished material means.

The breakup of the Empire began while Justinian was still sitting on the throne. Contained by the valiant efforts of his immediate successors, it could not be prevented for long and led to a succession of disasters that are known to us chiefly in their military and political aspects: the breaching of the Danube frontier about 580 and its complete abandonment twenty years later; the permanent settlement of the Slavs in the Balkans as far down as the Peloponnese; the epic war with Persia, beginning in 605 and culminating in the siege of Constantinople in 626; the rise of the Arabs under the banner of Islam; the definitive loss of Palestine, Syria, and Egypt in the 630s and 640s; the conquest of all of North Africa as far as Gibraltar; the sieges of Constantinople by the Arabs in 674–78 and 717–18. These catastrophic events are known to us in outline, but we are far less informed concerning the underlying developments which made these catastrophes possible. One of them we can point out, namely, a steady process of depopulation, starting with the great bubonic plague of 542, which is said to have claimed in Constantinople alone 300,000 victims, that is, about half its inhabitants. Further aggravated by long periods of drought and a succession of destructive earthquakes, this demographic crisis was probably the chief reason why Justinian's Empire, with its enormously long frontiers, could not be held together. Furthermore, it affected the entire Mediterranean basin. Italy in the mid-sixth century is described as being "empty of men."

The result of these catastrophic events can readily be imagined, but we do not have to depend on imagination. There is ample archaeological evidence from the regions that remained within the Empire—essentially Asia Minor and small portions of Greece—indicating that urban life was to all intents and purposes destroyed. Allowing for local differences, the picture is remarkably consistent. In Greece darkness falls about the year 580. Thereafter only a few coastal outposts, like Thessalonica, Athens, Corinth, and Monemvasia, remained in Byzantine hands, while the country was entirely occupied by the Slavs. At Athens the lower town was abandoned. One of the excavators of the Athenian agora speaks of "a period of well-nigh complete desolation until the area was re-occupied as a residential district in the tenth century."[1] At Corinth the situation was similar.[2] Thessalonica held out behind its walls, but it is doubtful if the life it sheltered could be described as urban. It is recorded that at the time of an attack by the Avars and Slavs about 617, many of the inhabitants were caught outside the walls gathering their own harvest; in other words, they had adopted a rural way of life. It is also worth observing that, with the exception of Thessalonica and Paros (an island which was deserted in the ninth century), not a single Early Byzantine church has remained standing in Greece.

In Asia Minor the conditions were different, but the results quite similar. Here there was no foreign occupation of the countryside; instead, it was subjected to yearly devastation by the Arabs over a period of nearly two centuries. Many cities disappeared altogether, others retreated to their fortified citadels, which served as shelters in time of danger, but could hardly have supported normal habitation for more than a very small number of people.

One cannot speak with any assurance of the development of Byzantine architecture in the period between about 610 and 850. Utilitarian work, such as fortification and water supply, was, of course, undertaken, mostly in the way of patching up existing facilities. When, for example, Constantinople was severely shaken by an earthquake in 740, very extensive repairs of the Land Walls had to be carried out. On the other hand, we ought to be very cautious in ascribing to this period churches which appear from the evolutionary point of view to be later than the sixth century and earlier than the tenth. Such an approach, especially when it is based on comparing ground plans, can be extremely misleading, as demonstrated by two examples. The main church of the monastery of the Chora (Kariye Camii) at Constantinople has been ascribed for a long time to the early seventh century; actually, it is no earlier than the eleventh.[3] Likewise, the church known by its Turkish name of Kalenderhane Camii, confidently attributed to the mid-ninth century, has turned out to be of the late twelfth.[4]

The number of churches that can be dated with some certainty in the two and a half "dark centuries" is extremely limited. We may mention first the partial rebuilding of St. Irene at Constantinople, carried out after the aforementioned earthquake of 740. Most of the superstructure above the springing of the aisle vaults was reconstructed at this time and is easily distinguishable by its masonry from the Justinianic portions which remained in place. This was a patch-up job, difficult no doubt because of the size of the church, but one that cannot claim much originality. The western bay of the nave was covered with a more or less elliptical, domical vault without windows, supported on the north and south sides on roughly elliptical arches, and the main dome was heightened by comparison to its presumed sixth-century form. The effect is decidedly clumsy.

To the end of the eighth century belongs St. Sophia at Thessalonica.[5] This is a large church (external measurements 115 by 141 feet) whose construction may well have been politically motivated. The mosaic inscriptions in the bema mention the empress Irene and the emperor Constantine VI, whose joint reign (780–97) coincided with a successful Byzantine offensive against the Slavs in Greece, an offensive that was given considerable publicity and whose conclusion

◁174. *Constantinople, St. Irene, interior looking west.*

175. *Thessalonica, St. Sophia, ground plan (after Diehl, Le Tourneau, and Saladin, 1918).*

176. *Thessalonica, St. Sophia, longitudinal section (after Diehl, Le Tourneau, and Saladin, 1918).*

was marked by triumphal celebrations at Constantinople in 783. One may therefore regard St. Sophia as a memorial of this offensive, which severely undermined, if it did not entirely eliminate, the hold of the Slavs over the country.

The design of the building is unoriginal and the execution heavy-handed. Basically, it is a sixth-century design, like that of St. Irene or Qasr ibn-Wardan, which has been called the "compact domed basilica."[6] The masonry resembles that of St. Irene, and the walls are unnecessarily thick, up to 6 1/2 feet. The dome is encased in a massive square drum so that the windows, three to each side, assume the form of tunnels radiating from the center. The interior is equally heavy, with a great deal of wall space and small openings. The lateral colonnades of the nave are interrupted by a central pier, which breaks up the undulation of the arches. The columns and capitals (a medley of fifth- and sixth-century types) are spoils. In spite of the great thickness of masonry on the ground floor, the galleries over the aisles and narthex were timber-roofed, as shown by the surviving corbels. St. Sophia need not be considered the work of a provincial architect: it was probably the biggest and best that eighth-century Byzantium could produce.

A number of fairly important churches belong to the same architectural group as St. Sophia at Thessalonica. Among them we may mention the Dormition church at Nicaea (Iznik), the cathedral of Bizye (Vize) in European Turkey, St. Clement at Ankara, St. Nicholas at Myra, and the ruined church of Dereağzı in Lycia. None of them can be dated with any accuracy. Since all are situated in present-day Turkey, that is, in what remained of the Byzantine Empire after the great wave of invasions, they could be regarded as representing the survival of a sixth-century formula into the Middle Ages, although one should not exclude the possibility that some of them belong to the sixth century.

The Dormition church at Nicaea (originally the Hyakinthos monastery) was, unfortunately, destroyed in 1922, but is well documented from photographs and publications previous to that date.[7] Today, only the lower portions of the walls, the pavement, and some marble elements remain. The church had a cruciform nave defined by four massive piers and crowned by a dome only twenty feet in diameter, a little over half the span of the Thessalonica dome. The nave was separated from the aisles by an arcade supported not on columns but on rectangular marble piers. There was originally a gallery over the aisles. In examining the preserved records of this monument, we must remember that much of it was rebuilt after the disastrous earthquake of 1065, in particular the tympana, dome base, and most of the narthex. The dome itself dates from 1807. But when was the

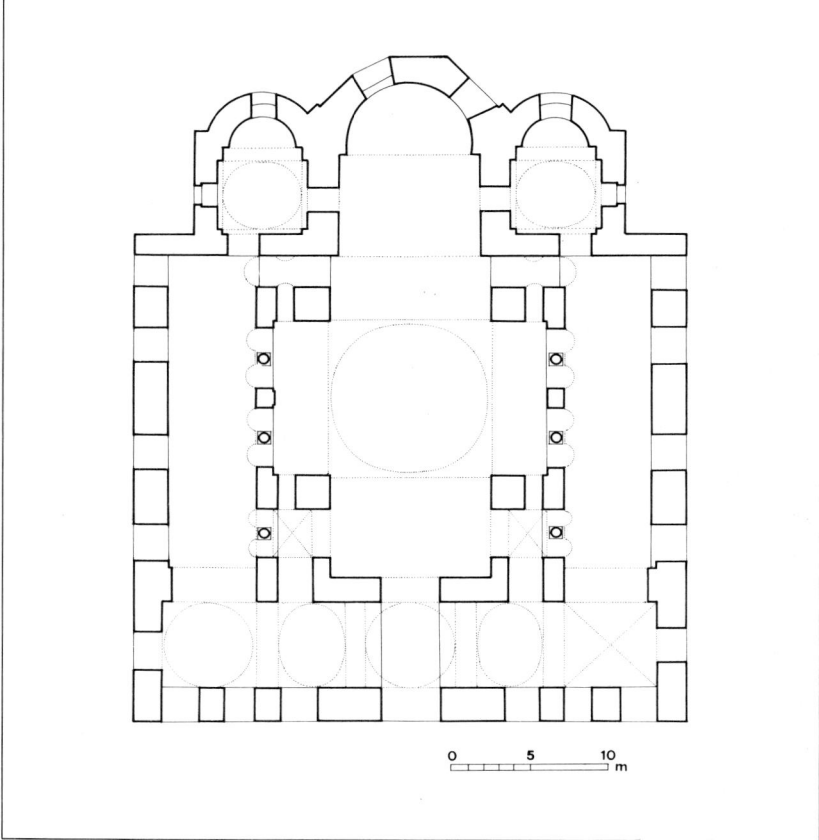

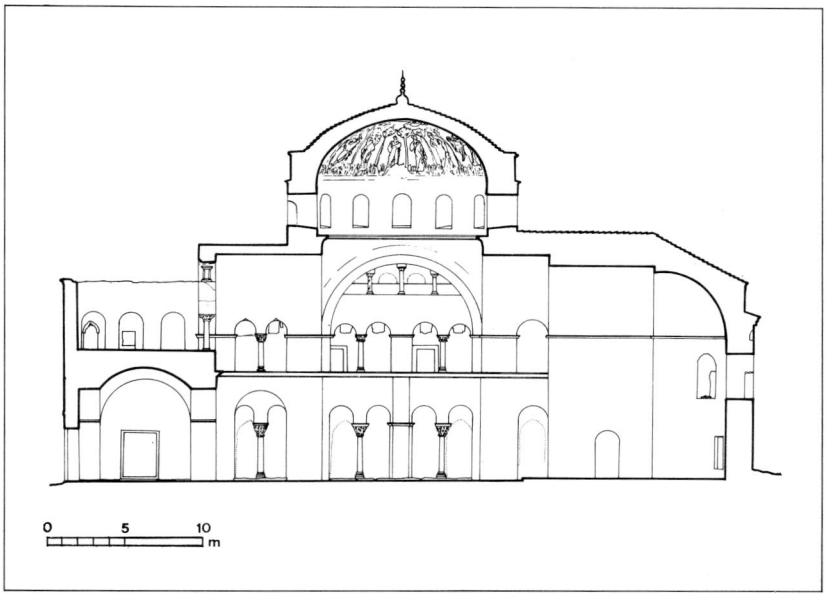

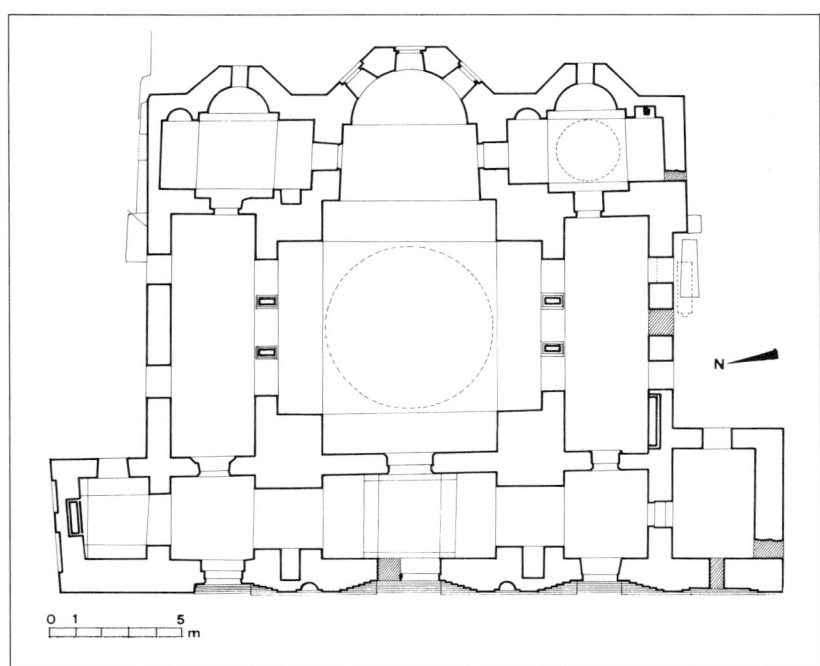

177. *Thessalonica, St. Sophia, interior.*
178. *Nicaea (Iznik), Dormition church, ground plan (after T. Schmit, 1927).*
179. *Nicaea (Iznik), Dormition church, exterior from the southeast as in 1912.*

180. *Nicaea (Iznik), Dormition church, interior, south aisle.*
181. *Myra (Demre), St. Nicholas, ground plan (after Y. Demiriz, 1968).*
182. *Myra (Demre), St. Nicholas, interior looking east.* ▷

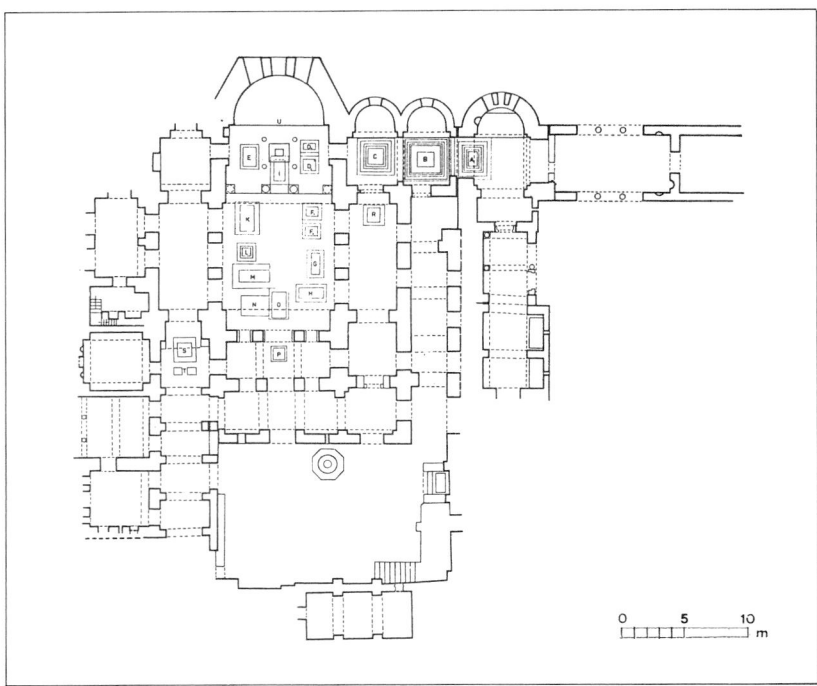

183. *Ankara, St. Clement, isometric section (after G. de Jerphanion, 1928).*

184. *Bizye (Vize), St. Sophia, interior looking northeast.*

185. *Bizye (Vize), St. Sophia, exterior from the south.* ▷

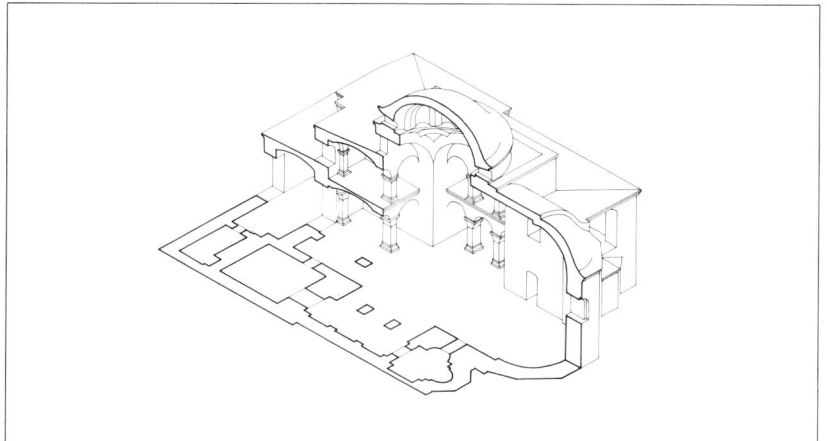

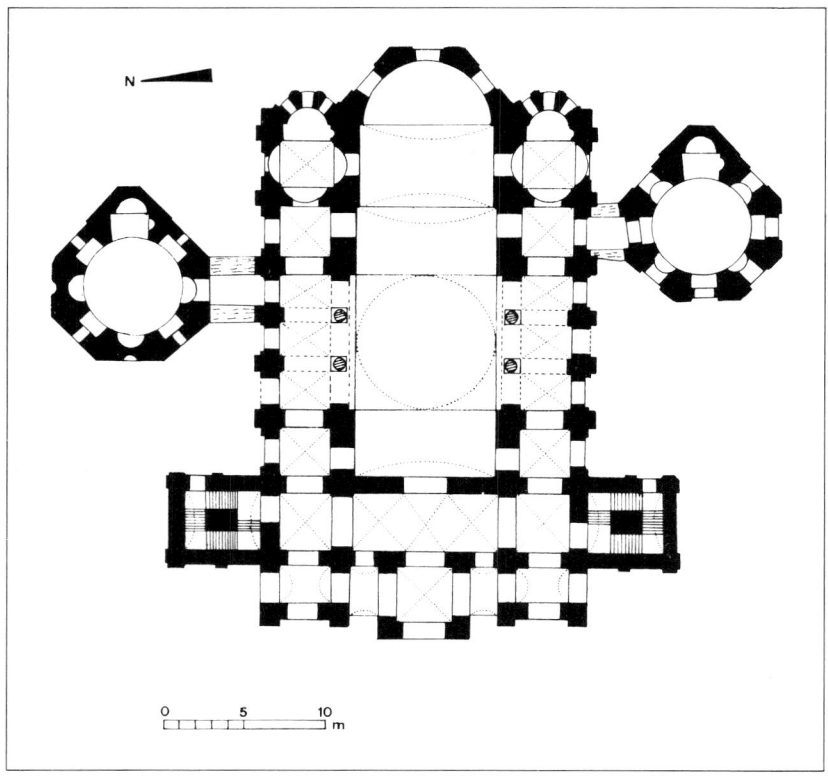

original church built? The famous mosaics of the bema, which were altered by the Iconoclasts and restored after 843, give a *terminus ante quem* of about 730. The regular brickwork of the surviving walls and the sober but neat carving of the marble pilasters, whose capitals bore a monogrammatic inscription of the founder Hyakinthos, suggest a good building period, perhaps as early as the end of the sixth century.

Equal uncertainty still surrounds the church of St. Nicholas at Myra (Demre), in spite of the fact that it is preserved.[8] This is a fairly large domed basilica with galleries supported not on columns but on masonry piers. The apse contains a synthronon with an annular passage under the seats as in St. Irene at Constantinople, but the ambo, recorded in the early years of this century, has been removed. The form of the church was drastically changed by a barbarous restoration carried out at the behest of the Russian government in 1862. Much of the superstructure was then rebuilt and the original dome replaced by a cross-groined vault. The existence of a martyrium of St. Nicholas is recorded in the late sixth century, and it is not impossible that portions of the existing building may go back to this period. Restorations appear to have been carried out in the ninth century (a period when the cult of St. Nicholas was greatly expanded), in 1043, and again in the twelfth century. The complicated ground plan of the complex, with two mortuary chapels abutting on the south aisle, and various other annexes, reflects the requirements of an important pilgrimage center, which continued functioning even after the saint's relics had been removed to Bari in 1087. The building, which has recently been cleared all around of the alluvial deposit that had buried it twenty-six feet into the ground, deserves a more thorough investigation than it has received until now.

Many features of the Dormition church are repeated in another destroyed monument, St. Clement's at Ankara, known to us from a few old photographs and a survey made in 1927.[9] This, too, was a fairly small cruciform church with a gallery running over the aisles as well as the narthex. The gallery was supported on rectangular marble piers, two on each side. The same arrangement of piers was repeated on the triforium level. The dome was carried on squinches and had no drum. Its shell was scalloped, with twelve concave segments separated by ribs and lit by only four windows. The main structural elements were built entirely of brick; elsewhere zones of brick alternated with several courses of irregular rubble. The marble elements, namely, the piers with their capitals and the gallery cornice, all made specifically for this church, were competently carved, the dominant motif being the "arch and dart," which is standard in Byzantine architectural sculpture of the fifth and sixth centuries. The

187. *Dereağzı, church, west facade.*

squat proportions of the church and especially the character of the carving point to a pre-Iconoclastic date, in the sixth or seventh century.

The mosque popularly known as Ayasofya (St. Sophia) at Vize, for which I have elsewhere suggested a *terminus ante quem* of 900,[10] should probably be dated in the end of the eighth or the ninth century. It survives in a dilapidated and somewhat precarious condition. This was, I believe, the cathedral of Bizye, which accounts for its fairly large size. The plan is basilican on the ground floor (the four corner piers under the dome were thickened at a later period) and cruciform on gallery level. The dome, carried on pendentives, is somewhat elliptical in plan and has a sixteen-sided drum and as many windows. The construction, largely of rubble, is crude and the exterior aspect of the monument plain and stark.

The ruin at Dereağzı in Lycia is probably the most recent member of the architectural family we have been studying (late ninth century?).[11] Nothing is known concerning its history, so that we cannot offer any plausible explanation for the presence of this elaborate church in a remote mountain area some fifteen miles northwest of Myra, except perhaps that it may have marked a pilgrimage site. The surviving ruins comprise a cross-domed basilica and two octagonal structures of uncertain destination, both with oriented apses, one to the north, the other to the south. The main church (total exterior length 128 feet, width across the nave 69 feet, dome span 26 feet) had a U-shaped gallery over the narthex and side aisles accessible by two external stair turrets, and a single-storied outer narthex. In the north and south bays under the dome the galleries must have been supported on a pair of columns, which have since been removed. Fragments of wall mosaic bear witness to the richness of the original decoration. Even in its present condition the ruin of Dereağzı shows the added regard for exterior appearance that differentiates Middle Byzantine from Early Byzantine architecture: note in particular the stepped recession of planes on the west facade and in the octagonal annexes.

The above group of cross-domed basilicas is usually regarded as marking the transition between the architecture of the sixth century and that of the ninth and tenth. It would, I think, be more exact to say that they represent a Justinianic type that was suitable for fairly large congregational churches, since they normally included a gallery, a type that was abandoned after the ninth century because there was no further need for such churches. It admitted of reduction, as shown by the church of the Archangels at Sige (on the southern shore of the Sea of Marmara), dated by a nineteenth-century inscription to the year 780.[12] Here we have, so to speak, only the core of

189. *Sige, Church of the Archangels, exterior from the southeast.*
190. *Sige, Church of the Archangels, interior looking east.*
191. *Trilye, Fatih Camii, exterior from the northwest.* ▷

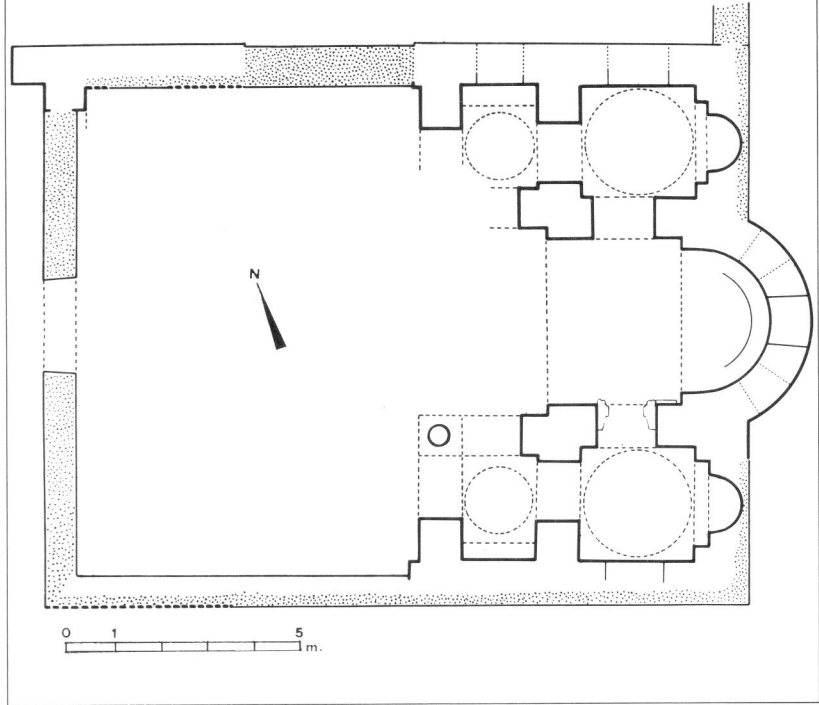

tects turned to another formula, that of the cross-in-square or four-column church, which was to remain dominant in Byzantine ecclesiastical architecture until the close of the Middle Ages.

In speaking of the genesis of the cross-in-square plan, we should lay aside the evolutionary approach, which demands a gradual, step-by-step transformation of forms which, in any case, cannot be documented with the few surviving monuments, most of them of uncertain date. We must also discard certain fantastic derivations that have been proposed, for example, that from the Iranian fire temples. The Byzantine architects who, toward the end of the eighth or the beginning of the ninth century, introduced the cross-in-square plan had never heard of these fire temples, nor were they aware of the second-century "praetorium" of Musmiye in Syria, which has been dragged into the discussion because its ceiling was supported on four freestanding columns, nor, in all probability, of the audience hall of al-Mundhir at Resafa. The idea was very simple and based entirely on structural elements deeply rooted in the Byzantine tradition: that of a dome rising above four barrel vaults, arranged so as to form a Greek cross. This system, clearly visible on the outside, was inscribed within a square with the help of four internal supports, either columns or masonry piers. The four corner bays were covered with cross-vaults, domical vaults, or even smaller domes. This way the nave assumed a perfectly symmetrical, centralized form, to which a tripartite bema, usually terminating in three apses, was added to the east.

A basic feature of the cross-in-square church was its small size. We have observed that Syrian architects were reluctant to place upon freestanding columns masonry arches of a span greater than 11 1/2 feet, and this in the case of timber-roofed basilicas. Byzantine architects, who built in a lighter material—namely, brick—faced nevertheless the same problem. In the average cross-in-square church the span of the major arches, which is equivalent to the diameter of the dome, is seldom greater than thirteen feet. Theoretically, of course, a marble column of what was then standard size (say, 20 inches in diameter) is capable of supporting a much larger arch, provided the whole arcade is sufficiently secured at the two ends. However, we are speaking here of builders who worked by rule of thumb. We may affirm, therefore, that the cross-in-square church on columns was specifically designed to be small, that is, to hold a congregation of about one hundred. Another important feature is the lack of any internal subdivisions: the whole nave is a single space, which does not readily lend itself to the segregation of the sexes. I conclude from these observations that the cross-in-square church arose in a monastic milieu. A Byzantine monastery normally numbered a brotherhood of between twenty and one hundred and was by definition "unisex."

the cross-domed basilica, minus the aisles and the bema vault: a unified space almost completely covered by the dome. Such a solution, however, did not prove popular, perhaps for the reason that the dome did not receive sufficient lateral abutment. Instead, Byzantine archi-

In the period under review monasticism witnessed a great revival in spite of, or perhaps because of, imperial opposition. The Iconoclastic emperors, in particular Constantine V (741–75), persecuted the monks because of their adherence to the cult of icons. It was to no avail: monasticism was only fortified by this trial and became adorned with a new set of martyrs and confessors. The center of Byzantine monasticism now lay out in Bithynia, roughly between Mount Olympus (Uludağ) to the east and the ruins of ancient Cyzicus to the west. It was a fertile region, yet one that afforded sufficient seclusion on its mountain slopes. It was also one of the few parts of Asia Minor that had remained untouched by the Arab raids. The leaders of Byzantine monasticism in the second half of the eighth and the first half of the ninth century had little in common with St. Anthony or St. Simeon Stylites. Far from being illiterate fanatics, they included some of the most cultivated and richest men of the period: Theodore the Studite, his uncle Platon, Theophanes Confessor, Methodius, and Nicetas the Patrician all belonged to the ruling bureaucratic caste and furthermore owned estates in Bithynia, where they founded monasteries. We have ample documentary evidence that monasteries sprouted up in Bithynia, particularly during the reign of the empress Irene (780–802), who reversed the Iconoclastic policy of her predecessors and showed great favor to monks.

Some of the monasteries in question have survived, although they have received very little attention. I have in mind a group of four-column churches in or near a little town called Trilye, on the south shore of the Sea of Marmara. Two of them can be identified with the monasteries of Pelekete and Megas Agros ("Big Field"), which played a leading role in the Iconoclastic period; the Byzantine name of the best-preserved of these monuments, the Fatih Camii at Trilye, is, unfortunately, unknown.[13] Pelekete, destroyed by the Iconoclasts about 764, was rebuilt before the end of the century; M′gas Agros was erected about 785. In the present state of our knowledge we cannot positively assert that these surviving churches were not reconstructed at some later period, say, in the tenth or eleventh century; such a supposition, however, would have to be proved by archaeological investigation rather than by reference to general trends. Until this is done, we must entertain the presumption that cross-in-square churches were built for Bithynian monasteries at the end of the eighth century, and this may shed some light on the use, or rather reuse, of columns in them. At a time when such objects were no longer produced it may not have been altogether easy to procure four large columns of uniform size and four fitting capitals, but in Bithynia the vast ruins of ancient Cyzicus provided an almost unlimited supply of carved marble pieces. To a cultivated person like Theophanes Confessor, the founder of Megas Agros, there may have been a special attraction in embellishing his church with such relics of a bygone age.

Before we leave the Dark Ages, we should make a brief excursion to Armenia. It is not my intention to present here a comprehensive sketch of the remarkable school of architecture that developed in Armenia and neighboring Georgia, a school that cannot be regarded as merely a provincial branch of Byzantine architecture and would require separate treatment. On the other hand, I do not share the exaggerated claims that have been made by Joseph Strzygowski and his followers, who regarded Armenia as a major creative center of architectural concepts that allegedly originated farther east, in the Iranian world, and were then disseminated throughout Christian Europe.[14]

The reason for our excursion is more pragmatic: beginning in the last quarter of the sixth century, the Armenian element acquired an extraordinary prominence in Byzantine society. There were, of course, many Armenians living within the Empire, especially in eastern Asia Minor; in addition, large groups of them either emigrated voluntarily or were forcibly transplanted from their homeland, which was constantly a battleground between Persia and Byzantium. Recruited as soldiers, they came to dominate the Byzantine army; and at a time when the Empire was obliged to be thoroughly militarized, the army held the key to social advancement. The Byzantine aristocracy that emerged during the Dark Ages was to a considerable extent Armenian; and several Armenians mounted the imperial throne, beginning with the great Heraclius himself.[15] Furthermore, the Armenians had a sturdy sense of identity, acquired from centuries of fighting for their independence, and did not always allow themselves to become thoroughly "Byzantinized." Under the circumstances, it is legitimate to inquire whether this Armenian presence exerted any influence on Byzantine architecture.

The earliest Christian monuments of Armenia date from the fifth or sixth century. They are barrel-vaulted basilicas supported on two rows of masonry piers.[16] The arches are usually horseshoe-shaped; the carved ornament, though sparse and debased, is of classical and, more specifically, Syrian derivation. Comparable basilicas are found in the Tur 'Abdin in northern Mesopotamia and, farther west, at Binbirkilise ("The Thousand and One Churches") in the Anatolian highlands.[17] The closest analogies between Armenia and Syria may be found in the basilica of Ereruyk, which, though supported on L-shaped piers, appears to have been timber-roofed. It had a flat sanctuary wall, open lateral colonnades, and a facade flanked by two rectangular towers. The detail is also typically Syrian: pedimented portals supported on engaged columns, strings of dentil and U-shaped moldings that frame the windows. It is entirely natural that Armenian architects should have sought their models from their southern neighbors: it was from the same region, from Edessa and Samosata, that Armenia received its Christian culture and its alphabet. By joining the Monophysite camp, the Armenian Church perpetuated this connection that was imposed by geography and the interplay of political forces.

The basilica did not have a long life-span in Armenia and gave way toward the end of the sixth century to the domed church, which attained a surprising degree of elaboration in the first great period of Armenian architecture, roughly between the years 610 and 670. These dates are significant: Armenian architecture developed at the very time when Christian Syrian architecture came to a halt; at a time, moreover, when the Byzantine Empire was entering its Dark Age. It may be said without exaggeration that in the seventh century Armenian architecture was leading the entire Christian East. It proved a short period of supremacy: the occupation of that country by the Arabs put an end to this remarkable development, and it was only two centuries later that Armenian builders were able to resume their work on a monumental scale.

The following architectural types appear in Armenia more or less simultaneously. First, the domed tetraconch, usually encased in a rectangle.[18] This type is common to both Armenia and Georgia, being represented in the former country by the churches of Avan near Erevan (before 609), Aramus, Sisian, St. Ripsime at Echmiadzin (618–30), and others; in the latter by the Holy Cross (Džvari) near Mtzkheta (before 605), Ateni, and others. The adaptation of a quatrefoil to a rectangle created an awkward problem of internal planning, namely, how to integrate the four outer corners. It was solved by inserting between the larger apses of the tetraconch four smaller exedrae of horseshoe shape, and these smaller exedrae, placed on the diagonals, led to corner rooms, circular at Avan, rectangular in the other churches. If the interior suffers from fragmentation, the exterior, on the other hand, acquires a massive monumentality; the four facades are practically identical, but each is deeply indented by a pair of wedge-shaped niches, creating areas of deep shadow. The dome, which is always of masonry, is supported on a system of squinches: four large squinches over the diagonally placed exedrae, and eight smaller squinches placed a little higher so as to form the transition from an octagon to the circular base of the drum.

Second, the octagon, represented by two rather small, ruined churches, namely, Zoravor near Evgard (662–85) and that of Irind.

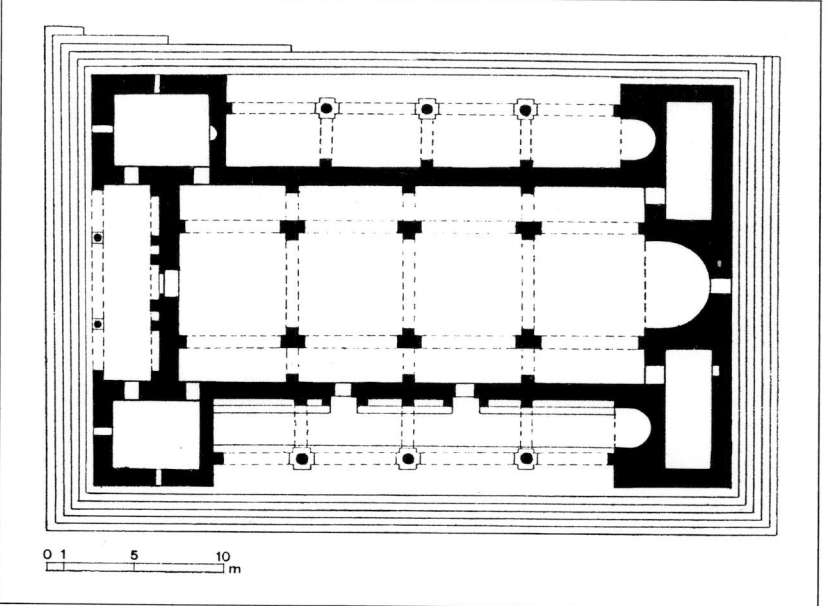

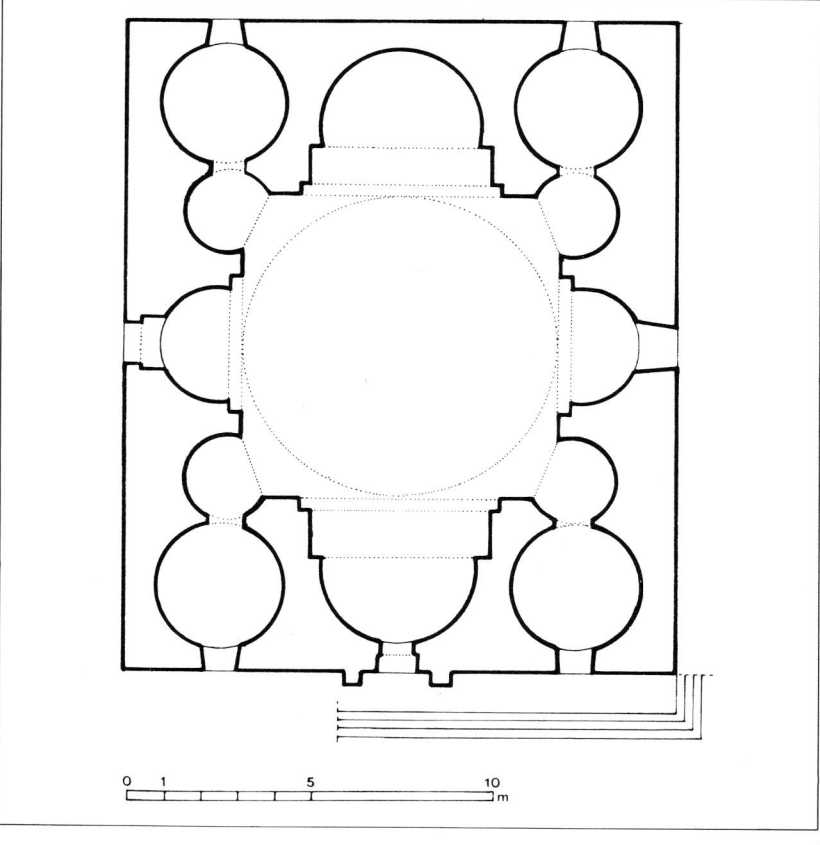

197. *Avan, Church of the Virgin, remains of portal.*
198. *Avan, Church of the Virgin, remains of apse.*
199. *Avan, Church of the Virgin, remains of interior.* ▷

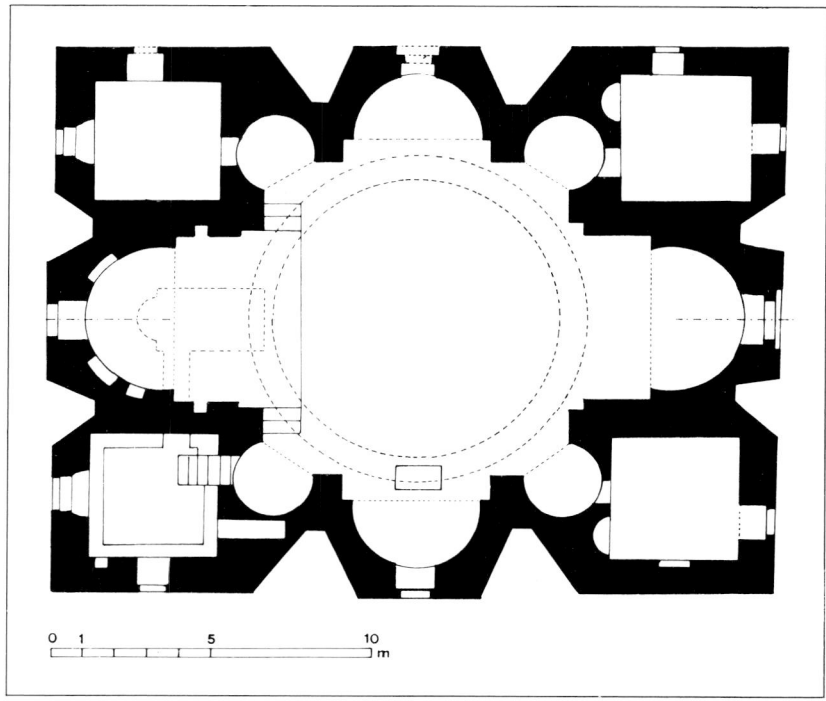

These comprise eight apsed exedrae arranged radially. On the outside each apse is three-sided, creating the same kind of wedge-shaped niche that we have noted in the first group. The entire interior space is covered by a dome on a relatively high drum.

Third, the double-shell quatrefoil, represented by one remarkable building, the church of the Vigilant Powers (Zvartnotz) near Echmiadzin (645–60), erected by the Greek-oriented *katholikos* (archbishop) Narses II. Only the lower portions of the walls remain, but the building can be reconstituted with reasonable accuracy. Seen from the outside, it must have presented the appearance of three gradually diminishing cylinders, placed one on top of the other. The lowest cylinder, that of the outer shell, had a diameter of 123 feet and was enlivened with blind arcading on the outside. Within its perimeter was placed the quatrefoil—four exedrae of six columns each, opening out between four W-shaped piers. This arrangement was repeated on gallery level. The whole tall structure was topped by a dome on squinches. It is reasonable to suppose that this ambitious design was adapted from the Syrian quatrefoils, such as those of Bosra, Amida, and Resafa. The use of columns, normally eschewed by Armenian architects, the basketwork capitals, and the Greek monograms of Narses all point to foreign inspiration.

Fourth, a group of fairly large domed churches having four freestanding internal supports, which are most significant for our inquiry. They are represented by three almost contemporary monuments, erected at a time of maximum Byzantine ascendency over Armenia: the church of St. Gayane at Vagarshapat, built by Archbishop Ezr (Esdras) in 630–36, that of St. John at Bagavan, commissioned by the same prelate in 631–39, and the church of Mren (just inside the Turkish frontier), dating from 639–40.[19] The significance of these churches is that they embody, to all intents and purposes, the cross-in-square principle, except for a slight longitudinal elongation. In all three cases the dome is carried on four masonry piers and on squinches. The four barrel-vaulted cross-arms, covered with gabled roofs, are clearly expressed on the outside. The drum of the dome is eight-sided, tall and elegant at St. Gayane and Mren, squat in the larger church of Bagavan. The diameter of the dome ranges from 18 feet at St. Gayane and 20 1/2 feet at Mren to 29 1/2 feet at Bagavan.

The virtuosity displayed by the Armenian architects of the seventh century is beyond doubt; their originality is harder to assess. A consideration that cannot be overlooked is that the wide variety of domed forms I have described was introduced all at once and had no prior development in Armenia. It may be suggested as a working hypothesis that the center of inspiration was provided by northern Mesopotamia, that is, the region extending from Samosata and Edessa (Urfa) to Amida (Diyarbakır) and farther east to Martyropolis (Silvan), where Armenians and Syrians came into direct contact. The almost total disappearance of Early Christian monuments in the cities of this region does not allow us to support this hypothesis by sufficiently convincing comparisons; nevertheless, a number of specific traits point in the direction I have indicated. The dome on squinches, the horseshoe arch, and a predilection for multilobed plans are all to be found in Mesopotamia, witness, for example, the church of the Virgin at Hah in the Tur 'Abdin.[20] If we extend our search to central Anatolia, we shall find at Binbirkilise the high octagonal drum and tentlike covering of the dome that are so characteristic of Armenian architecture. It is certainly no coincidence that the closest parallels to the Armenian vaulted basilicas are offered by the same areas.

If my views are correct, the importance of Armenian and Georgian architecture resides not only in its inherently high quality, but also in that it reflects otherwise unknown developments in the eastern provinces of the Empire. By way of Armenia these Oriental forms reentered the main current of Byzantine architecture during the period to which we must now turn our attention.

202, 203. *Vagarshapat (Echmiadzin), St. Ripsime, interior, view of dome.*

204. *Zoravor, near Evgard, ground plan (after A. L. Jakobson, 1950).*

205. *Zvartnotz (Church of the Vigilant Powers), ground plan (after T. Toramanian, 1918).*

206. *Zvartnotz (Church of the Vigilant Powers), reconstruction of exterior (after T. Toramanian, 1918).*

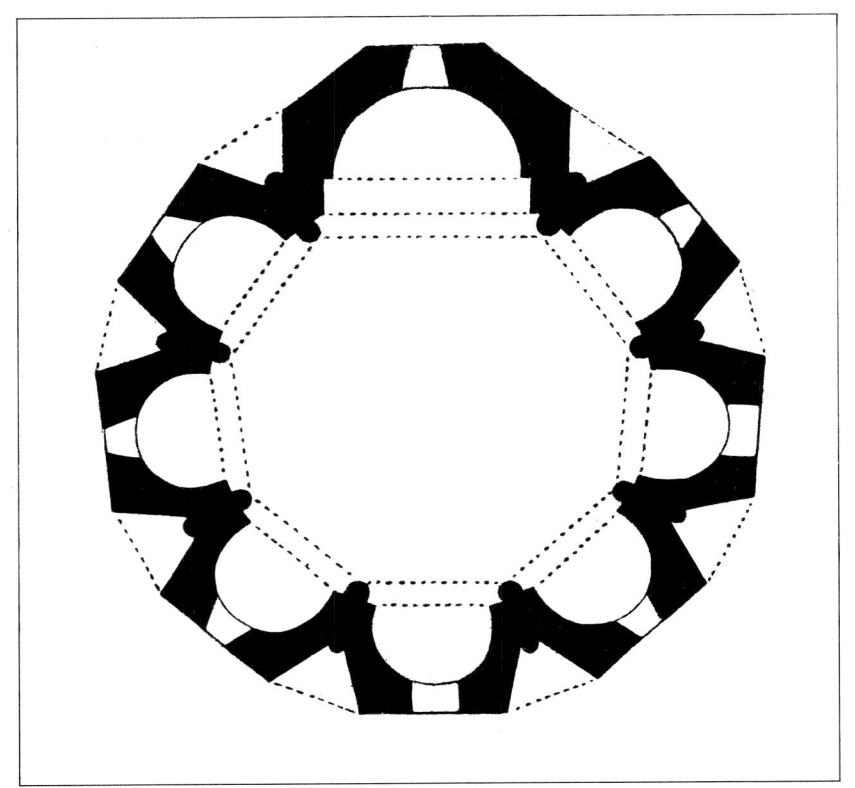

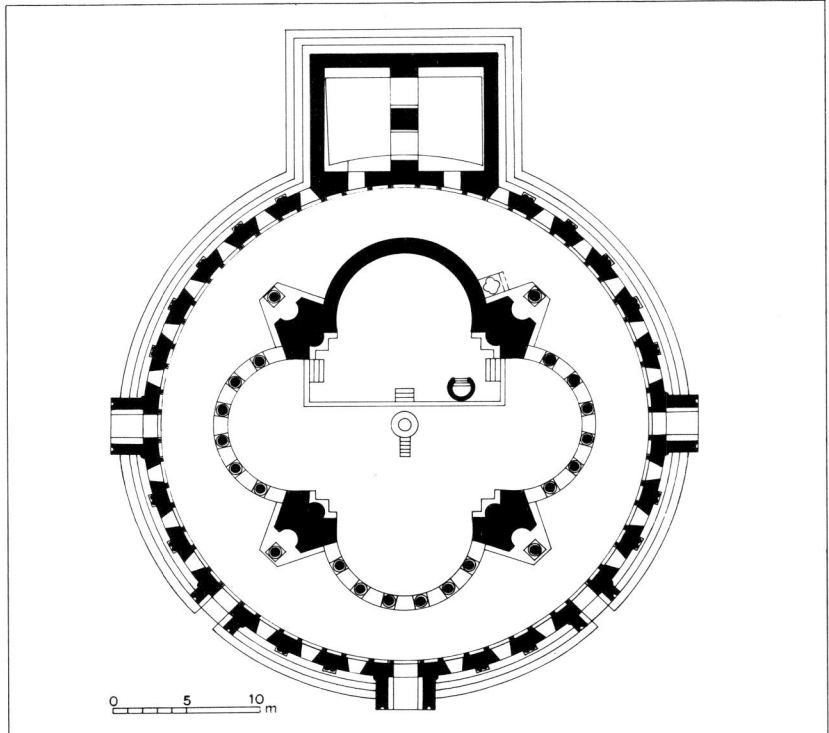

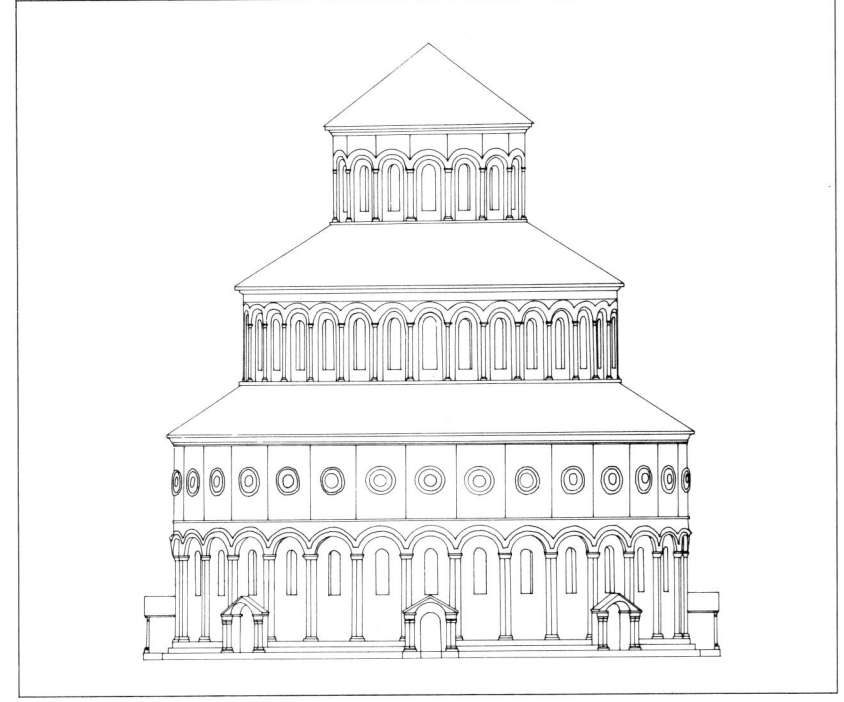

208. *Vagarshapat (Echmiadzin), St. Gayane, exterior.*
209. *Mren, cathedral, ground plan (after T. Toramanian, 1918).*
210. *Mren, cathedral, exterior from the southeast.* ▷

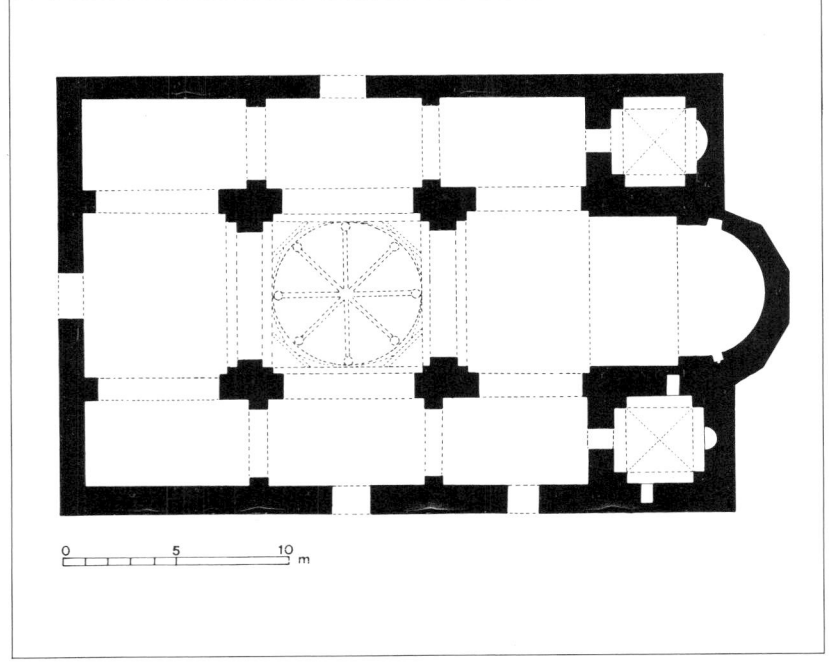

211. *Hah, Church of the Virgin, interior looking into dome.*

212. *Hah, Church of the Virgin, ground plan (after U. Monneret de Villard, 1940).*

213. *Hah, Church of the Virgin, interior looking north.*

214. *Madenşehir (Binbirkilise), general view (19th-century engraving).*

215. *Madenşehir (Binbirkilise), church no. 1, interior looking northeast.*

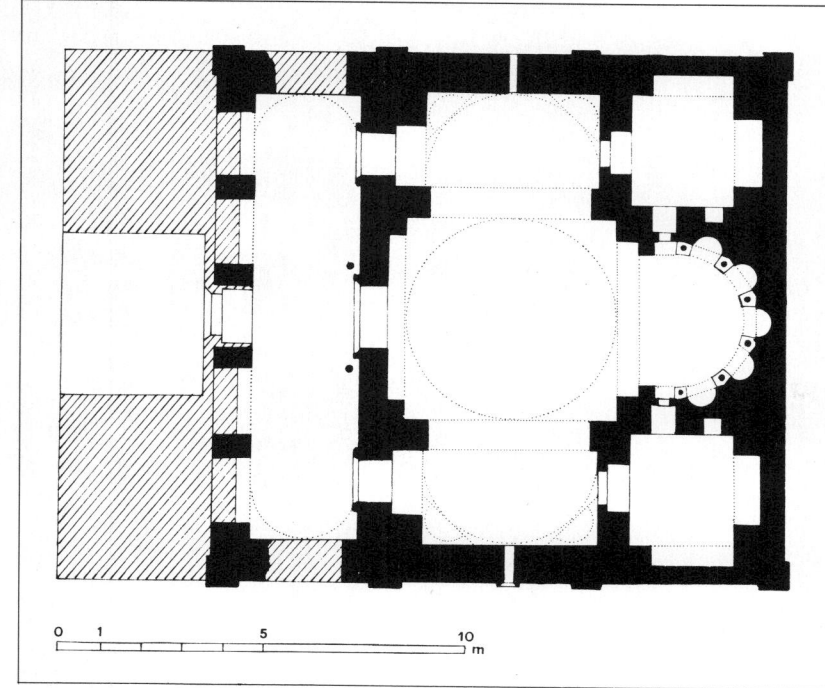

In the first half of the ninth century the Byzantine Empire began to emerge from the cloud of darkness that had hung over it for some two hundred years. It was no longer a great Mediterranean empire. The inheritance of Rome had passed in large part to the Arabs, who now controlled an immense area, from Central Asia to Spain, within which a prodigious urban development could take place. Compared with the domains of the caliph, those of the *basileus* were both small and underdeveloped: Asia Minor, devastated by continuous Arab incursions; Greece, which had just been regained from the Slavs; and the distant provinces of the Crimea, South Italy, and Sicily, which lived their own lives. What is more, this shrunken state no longer controlled the major routes of international communication and trade. It was a rural state with one large city, Constantinople, which now enjoyed an exclusive monopoly on culture and art. The architectural pattern of the Middle Byzantine state was necessarily very different from that of Justinian's period.

The contrast can be illustrated by specific examples. For just as we have a catalogue of Justinian's buildings, so we also possess catalogues of buildings erected by Theophilus (829–42), the last Iconoclast emperor, and Basil I (867–86).[1] The two latter are limited exclusively to Constantinople and its immediate vicinity. In addition to repairing the Sea Walls of the capital, Theophilus appears to have concerned himself only with the building of palaces. It is reported that in 830 a Byzantine envoy who went to Baghdad was so impressed by the splendor of Arab architecture that on his return he persuaded the emperor to build a palace exactly like the ones he had seen in "Syria." Theophilus was glad to comply, and such a palace was constructed at Bryas, an Asiatic suburb of the capital; the only departure from the Arab model consisted of the addition of a chapel next to the imperial chamber and of a triconch church in the middle of the courtyard. The substructures of this palace, probably still preserved, consist of a large rectangular enclosure that does indeed call to mind the layout of Umayyad and Abbasid palaces.[2] It was, however, in the Great Palace that Theophilus constructed his best-known buildings—a series of pavilions of which the principal one had, once more, the shape of a triconch. The minute description of these buildings that was compiled some one hundred years later by the emperor Constantine VII Porphyrogenitus evokes the atmosphere of *A Thousand and One Nights*. It was not for nothing that Theophilus was the contemporary of Harun al-Rashid.

If the art of Theophilus was a courtly art, the same could be said in large measure of Basil I. The latter emperor, an Armenian adventurer of lowly birth, was, however, animated by the loftier ideal of a *renovatio imperii Romani*. The same ideal had inspired Charle-

◁ 216. *Maltepe, near Istanbul, substructures of Bryas palace looking northeast.*

217. *Maltepe, near Istanbul, substructures of Bryas palace, ground plan (after S. Eyice, 1959).*

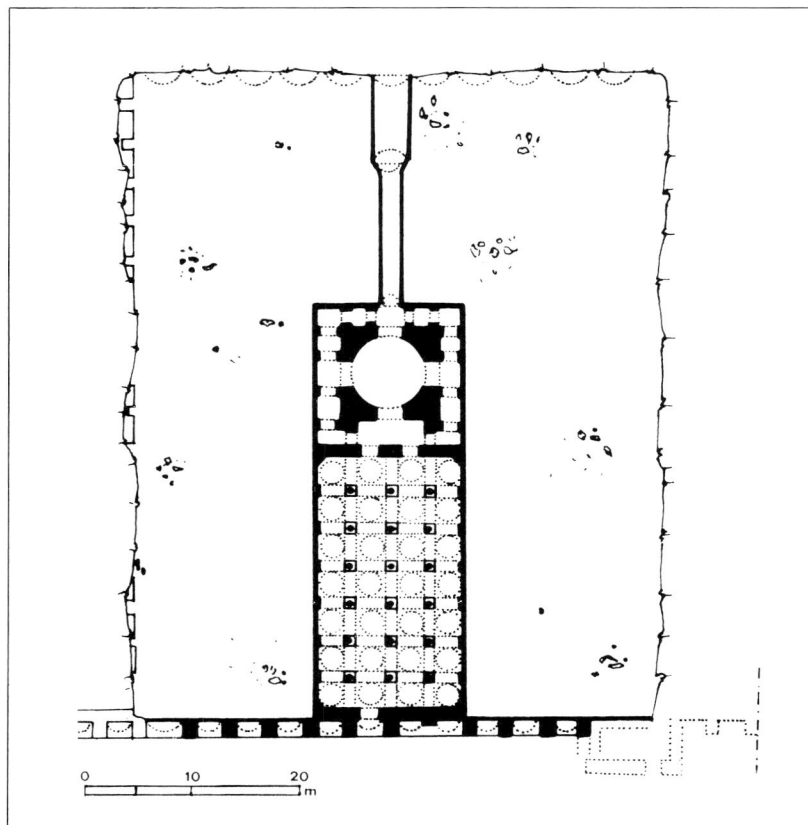

magne more than half a century earlier, and it would be interesting to speculate whether the Byzantine *renovatio* was not a response to the Frankish one. However that may be, the Byzantines had their own reasons for believing that their Empire was on the threshold of a new era. The liquidation of Iconoclasm in 843 was interpreted as signaling the defeat of the last major heresy—a heresy that went to the very root of the dogma of the Incarnation. Christianity had, therefore, attained its ultimate perfection. It was the church of the Seven Councils, to which nothing could be added, from which nothing could be taken away. No further development was conceivable.

This "definitive" reestablishment of true Christian religion coincided, moreover, with a series of military and political successes. The perennial war against the Arabs entered on a new course after the decisive defeat in 863 of the emir of Melitene (Malatya): henceforth it was to be an offensive not a defensive war. And in 864 or 865 the other major enemy, Bulgaria, was drawn into the orbit of Byzantine Christianity. The great patriarch Photius made himself the mouthpiece of the idea of "renovation." And although the emperor he served, namely, Michael III, was murdered by Basil I, and Photius himself was dismissed, to reappear on the patriarchal throne only ten years later, "renovation" remained in the air. The words for "new"—*neos, kainos, kainourgios*—appear with remarkable frequency in the vocabulary of the time. We must not interpret this term in the sense of "new and different"; it stood rather for rejuvenation, for the repair and consolidation of the old. This is a concept of fundamental importance for the understanding of all Byzantine cultural manifestations, architecture included.

But to return to Basil I and his building activity. The catalogue of his constructions lists twenty-five churches at Constantinople and six in the suburbs which he "made new." Among them were some of the largest and most highly venerated churches of the capital: St. Sophia, the Holy Apostles, St. Mocius, and St. Mary Chalkoprateia. We need not doubt that this represented a major effort, and it is worth observing that so many famous churches had been allowed to become dilapidated. Basil also built eight churches *de novo,* and all of them were inside the Imperial Palace. The most important of these was the Nea Ekklesia or New Church, as it was significantly named (dedicated in 880). It disappeared at the end of the fifteenth century, so that our knowledge of it is based on medieval descriptions and a few summary drawings. The Nea was crowned by five domes and was in all probability of the cross-in-square type. The extraordinary diffusion in subsequent centuries of the five-domed church testifies to the importance of the Nea as a model. The domes of the Nea shone with mosaics, while on the outside they were covered with brass tiles. The walls were reveted with multicolored marble: the chancel screen, synthronon, and altar table were sheathed with silver, enlivened with gilding, and studded with precious stones. The pavement consisted of marble slabs framed by bands of mosaic. To the west the church was preceded by an atrium with two fountains, while to the north and south were barrel-vaulted porticoes.

The description of the Nea reminds us of the earlier descriptions, by Procopius and Paul the Silentiary, of Justinian's St. Sophia. This impression is reinforced when we pass to the halls and pavilions which Basil erected in the Imperial Palace. The most notable of these was called Kainourgion, that is, the New Hall. Its architectural form is not known exactly, except that it had a semidome to the east and its roof was supported on sixteen columns of different materials and design—eight of verd antique, six of onyx carved with an "animated scroll," and two with spiral fluting. Unless these elements were reused, they represented a deliberate return to the art forms of the Late Roman Empire. Particularly interesting, furthermore, were the mosaics that decorated the ceiling of the Kainourgion. They represented Basil enthroned (in the apse?), escorted by his victorious generals, who were offering him the towns they had captured; in other words, this was a replica of the mosaics which Justinian caused to be represented in the vestibule of the palace called Chalkê.

The architectural renovation of Basil I included, therefore, a reversion in smaller format to the glorious monuments of Justinian, but with one important difference: whereas the greatest of Justinian's monuments had been public, those of Basil I, like those of Theophilus, were private, or, to put it more accurately, they were intended for a restricted group, the dignitaries and courtiers who had access to the palace. The social basis of "imperial" art had thus been restricted. And what was done by the emperor was repeated by lesser patrons. From this time onward the bulk of ecclesiastical architecture also became, in a very real sense, private: the parochial or episcopal church gave way to the monastic church.

In view of the ever-increasing place occupied by monastic architecture, we should inquire briefly into the development of Byzantine monasticism in its "material" manifestations. The essential point is that the monastery was an agricultural enterprise. It acquired this character at an early date, when eremitic life, generally regarded as being fit only for a chosen few, gave way to the *koinobion*. The monastic community, which in the early centuries was occasionally very large, consisted of ordinary people who were not ordained; they had simply renounced "the world," been admitted by an abbot, and served a novitiate. However much time they may have spent in attending services and in meditation, they were also bound to manual

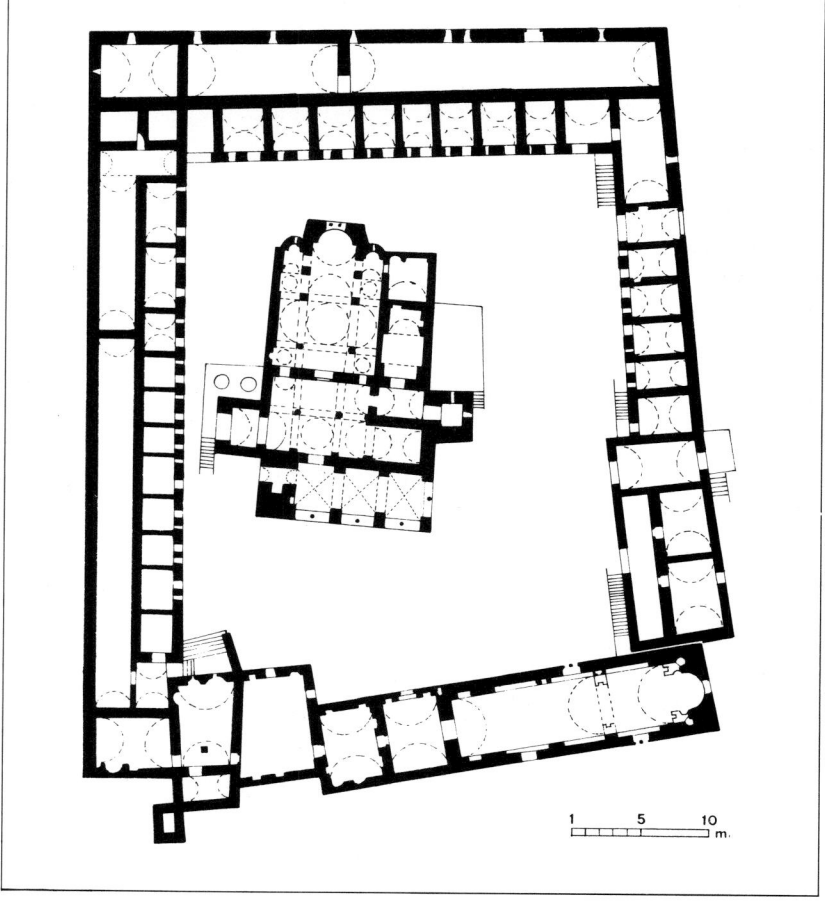

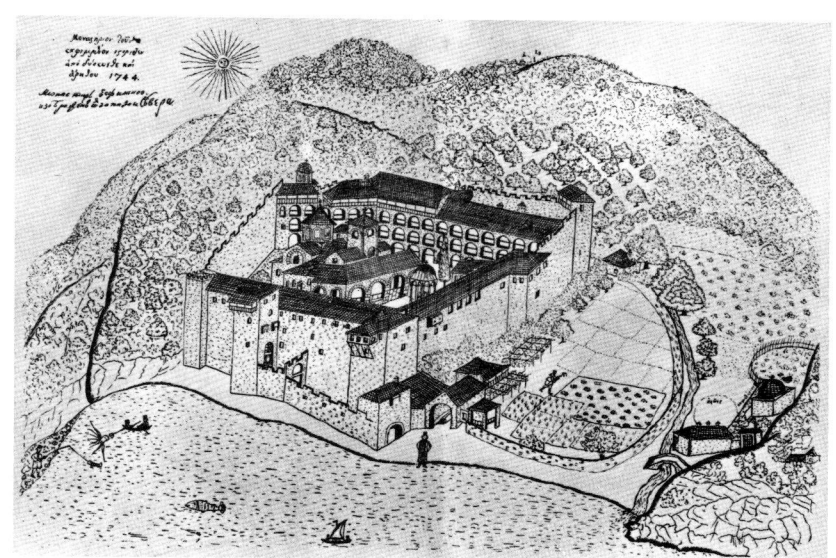

labor, which made them economically self-sufficient. The monastery inserted itself, therefore, into the context of rural life. It was usually situated on the edge of a village, and it absorbed the surrounding fields. In its architectural aspect the Early Byzantine monastery (fifth to sixth centuries) can best be studied in northern Syria.[3]

An important development of the Middle Byzantine period is that monasteries were removed more and more from episcopal control, under which they had been placed by the Council of Chalcedon and by Justinian's legislation. In this respect Iconoclasm must have played a role: for at a time when the secular clergy was considered heretical, the republic of monks had to organize itself into an autonomous underground movement. The monks won the day. Having once tasted their power, they were not anxious to submit themselves to a clergy that was appointed directly by the government.

If this statement contains some truth, it may serve to explain two parallel developments: on the one hand the impoverishment of the secular clergy, which now found itself deprived of the economic resources of the monasteries (hence the diminishing number of parochial and episcopal churches that were built); on the other, the need of the monasteries to integrate themselves into another kind of social structure, which was provided by the rich benefactor. The final crystallization of this new institution, known by the name of *charistikê,* did not occur until the eleventh century, but we can safely suppose that it was long in the making. We are not here concerned with the moral effect of this arrangement; the fact remains that monasteries were assigned to prominent laymen who could transmit them to their heirs, exchange them, or even sell them.[4] The monastery often benefited in having a highly placed protector who could invest his resources toward a fuller exploitation of the monastic properties; the beneficiary, for his part, drew the excess profit in addition to having prayers offered up for the salvation of his soul, a place of retirement for himself and his clients and of burial for his family. Judging by the surviving monuments, a major part of the building activity of the Middle and Late Byzantine periods went into the construction of monasteries which were privately owned.

One more development may be mentioned here, namely, the invasion of the city by monastic establishments. In the early period monks gravitated toward the country in a quest for solitude and an attempt to escape the temptations of secular life; urban monasteries were exceptional. But as the cities became depopulated, more and more monasteries were set up *intra muros.* This is especially clear in the case of Constantinople. Influential persons could thus enjoy the convenience and, perhaps, prestige of having their own family monasteries right in the capital, while the estates, which assured the livelihood of the monks, were situated in the suburbs or even in more distant provinces. Conversely, the more important provincial monasteries possessed dependencies (known as *metochia*) in the capital, in which their monks could be housed when they traveled on business.

The Middle Byzantine monastery presented an architectural complex with fairly well-defined characteristics.[5] It was normally surrounded by a wall and had a fairly elaborate covered portal, sometimes provided with benches. Beggars congregated here to receive alms from the monks. In theory access to the interior was limited, young boys and members of the opposite sex being rigorously excluded. After passing the portal, the visitor found himself in a large, open courtyard. In the middle stood the church, visible from all sides. This isolation of the church contrasted with the practice of the Early Byzantine period and led to the elaboration of its exterior appearance. The living quarters were arranged all around, following the lines of the enclosure. The cells were rectangular and usually barrel-vaulted. Often they were built in two or more stories and had an open arcade in front of them. Next to the church, the most important building was the refectory, which was either isolated or formed part of the residential rectangle. It was an elongated, apsed structure furnished with long tables and benches. Close to the refectory was the kitchen, with a raised hearth and an open domical lantern through which the smoke escaped. Storerooms equipped with large earthenware jars for keeping grain, pulse, oil, and wine were standard. Other subsidiary structures included a fountain, a bakery, a guesthouse, sometimes an infirmary, and a bath (bathing was normally allowed three times a year, except in cases of illness).

The call to prayer was given by striking a wooden or metal beam with a mallet. This beam *(sêmantron)* was sometimes suspended in a tower, which after the introduction of bells from the West (they are attested by the twelfth century) was often converted into a belfry. Burials were usually made outside the monastery, except for venerated persons such as the founder or the lay patrons, who were interred in sarcophagi either in the nave or in the narthex. In short, the monastery was a miniature, self-enclosed city. In most cases the monastic complex has disappeared, leaving only the church; or if the monastery has continued functioning until today, as is the case on Mount Athos, the residential and utilitarian buildings have usually been reconstructed. Even so, the general dispositions of a Byzantine monastery are reasonably well attested.

Turning next to the evolution of the church, we may note that the first phase of Middle Byzantine architecture at Constantinople is associated with the four-column plan. We may begin with two dated monuments, the north church of the monastery of Lips (Fenari Isa

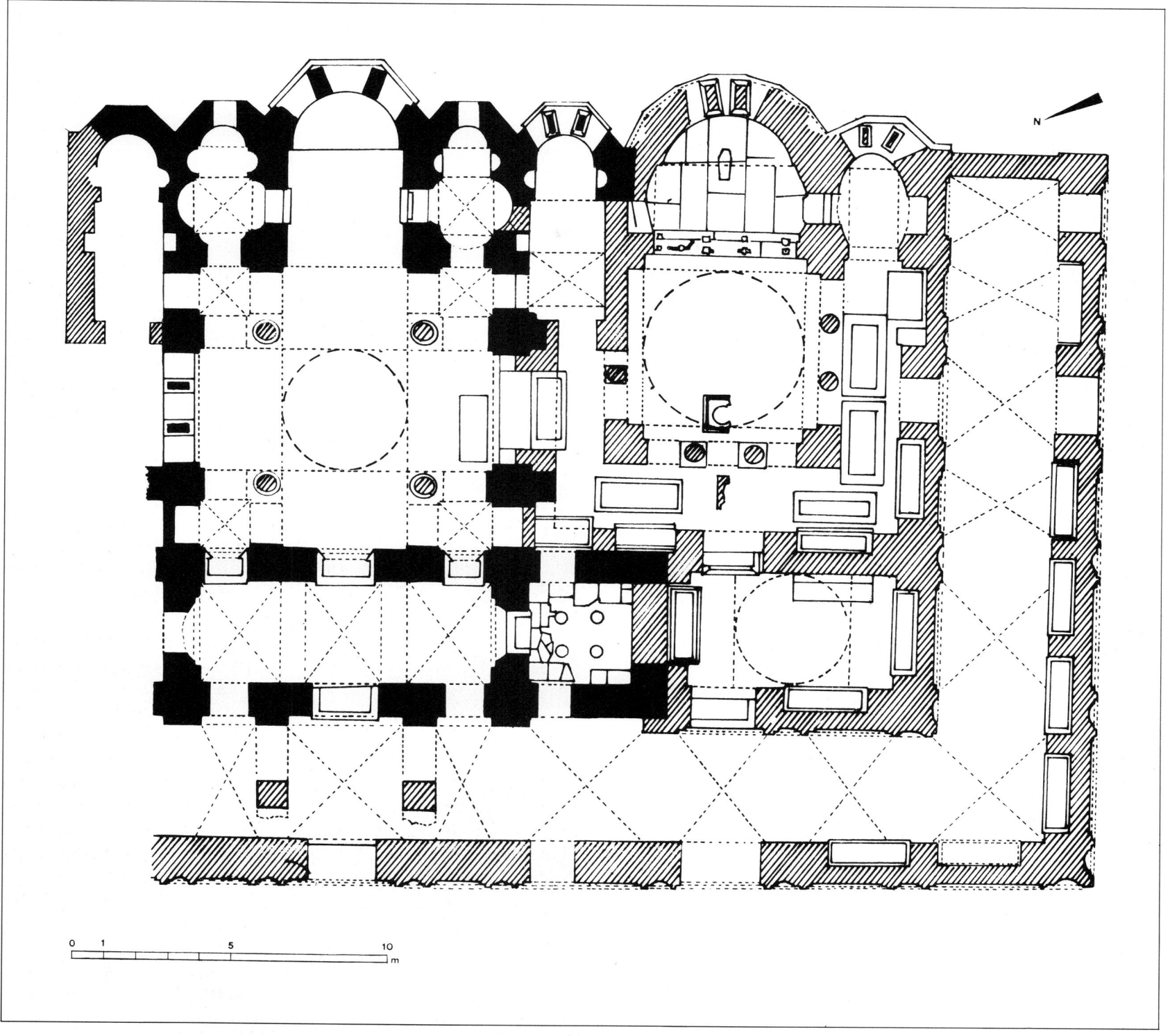

220. *Constantinople, Monastery of Constantine Lips (Fenari Isa Camii), ground plan of the two churches (after A. H. S. Megaw, 1964).*

N

0 1 5 10
m

221. *Constantinople, Monastery of Constantine Lips (Fenari Isa Camii), north church, reconstruction of exterior from the northwest (after A. H. S. Megaw, 1964).*

222. *Constantinople, Monastery of Constantine Lips (Fenari Isa Camii), north church, exterior.* ▷

Camii) of 907, and that of the Myrelaion (Bodrum Camii) of about 920. Both deserve detailed treatment.

The north church of Fenari Isa Camii[6] was built by the patrician Constantine Lips; its dedication was attended by the emperor Leo VI. We can be sure, therefore, that we are dealing with a building belonging to the highest social stratum. Despite the severe damage it has suffered, in particular the removal of the four columns and the rebuilding of the dome, its original features and decoration may be reconstructed with some accuracy. Though small (the dome span is 12 1/2 feet), this was a building of considerable sophistication. In plan we may notice the two lateral chapels that are added to the cross-in-square core, the scalloped pastophoria, the big lateral windows illuminating the nave, and the staircase tower attached to the narthex. The staircase led to the roof, where four more chapels, each covered with a separate little dome, were disposed in the corners of the rectangle—two over the narthex, the other two over the pastophoria. The two eastern chapels, which today have no visible means of access, were probably approached by a cantilevered passageway supported on corbels.

Seen from the outside, this was, therefore, a five-domed church, like the Nea Ekklesia built twenty-seven years previously. Another link between the two churches is provided by the multiplication of chapels: we happen to know that the Nea Ekklesia was dedicated to Christ, the Virgin, the archangels Michael and Gabriel, Elijah, and St. Nicholas, which means that it had at least four chapels, if Michael and Gabriel are counted together. The church of Lips may, therefore, be considered as the closest surviving relative of the Nea. Its interior decoration was, moreover, of quite exceptional richness and quality. The mosaics have disappeared, but a great quantity of carving remains—on the slender mullions of the apse windows and the great north window of the nave, on the cornices, corbels, and closure slabs. The ornamental repertory consisted of Sassanian palmettes, bouquets of complicated shape, rosettes, peacocks, and eagles, all very crisply carved. Moreover, the sculpture was duly proportioned to the position it occupied in the church: the dome cornice, which exhibited six eagles, had a greater overhang than the lower cornices and was more deeply cut. Excellent as this sculpture is by Byzantine standards, two interesting facts have come to light: first, much of the marble used in the church consisted of recut gravestones, removed from a Late Roman cemetery at Cyzicus; second, the major carved elements appear to have been likewise reused. We cannot be positive about the capitals of the four main columns, but those of the eight-pilaster responds that were linked to the columns by arches had fifth-century capitals, carefully cut in half and even mended.

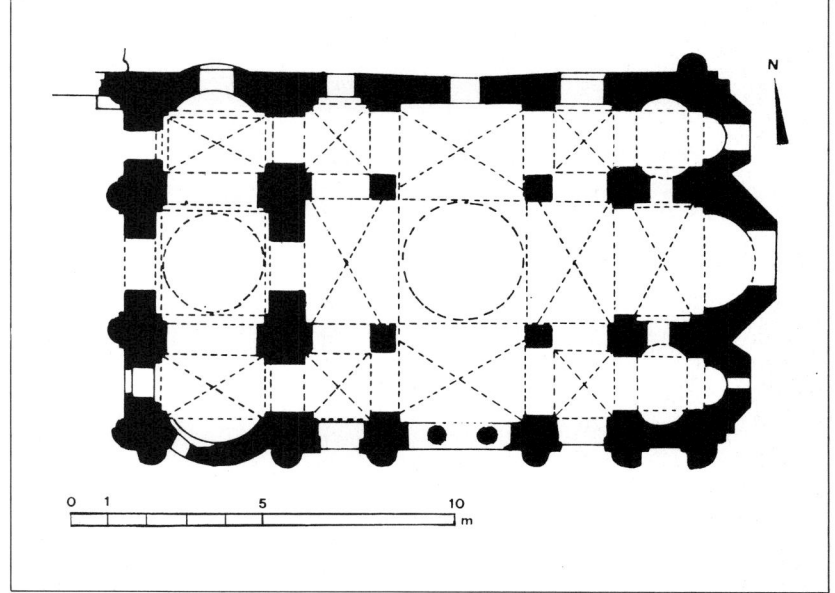

Two other kinds of decoration were used in the church of Lips: inlay and glazed tiles. Fragments of a great number of inlaid icons and roundels, including a complete icon of St. Eudocia (now in the Istanbul Archaeological Museum), have been brought to light: some had a matrix of white marble and were inlaid with colored materials, others had a matrix of dark marble and were inlaid with white limestone. As for the ceramic tiles, they appear to have been used as borders or frames. This was a new kind of decoration, probably inspired by Muslim practice. When, beginning in 1909, a series of similar glazed tiles, some decorative, others forming icons of saints, was brought to light at Patleina, near the ancient Bulgarian capital of Preslav, in a context of about 900, this appeared to be an unparalleled discovery and led to the wildest speculations. By what means, was it asked, did a workshop of Mesopotamian craftsmen reach Preslav? Were they, perchance, Iranians whom the Bulgar tribes had swept along in their migration from Asia into the Balkans?[7] Subsequent discoveries in Constantinople have amply demonstrated that glazed tiles bearing a deceptively Sassanian ornamentation—the same that we encounter at Fenari Isa Camii—had a wide currency in the capital in the ninth and tenth centuries. It may be that this technique, which was later abandoned by Byzantine artists, was inspired by the contact between Byzantine and Muslim art, which is documented for the reign of Theophilus. It should be observed, however, that apart from some instances of stylized Kufic script, the ornamental vocabulary of the Byzantine tiles is not of Arab inspiration.

225. *Constantinople, Myrelaion (Bodrum Camii), exterior from the south.*

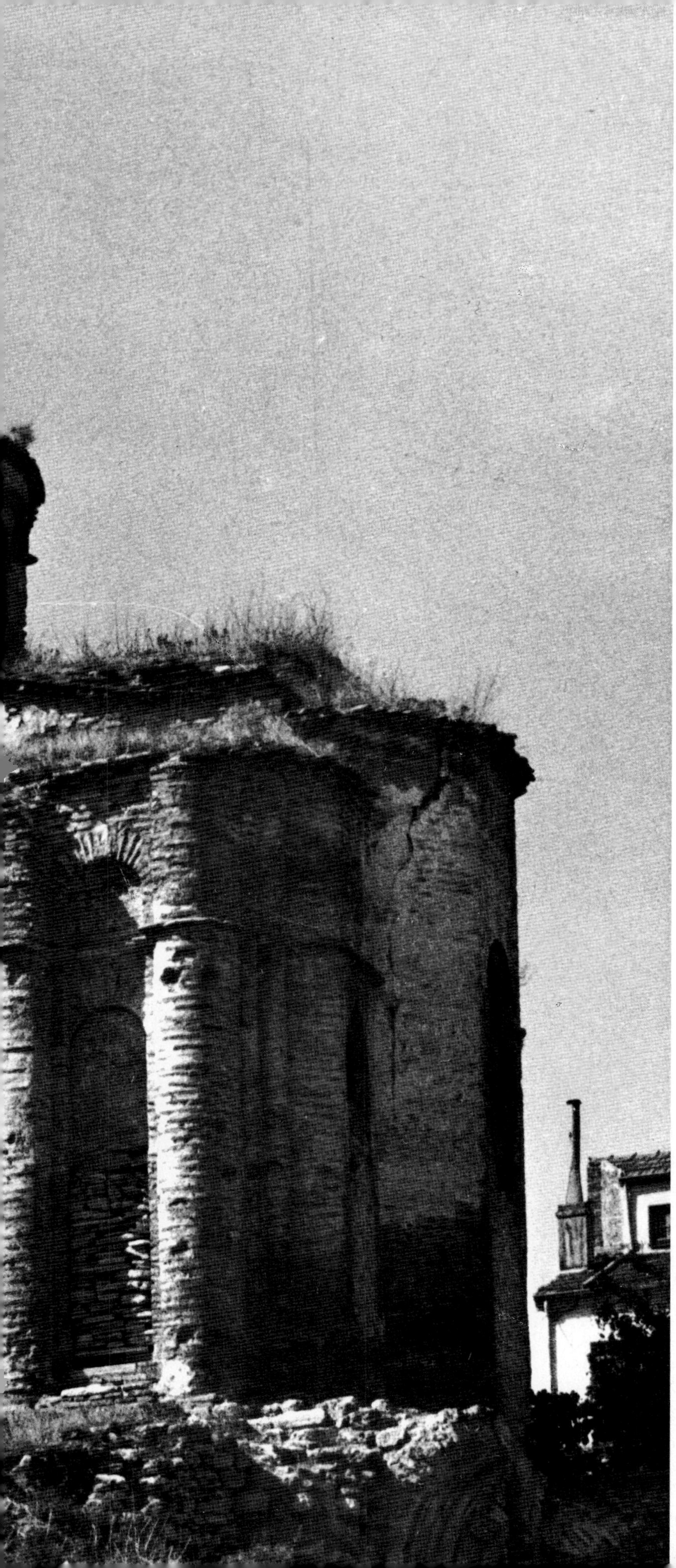

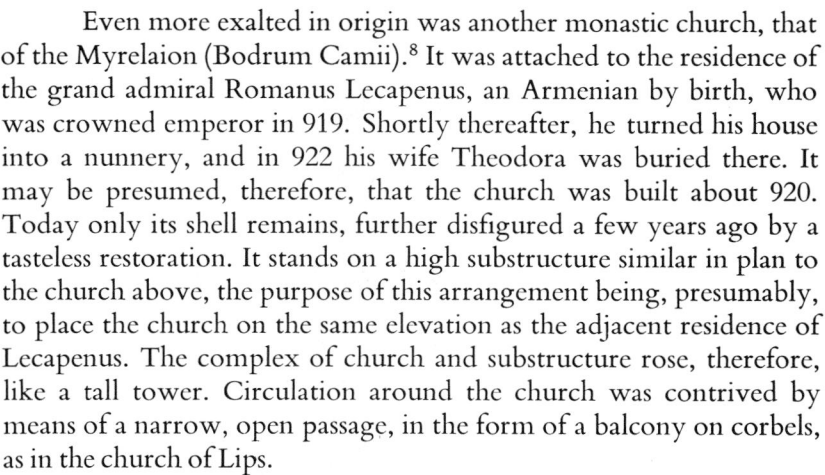

Even more exalted in origin was another monastic church, that of the Myrelaion (Bodrum Camii).[8] It was attached to the residence of the grand admiral Romanus Lecapenus, an Armenian by birth, who was crowned emperor in 919. Shortly thereafter, he turned his house into a nunnery, and in 922 his wife Theodora was buried there. It may be presumed, therefore, that the church was built about 920. Today only its shell remains, further disfigured a few years ago by a tasteless restoration. It stands on a high substructure similar in plan to the church above, the purpose of this arrangement being, presumably, to place the church on the same elevation as the adjacent residence of Lecapenus. The complex of church and substructure rose, therefore, like a tall tower. Circulation around the church was contrived by means of a narrow, open passage, in the form of a balcony on corbels, as in the church of Lips.

The church itself is small but very neatly built of brick without any stone courses. The four columns were replaced by piers, probably in the Turkish period, and the three large windows of the apse filled up. The melon dome, consisting of eight concave segments, is, however, original. The interior decoration included mosaic, marble revetments, and ceramic borders. The most striking feature of the building today is its exterior aspect. The side walls of the narthex curve gently outward, while six rounded pilasters on each of the long sides express the main interior articulations. These pilasters are built of specially manufactured, rounded bricks, a complicated procedure, which suggests that the idea was inspired by architecture in stone. In terms of plasticity Bodrum Camii represents an advance on Fenari Isa Camii.

A century later, in the church now known as St. Mary of the Coppersmiths (Panagia tôn Chalkeôn) at Thessalonica, built in 1028, we find a further development of the architectural concepts embodied in the two Constantinopolitan monuments we have discussed.[9] This, once again, was probably a monastery, but we do not know its original name. The inscription over the door names the founder, who was governor of Longobardia (the Byzantine province of South Italy), his wife, son, and two daughters; in other words, it was a family affair, and the arcosolium in the south aisle was probably intended for the founder's sarcophagus.

The plan of the church is of the normal four-column type and, as at Fenari Isa Camii, there is an overnarthex with two domed bays. Thus, there are three domes in all, instead of five; and since the pair over the narthex stand fairly high, the central dome had to be correspondingly raised. This was achieved by giving it a taller than normal drum, pierced by two tiers of windows. The effect is rather top-heavy. The interior, too, is somewhat ponderous, owing to the

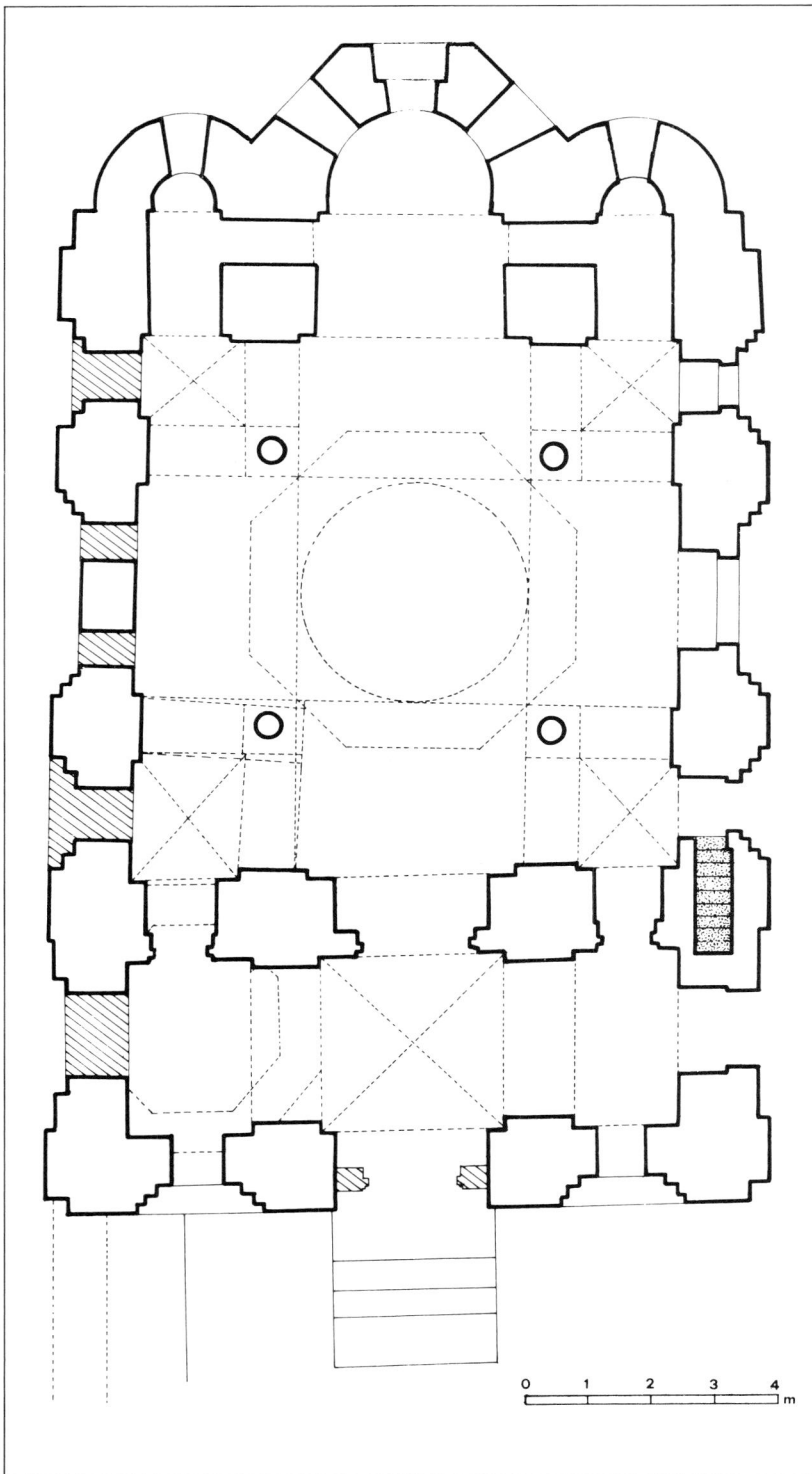

0   1   2   3   4
m

reduction of the windows. The airiness of Fenari Isa Camii is due to the large openings in the apse and side walls and the slenderness of the dividing mullions; at Thessalonica there are two tiers of small windows in the apse and three tiers in the tympana.

The exterior, though not altogether successful, shows some interesting advances. The construction, like that of the Myrelaion, is exclusively of brick and, once again, we have rounded pilasters, which, however, instead of rising from the ground, start above the cornice, while below the cornice the pilasters are rectangular. There is, thus, an emphatic division of the exterior into, as it were, two stories. Instead of accentuating the tall proportions of the building, the architect sought to stunt them. He also failed to integrate the west end of the church with its main body: in the former he used a scalloped roof line, in the latter a gabled one. What is new—and this represents a general trend in the eleventh century—is the growing recession of planes. All arched openings and blind arches (except, strangely enough, at the east end) have two, three, or even four setbacks. The little domes over the narthex have deep blind niches alternating with windows. In this way a sculptured effect is created. The architect has also enlivened the facades by introducing strings of dogtooth under the eaves and a row of little glazed tiles bearing a Kufic decoration under the cornice. Clumsy as it is in some respects, the Panagia tôn Chalkeôn shows, nevertheless, a striving toward new effects.

The first half of the eleventh century appears, indeed, to have been a time of architectural innovation. With the reign of Basil II (976–1025), the Empire had reached the apogee of its power: at the cost of unceasing wars, the frontier had been pushed forward to the Danube, thus making Byzantium ruler of the entire Balkan peninsula, while in the East its sway extended from Armenia to the Syrian coast. But Basil II was an austere soldier, who did not waste the resources of the state on architectural projects. No building is associated with his name. It is even reported that when he deposed from power his chief minister, the eunuch Basil, he sought to destroy and deprive of its revenues the splendid monastery which the latter had erected.[10] The emperor Basil accumulated an enormous treasure. His successors, who were given to the good life, to luxury and ostentation, had little trouble in dissipating it. The period from 1025 until the eruption of the Seljuk Turks into Asia Minor in 1071 is one of the most fertile in the history of Byzantine architecture.

Owing to the accidents of preservation, the most notable buildings associated with this renewal of artistic activity are situated in continental and insular Greece. In view of the growing importance which the territory of Greece assumes at this point, a brief digression

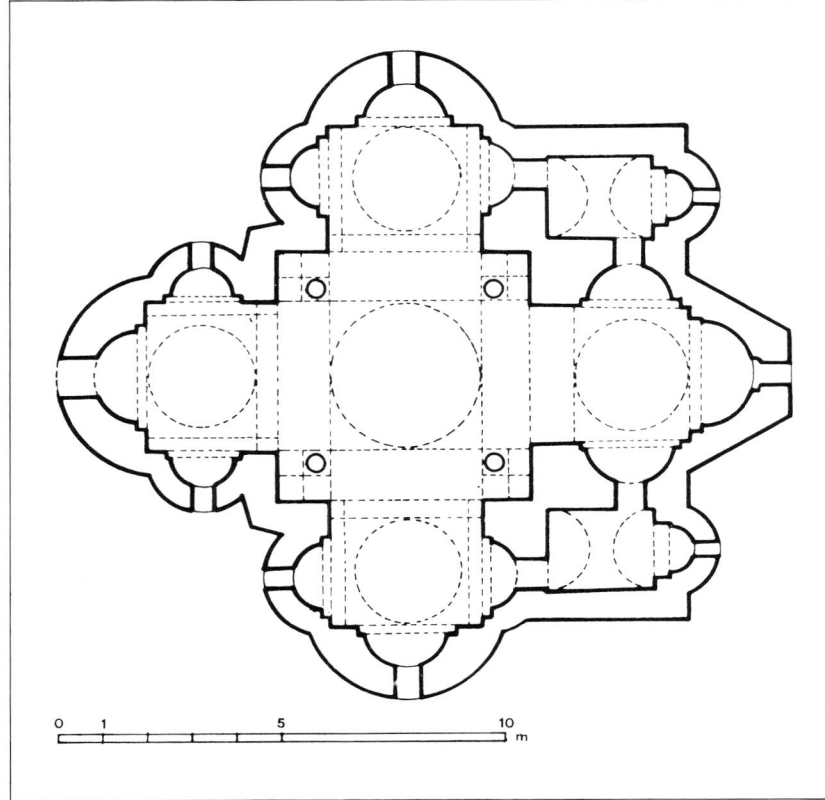

may be justified. Today, more than 230 Byzantine churches are preserved in Greece, a sufficiently large number to permit some fairly rough statistics.[11] Of the total, fifty-three are of the Early Byzantine period (mostly excavated ruins); one, namely, St. Sophia at Thessalonica, of the Dark Ages; four dated in the ninth century; about fifteen of the tenth; thirty-three of the eleventh; forty-nine of the twelfth. Approximate as these figures are, they show that after the reestablishment of Byzantine authority in Greece about 800, the progress of the Orthodox church was very slow and did not gather momentum until the tenth to eleventh centuries.

The first half of the ninth century has left us no monuments whatever; among those of the second half we may notice, in the first instance, that of St. Andrew at Peristerai, some twenty miles southeast of Thessalonica, that is, strictly speaking, outside the Byzantine province of Greece. This appears to have been the monastic church erected in 870–71 by St. Euthymius the Younger, a native of Galatia in Asia Minor. The *Life* of Euthymius relates how the hermit himself built the church with the help of three or four workmen and in so doing had to overcome the resistance of the demons that infested the place.[12] The church, indeed, is roughly built without any adornment, but its design is interesting: it is a quatrefoil crowned by five domes, one over the central square, the others over the arms. The eastern arm is slightly longer than the other two and is flanked by the prothesis and diaconicon, both barrel-vaulted. There is no narthex.[13] The closest analogies to this plan, including the absence of the narthex, are found in Armenia.

The big heavy church of Skripou in Boeotia was built in 873–74 by a certain Leo, a high imperial official and local landowner.[14] Its dominating element is the cross with barrel-vaulted arms, crowned by a dome (rebuilt in the eighteenth century). The lateral aisles are very low, while the narthex, badly connected with the rest of the building, stands a little higher. The church is constructed of reused stone blocks which are mostly antique. The clumsiness of the architecture was to some extent compensated for by the proliferation of carved ornament, both inside and out. Less well executed than the sculpture of Fenari Isa Camii, it belongs nevertheless to the same orientalizing current that seems to have emanated from the capital.[15] The use of exterior carved ornament suggests, however, some connection with Armenia.

The example of Skripou shows us the slow beginnings of Byzantine ecclesiastical architecture on Greek soil. This phenomenon is explainable not only by the rude and backward condition of the country, but also by the constant invasions to which Greece was subjected. The coastal areas were continuously ravaged by the Arabs

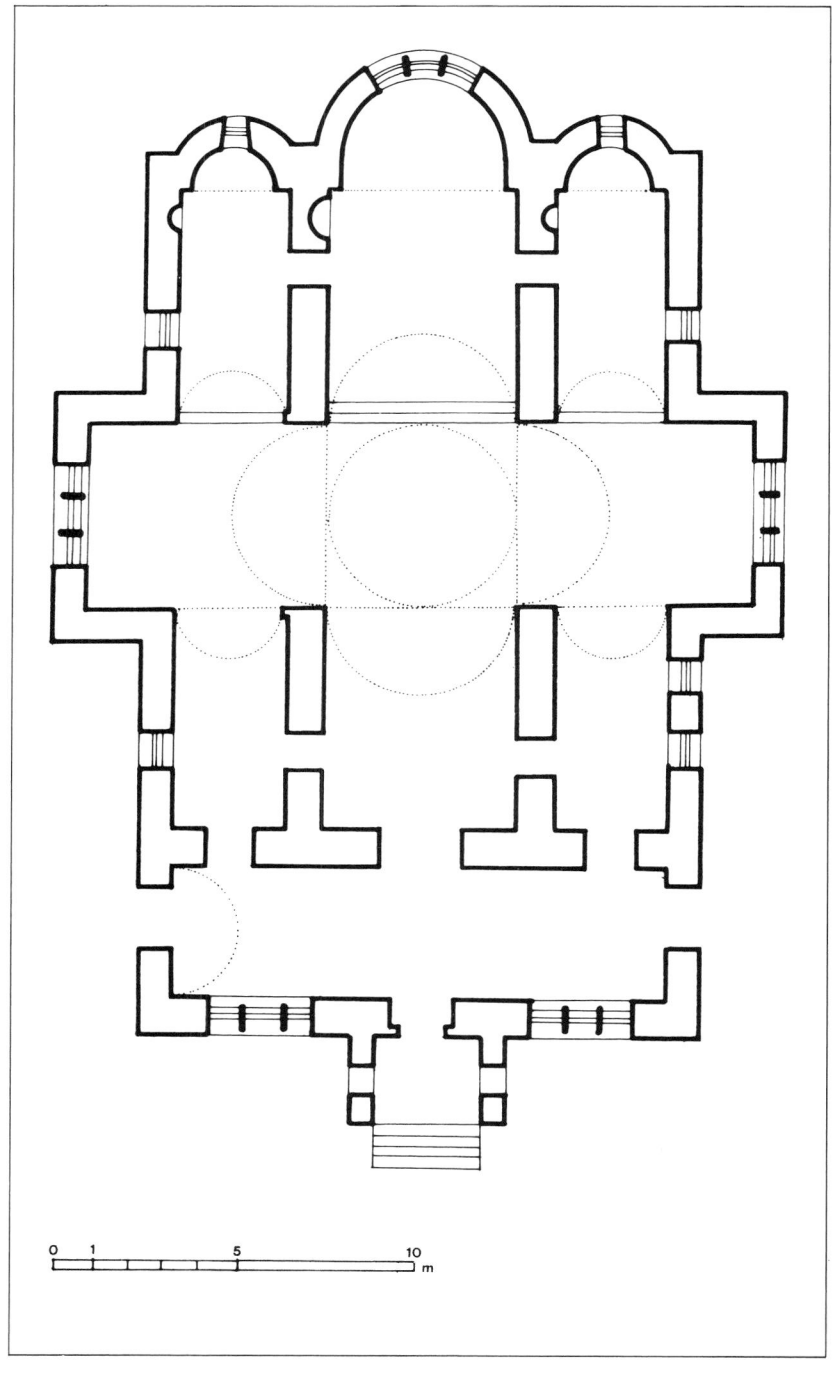

230. *Skripou, Dormition church, ground plan (after M. G. Soteriou, 1931).*
231. *Skripou, Dormition church, exterior from the northeast.* ▷

0 1   5   10
                         m

232. *Phocis, Hosios Loukas, ground plan of the two churches (after E. Stikas, 1970).*

233. *Phocis, Hosios Loukas, Theotokos church, exterior from the east.* ▷

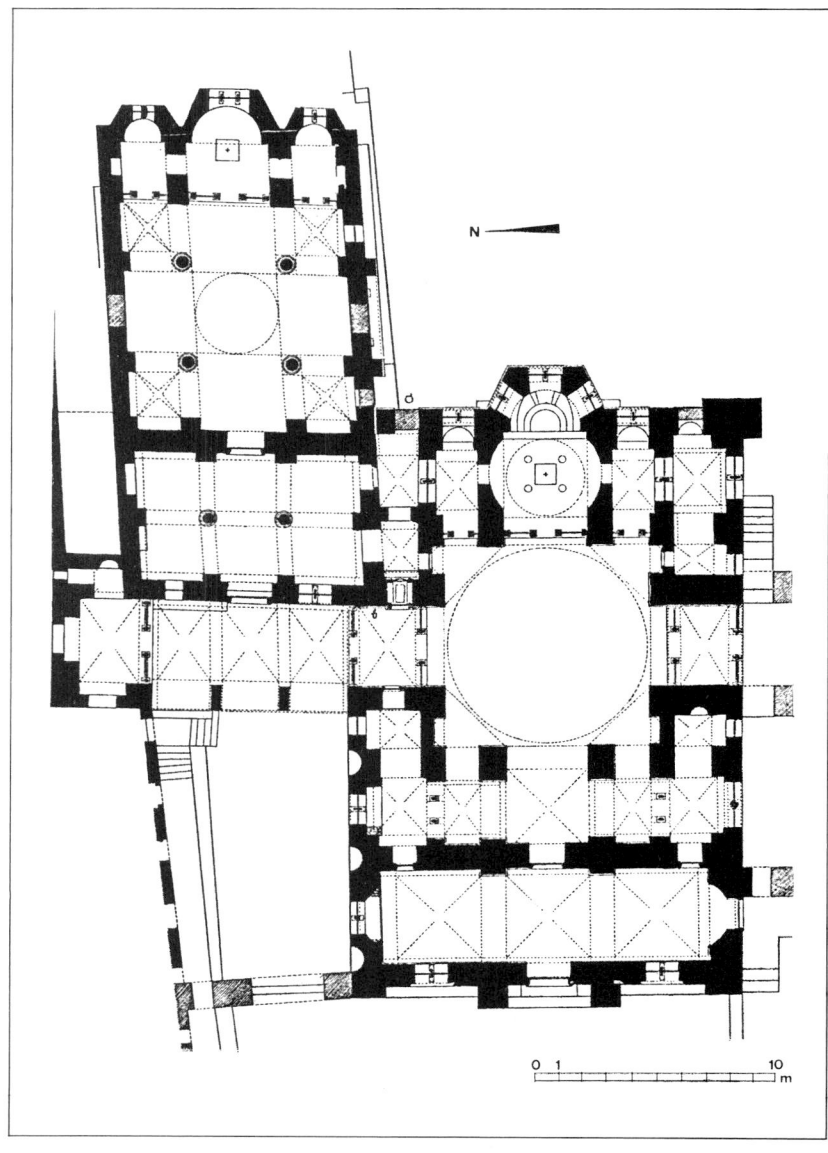

based on Crete, North Africa, and Sicily, while the Bulgarians and Magyars made incursions from the north. A perusal of the *Life* of St. Luke of Steiris, to whose monastery we shall shortly address ourselves, gives a vivid impression of the dangers that beset the inhabitants of Greece in the first half of the tenth century. The Byzantine conquest of Crete in 961 contributed greatly to an improvement of the situation, which was further stabilized by the annihilation of Bulgaria in the early eleventh century. It was under these more peaceful and increasingly more prosperous conditions that architecture developed in Greece.

In the second half of the tenth century the cross-in-square plan was imported from the capital. Its most outstanding representative is the Theotokos church of the monastery of St. Luke (Hosios Loukas), which has recently been shown to be older than the adjoining *katholikon*.[16] If it is the same as the church of St. Barbara mentioned in the saint's *Life*, it was built between 946 and 955, in which case it may be the earliest representative of certain characteristics that were to become typical of the Greek "school." These concern not the interior planning, which is Constantinopolitan, but the treatment of the exterior. The walls are built in the "cloisonné" technique, which means that the stones, laid in single courses, are individually framed by bricks, both horizontally and vertically. Above cornice level the surface is further punctuated by strings of dentils which run lengthwise as well as around the arched windows. Even more exotic are the motifs based on the Kufic alphabet that have been introduced in great profusion into the walls. Finally, the dome (its low pyramidal top appears to have been rebuilt) is encased on the outside in carved marble slabs. This decorative treatment of the exterior is foreign, as far as we know, to the contemporary art of Constantinople; and while Islamic influence is obvious, it is by no means clear by what channels it reached the architecture of Greece.

The clearest manifestation of this Islamic influence is provided by the simulated Kufic letters which, executed in cut brick, are found on the facades of a great many Greek churches from the tenth to the twelfth century, especially in Attica, Boeotia, and the Argolid. They are also used in sculpture and painting.[17] The horseshoe arch also occasionally makes its appearance in the same group of monuments.[18] Indeed, one may wonder whether the very idea of enlivening exteriors with patterns of brick—an idea that was to gain an extraordinary diffusion in later Byzantine architecture, more in Greece and the Balkans than in Constantinople (where it appears in the eleventh century)—was not itself of Oriental inspiration. The use of such patterns is attested in Early Abbasid buildings, such as the Baghdad gate at Raqqa (772) and the nearly contemporary palace of Ukhaidir.[19]

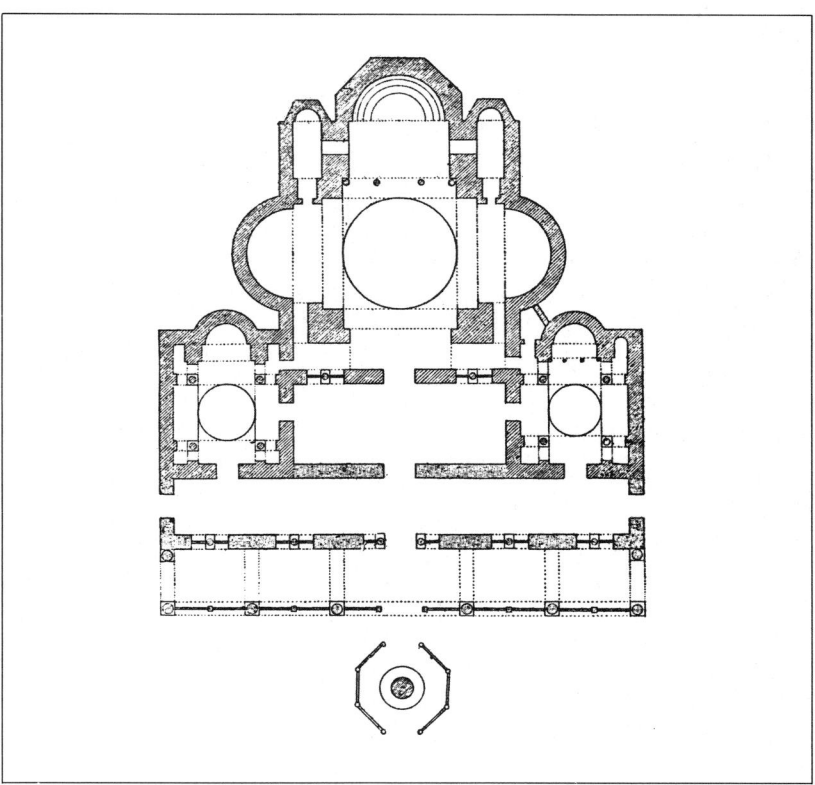

237. *Mount Athos, Lavra,* katholikon, *exterior from the northeast.*

Standing somewhat apart from the architectural development in Greece are the monasteries of Mount Athos, which, after the foundation of the Great Lavra of St. Athanasius in 961, gradually supplanted the Bithynian Olympus as the main center of Byzantine monasticism. Unfortunately, one cannot be very precise about the Athonite churches, since their architectural aspect has not been seriously studied.[20] The earliest church on the peninsula appears to be the Protaton of Karyes, the administrative capital. It is a fairly large, almost square building of the inscribed-cross type, with three projecting semicircular apses. There is some resemblance to Skripou, although the Protaton could not have been domed: the present high roof with a clerestory is, however, a modern addition. Except for the Protaton, practically all the other Athonite churches are built on the same model, that of a trefoil. The fashion appears to have been set by the *katholikon* of Lavra, said to have been built by Athanasius himself shortly after 961.

The churches of Vatopedi and Iviron are believed to be slightly later. Their design has an obvious affinity to that of Peristerai, including the four columns set very close to the corners of the central square, with a view to diminishing the space covered by the dome (these are, however, absent at Lavra, where the large dome rests on corner piers). The Athonite churches have certain other distinctive features, such as a very deep narthex, called *litê,* in which some offices were celebrated. This vestibule is usually divided into six vaulted bays by means of two internal columns. The date of its introduction is not, however, clear. Once consecrated by the prestige of the Holy Mountain, the Athonite type of church enjoyed a wide diffusion in the Orthodox world, even after the fall of Constantinople.

The developments in Greece and neighboring Macedonia, which we have briefly noted, do not pave the way to a series of large and, in some cases, lavish monuments that we encounter starting in the 1040s at the latest. They are distinguished by their relatively wide domes that are carried not on pendentives but on corner squinches, that is, on an octagonal base. Structurally, they may be subdivided into two classes: the simple, where the dome is supported directly on the exterior walls, and the complex, where the central core is enveloped by subsidiary spaces.[21]

The earliest-known example of the "simple" type is the *katholikon* of the Nea Moni (New Monastery) on the island of Chios. This is a dated monument (1045), and we are fortunate in knowing something of its origin.[22] Its founders were two Chiote monks, Niketas and John, who, being possessed of the gift of prophecy, foretold to the exiled nobleman Constantine Monomachos that he would become emperor. When the prediction was confirmed in

238. *Mount Athos, Karyes, Protaton, exterior from the southeast.*

1042, Constantine rewarded the monks by building a splendid monastery for them and showering them with gifts: a series of chrysobulls (imperial decrees) detail the donations, exemptions from taxes, and other benefits which the Nea Moni received from the same emperor. Niketas and John were often at Constantinople and gained ascendency over the powerful patriarch Michael Kerularios; it was rumored, however, that they dabbled in magic and uttered their prophecies through the intermediary of a young woman who was disguised as a man. Whatever truth there may be to these stories, which were current at the time, it is probable that the generous and gullible Constantine IX was the victim of a deception on the part of the two monks, who thereby made their fortune and that of their monastery. Later tradition affirms that the builders of the Nea Moni were sent from Constantinople and that the *katholikon* was modeled after "the small church of the Holy Apostles," whatever that may mean. Considering the history of the two monks and their access to the very pinnacle of Byzantine society, there can be no doubt that Nea Moni is indeed a monument of Constantinopolitan art.

The *katholikon* consists at ground level of a square nave without aisles or other subsidiary spaces. As we mount above the lower cornice, however, the central square is scalloped out by means of four semicircular niches at the corners and four wider but shallower niches on the sides. The corner niches are covered with squinches, thus producing an octagonal base upon which rests a circular corona, which may be described as eight pendentives joined together. The dome is proportionately very large (just under 23 feet across), spanning as it does practically the entire width of the nave. The interior effect, with its undulating surfaces, is decidedly baroque as compared with that of the cross-in-square church, and contains some exotic elements, such as the depressed arches in the lower zone and the slender, geminated colonnettes in two tiers which mark the eight corners of the octagon. The elaborate marble revetment of the walls, the mosaics, and the patterned floor give evidence of the initial wealth of the monastery. The exterior, now covered with plaster, is somewhat top-heavy, owing to the disproportionate size of the main dome, but is enlivened by blind arcading and by the three little domes set over the outer narthex, which has apsed side walls.

The design of the Nea Moni produced a number of imitations on Chios and reappeared, somewhat modified, in several Cypriot churches, the earliest of which may be the *katholikon* (destroyed at the end of the nineteenth century) of the Chrysostomos monastery of the year 1090.[23] It continued to be used well into the twelfth century, as shown by the monasteries of Antiphonitis and Apsinthiotissa (where the octagon is reduced to a hexagon), also in Cyprus.

239. *Chios, Nea Moni*, katholikon, *ground plan (after A. Orlandos, 1935).*

240. *Chios, Nea Moni*, katholikon, *perspective view of interior (after A. Orlandos, 1935).*

241. *Chios, Nea Moni*, katholikon, *exterior.*

242. *Christianou, church, perspective section (after E. Stikas, 1951).*

243. *Phocis, Hosios Loukas*, katholikon, *interior looking east.* ▷

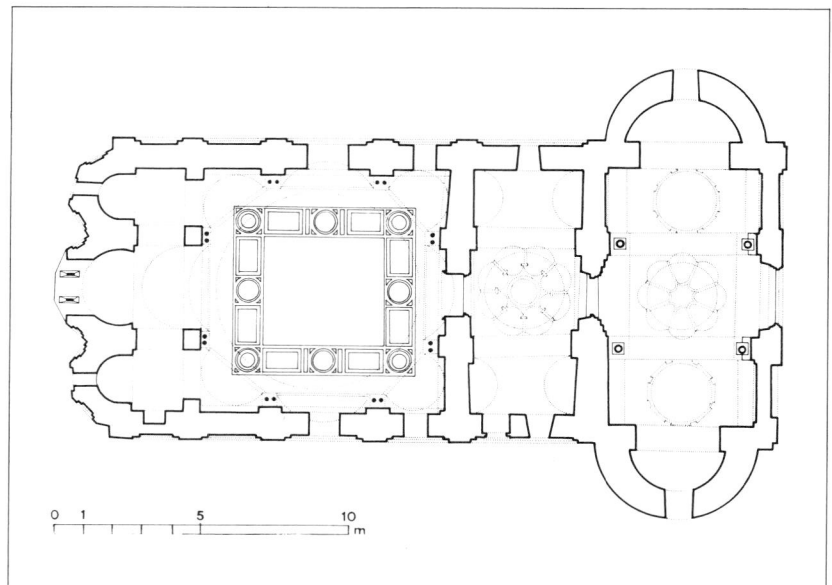

The "complex" type of the church on squinches may be illustrated by the *katholikon* of Hosios Loukas, probably the most important Byzantine monument to have survived in Greece.[24] Here, too, the central square is quite large (close to 30 feet across) and nearly equal to the span of the dome. The nave is, however, bordered on all sides by subsidiary cross-vaulted spaces, which support a gallery. These spaces cannot be described as aisles since they are broken up by thick transverse walls which provide lateral buttressing for the dome. The interior effect is soberer than that of Nea Moni, and the exterior better balanced, since the dome is in proportion to the mass of the entire structure.

It is astonishing that there is no trace in documentary records of a building as big and sumptuous as the *katholikon* of Hosios Loukas, with its famous mosaics, its expensive marble revetments, carved marble, and stucco, yet such is the case. We do not know, therefore, when and by whom it was built, beyond the fact that its construction, next to the preexisting church of the Theotokos, must have been dictated by the growing popularity of St. Luke's miraculous tomb as a center of pilgrimage.[25] The mosaics are usually dated on stylistic grounds in the first half of the eleventh century.

Among related architectural monuments, the only one that bears an approximate date is the Panagia Lykodemou at Athens, the largest of the medieval Athenian churches, which contained a funerary inscription recording the death of its founder in 1044.[26] Next to the Panagia Lykodemou, which was drastically altered in 1847, I may mention the church at Christianou in Triphylia (Peloponnese), the famous monastery of Daphni near ancient Eleusis, St. Sophia at Monemvasia (twelfth century?), and the Sts. Theodoroi at Mistra (end of the thirteenth century). Both the Panagia Lykodemou and Christianou have galleries, like Hosios Loukas; Daphni and the later examples do not. The church of Christianou (now in large part restored) is exceptional in that it was—or so it has been maintained—an episcopal church, erected when the town of Christianoupolis was raised to metropolitan rank (before 1086); Daphni, a monastery, is not dated, but there is general consensus that it should be placed in the last quarter of the eleventh century.[27]

The design of the church on squinches was intended, no doubt, to unify the interior and to enlarge the dome by giving it eight points of support instead of four. It has long been thought (I think correctly) that the idea came, by way of Constantinople, from Armenia, where we have encountered it as early as the seventh century, since it could hardly have been invented on Greek soil. Recently, a very small church on the island of Heybeliada (Chalki), one of the Princes' Islands near Constantinople, has been brought into the

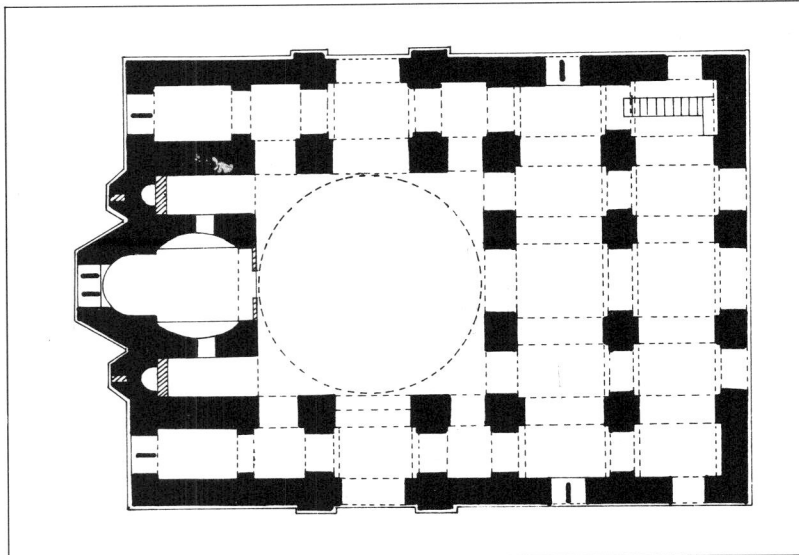

discussion: it combines a quatrefoil plan with the use of corner squinches and dates, in all probability, from the eleventh century.[28] This church is valuable in proving that the architectural concepts, known to us mainly from Greece, were also used at Constantinople, but it is itself too unpretentious a building to have served as the intermediary.

There is a good chance, on the other hand, that the missing link was provided by the great imperial foundations of the late tenth and eleventh centuries at Constantinople. Indeed, it has been suggested that the monastic church of St. Mary Peribleptos (1028–34), built with mad extravagance by the emperor Romanus II, was to be considered in this connection. This church disappeared long ago, but we have a description of it written in 1403 by the Spanish ambassador Ruy González de Clavijo, who says that the nave was surrounded by three aisles, and that the ceilings of the nave and of the aisles were one and the same.[29] This is, unfortunately, rather too vague to be of much help. We may think, therefore, of other prestige monuments that are known to us from historical sources. These include a splendid church of the Savior, built at the gate of the Imperial Palace by John I Tzimiskes shortly after 972; the monastery of Sts. Cosmas and Damian (1034–41) at Cosmidion, a suburb of Constantinople, reconstructed at enormous expense by Michael IV;[30] and, above all, the monastery of St. George of Mangana, a foundation of Constantine IX, who, we are told, was so intent on rivaling St. Sophia that he erected costly structures only to tear them down and was not satisfied until the third attempt, to the great detriment of the exchequer.[31] Could any of these lost monuments have been the intermediaries we are seeking?

The church of the Savior at the Chalkê gate of the palace, converted after the fall of Constantinople into a menagerie and later into the dwelling of the painters attached to the sultan's court, was destroyed in 1804.[32] By piecing together various scraps of evidence, including a number of old drawings, we can offer the following reconstruction of it: it was a church in two stories somewhat after the manner of Bodrum Camii, both levels being decorated with mosaics; the upper church had a dome on a tall drum pierced by twelve windows; it served as the burial place of the founder, John Tzimiskes, and as the repository of several precious relics. What is, however, of particular interest to us is that after the building had been severely ruined on the north and south sides, it still retained a dome and two semidomes. In 1795 the Italian dragoman Cosimo Comidas de Carbognano speaks of it as being "ornata di due mezzecupole, e di una intiera," just like St. Sophia.[33] The presence of two semidomes is, however, almost unthinkable in a church of the Middle Byzantine

◁ 248. *Monemvasia, St. Sophia, exterior from the northwest.*

249. *Chalki (island of Heybeliada), Panagia Kamariotissa, exterior from the southeast.*

250. *Chalki (island of Heybeliada), Panagia Kamariotissa, ground plan (after A. Pasadaios, 1971).*

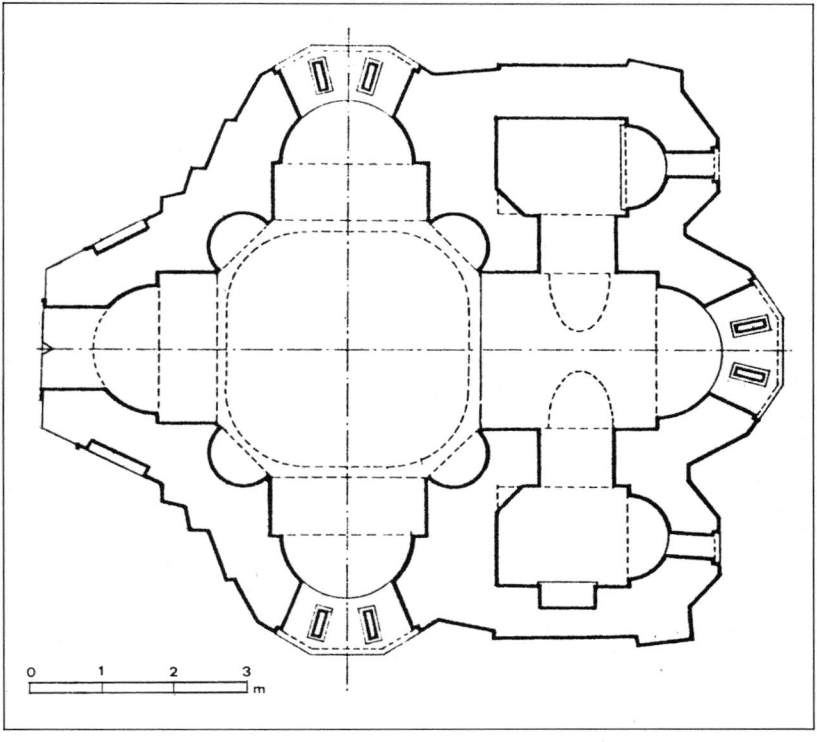

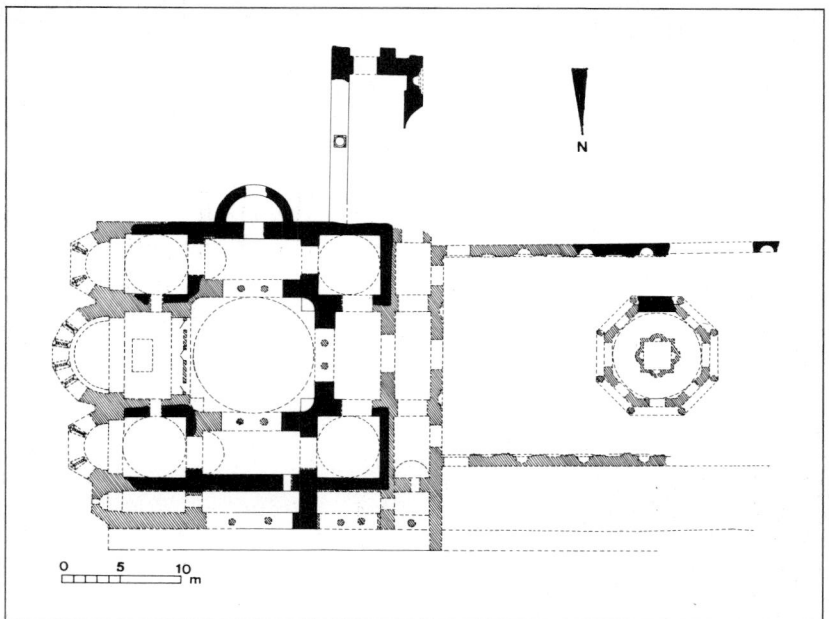

251. *Panorama of Constantinople, detail (16th-century Turkish miniature). University Library, Istanbul.*

252. *Constantinople, St. George of Mangana, ground plan (after E. Mamboury, 1939).*

253. *Aght'amar, Church of the Holy Cross, ground plan (after J. Strzygowski, 1918).*

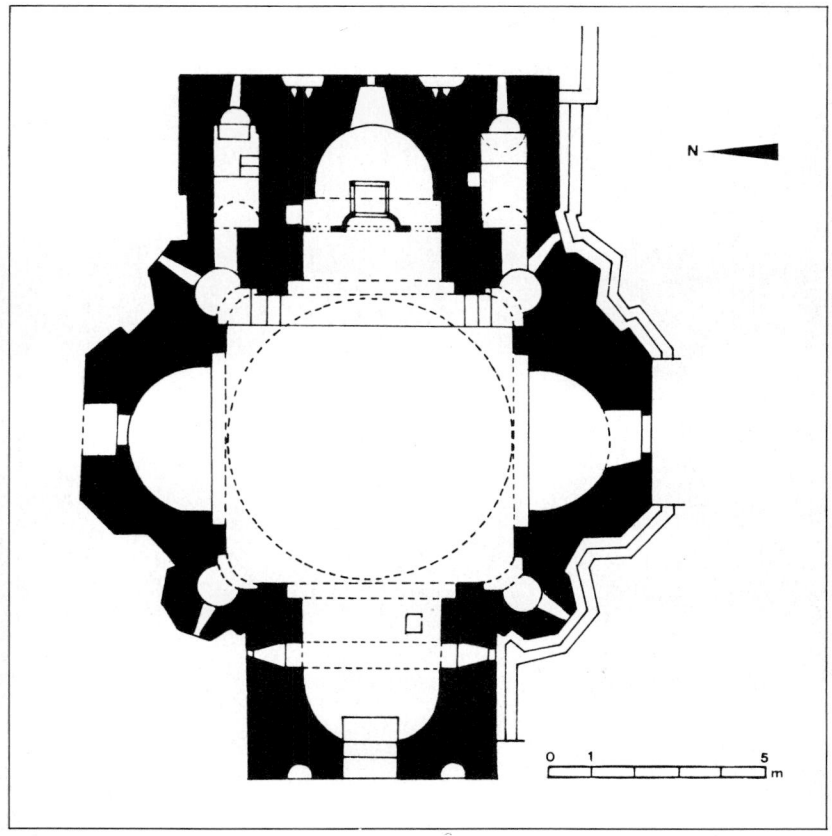

period, which makes me suspect that there were originally four. I would suggest, therefore, that the church of the Savior was a quatrefoil, which accords well with a Turkish miniature of 1537–38 in which it is represented. What is more, we know that this church was designed by the emperor himself;[34] and John Tzimiskes was an Armenian.

We can be a little more specific concerning the church of St. George of Mangana on the Seraglio Point, since it was partly excavated by the French occupational force at Constantinople in 1922–23. The published report[35] gives very few particulars concerning the superstructure, but the few photographs and drawings that have been made available are of the highest interest. By Byzantine standards this was a large church, the main structure measuring about 75 by 108 feet (these are the external dimensions, including the narthex). It was preceded by an atrium having an octagonal fountain in the middle. The *naos* was a cross-in-square with four corner compartments, the central space measuring thirty-three feet across. A feature that attracts attention is the reentrant dome piers, which present a curved angle. This is a most unusual disposition, which proves that the dome could not have been carried on normal pendentives tapering to a sharp point; for a similar arrangement we have to turn to the Armenian church of Aght'amar (915–21), where the curved corners of the central square open by means of tall arched slits into little chambers.[36]

The church of St. George presented some other interesting features: the exterior had patterns of brick, while the side walls of the atrium were enlivened with niches and clustered pilasters executed in brick but clearly inspired by stonecarving. Here, too, an Armenian influence may be suspected, for the same clustered forms, alternately rounded and angular, occur in the cathedral of Ani (988–1000) and other contemporary Armenian buildings. We may also remember that the architect Trdat, to whom the cathedral of Ani is ascribed, was also responsible for the rebuilding of St. Sophia at Constantinople, which, following the earthquake of 989, suffered the collapse of its main western arch and a portion of the dome.[37]

There is, therefore, good reason to believe that the Oriental features which have been observed in Greece were transmitted by way of the capital, where they appeared in the prestigious imperial foundations of the late tenth and eleventh centuries. Even on the basis of historical documents alone, one may observe the connections linking Greece with Asia Minor and the Caucasus. St. Athanasius the Athonite was half Georgian and a native of Trebizond. He spent his formative years in the "lavra" of the aristocratic saint Michael Maleinos, who himself hailed from Charsianon in eastern Asia Minor.

256. *Armenia, Monastery of Marmašen.*

257. *Constantinople, Christ Pantepoptes (Eski Imaret Camii), exterior from the southeast.*

258. *Constantinople, Christ Pantepoptes (Eski Imaret Camii), interior looking east from gallery.*

259. *Constantinople, Christ Pantocrator (Zeyrek Kilise Camii), ground plan of the three churches (after A. H. S. Megaw, 1963).*

260. *Constantinople, Christ Pantocrator (Zeyrek Kilise Camii), exterior from the east.* ▷

Would it not be tempting to imagine that the Great Lavra was modeled on that of Maleinos (built about 925), situated on Mount Kyminas on the confines of Paphlagonia and Bithynia?[38] Nor should we forget that the great Georgian monastery on Mount Athos, still known today as Iviron, was founded about 980.

The building phase which corresponds to the period of "government by the civil aristocracy of the capital" (1025–81), as historians often call it, ends with the eruption of the Seljuk Turks into Asia Minor and the First Crusade. The task of restoring the Empire fell to the dynasty of the Comneni (1081–1204), whose power rested on the provincial military aristocracy. The twelfth century witnessed an intensification of the quasi-feudal tendencies of Byzantine society, which, without exactly paralleling the feudal structures of the West, led to rather similar results. The Comneni governed not so much as leaders of a centralized state but as a family clan, the foremost of many other clans that divided among themselves the ownership of the Empire's lands.[39] The architecture in which this period expressed itself may, therefore, be called seigneurial. The dwellings of the nobility have not, unfortunately, survived, but we may quote the statement of a contemporary historian to the effect that the emperor Alexius I distributed so much money to his relatives and followers that "they made for themselves houses which, in point of size, resembled cities, and, in point of magnificence, were no different from royal palaces."[40] The Comneni themselves finally abandoned the old Imperial Palace by the Hippodrome, in which the *basileus* had resided for seven hundred years, and moved to the smaller palace of Blachernae, which, dominating the northern corner of the city's defenses as it did, must have had the character of a castle. In ecclesiastical architecture the predominance of monasteries continued, if it was not intensified, and in this respect the imperial family took the lead.

A number of foundations associated with the imperial dynasty have survived, and they give us some idea of what was evidently the best work of Byzantine architects of the late eleventh and twelfth centuries. In this group we may place, first, the monastic church of Christ Pantepoptes (Eski Imaret Camii), overlooking the Golden Horn.[41] It was founded about the year 1100 by the mother of Alexius I, the famous Anna Dalassena. This quite small church is a classic example of the four-column type (the present octagonal stone piers must have been substituted for the original columns in the Turkish period). The construction is very careful, the carving of the cornices and door jambs competent, but there is hardly anything in this building that could not have been done 150 or 200 years earlier: the ribbed, twelve-sided dome (diameter 13 feet), the scalloped pastophoria, the narthex

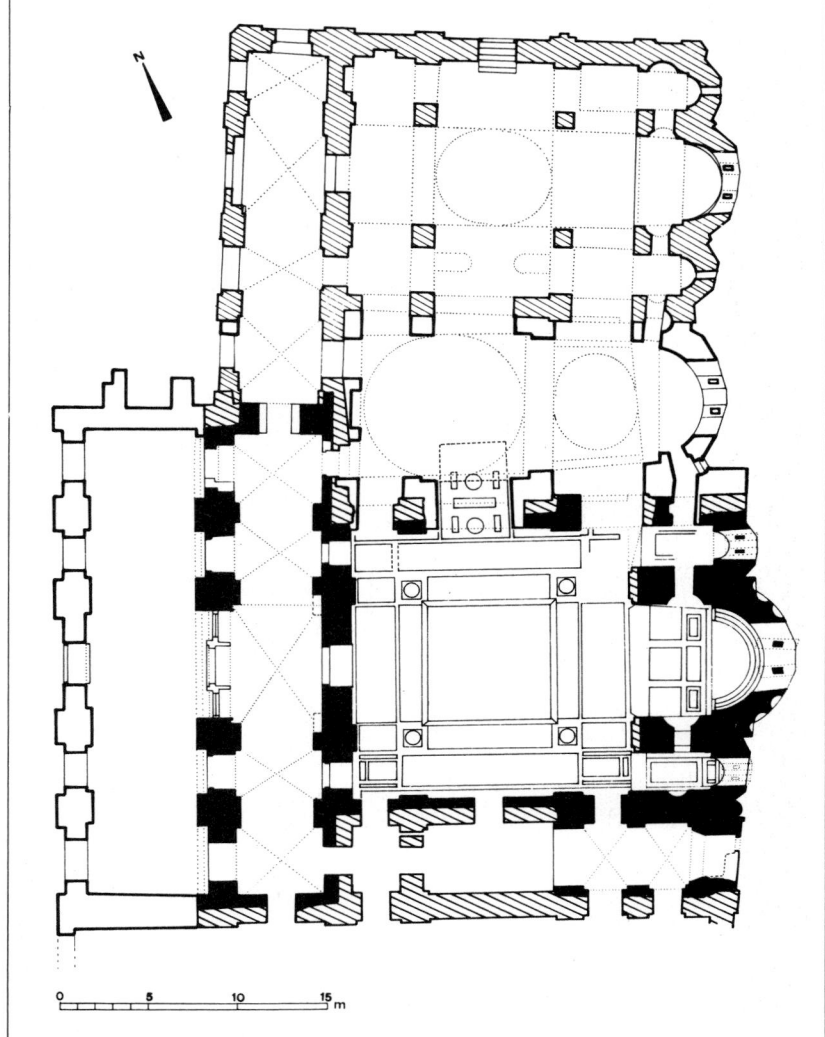

261. *Constantinople, Christ Pantocrator (Zeyrek Kilise Camii), south church, interior, detail of pavement.*
262. *Constantinople, Gül Camii, apses.* ▷

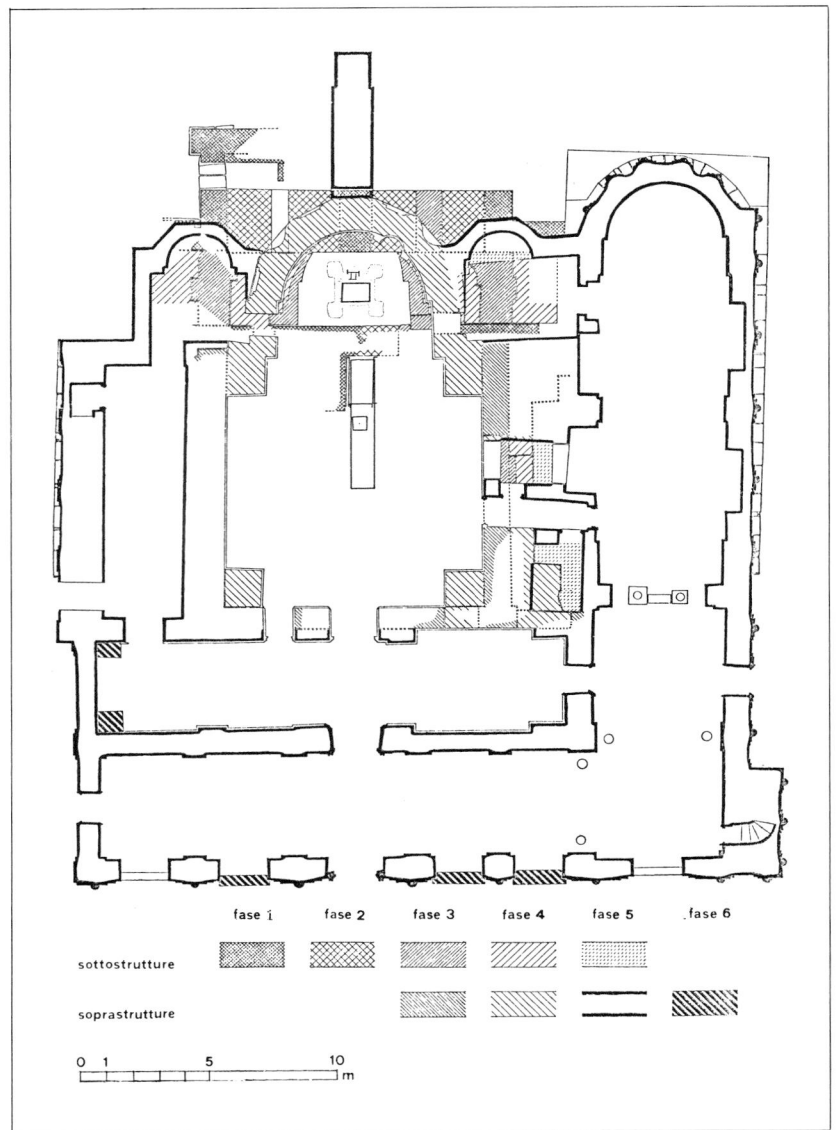

263. *Constantinople, Christ of the Chora (Kariye Camii), ground plan (after P. A. Underwood, 1966).*

fase 1   fase 2   fase 3   fase 4   fase 5   fase 6

sottostrutture

soprastrutture

0 1   5   10
                           m

264. *Constantinople, Christ of the Chora (Kariye Camii),* katholikon, *interior looking toward apse.*

of three bays surmounted by a gallery which opens into a nave through an elegant *tribelon*—all these are standard features of the tenth century. Only in the patterned brickwork of the exterior do we find a reminder of the intervening development.

The same apparent retrogression confronts us in the dynastic monastery of the Comneni, that of Christ Pantocrator (Zeyrek Kilise Camii).[42] This large complex consists of three juxtaposed churches. The south one, dedicated to Christ, was built by the empress Irene between 1118 and 1124, then the north church, dedicated to the Virgin of Mercy (Eleousa), and finally the intervening domed mausoleum which bore the name of St. Michael; the latter two were erected by the emperor John II before 1136. Here were buried the greatest emperors of the Comnenian house, John II and Manuel I, and later, in the fourteenth and fifteenth centuries, the emperors of the house of Palaeologus. The monastery, lavishly endowed, is alleged to have accommodated seven hundred monks, an improbably high figure. Included in the complex were a hospital of fifty beds, a home for the aged, and a bath.

Dilapidated as it is today, the monastery of the Pantocrator bears many traces of its former glory. The south church is the largest specimen of the four-column type at Constantinople, the nave measuring about 52 feet square and the dome 23 feet across. This exceptional size appears to have been achieved thanks to the availability of four very large columns of red marble, said to have been seven feet in circumference—surely spoils from an earlier building. These columns have been removed and replaced by stone piers in the Turkish baroque style. The dome is sixteen-sided and has as many windows. The *naos* was flanked by two lateral galleries—the south one is still preserved, though not accessible, while the north one must have been destroyed when the mausoleum was built. The narthex was in five vaulted bays and carried a gallery: the dome over its central bay represents a later alteration, designed to improve the lighting after the addition of the exonarthex.

The south church was particularly remarkable for its decoration. The marble placage has survived in the apse, but originally it extended all around the nave, above a skirting of verd antique. A magnificent pavement of *opus sectile* has recently been recovered and consists of a pattern of roundels with interlace borders and corner panels filled with a rinceau and figures of animals—a continuous carpet that enables us to visualize the descriptions of such pavements in Byzantine texts. Most unexpected of all has been the discovery of many hundreds of fragments of stained glass, some of them pertaining to figural representations. If these fragments, which were set in lead, go back to the original decoration of the church (and there is some

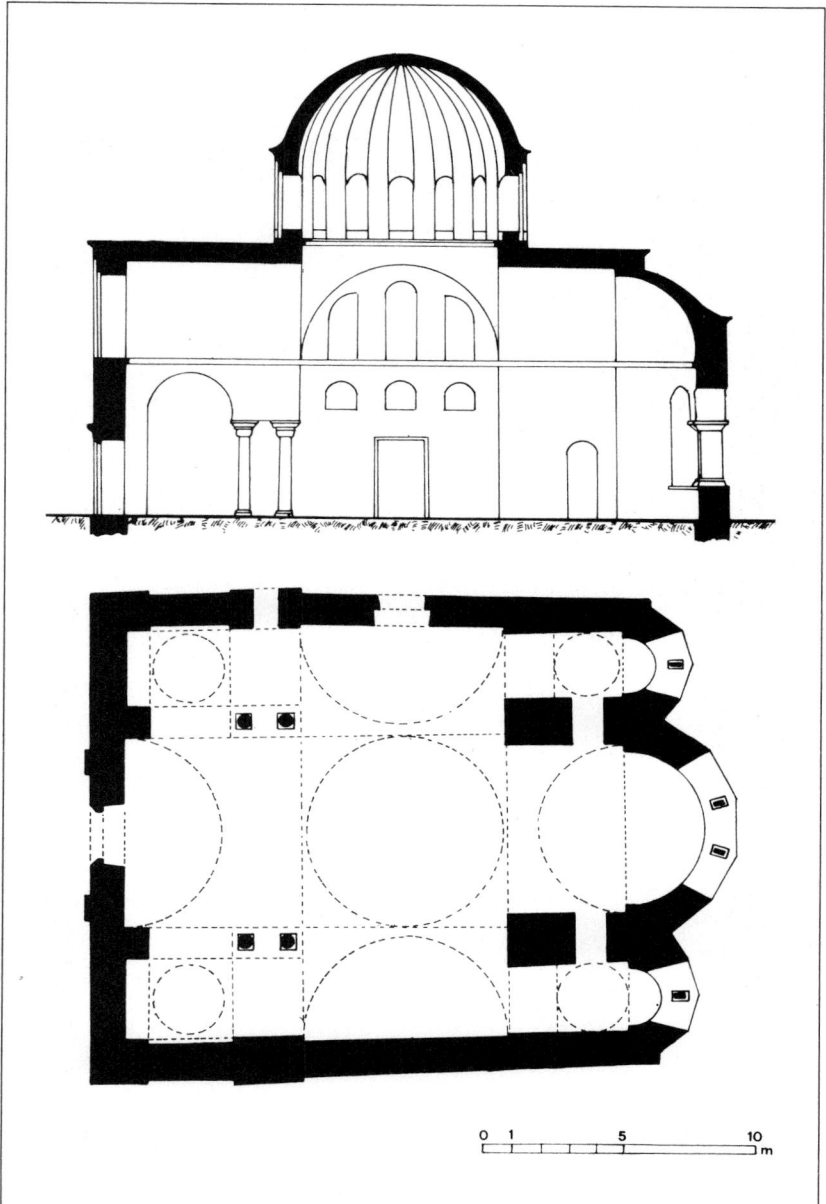

268. *Pherrai, Panagia Kosmosoteira, exterior from the southwest.*
269. *Kastoria, St. Stephen, exterior from the east.*
270. *Kastoria, Kumbelidiki, exterior from the southwest.* ▷

reason to believe that they do), we may have to reconsider not only the origins of stained glass, but also the aesthetic impact of a high-class Byzantine church of the twelfth century.

The north church—that of the Virgin Eleousa—is somewhat smaller than the south church, but belongs to the same architectural type. It, too, had four columns, for which the Turks have substituted stone piers. Traces of mosaic survive in a window, and there is a fine carved cornice that runs all around the church. The mausoleum, which had to be squeezed into a narrow, predetermined space, is divided into two bays and covered by two domes of elliptical shape. It had an *opus sectile* pavement similar to that of the south church. On the exterior the multiple apses of the complex are enlivened by slender niches and patterns of brick.

A third church that may be associated with the Comnenian dynasty is that of Christ of the Chora (Kariye Camii), famous for its fourteenth-century mosaics. Its structural history is too complex to describe here.[43] It will suffice to say that the nave as it stands today as well as the central apse are largely of the Comnenian period and were probably built in the early twelfth century by Isaac, the youngest son of Alexius I. Here a fairly large dome (nearly 23 feet in diameter) rested directly upon masonry piers whose corners projected into the nave so as to form a cruciform ground plan with shallow cross-arms. This disposition recalls a much earlier stage of Byzantine architecture, represented by buildings such as the Dormition church at Nicaea and St. Sophia at Thessalonica; indeed, by virtue of this resemblance, the central part of the Kariye Camii was regarded for a long time as dating from the seventh century, until the true facts were exposed by archaeological investigation. Today, however, we can assert that this kind of plan came back into vogue in the twelfth century. We find it, for example, in the monastic church built in 1162 at Elegmi (Kurşunlu) near Mudanya, on the south coast of the Sea of Marmara,[44] and in the large church known by its Turkish name of Kalenderhane Camii at Istanbul, previously regarded as being of the ninth century.[45] It is worth recording that Kariye Camii in its Comnenian stage also appears to have had stained-glass windows.

Isaac Comnenus, the patron of the Chora monastery, founded, toward the end of his life, another establishment, the monastery of the Virgin Kosmosoteira (Savior of the World) at Vira or Pherrai on the Maritsa River. The charter which he issued for the latter foundation in 1152 paints a vivid picture of his extensive landholdings, including two castles, several villages, and fisheries on the river. The monastic church in which Isaac was ultimately buried has survived:[46] it is a fairly large but not very elegant building, which may be described as a variant of the cross plan on piers. The dome (diameter

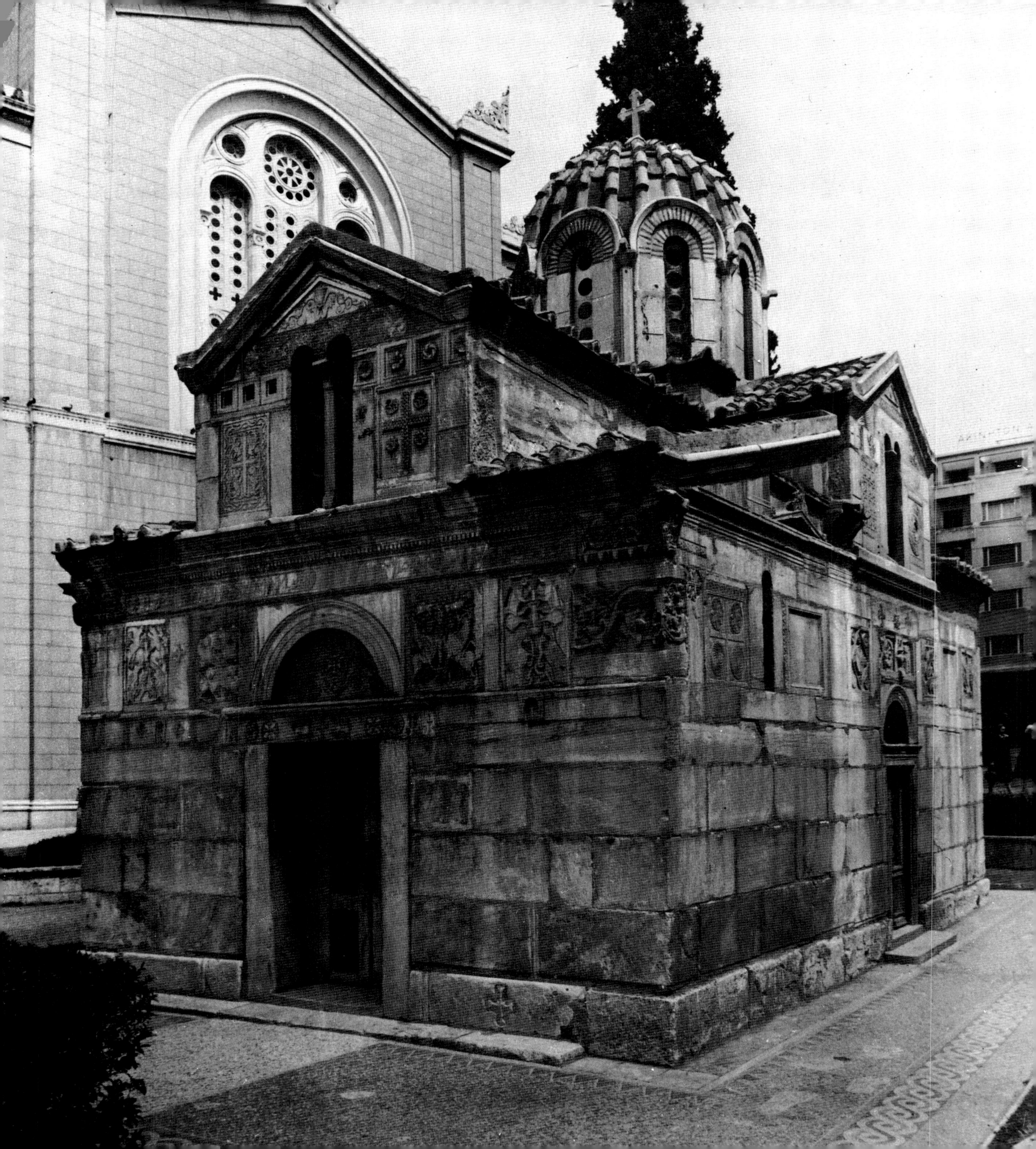

21 1/2 feet) is supported on 2 masonry piers to the east and 2 pairs of columns to the west. The column shafts are reused, and since they were too thin for the purpose, they had to be surmounted by disproportionately wide capitals and an impost block, which provide, incidentally, a good example of contemporary carving. We may note here the value that was attached to marble columns: introduced into the building for reasons of prestige, they caused a noticeable asymmetry in the plan, since, in spite of their flaring capitals, they could not attain the width of the two eastern piers. As a result, the corner compartments of the church, which are covered with little domes, are considerably wider on the west side than they are on the east.

The monuments we have enumerated, most of them associated with the imperial family, offer a sufficiently large sample of metropolitan architecture to support the view that the interesting experiments of the eleventh century were abandoned in Constantinople under the Comneni. The desire for wide, unencumbered interiors persisted, but instead of further developing the octagonal plan on squinches, Byzantine architects reverted to older traditions. One may suspect here a deliberate attitude, an attempt to maintain certain forms that were thought to be truly Byzantine and Orthodox in the face of the double thrust—from the Catholic West and the Muslim East—which the Empire had to sustain.

The chief contribution of Middle Byzantine architecture consisted in the elaboration of a type of church that was, in its own way, perfect. It was never very large and in fact was often tiny, because it did not have to serve a large public. At Constantinople there was an abundance of enormous congregational churches bequeathed by an earlier period, churches that were, for reasons of *pietas,* maintained (we may recall the great effort made in this direction by Basil I). These were sufficient, indeed excessive, for the needs of a diminished urban population. The same must have been true of Thessalonica. The precarious financial position of the episcopate prevented the construction of large congregational churches in provincial centers, even if there was some call for them: the trend, as we shall see presently, was toward a great number of small neighborhood churches. The main architectural effort was directed, however, to monasteries, for reasons that I have tried to explain, and it was the monastic church that set the pace.

In terms of architectural concepts there was no break between the Early and Middle Byzantine periods. The chief innovation lay in a growing concern for exterior appearance, a concern that may have been motivated, at least in part, by the isolation of the church in the courtyard of the monastery; but this was not done to the detriment of

the interior, which remained of primary importance. Middle Byzantine architecture continued to be an architecture of interior space, and whenever plastic articulations were introduced on the outside, they reflected the interior divisions. The enclosed space, moreover, was centripetal rather than one-directional, as in the basilica, and it was hierarchically organized: starting in the dome, it descended, as it were, to the vaults, spread out into the bema and apse, and finally came down to earth. This hierarchy was emphasized by marble cornices, which divided from one another the three zones of dome, vaults, and vertical walls.

The spatial construction and medium scale of such a church were ideally suited for a pictorial decoration that reflected the hierarchical and immutable nature of the Christian cosmos. Best expressed in mosaic, this decoration consisted of two elements: a hierarchy of figures, beginning with Christ in the dome and the Virgin Mary in the semidome of the apse, and going on to the archangels, Prophets, Apostles, Fathers of the Church, and other saints; and a cycle of narrative images depicting the major "feasts" of the Christian calendar, from the Annunciation to the Ascension and the Dormition of the Virgin.

Placed on a background of gold tesserae, these figures appeared to inhabit the actual space of the church and to be in converse with one another.[47] The angelic host escorted the Lord; the Prophets

exhibited their testimony concerning the Incarnation on the inscribed scrolls they held; the Evangelists, usually placed in the four pendentives, supported in a very real sense the edifice of Christian doctrine; the Fathers stood around the altar table, upon which they offered their timeless sacrifice. This pictorial program, as seen in the great mosaic decorations of Hosios Loukas, Daphni, Nea Moni, and St. Sophia at Kiev, could not readily adapt itself to a radically different form of architecture; furthermore, the intimate relationship between the figures was disrupted if the church they decorated was too large. In St. Sophia of Constantinople figural mosaics were set up in the second half of the ninth century after the suppression of Iconoclasm. Excellent as they are in themselves, they are, however, completely lost in the vast spaces of the cathedral.

While the mosaics occupied the upper reaches of the church— the zones of dome and vaults—the walls below the lower cornice continued in high-class churches to be reveted with marble, as they had been in the Imperial Roman and Early Byzantine periods. The supply of marble was, however, predicated on its reuse, and mosaics were very expensive. In more modest Middle Byzantine churches, which is to say the majority of them, the entire interior was painted. The figural decoration (normally on a plain blue background) came farther down the walls, but there was always a dado imitating in paint the more expensive effects of veined marble and incrustation.

If from the individual church we pass on to planned architectural complexes, we may say that the monastery, such as we have described it, best expresses the contribution of the Middle Byzantine period. The town, on the other hand (setting aside the peripheral case of Kiev, which I shall discuss in the next chapter), appears to have lost all monumental character. Take the example of Kastoria in northern Greece, which remained in Byzantine hands with some interruptions between 1018 and 1331. It was a fortified town situated on the neck of a peninsula jutting out into a lake. Here we find some thirty tiny churches, dating from the Byzantine and post-Byzantine periods, scattered more or less at random. There is no recognizable urban center, no main street: the whole town is covered by a maze of tortuous alleys bordered by a picturesque agglomeration of old houses, some of them going back to the seventeenth and eighteenth centuries. With one exception (the so-called Kumbelidiki), the churches are not domed. The biggest of them, that of the Anargyroi of the eleventh century, measures 26 by 29 1/2 feet, including the narthex. It is of basilican plan, that is, it has three aisles separated by piers and a clerestory. Most of the other churches are simple rectangular rooms. They were put up by local initiative: the most exalted personage that appears in the dedicatory inscriptions is a certain *magistros* Nikephoros

251

Kasnitzis, whose title corresponded roughly to the post of provincial judge or tax assessor.[48]

Athens was a more important center than Kastoria, but here, too, the main legacy of the Middle Byzantine period consists in a scattering of churches. Owing to their wholesale demolition in the nineteenth century, their number is difficult to estimate: there were probably more than forty, of which eight have survived. The earliest one on record, that of St. John Mangoutis (now destroyed), was a small basilica of the year 871, but by the late tenth or eleventh century a variety of domed types were introduced. The administrative and ecclesiastical center was in the Acropolis, and the Parthenon, rededicated to the Virgin Mary, served as the cathedral. The ancient citadel was further fortified by a circuit wall known as Rizokastron, which enclosed a total area of only 470 by 305 yards. Another line of fortification, dating from the third century, lay immediately to the north of the Acropolis and included the ancient Agora. Byzantine habitations and churches spilled beyond this double enclosure. The medieval houses that have been excavated were all extremely modest and so badly built that in most cases even their ground plans could not be ascertained. Unlike Thebes, which was the capital of the Byzantine province of Greece and sustained a flourishing silk industry, Athens does not appear to have been very prosperous. Its miserable condition is graphically described by its bishop Michael Akominatos (1182–1204), who says that the city walls were in ruins and many dwellings had been pulled down and replaced by plowed fields. Here, as elsewhere, the most notable Byzantine buildings were monastic: Panagia Lykodemou, which I have already discussed, and the neighboring monasteries of Daphni and Kaisariani.[49]

The fragmentation of the medieval Byzantine state into feudal "duchies" began in the late twelfth century: Cyprus seceded in 1185 under Isaac Comnenus, a member of the imperial family; in 1189 a certain Theodore Mankaphas set himself up as the independent ruler of Philadelphia in western Asia Minor. When, in 1204, Constantinople fell to the knights of the Fourth Crusade, this internal process was further accelerated. The history of the Late Byzantine period is concerned, therefore, not with a single state, but with a series of minor principalities: the "Empire" of Nicaea, which, under the house of Lascaris, controlled the northwest corner of Asia Minor; the "Empire" of Trebizond under the Grand Comneni, who ruled the Black Sea coast from 1204 until 1461; the Despotate of Epirus, centered on Arta; the reconstituted "Empire" of Constantinople under the house of the Palaeologi (1261–1453); the principality of the Morea (Peloponnesus), with its capital at Mistra, which maintained its independence until 1460.

The architecture of this period naturally shows a diversity of regional manifestations which cannot be described here in exhaustive detail. Each of the Greek principalities found itself in a different political configuration and was subject to a different set of influences: the Empire of Trebizond was wedged between the kingdom of Georgia to the east and the Turks to the south; the Empire of Nicaea was an enclave within a vast territory controlled by the Sultan of Konya and various Turkish emirates; the Despotate of Epirus had to face the "Franks" in Greece as well as its Balkan neighbors—Albanians, Serbians, and Bulgarians. The Latins were omnipresent, not only as temporary conquerors but also, and in more lasting fashion, as the commercial imperialists of Venice and Genoa. Another new factor was that the two great cultural blocks which now enfolded the Greek domains, namely, the Roman Catholic and the Islamic, had an architecture that was more advanced than the Byzantine. It is well to remember that the thirteenth-century Seljuk mosques, medreses, and hans of Konya, Kayseri, Sivas, and Divriği surpass in size and technical competence anything that the Byzantines had built since the days of Justinian, even if the influence exerted by Seljuk on Byzantine architecture appears to have been very slight.[1] In the case of Romanesque and Gothic architecture, on the other hand, there was greater receptivity.

With the establishment of Latin principalities in lands previously belonging to the Byzantine state, a considerable number of castles, abbeys, and churches of Western style were erected from the early thirteenth century on. In Constantinople itself the period of Latin domination (1204–61) does not seem to have been very productive architecturally: the only construction that has been attributed to

276. *Arta, Katô Panagia, church, exterior from the southwest.*

it is the southeast porch of St. Sophia.[2] We should not rule out the possibility that at an even earlier period, in the eleventh and twelfth centuries, the various Italian colonies that were established along the Golden Horn—those of the Amalfitans, Venetians, and Pisans—could have put up buildings in their native style. There can be no doubt, on the other hand, that when Galata was ceded to the Genoese in 1303, there sprang up opposite Constantinople a Western town with its palazzi and churches, one of which, that of St. Paul (Arap Camii), has come down to us in a greatly altered condition.[3]

In Greece the number of surviving Frankish structures is more considerable. There are several important castles, such as Chlemoutsi (Clermont) on the west coast of the Peloponnese, erected in 1220–23, and Bodonitsa near Thermopylae of about the same period.[4] There are also several churches, such as Our Lady of Isova, St. Sophia at Andravida, the Cistercian monastery of Zaraka, the monastery of Blachernae in Elis (presumably begun before the arrival of the Crusaders and completed in the Gothic style), St. Paraskevi at Chalkis —long rectangular structures whose size alone (St. Sophia measured 62 by 164 feet) stands in sharp contrast to that of Byzantine churches.[5] Gothic architecture was thus transplanted to Byzantine lands and left a noticeable, if not a major, imprint in features such as the pointed arch, the rib vault, the belfry, and the elongation of church plans.[6] It also gave a new impetus to figural sculpture, an art that had been dormant in Byzantium for several centuries.[7]

Of the Greek principalities that were formed after 1204 the most dynamic was the "Empire" of Nicaea. Its rulers brought a measure of prosperity to western Asia Minor, and they are known from documentary sources to have been active builders. Unfortunately, very little of their work has been identified other than fortifications, for example, those of Magnesia (Manisa), Smyrna, Ephesus, and Priene.[8] The ruins of a four-column church found at Nicaea have been attributed to this period,[9] as have the remains of a church recently excavated at Sardis. We may also mention the shell of the palace at Nymphaion (Kemalpaşa) near Smyrna, the favorite residence of the Nicene emperors. It is a rectangular structure of three stories, lacking any attempt at elegance. The ground floor, which must have been vaulted, is built of cut stone, the superstructure of alternating bands of stone and brick.[10]

The Despotate of Epirus, which was the chief rival of Nicaea for the crown of Constantinople, is better known through its architectural monuments, several of which are directly associated with the royal family. They deserve the epithet "provincial," for there is something about them that is "home-made," a clumsy naiveté that is yet coupled with a desire to achieve expensive and grand effects. Of the

278. *Arta, Monastery of Blachernae, church, iconostasis fragments built into door.*

279. *Arta, Monastery of Blachernae, church, exterior from the south.* ▷

monuments in question, two are almost identical in form: they are the Katô Panagia near Arta, built by the despot Michael II between 1231 and 1271,[11] and the Porta Panagia near Trikkala, a foundation of this prince's son, John Doukas, and erected in 1283.[12]

Both belong to the "cross-vaulted" type, which is very common in Greece from the thirteenth century on. The plan is three-aisled, and the nave is covered by a longitudinal barrel vault, which is interrupted at the crossing by a slightly higher transverse barrel vault. The effect is rather like that of a cross-in-square church deprived of its dome. The Katô Panagia even has the suggestion of a dome, for the central bay of the barrel-vaulted crossing is raised by fifty-one inches above its lateral bays. The tall, narrow crossing, accentuated by a gable that projects above the roof line, is the dominant element in the exterior appearance of both churches. The resulting lack of unity is particularly noticeable in the Katô Panagia, where the barrel vault over the bema is considerably lower than that over the west arm of the nave, the difference in height being concealed by a false pediment. An exuberant geometric decoration consisting of tile patterns and dentils has been applied to the exterior of both buildings, with a charming disregard for symmetry. The Porta Panagia also boasts an elaborately carved chancel screen flanked by mosaic icons of Christ and the Virgin Mary.

The dynastic burial church of the despots of Epirus was that of the Blachernae near Arta.[13] Its architectural history is rather confused. It appears that the original church, built at the end of the twelfth or the beginning of the thirteenth century, was a three-aisled vaulted basilica with an arcade of two columns on either side. A few decades later it was given a grander aspect: three domes were added, one over the nave, the others over the aisles. This was done without any regard for the architectural articulations of the building. Arches on corbels were thrown across the nave and aisles, and an additional slender colonnette inserted between each pair of preexisting columns. The nave and south aisle were divided into three bays each, unrelated to the system of supports, with a dome over the central bay; the north aisle, on the other hand, was divided into four bays, of which the second from the west was domed and the third covered with a vault. Not content with this, the architect concealed the two lateral domes behind false gables for no other reason, it would seem, than the desire to give the illusion of a transverse vault. In contrast to the clumsiness of the architecture, the interior decoration of the church was given particular attention: the floor was elaborately inlaid, while the chancel screen and the royal tombs were enlivened with some of the most interesting carving that has survived from the Late Byzantine period.

The masterpiece of the Epirote school is, however, the church

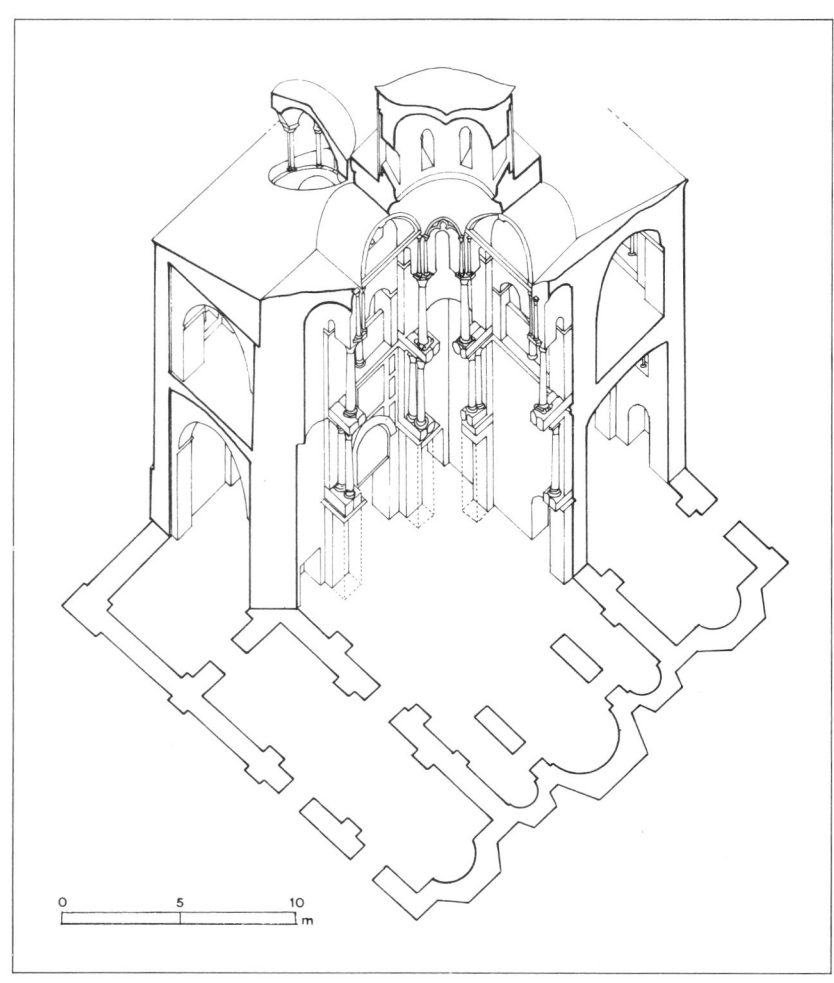

281. *Arta, Parigoritissa, isometric section (after A. Orlandos, 1963).*
282. *Arta, Parigoritissa, exterior from the northwest.* ▷

0   5   10
m

285. *Constantinople, Monastery of Constantine Lips (Fenari Isa Camii), south church, ground plan (after E. Mamboury, 1964).*

286. *Constantinople, Monastery of Constantine Lips (Fenari Isa Camii), south church, interior looking southeast.*

287. *Constantinople, Monastery of Constantine Lips (Fenari Isa Camii), south church, exterior from the east.* ▷

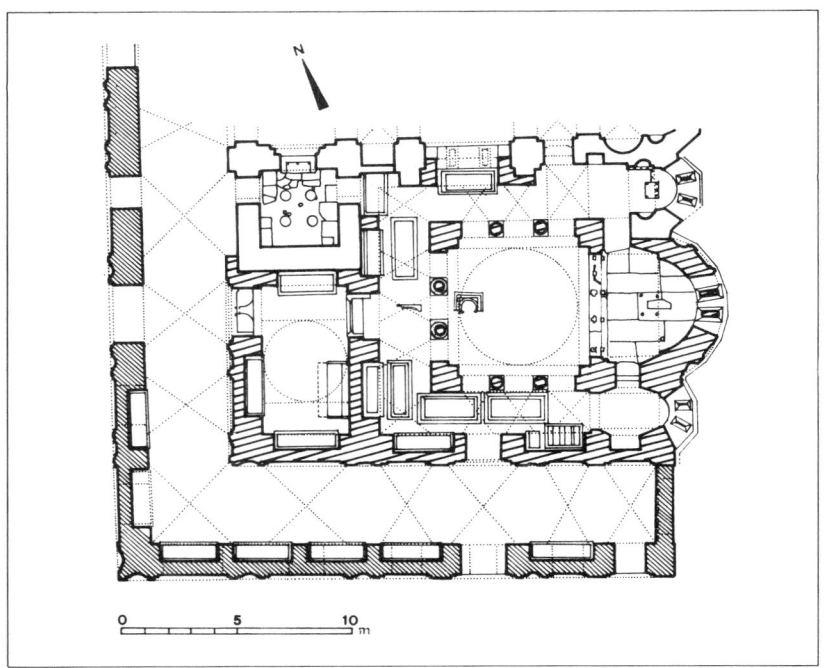

of the Parigoritissa at Arta.[14] Its cubic mass, seen from the outside, reminds one of an Italian palazzo, except that five domes and an open lantern (possibly used as a belfry) project above the horizontal roof line. A basic principle of Byzantine architecture, whereby the interior vaulting system was plastically expressed on the outside, has here been sacrificed in favor of the flat facades which encase the church on three sides. Each of these facades is divided into three stories: two zones of bilobed windows and a podium of rough rubblework with projecting pilasters, which was probably surrounded by a wooden porch with a lean-to roof. The narthex and side aisles are relatively very wide and are surmounted by a gallery, to which no means of access was, however, provided; the *naos* is correspondingly small, occupying, as it does, less than a third of the interior floor space and is unusually steep. For its roofing the architect devised an unprecedented and rather hazardous scheme: taking eight points of support, as in the Greek church on squinches, he gradually corbeled them out by using a great number of column shafts, obtained, no doubt, from the ruins of nearby Nicopolis. These were let into the walls in pairs so as to form securely anchored brackets: a first set halfway up the lower story and a second set, with greater overhang, at gallery level. Upon these improvised brackets were placed columns: paired columns on the lower brackets, single columns set farther away from the wall on the upper ones. This whole precarious system was surmounted, just below the dome, by ornamental colonettes subtending trefoil arches and carved archivolts of Italian style.

The Parigoritissa was erected sometime between 1283 and 1296 and was a foundation of the royal house of Epirus, which had intermarried with the Orsinis of Cephalonia, with the Hohenstaufens of Sicily, and with the Villehardouins and St. Omers: the presence of purely Western features in the building is, therefore, easily explainable. Precisely because the architect was a provincial, free from the constraints of a strong tradition, he was able to experiment with forms borrowed from the West and so produced an *ad hoc* solution which, though not successful, is an interesting hybrid. Such latitude was not encouraged in the reconstituted Empire of Constantinople, which, no doubt deliberately, reverted to older formulas.

The house of the Palaeologi has given its name to the last phase of Byzantine history and art. The "Palaeologan Renaissance" is a term that has often been used and may have some justification in the domain of painting; it is hardly applicable to architecture. In the relatively short period between 1261 and about 1330 (when, owing to the deteriorating condition of the state, building activity practically came to a halt in the capital), some attractive structures were erected at Constantinople and Thessalonica, but they perpetuated the tradi-

tions of the Middle Byzantine period without any attempt at reviving Early Christian, let alone antique, forms. The social class responsible for this architecture was a closely knit aristocracy which, as previously, spent its resources on palaces and family-owned monasteries. A characteristic feature of the latter is the important place reserved for burials: along the walls of church and narthex, in specially constructed chapels and ambulatories, were arched recesses containing sarcophagi as well as portraits of the deceased and pompous epitaphs detailing the noble ancestry and high connections of all those Palaeologi, Doukai, and Cantacuzenes.

Of the surviving ecclesiastical buildings of this period at Constantinople the most important is the south church of the monastery of Lips (Fenari Isa Camii), founded by the empress Theodora, wife of Michael VIII Palaeologus.[15] The exact date of construction is unknown: it is, in any case, earlier than the charter *(typikon)* which was drawn up by the foundress sometime after 1282. Instead of building an entirely new monastery, Theodora chose to enlarge an existing one, perhaps with the intention of imitating the complex of Christ Pantocrator, the dynastic mausoleum of the Comneni.

The original church of Constantine Lips was left practically untouched, and a somewhat wider church was built against it. The latter is of the "ambulatory" type, which means that the dome is supported on four masonry piers, and that between each pair of piers two columns were inserted; in this way the lateral aisles and western part of the church formed a continuous vaulted passage. The principle can be traced as far back as the Dormition church at Nicaea and St. Clement's at Ankara, but there is no need to evoke such distant predecessors, since the main church of St. Mary Pammakaristos (Fethiye Camii)—a building of, probably, the twelfth century—was constructed on the same formula.[16] Theodora's church is preceded by a domed narthex which does not extend the full width of the *naos* because the preexisting staircase tower of the north church was left in place; and the whole complex is enveloped on the west and south sides by a vaulted ambulatory. The aesthetic qualities of the building are today best appreciated by viewing its exterior from the east, where the plain, three-sided apses of the tenth-century structure contrast with the multifaceted and elaborately decorated apses of Theodora's church.

The interior has suffered too much transformation to convey its intended appearance. However, a glance at the plan will reveal one essential feature, namely, the profusion of arcosolia that were specifically provided by the architect: there are five in the *naos,* four in the narthex, and seven in the ambulatory. The one that has the place of honor, the east arcosolium of the south aisle, was intended for Theo-

dora herself; and probably the beautiful carved archivolt with busts of the Apostles (now in the Istanbul Archaeological Museum), the most outstanding example of Palaeologan sculpture, pertains to this tomb.

The same preoccupation with the afterlife confronts us in the elegant pareeclesion of St. Mary Pammakaristos of about the year 1310.[17] This was a memorial chapel erected in honor of the prominent general Michael Doukas Glabas Tarchaniotes by his widow, Maria, as explained in a long carved epigram that still survives on the south facade. The chapel is of the classical four-column type and is preceded by a two-story narthex covered by two tiny domes. The sepulchral arcosolia, four or five in number, were placed in the narthex. The exterior provides one of the best examples of the Palaeologan style in the capital. Because of the two-storied narthex, the chapel has a cubic form divided into three zones of blind arcading—wide arches alternating with narrow ones (note the little ogee arch at the center of the south facade), slender niches, and concave roundels. The masonry is of the regular Constantinopolitan type, and the ornamental patterns are more restrained than in Greece and the Balkans. Originally, the west facade of the chapel was free (the U-shaped ambulatory is a later addition) and may have had a scalloped roof line. The interior, tiny as it is, gleams with marble and mosaic; it is the traditional scheme but contains some minor Palaeologan innovations, like the champlevé frieze with heraldic emblems that runs at window level.

Between the years 1316 and 1321 the statesman and scholar Theodore Metochites restored the monastery of the Chora (Kariye Camii). Thought not a member of the highest aristocracy, Theodore attained the position of prime minister, married his children into the imperial family, and, above all, made himself fabulously rich.[18] Unfortunately, the palace that he built for himself (and which he described in a poem) as well as the conventual structures of the Chora have not survived; yet, in considering Kariye Camii we can safely assume that we are dealing with a monument emanating from the most exalted stratum of Byzantine society.

Once again, this is not an entirely new building but an enlargement of an older one. The shell of the Comnenian nave was left in place, but its dome was built anew; the two narthexes and the mortuary pareeclesion to the south of the church are due to Metochites. For such an ambitious enterprise, the architectural work may strike us as mediocre. The additions had, of course, to be adapted to the older elements and to certain functional requirements, and this led to considerable irregularity. The inner narthex is not centered with regard to the nave, and the two domes that cover its end bays are consequently off axis, with the result that the south dome, which is the larger of the two, obstructs the exterior view of the west tympanum

269

of the church. The outer narthex, too, is divided into very unequal vaulted compartments. The parecclesion, which was built *de novo,* is more rationally laid out, with one domed and one vaulted bay, but here, too, the north and south walls are not symmetrical. The exterior aspect is pleasing and was even more attractive before the scalloped roof line of the outer narthex and of the parecclesion was replaced by a horizontal one about a hundred years ago. The facades, built in the same masonry as the parecclesion of St. Mary Pammakaristos, are articulated by means of rounded pilasters and setbacks, and the western facade in particular must have looked more elegant before its arched openings had been filled up. Even so, the architecture hardly stands comparison with the deservedly famous mosaics and frescoes of the interior, upon which, as well as on the marble revetments, Metochites lavished the greater part of his attention.

Another example of Palaeologan church architecture at Constantinople is provided by the outer narthex of Kilise or, more correctly, Molla Gürânî Camii (its Byzantine name is unknown).[19] This building has never been thoroughly investigated, but it is safe to say that it presents a case analogous to that of Kariye Camii: an earlier, four-column church of about the eleventh century must have been taken over by a rich patron, who enlarged it by means of subsidiary structures, including, it would seem, a belfry. The outer narthex, which today is the most notable part of the addition, extends beyond the older *naos* on both north and south and gives access to annexes. That on the south was still preserved in the early nineteenth century and was recorded in 1833–35 by Charles Texier, whose drawing shows an arcaded front supported on four, surely reused columns: a pair of tall columns and a pair of shorter ones with a marble doorframe between them.[20] The same principle has been used with considerable success on the west facade of the outer narthex, which, because of the declivity of the ground, stands on a podium and consists of two zones: a lower zone of two triple arcades flanking the central door, and an upper zone of five arched windows. The articulations of the two zones do not line up, since the five windows correspond to the five bays into which the interior of the narthex is divided; furthermore, all the marble elements—namely, the four columns, their capitals, and the carved parapet slabs inserted between the columns—are spolia. Working with such disparate material, the architect was nevertheless able to impart to the facade a well-proportioned elegance. The outer narthex is crowned by three domes, which are decorated with mosaics.

The "portico facade," of which Kilise Camii offers a fine example, appears to have been a more prevalent feature of Late Byzantine architecture than has been suspected hitherto. In addition

294. *Constantinople, Kilise Camii, exterior from the northwest.*

295. *Constantinople, Kilise Camii, exterior from the south (19th-century drawing by Charles Texier). Library of the Royal Institute of British Architects, London.*

296. *Selymbria (Silivri), St. John Prodromos, exterior.*

to St. Sophia at Ohrid, which I shall consider in the next chapter, I may mention a building that has received very little attention, namely, the Fatih Camii at Enez (Ainos) on the Turkish side of the Maritsa River.[21] This is a very large church (external dimensions 69 by 111 1/2 feet, discounting the apses) of a somewhat elongated cross-in-square plan, preceded by an inner narthex and an open porch or outer narthex. The monument is today ruined, and its date is difficult to determine: in view of the fact that it is built in the "concealed course" technique and has some ornamental brickwork on the exterior, there may be some justification in assigning it to the twelfth century. It is, however, to the porch that I should like to draw attention. It consists of a triple arcade in the middle, flanked by two double arcades. Originally there may have been a second zone of windows that has fallen down. The porch is an addition to the main body of the building, but it also displays the "concealed course" technique, which, as far as we know, was not used in the Palaeologan period. Whatever the exact date of this porch, it is of some relevance to the problem of the "portico facade," which is characteristic of the thirteenth-century Venetian palazzi such as the greatly altered Fondaco dei Turchi. In the present state of our knowledge it appears more likely that the idea traveled from Venice to the East rather than vice versa; but it may be prudent to reserve final judgment.

In the domain of domestic architecture, with which the "portico facade" is associated more closely, perhaps, than with ecclesiastical architecture, the only surviving Palaeologan monument at Constantinople is the so-called Tekfursarayı, which overlooks the Land Walls of the city a short distance from the Kariye Camii.[22] This was originally known as the palace of the Porphyrogenitus, referring not to the emperor Constantine VII Porphyrogenitus (913–59) but probably to his namesake, the third son of Michael VIII: if so, the date of construction would fall between 1261 and 1291. It is a three-story rectangular building, a more elegant version of the palace of Nymphaion. The ground floor was vaulted and supported on columns, while the first floor had a flat wooden ceiling, and the second floor was covered with a low-pitched roof. The palace was set between two fortified walls and was preceded on the north side by a protected courtyard, which accounts for the open north facade. The interior arrangements are difficult to reconstruct, except that the first floor appears to have been divided and had a number of built cupboards next to the windows, while the second floor had a tiny chapel corbeled out on the south side. The two main facades, north and south, are elaborately decorated with a variety of diaper patterns consisting of tiles and stone. Certain interesting details have, however, disappeared: the ground-floor arcades, composed of joggled voussoirs, had on their keystones escutch-

297. *Enez (Ainos), Fatih Camii, outer narthex from the southwest.*
298. *Constantinople, Tekfursarayĭ, exterior from the north.*

299. *Constantinople, Tekfursarayĭ, south facade (19th-century drawing).*
300. *Constantinople, Tekfursarayĭ, interior looking northeast.*

eons of Western form, engraved, it would seem, with the emblem of the Palaeologi, while on the east side of the building, facing the city, was a balcony supported on consoles terminating in lions', rams', and eagles' heads.

Thessalonica, always more closely connected with the capital than with Greece, experienced in the Early Palaeologan period a time of prosperity, which expressed itself in the construction of several churches, most if not all of them monastic.[23] The most remarkable of these is the church of the Holy Apostles (originally a monastery dedicated to the Virgin), founded by the patriarch Niphon between 1312 and 1315, which offers points of similarity with the undated churches of St. Panteleimon and St. Catherine as well as a few smaller ones. A striking feature of these churches is that they are enveloped on three sides by a covered gallery which often takes the form of a portico. At the Holy Apostles, the *naos,* which is of the normal four-column type, has an internal floor area of 550 square feet, that is, less than one-third of the total area of the monument, the rest being occupied by a U-shaped gallery, surmounted by domes at its four corners, and an additional open porch to the west consisting of two triple arcades on either side of the entrance door. The south wall of the church, which is today solid, also had the form of an open portico. At St. Catherine's, as restored after World War II, the portico is open on three sides, and, once again, it has four domes at the corners. The proportion of the internal area of the *naos* to that of the whole building is 565 square feet as against 1,830 square feet. At St. Panteleimon the U-shaped gallery was demolished at the turn of the century, but its original aspect is recorded in old photographs and drawings.

The prevalence of these galleries at Thessalonica throws some light on the Constantinopolitan monuments we have been considering, for there, too, the contribution of the Palaeologan period consisted largely in the addition of annexes enveloping earlier churches on three sides. The precise function of these galleries has not yet been explained: at Constantinople they were used, in part, for burials, but this does not appear to have been the case at Thessalonica. At the church of the Holy Apostles the east bay of the north gallery, judging by its fresco decoration, served as a chapel dedicated to St. John the Baptist. The amount of shace devoted to the galleries and their "highlighting" by means of domes shows, in any case, that they had acquired a particular significance that may be explained by some peculiarity of monastic ritual.[24]

The building of churches continued at Thessalonica rather longer than it did at Constantinople. The fairly large church known as that of the prophet Elijah appears to date from about 1360, if, as seems likely, it was the *katholikon* of the New Monastery founded by

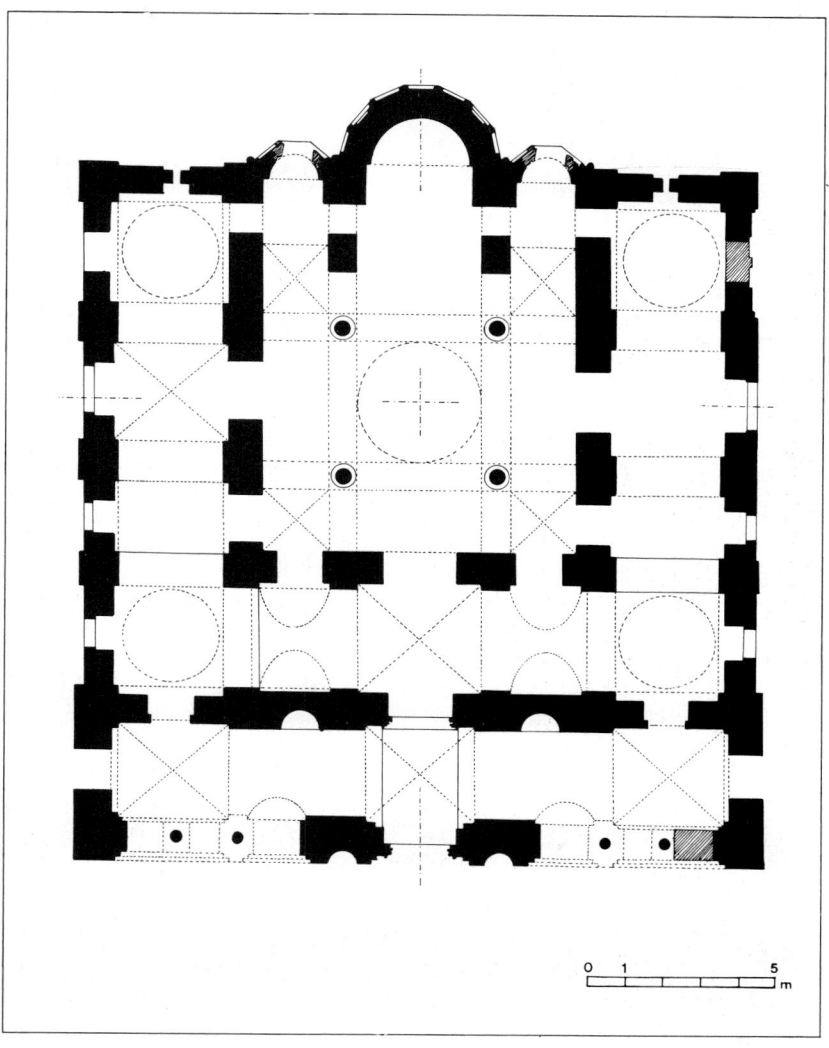

Makarios Choumnos. It is of the triconch Athonite plan and, like the churches of the Holy Mountain, has a deep narthex or *litê* supported on four columns. The smaller church of the Vlattadon monastery, of about the same date, was built on the perambulatory pattern.[25]

The principality of the southeastern Peloponnese, centered on the fortress of Mistra, was ceded to Constantinople in 1262. Divided from Byzantine territory by the Latin possessions in central Greece, it was administered at first by governors appointed for one year. Sometime after 1282, however, the governor obtained a more durable term of office and was thus able to set up his own court. In 1348 the Morea, as it was called, was erected into a Despotate, the appanage

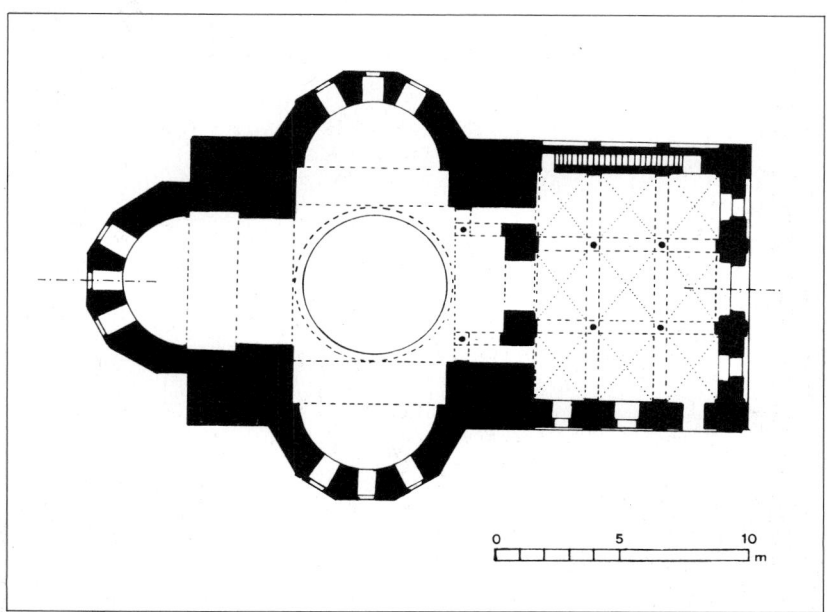

304. *Thessalonica, St. Catherine, exterior from the southwest.*

305. *Thessalonica, St. Elias, ground plan (after Diehl, Le Tourneau, and Saladin, 1918).*

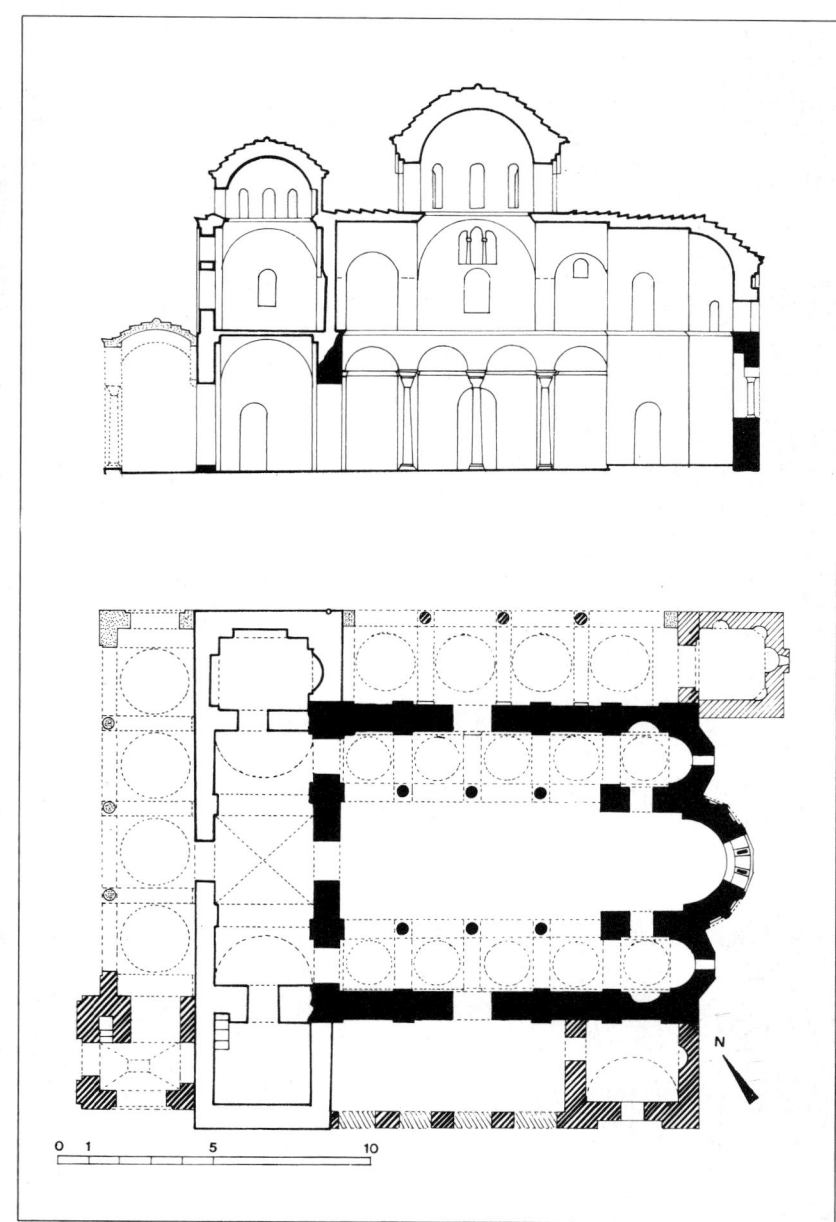

308. *Mistra, Hodegetria, exterior.*
309. *Mistra, Hodegetria, longitudinal section and ground plan (after H. Hallensleben, 1969).*

of a prince of the imperial family, first of the Kantakouzenoi (until 1383), then of the Palaeologi (until 1460). The Morea had, therefore, a special bond with Constantinople; at the same time it had close ties with the Frankish world by virtue of its immediate past, of the surrounding Frankish principalities, and of the mixed marriages that were so common among the Greek gentry. The monuments of Mistra reveal this double connection.

The citadel of Mistra, perched on an inaccessible mountaintop to the west of Sparta, was founded by William II Villehardouin, the same prince who thirteen years later had to surrender it to the Byzantine emperor. Below the castle a town grew up, which became the seat of the Greek administration and of the metropolis of Lacedaemonia. It was still a flourishing town in 1700, but in 1825 it was burned down and has remained a ruin ever since. Mistra is not entirely medieval, but it preserves, better than any other site, the flavor of a Late Byzantine town.[26] Built on very steep terrain (within the fortifications the ground rises by 800 feet over a width of 1,000), it has no recognizable street plan. The focus was provided by a piazza bordered on two sides by the L-shaped palace of the Despots, but this did not serve as a religious center. The metropolitan church, built in 1291–92 on a basilican plan, was situated much farther down, on the very edge of the fortified enclosure, and parish churches were not much in evidence. The main religious monuments of Mistra were monasteries—the complex of the Brontochion, the Peribleptos, St. Sophia, the Pantanassa—intramural monasteries occupying wide enclosures and enjoying ample revenues from their estates.

Next to the Metropolis, the earliest religious building of Mistra is the monastic church of the Hagioi Theodoroi, which dates from about 1290–95. It is the last representative of the octagonal plan on squinches, probably inspired by St. Sophia of Monemvasia. The abbot Pachomius, who completed this church, built a second one close by, dedicated to the Virgin Hodegetria (c. 1310), which served as the *katholikon* of the monastery called Brontochion. In an annex of its narthex are painted four chrysobulls (imperial decrees) which detail the possessions and immunities enjoyed by the monastery—possessions which the influential Pachomius continued enlarging until the year 1322. The Hodegetria was an ambitious building which set the architectural tone at Mistra for another century and was the model of what has been called the "Mistra type." Its distinguishing feature is the superimposition of a domed, cross-in-square design upon a basilica with galleries. The idea as such is a very old one and takes us back to Justinian's St. Irene. There is, however, a difference: in St. Irene and other "compact basilicas" of the sixth century the four piers supporting the dome rise from the ground up, while the colonnades serve the secondary purpose of upholding the gallery.

311. *Mistra, Pantanassa, exterior from the east.*
312. *Mistra, general view of the palace.*

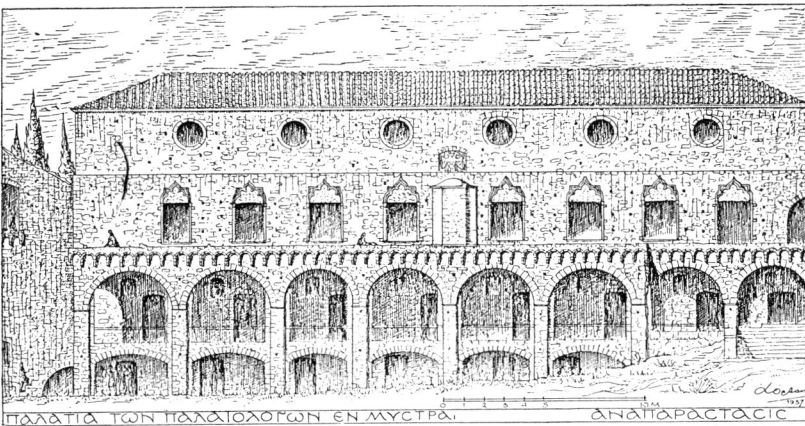

In the Hodegetria, on the other hand, we have a basilica on ground level with a row of three columns on either side of the nave, while the masonry piers upon which the dome rests have their footing on the gallery floor. There is some reason for thinking that this solution represents a change of mind that took place when the church was already under construction,[27] and it has been suggested that the introduction of the gallery was connected with the appointment of a permanent governor of the Morea—on the assumption that the gallery played a role in the court ceremonial of Constantinople and that a similar arrangement was re-created at Mistra with the establishment of a princely court.[28] While this explanation can hardly be substantiated, there is no doubt that Pachomius did his best to endow the Hodegetria with a Constantinopolitan look: the cross-in-square design with four little domes over the corners, the coursed (as opposed to cloisonné) masonry of the walls, the seven-sided outline of the main apse, and especially the interior marble revetment of the walls (now almost completely gone),[29] all point to this conclusion. The only missing ingredient was mosaic, for which fresco had to be substituted.

The Hodegetria must have been greatly admired at Mistra: the Metropolis was remodeled to look like it, and the same design was used in 1428 for the monastery of the Pantanassa, founded by John Frangopoulos, the prime minister of the Despotate. The latter church, situated on a terrace commanding a superb view, is the best-preserved and most picturesque of all the Mistra churches. It is particularly noteworthy for its Frankish elements—the tall belfry with pointed arches and the Gothic treatment of the apses—elements which do not alter the basically Byzantine character of the building but which impart to it a peculiar fancifulness.

The palace complex of Mistra has an even more markedly Frankish look.[30] It was built in stages: first a somewhat austere two-story building with an undivided hall on the ground floor (18 by 49 feet), barrel-vaulted and sparsely lit through ogival windows; then a residential block divided into 6 unequal rooms, with an open porch in the rear and a flanking tower; finally, a large rectangular building with a single audience room, measuring 34 1/2 by 119 feet, on the *piano nobile*. The three stages are not dated, but it is presumed that the first falls roughly in the period 1250–1350, the second in 1350–1400, and the third in 1400–1460. All the architectural detail is Western: the flat, "basket-handle" arches, the multilobed ogee window frames, the strings of consoles resembling machicolations; in fact, one may well wonder whether the palace of Mistra has much in common with a specifically Byzantine tradition. Since all that remains now is an empty shell, the living arrangements are difficult to visualize. It would seem that the princely family resided in the middle building, whose biggest room measures about 16 1/2 by 26 feet, and where there was an improvised private chapel. They could not have had much comfort or privacy, since all the rooms communicated with one another and no corridors were provided. From this middle building there must have been a hidden entrance to the great audience chamber (none is visible today), it being the custom of Byzantine sovereigns to move about *mystikôs*, that is, "privately" or "secretly." The quarters below the audience chamber—they consist of eight sparsely lit barrel-vaulted rooms, each one with a fireplace—were probably occupied by servants or guards. In short, the despots of Mistra do not appear to have lived in great style.

The houses of the gentry and burghers were, naturally, even more modest.[31] They were freestanding and, being built on a steep slope, comprised a vaulted half-basement which was used as a stable for animals or as a storeroom. Above this was the living space, normally a single large room, without any subdivisions, provided with a hearth and cupboards. There were no separate kitchens, so that cooking must have been done on the hearth or, perhaps, in the neighborhood bakery; even the privy was in the form of an alcove opening into the living room, screened off, perhaps, with a hanging curtain. Within this one room or *triklinos* the Mistriote family ate and slept; the women, we may imagine, spent most of the day at the window. The richer houses had towers with loopholes and crenellations for storing away valuables, since life was not without its dangers.

When we move from Mistra to Trebizond we find ourselves in a different and as yet rather hazy world. The Empire of Trebizond (1204–1461) has left a number of buildings, but, with the exception of St. Sophia, they have not been sufficiently explored. Trebizond itself was a walled city situated on a spur of ground between two deep ravines running into the Black Sea. The circuit of walls was approximately wedge-shaped, with a maximum length from north to south of half a mile. The southernmost corner, which was the highest, was occupied by the citadel and contained the royal palace. An account of it, written in the fifteenth century, speaks of a large oblong building decorated with paintings in which the emperor gave audience, and of many suites of rooms with balconies all around[32]—a complex that must have resembled the palace of Mistra but was probably more extensive. Many remnants are still visible, including a high façade pierced by bilobed windows, but they have not been properly recorded. Within the walled city stood the metropolitan church of Trebizond, called Panagia Chrysokephalos (the Golden-Headed), which has survived as a mosque.[33] It is a large, elongated

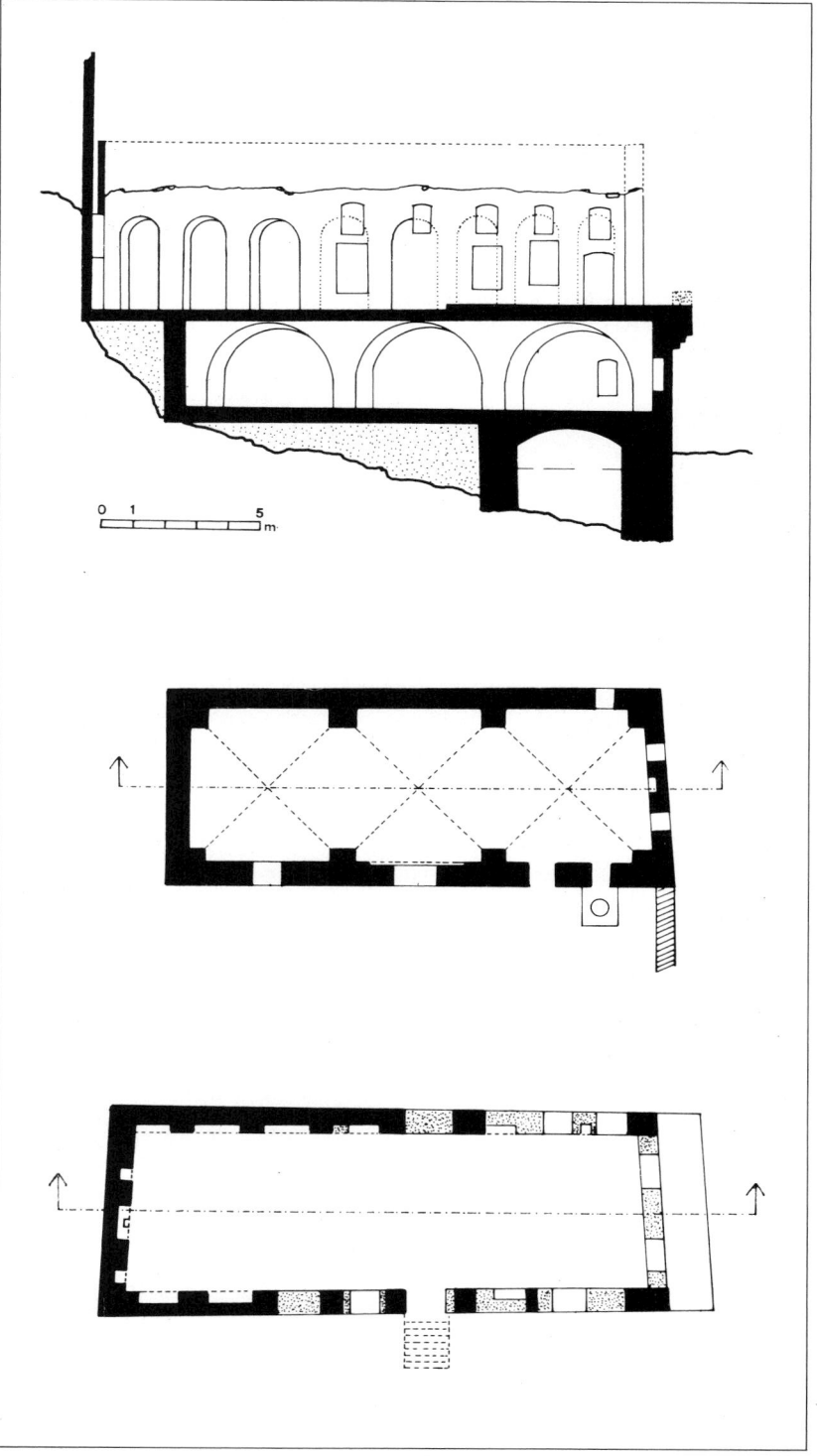

316. *Trebizond, ruins of palace.*

building (the nave measures 49 by 79 feet), covered with a single dome. Originally it may have been a vaulted basilica, but it has undergone many changes; both its date and its structural history remain undetermined. The town spilled outside the walls to the east, and it is there that several Byzantine churches are still to be seen. Among them is the tiny St. Anne, a vaulted "basilica" with a clerestory, dated by an inscription to 884–85, and the larger church of St. Eugenios, which appears to have been designed as a basilica but was rebuilt as a domed cross-in-square in the thirteenth or fourteenth century.

To gain a more direct insight into Trapezuntine architecture, we must proceed to the monastery of St. Sophia, situated 1 1/4 miles to the west of the walled city.[34] The complex, overlooking the sea, consists of the main church, a smaller church to the north of it (only its foundations have been preserved), and a tall belfry dated 1427. The main church was built between 1238 and 1263 by the emperor Manuel I and shows no sign of alterations. It is set on a raised podium whose retaining wall contained a great number of niches used for burial—a unique arrangement. The church itself is a somewhat elongated four-column structure crowned by a single dome on a twelve-sided drum. Its most conspicuous feature, unknown in Byzantine architecture and certainly borrowed from Georgia, are the three open porches which project from the church on the north, south, and west sides. Another peculiarity is the overnarthex, which must have served as a separate chapel rather than a gallery, since its central bay has an apse pointing to the east.

It is, however, in the decoration of St. Sophia that we see most clearly the mingling of several heterogeneous traditions that confers on this monument its chief interest. The columns and capitals, namely, the four big ones under the dome and the six smaller ones placed in pairs in the three porches, are Byzantine spoils of much earlier date (fifth to sixth centuries). The pair in the west porch were found to be too short and were capped by a second set of capitals in a purely Seljuk, "honeycomb" style. The two niches on either side of the west porch, shaped like *mihrabs*, and a number of carved roundels of intricate design are also unmistakably Seljuk. On the face of the south porch, on the other hand, below a quatrefoil oculus of Western inspiration, is a long carved frieze representing the Expulsion from Paradise, which could have been lifted from the facades of Aght'-amar. It is not particularly important to know (assuming we could ever find it out) whether this work was carried out by a team consisting of Georgians, Armenians, Turks, and Greeks, with one or two Italians standing by. For Trebizond was a melting pot of nationalities that coexisted under the thin veneer of the Greek administration.

What is perhaps rather more instructive for our purpose is to note the relative tenacity of the different branches of Byzantine art—painting, architecture, and sculpture. The frescoes that decorate St. Sophia are purely Byzantine; the architecture contaminated; the sculpture entirely alien. We shall encounter a similar situation when we review the impact of Byzantine artistic forms on southern and eastern Europe.

A hundred years ago Texier and Pullan, whose pioneering work was mentioned in Chapter One, expressed the view that the church of the Holy Apostles at Thessalonica "possesses all the elegance of the Byzantine architecture of the seventh century."[35] The fact that they were mistaken by seven hundred years is deserving of notice, yet there is some excuse for their error. They recognized that this monument was later than the age of Justinian. But later by how much? Today we know the answer, but we may well ask a related question: "In what respect does the church of the Holy Apostles, taken as a representative example of the last phase of Byzantine architecture, differ, say, from the north church of the monastery of Lips, dated 907?" We shall have to admit that the similarities are more striking than the differences. Both churches are of the four-column type; both are crowned by five domes rising in a pyramidal formation; both were intended to have the same form of interior decoration, namely,

318. *Trebizond, St. Sophia, ground plan (after D. Talbot Rice, 1968).*
319. *Trebizond, St. Sophia, south facade (19th-century drawing).*
320. *Trebizond, St. Sophia, south porch, exterior carving.*

321. *Trebizond, St. Sophia, west porch.*
322. *Trebizond, St. Sophia, west porch, detail of Seljuk carving.*

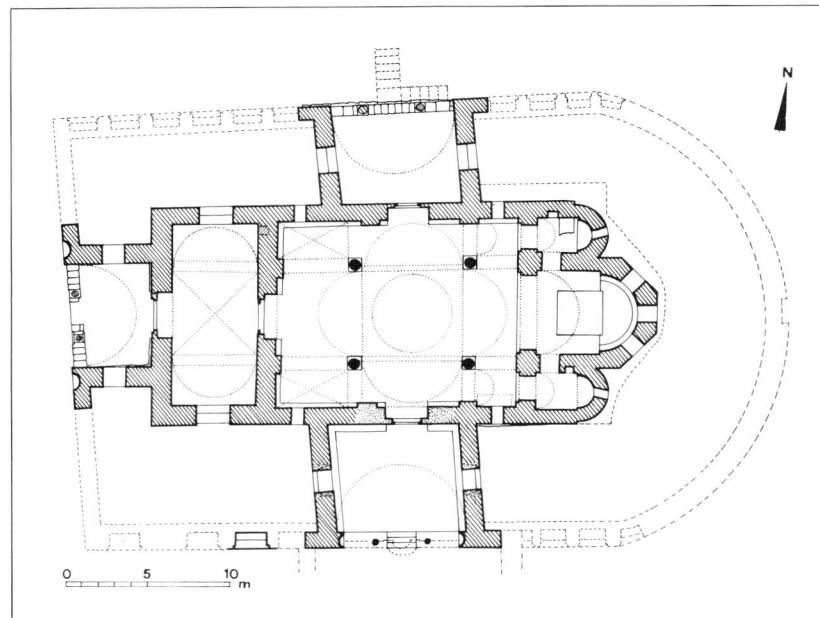

marble revetment and mosaic. The differences are not fundamental and require a trained eye to recognize them. The church of the Holy Apostles has a slenderer form than its predecessor, its facades are more open, and its exterior decoration is richer and "fussier." In other words, there was no architectural revolution between the years 900 and 1300, and yet, by slow degrees, a change did take place.

In an earlier Byzantine church, even in a church like that of Daphni of about 1100, it is the interior that counts. The interior is a closed system, covered by the dome of heaven. In a Palaeologan church this illusion does not exist. The dome is usually so steep that it resembles an inverted well. It no longer embraces the interior with its majestic curve, and the bust of Christ Pantocrator has grown smaller and more distant. The evolution of Byzantine painting, more rapid than that of architecture, has also introduced a new element. As the churches diminished in size, so the number of painted scenes, especially narrative ones, multiplied; and the desire for greater realism created a form of perspective, which meant in turn that each picture became an entity in itself and lost its relation to the architectural space.

The first impression one obtains upon entering a well-preserved Palaeologan interior is of the proliferation of painted figures that cover every inch of available surface. They are not the monumental figures of the earlier period, standing before a gold or blue background, but a multitude of little ones moving before a backdrop of fantastic structures, billowing curtains, and jagged rock formations. The Palaeologan period also saw the introduction of the *ikonostasis*, a tall partition between the nave and the bema. Instead of the open marble screen that afforded a view of the apse, a solid wall of icons now stood between the worshiper and the mystery of the Christian service, barely revealing the figure of the Virgin Mary in the semi-dome of the apse. The interior space was thus entirely overrun and obscured by painting.

By contrast—and here we see a gradual reversal of the principle that had governed Byzantine architecture since its inception—the exterior assumes a dominant role. It is enlivened plastically by means of niches, arcading, corbels, and strings of dentils—that is, elements that create a play of light and shadow—and coloristically by means of patterns of tile and stone. What is more, the multiplication and heightening of the domes, designed for external effect, have altered the perfect balance of the interior space that was the chief glory of the Byzantine church. With this "picturesque" phase, Byzantine architecture comes to a conclusion on home ground; it remains to consider its development in the wider sphere of the Orthodox world.

Chapter Nine THE DIFFUSION OF BYZANTINE ARCHI-
TECTURE IN EASTERN EUROPE

When we speak of the influence or diffusion of Byzantine architecture in countries that did not form part of the Empire, we should begin by explaining that we are dealing with different kinds of phenomena that cannot all be set on the same plane. On the one hand, there was eclectic borrowing, that is, when a state that had its own architectural traditions adopted Byzantine forms on a given occasion and for particular reasons; on the other hand, a newly constituted barbarian state that had had no tradition of building could take over Byzantine architecture lock, stock, and barrel or, at any rate, as much of it as it could use. Further distinctions can be made: a barbarian state may have been situated on lands that had previously belonged to the Empire (as was the case with Bulgaria and Serbia), or in more distant lands that had not at any earlier time come within the orbit of Byzantium (as was the case with Russia); it may have drawn its architectural expertise from Byzantium or from other quarters.

A famous example may be used to illustrate the distinction. The church of S. Marco in Venice is rightly regarded as a monument of Byzantine architecture. If we peel away all the accretions it has received in the past nine hundred years, we shall discover the cruciform church that was begun about 1063 by Doge Domenico Contarini and completed some thirty years later by Doge Vitale Falier.[1] This church is still standing today, and we can see more of its interior than of its exterior. It is well known that S. Marco was modeled on Justinian's church of the Holy Apostles at Constantinople and that it reproduced the principal features of the latter. Both churches were cruciform; both were crowned by five domes; both had quadripartite (or "four-footed") piers; both had galleries supported on columns; both, we may imagine, were approximately of the same size. There were also differences: for example, the Holy Apostles had two tiers of columns, S. Marco only one. Yet, as an instance of medieval imitation, S. Marco stood remarkably close to its model.

The fact to which I should like to draw attention is not that the Venetians (who had very close ties with Byzantium) should have imitated a Byzantine church, but that they should have imitated one that was five hundred years old at the time. They did so because they wanted to enshrine the relics of St. Mark in a building as prestigious and "authentic" as the Apostoleion of Constantinople, which contained the bones of Sts. Andrew, Luke, and, perhaps, also Matthew. Which is why the architect of S. Marco—even if we assume that he was a Greek—did not reproduce the design of a contemporary Byzantine church. Here, then, we have a clear example of eclectic and, indeed, antiquarian borrowing inspired by political motives.

No such conditions could have been operative in the Balkan and East European countries that came under Byzantine cultural

influence in the ninth century. We must begin with the historical context, which will be described very briefly.[2] About 600, as we have seen, the Danubian frontier of the Empire was breached and the entire Balkan peninsula overrun by Slavic tribes, which settled to a fairly sedentary way of life but showed themselves incapable of a more advanced political organization and, incidentally, produced no architectural works whatever. Leadership was provided by alien groups, first by the Avars, whose short-lived Empire went into a decline after their unsuccessful attack on Constantinople in 626; then by the Bulgars, a Turkic tribe that set itself up, about 680, in the area corresponding to modern Bulgaria. Twenty years later the Bulgarian khan was already intervening in the affairs of the Byzantine Empire. Repeated attempts to neutralize the growing Bulgarian menace remained fruitless: in 811 the terrible khan Krum annihilated the army of the emperor Nicephorus I, and in 813 he laid siege to Constantinople.

The Bulgars did not control all the Balkan Slavs. The tribes that had settled in Greece remained independent until they were reabsorbed by Byzantium from about the year 780 on, while the northwestern part of the peninsula was occupied by the Serbs and Croats, of whose early history very little is known. Yet the Bulgars constituted a grave threat: they had a good military organization and were established at a short distance from Constantinople, unimpeded by any physical barriers.

Toward the middle of the ninth century a number of important developments occurred almost simultaneously on the international scene. First, a Russian state was formed along the waterways linking the Baltic with the Black Sea: as in the case of Bulgaria, the leadership was provided by a small foreign elite, the Scandinavian Vikings, while the population was Slavic. By 860 the Russians, too, were attacking Constantinople. Second, a short-lived entente was formed between Bulgaria and the German Empire, which was interested in extending its dominions toward the east. Third, Byzantium scored its first decisive victory against the Arabs in Asia Minor and was thus free to intervene more actively in European affairs. The Byzantine response to this new situation took the form of diplomacy and religious propaganda. To counteract the German threat, a mission headed by Sts. Cyril and Methodius was sent to faraway Moravia in 863. The following year the Bulgarian khan Boris was pressured into receiving baptism in the Orthodox Church and opened his country to an influx of Byzantine clergymen.

Even if the mission to Moravia failed in its immediate objectives, it proved to be a landmark of immense importance in the history of eastern Europe. It was, indeed, for this purpose that St. Cyril had invented a Slavonic alphabet and began the task of translating the Bible, the liturgy, and other essential texts. After Cyril's death in 869, Methodius kept the mission alive in Pannonia (wherever exactly this may have been), and then his disciples, led by Clement and Naum, migrated to Bulgaria, where they were enthusiastically received by King Boris. In the reign of the latter's son Simeon (893–927), who proved, incidentally, a highly dangerous enemy of Byzantium, Slavonic letters experienced their first flowering. At the two centers of the kingdom, Preslav in the east and Ohrid in the west, an impressive body of literature was translated from the Greek—the basis of a heritage which eventually was shared by all Orthodox Slavs.

I do not have to relate here how the Bulgarian kingdom collapsed after the reign of Simeon's feeble son Peter (927–69), how it was revived for a short time by Samuel, who fixed his capital at Ohrid, and how it was ruthlessly conquered by the emperor Basil II. By 1018 Bulgaria was no more; its lands were divided into a number of Byzantine provinces and, instead of a Bulgarian patriarch, a Greek archbishop was installed at Ohrid. His cathedral church, St. Sophia, still stands as a reminder of this wave of enforced Byzantinization.

The conversion of pagan Russia took a longer time to achieve. The first Byzantine mission, sent out soon after 860, met with little success. It was only a hundred years later, after the second (or possibly third) Russian attack on Constantinople had failed, that a member of the Scandinavian dynasty of Kiev, the princess Olga, accepted baptism in 957. Finally, in 989 her grandson Vladimir adopted Christianity as the official state religion and was allowed to marry the sister of Basil II, the same emperor who is remembered for the annihilation of Bulgaria. It so happened that, as Bulgaria was about to succumb, Russia came forward to receive the Cyrillo-Methodian heritage of Slavonic letters.

By these steps Bulgaria and Russia fell under the cultural domination of Byzantium. In both countries the foreign elite—Turkic in the former, Scandinavian in the latter—was soon absorbed by the Slavic population; and since the language of the Slavs was not, as yet, sufficiently differentiated, a single idiom of religion and culture—the Church Slavonic of the Cyrillo-Methodian mission—prevailed throughout a vast area, which extended from the Baltic to the Black Sea and from the Black Sea to the Adriatic. The conversion of the Serbs to Orthodox Christianity appears to have taken place at about the same time as that of the Bulgarians, but it passed almost unnoticed. It was not until the twelfth century that an important Serbian state emerged.

For the sake of convenience, the monuments that are discussed in this chapter have been divided according to present-day political

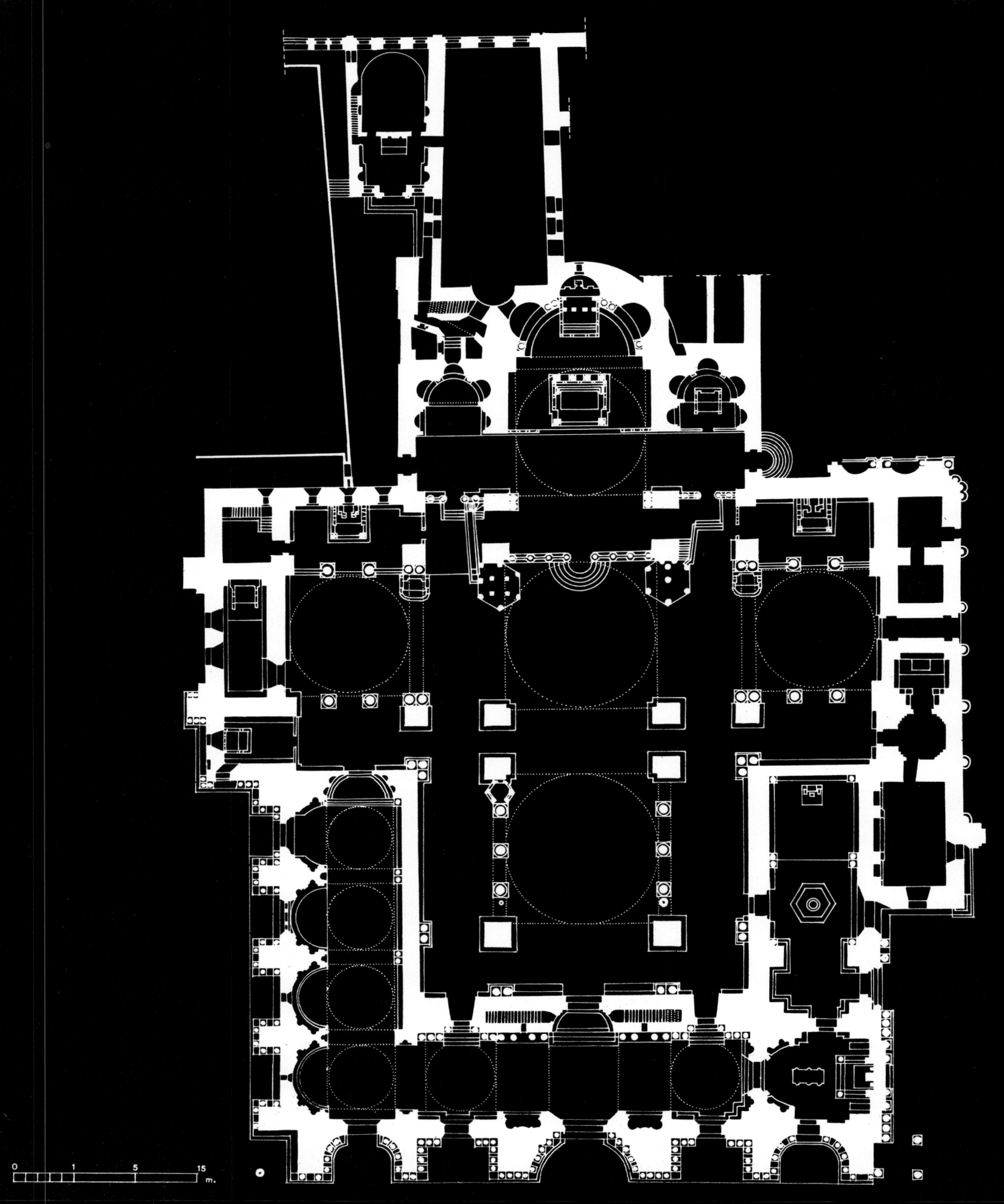

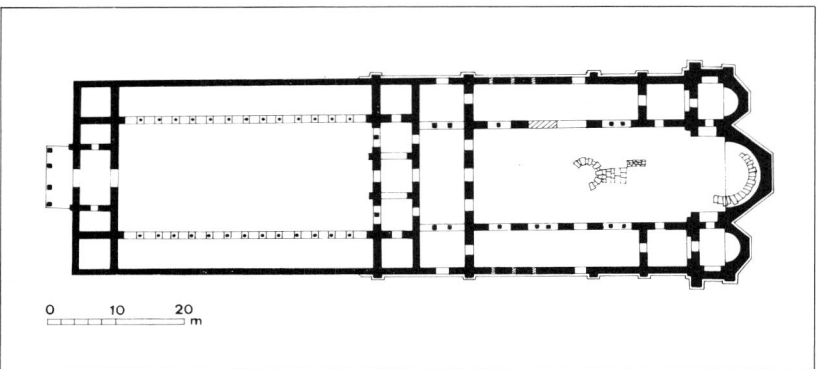

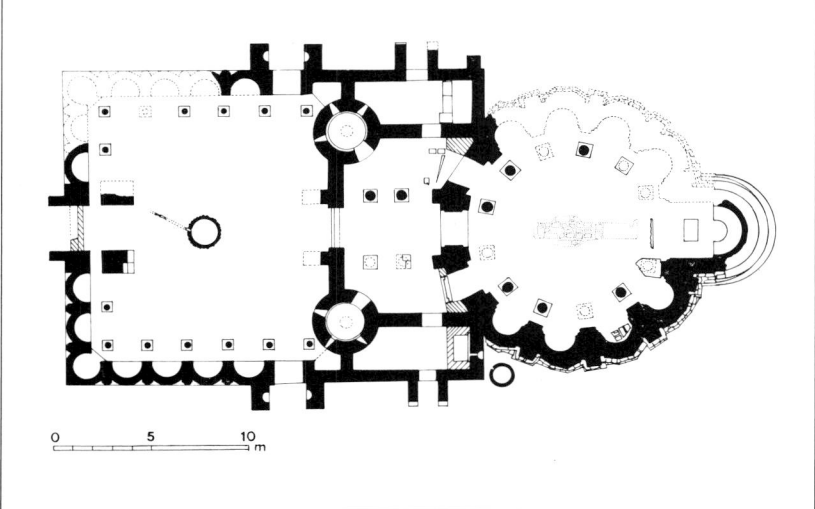

boundaries. It goes without saying that such a division is often misleading; any other form of classification would lead, however, to equal if not greater confusion. Consider the single case of Ohrid. This town was part of the Bulgarian kingdom in the second half of the ninth century and in the tenth century; it became Byzantine in 1018; in the thirteenth century it reverted to Bulgaria and then, once again, to Byzantium; it was taken by the Serbian king Dušan in 1334, subsequently occupied by the Ottoman Turks, and after several centuries of Turkish rule is now in Yugoslavia. Are we then to say that the cathedral of St. Sophia belongs to Byzantine art insofar as it is a building of the mid-eleventh century, but to Bulgarian art in any earlier elements it may incorporate? That St. Clement's should be classed as Byzantine because it dates from 1295, while St. Nicholas Bolnički is Serbian because it was built after Dušan's conquest? Or should we label all of these monuments "Macedonian," irrespective of whichever kingdom happened to be in power? The only sensible course, it seems to me, is to disregard the fantasies of modern nationalism and let the monuments speak for themselves. If they do not deviate from the Byzantine canon, they should be called Byzantine; only when they exhibit an appreciable number of distinctive traits is there any reason to attribute them to a national school.

1. *Bulgaria*

The medieval history of Bulgaria is marked by its discontinuity: short periods of glory alternated with much longer ones of obscurity. From the conversion of King Boris in 864 only one century elapsed until the downfall of the First Bulgarian Kingdom in 969, and nearly half of this century, namely, the reign of Peter (927–69), was a time of decline. The short-lived kingdom of Samuel at Prespa and Ohrid (987–1018) left, of course, no durable trace. After this, Bulgaria disappeared for two centuries. The Second Bulgarian Kingdom, centered on Trnovo, was a by-product of the decomposition of the Byzantine Empire shortly before the Fourth Crusade. For a few years, under John Asen II (1218–41), it dominated the Balkans; thereafter it lost its importance and vegetated until it fell to the Turks in 1393.

Of the two periods of Bulgarian prominence on the historical scene, the earlier one (ninth to tenth centuries) is potentially of some interest in the history of architecture. I say "potentially" because the evidence is puzzling and inconclusive. It can be taken for a fact that the Slavic tribes knew no architecture when they settled in the Balkan peninsula; it is also extremely unlikely that the Onogur Bulgars—who, in the seventh century, migrated from the mouth of the Volga to that of the Danube—should have brought with them any architectural tradition. And yet we are asked to believe that these same Bul-

327. *Preslav, Round Church, interior looking west.*
328. *Preslav, Round Church, reconstructed model, Museum, Preslav.*

gars, by the year 800, started building great palaces and cities and, after 864, great churches, which, moreover, did not resemble contemporary Byzantine monuments, while displaying a remarkable similarity to those of the sixth century. If true, this phenomenon would indeed be of considerable interest.

Controversy has centered especially around two archaeological sites that represent the early Bulgarian capitals of Pliska and Preslav. Pliska, identified with the former Turkish village of Aboba, has been under investigation since 1899.[3] It comprises a vast area of 9 square miles, trapezoid in shape, protected by an earth bank and a moat, within which is a much smaller (120 acres) quadrangular *castrum* enclosed by a stone wall with round corner towers. Within the *castrum* are the substructures of various buildings, including those of a large basilican hall (89 by 164 feet) that has been called a throne room and, presumably, those of a pagan temple that was later turned into a church. The biggest monument of Pliska is, however, a basilica situated outside the *castrum*: including a long colonnaded atrium, it measures 99 by 325 feet. As far as one can judge from the standing ruins, which rise to a maximum height of 6 1/2 feet, this was not a very elegant building. The nave was separated from the aisles by unevenly spaced piers as well as columns, somewhat after the manner of St. Demetrius at Thessalonica. The column shafts, bases, and capitals were of different sizes and design and so must have been spolia. On the longitudinal axis of the nave stood a circular ambo, and there was a synthronon in the apse.

The construction of the basilica was attributed by its first excavators to the ninth century because of a number of commemorative and funerary inscriptions that were found in it. These inscriptions, however, pertain to the second and third decades of the ninth century, when the Bulgars were still pagan; in other words, they have no bearing on the date of the basilica. There can be, of course, no question that the early Bulgars dwelt at Pliska; yet there appears to be no compelling reason for crediting them with the principal buildings, namely, the *castrum,* the "throne room," the pagan temple, and the basilica, all of which would fit much more comfortably in the Late Roman and Early Byzantine periods. The technique of construction, the sculptural fragments, and the great number of stamped Roman bricks that have been found on the site all point in the same direction. In this way the great basilica takes its place alongside other basilicas of the fifth and sixth centuries, like those of Mesembria[4] and St. Sophia at Sofia,[5] which survived the invasions and may even have been repaired in the Middle Ages.[6]

Preslav, the city which King Simeon (893–927) chose as his capital, presents a problem that appears at first sight to be analogous

329. *Mesembria (Nesebŭr), St. John the Baptist, exterior from the south-east.*

330. *Mesembria (Nesebŭr), St. John Aleitourgetos, exterior from the northeast.*

303

331. *Asenovgrad (Stanimaka), Church of the Virgin, exterior from the south.*

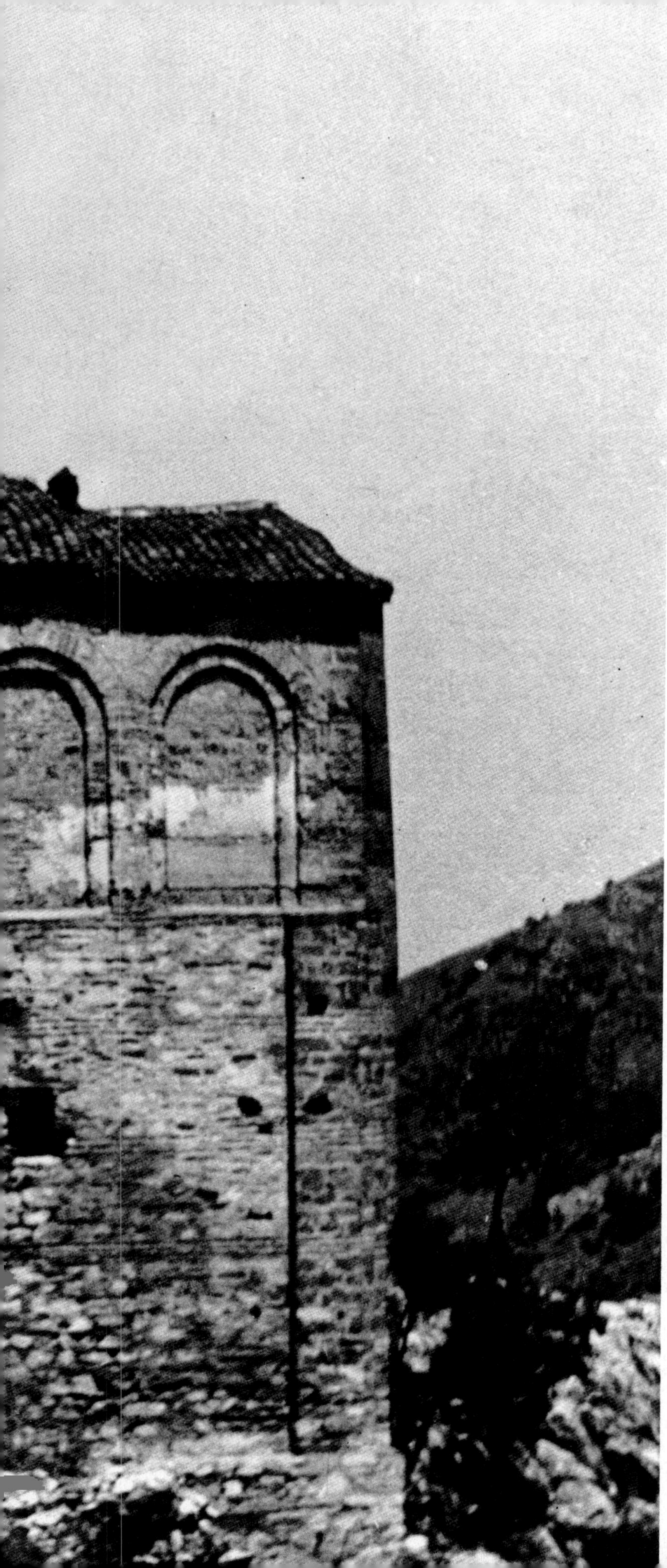

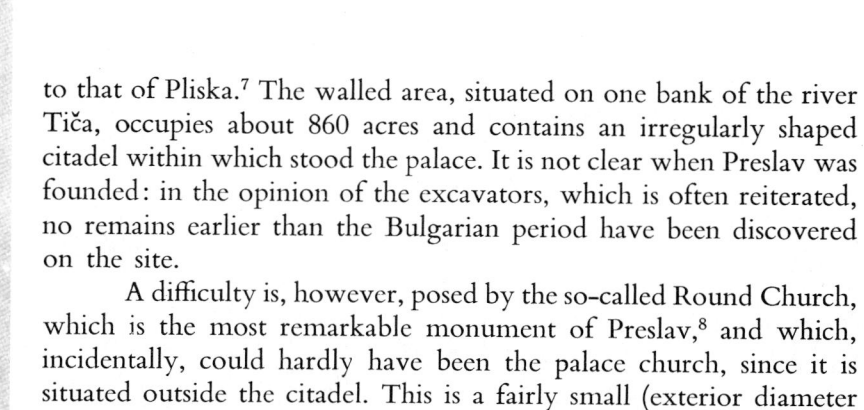

to that of Pliska.[7] The walled area, situated on one bank of the river Tiča, occupies about 860 acres and contains an irregularly shaped citadel within which stood the palace. It is not clear when Preslav was founded: in the opinion of the excavators, which is often reiterated, no remains earlier than the Bulgarian period have been discovered on the site.

A difficulty is, however, posed by the so-called Round Church, which is the most remarkable monument of Preslav,[8] and which, incidentally, could hardly have been the palace church, since it is situated outside the citadel. This is a fairly small (exterior diameter 49 feet), twelve-sided rotunda with radiating niches and projecting apse. The niches were separated by pilasters, in front of which were placed marble columns; upon this ring of columns the dome must have rested. The central space of the nave was occupied by a monumental ambo. Three doorways to the west gave access to a deep narthex provided with two corner turrets, which must have contained spiral staircases leading to an upper floor. The narthex opened into an atrium whose walls, like those of the church, were also enlivened with niches. A great variety of ornamental elements were recovered from the excavation of the church: carved cornices, inlaid colonettes and frames, mural mosaic, and, in particular, glazed tiles bearing both abstract and figural decoration. The accepted date of the church (c. 900) is appropriate for much of this ornament, which bears a close resemblance to that of Fenari Isa Camii at Constantinople; yet the architectural form appears to be alien to contemporary Byzantine practice, while it recalls a category of funerary and religious monuments of a much earlier period (fourth to sixth centuries). At first sight, then, the problem is the same as at Pliska: how is it that the Bulgarians, recently converted to Christianity, adopted building forms that had been in abeyance for several centuries in Byzantium, namely, the basilica and the rotunda?

Several explanations have been offered. Some scholars have simply affirmed that the Round Church was of the sixth century, and that it was restored and redecorated about the year 900.[9] Others, assuming the later date, have argued for a persistence of Early Christian forms in the Balkans, that is, for a local tradition uninterrupted by three centuries of barbarian occupation; or, alternatively, for a conscious return to early designs, a kind of Bulgarian "renascence." The first solution appears to be untrue, if the available archaeological evidence can be trusted; the other two are highly improbable on historical grounds.

In looking for a more realistic explanation, we ought to consider the following propositions: the case of the basilica at Pliska need not be similar to that of the Round Church, that is, the former may

be Early Christian, the latter medieval; the decoration of the Round Church was modeled on the latest Constantinopolitan fashions; King Simeon was educated at Constantinople in the 870s and 880s, and thus in the reign of Basil I; the columns of the church are of Proconnesian marble and, even if the shafts could have been reused, the bases were certainly made to order; the builders responsible for the Round Church must have been either imported from Constantinople or recruited among the numerous captives taken in Thrace (where, incidentally, there was a sizable Armenian colony), or both. In other words, if the Round Church dates from about 900, its model could have come only from Constantinople. Even if no such model has survived, we happen to know that a similar church was put up in the Great Palace by Basil I at the very time when Simeon was residing in the capital. It was the church of the prophet Elijah, which was circular, had seven *bemata* (chancels), and some kind of curved passages, probably an ambulatory.[10] This Constantinopolitan church may itself have been inspired by Armenian buildings, since the polygonal plan with radiating niches was, as we have seen, current in Armenia in the seventh century and was revived, once more, in the tenth to the eleventh. The Armenians, however, did not use internal columns, so that this feature must have been added at Constantinople before it was copied at Preslav.

A considerable number of smaller churches that have been excavated in the immediate vicinity of both Pliska and Preslav belong, for the most part, to the cross-in-square type and demonstrate that the Bulgarians did indeed use contemporary Byzantine formulas. It may also be said that all subsequent architecture on Bulgarian soil, down to the fourteenth century, is also predominantly Byzantine and does not show any consistent stylistic traits that would permit us to speak of a national school.

We shall content ourselves with a visit to the picturesque town of Mesembria (Nesebŭr), situated on a peninsula jutting out into the Black Sea. In fact, this "Bulgarian Ravenna," as it has been called, remained during the greater part of the Middle Ages in Byzantine hands, except for brief periods when it passed under Bulgarian control, as in 812–c. 864, 1308–23, 1328–31, and 1333–66.[11] The period of its greatest prosperity, connected with the development of the Black Sea trade under Genoese auspices, occurred in the fourteenth century, when most of the preserved churches were built. The earlier monuments comprise, in addition to the fortifications, the Old Metropolis (sixth century) and the church of St. John the Baptist (tenth or eleventh century), a cross-in-square on piers, with barrel-vaulted aisles. The exterior, built of coursed rubble, is almost unadorned and is marked by an unusually tall drum, perhaps the result

of a later heightening. The later churches, those of St. John Alei-tourgetos, Pantocrator, St. Theodore, St. Paraskeva, and Sts. Michael and Gabriel, are distinguished, on the other hand, by their exuberant exterior decoration and are closely related to the Palaeologan monuments of Constantinople, Thessalonica, and the Apokaukos church at Selymbria (Silivri), now, unfortunately, destroyed.[12]

St. John Aleitourgetos, a four-column, domed church of which only the lower part remains standing, had the richest exterior decoration—checkerboard, herringbone, zigzag as well as two rows of corbel table inspired by Romanesque models. The Pantocrator, also a four-column church of somewhat elongated shape, is particularly notable for the square belfry that surmounted its narthex, a feature that is found in the earlier church of the Virgin at Asenovgrad (Stanimaka), probably of the thirteenth century, and which must have come, ultimately, from the West, perhaps by way of Serbia.[13]

2. *Yugoslavia*

Within the boundaries of modern Yugoslavia, Byzantine monuments and monuments more or less marked by Byzantine inspiration extend, on a north-south axis, from Belgrade to the Greek border. This territory formed part of the Early Byzantine Empire, was occupied by various Slavic tribes in the sixth and seventh centuries, passed in part under Bulgarian control, was regained by Byzantium in the reign of Basil II, and was lost again, piecemeal, between the eleventh and the fourteenth century. Consequently, there are in

Yugoslavia, especially in Yugoslav Macedonia, monuments that are purely Byzantine—some of the early period, like those of Stobi and Heraclea Lyncestis (near Bitola); others of the middle period, like St. Sophia at Ohrid (mid-eleventh century), the tetraconch church of the Virgin Eleousa at Veljusa near Strumica, dated 1080, the monastery of St. Panteleimon at Nerezi near Skopje, founded by the imperial prince Alexius Comnenus in 1164; finally, a few of the Palaeologan period, like St. Clement (originally dedicated to the Virgin Peribleptos) at Ohrid of 1295. These buildings form an integral part of the history of Byzantine architecture and should be distinguished from those that were erected under Serbian auspices.

The basic classification of Serbian churches was established by Gabriel Millet[14] and has remained valid to this day. Millet distinguished between three schools: that of Rascia (Raška), that is, Old Serbia, corresponding historically to the kingdom of Stephen Nemanja and his successors between about 1170 and 1282; that of "Byzantine Serbia," marked by the glorious reigns of Milutin (1282–1321) and Stephen Dušan (1331–55), when Serbia expanded into the valley of the Vardar and became for a short time the dominant power in the Balkans; finally, that of the Morava, which corresponds to the period of the dismemberment of Dušan's Empire down to the surrender to the Turks of the castle of Smederevo on the Danube in 1459.

The kingdom of the Nemanids, being of the Orthodox faith, was naturally open to Byzantine influences, but its economic ties were mostly with the West through the coastal cities of Ragusa (Dubrovnik), Cattaro (Kotor), and Scutari (Shkoder). Hence, there was a mingling of currents. We should also remember that the last thirty years of the twelfth century and the beginning of the thirteenth witnessed on all sides the shrinkage of the Byzantine world and corresponding gains made by the Latin West. The Serbs did not have far to look: Durazzo and Thessalonica fell to the Normans in 1185, and less than twenty years later the Empire of Constantinople was dismembered. At the same time, important Romanesque churches were going up on the Dalmatian coast, at Zadar, Trogir, and Kotor. These developments are accurately reflected in the architecture of the school of Rascia, which arose rather suddenly and without, it would seem, any preliminary gestation.

The first religious foundation of Stephen Nemanja, the ruined church of St. Nicholas at Kuršumlija (c. 1168), may almost be called a Byzantine monument. It has the unencumbered, single-nave interior and large dome which Comnenian architects strove to achieve; typically Byzantine recessed arches and triple windows; and, most notably, the "recessed-brick technique" that was current at Con-

334. *Nerezi, Monastery of St. Panteleimon, church, exterior from the north.*

335. *Kuršumlija, St. Nicholas, ground plan (after A. Deroko, 1962).*
336. *Kuršumlija, St. Nicholas, exterior from the south.*
337. *Ohrid, St. Clement, exterior from the southeast.* ▷

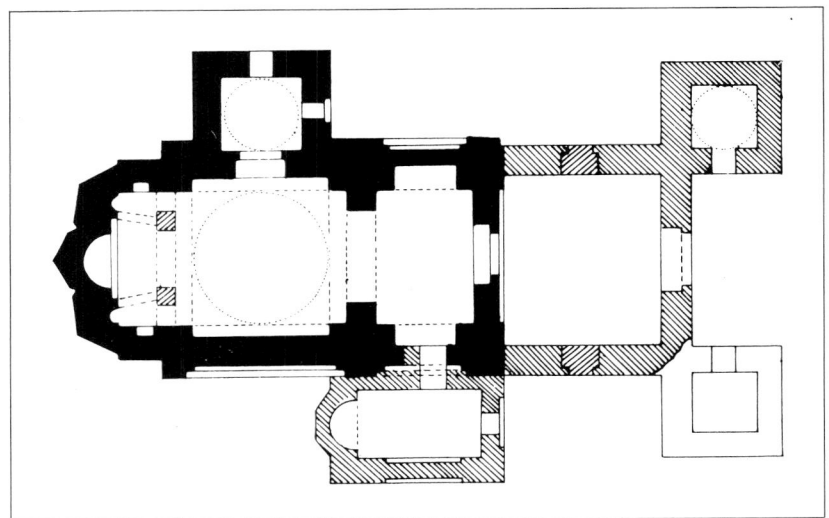

338. *Studenica, Church of the Virgin, ground plan (after V. Korać).*
339. *Studenica, Church of the Virgin, exterior from the southeast.*

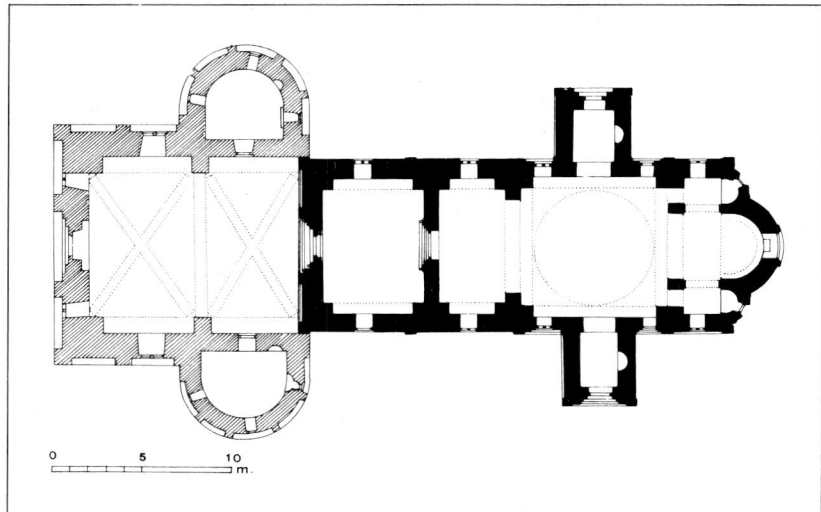

stantinople in the eleventh and twelfth centuries. Yet here already we notice some details that were foreign to the Byzantine tradition and subsequently became typical of the school of Rascia: the "rib arch," which interrupts the transition from the central square to the bema vault, and the lateral porch, in this case only on one side, but in other Serbian monuments attached to both sides of the church. The basic plan of St. Nicholas remained dominant in Serbia for the next hundred years, whereas its treatment in elevation showed an increasing influx of Romanesque forms, introduced by craftsmen from the Adriatic coast.

Already in the contemporary foundation of Durdjevi Stupovi (the Pillars of St. George), near Novi Pazar,[15] we find a false arcade on columns inside the drum of the dome and two tall towers flanking the west facade. A few years later, in the church of the Virgin at Studenica, a foundation of the same king, built after 1183,[16] the plan is still the same, except for the addition of a deep narthex. However, the exterior, built of dressed stone, has taken on the aspect of a longitudinal Romanesque church with a continuous gabled roof covering the nave and the narthex, except for the cubic mass of the dome bay. Particularly noteworthy are the carved portals, the apse window, and the exterior corbels, all purely Romanesque work.

While remaining faithful to the same general scheme—the single-nave interior, the lateral porches sometimes transformed into a low, closed transept, the cubic dome base that rises above the gabled roof, the "rib arches" which separate the central square from the barrel vaults of the bema and the western bay of the nave—the school of Rascia developed in the direction of taller, slenderer proportions. It is enough to compare Studenica with Sopoćani of about 1250,[17] and especially Arilje, between 1290 and 1307,[18] to notice the desire of raising the dome as high as possible on a successive series of arches that overhang, stepwise, the diminished central space. A belated product of the Rascian school is the monastery church of Dečani (1327–35), built for King Stephen Dečanski by a Dalmatian Franciscan, Vita of Kotor. This is a vast five-aisled pile faced with alternating bands of light and dark marble, like many cathedrals of northern Italy.[19] Except for the tall dome rising on its square base and the overpowering profusion of frescoes, nearly everything is Western here—portals, windows, ribbed vaults, and columns.

Dečani was, however, a throwback; for in the reign of Milutin, Serbia reoriented itself toward Byzantium. By force of arms the kingdom expanded into Macedonia; and in 1299, when Milutin married the infant Simonis, the daughter of the Byzantine emperor Andronicus II, he received as her dowry the territory he had already conquered, north of a line running from Ohrid to Prilep and on to

340. *Sopoćani, monastery church, exterior from the southwest.*

341. *Dečani, monastery church, exterior from the southwest.*
342. *Ohrid, St. Sophia, outer narthex from the west.* ▷

343. *Prizren, Church of the Virgin Ljeviška, ground plan (after S. Nenadović, 1963).*

344. *Prizren, Church of the Virgin Ljeviška, exterior from the west.*

345. *Staro Nagoričino, St. George, exterior from the southwest.* ▷

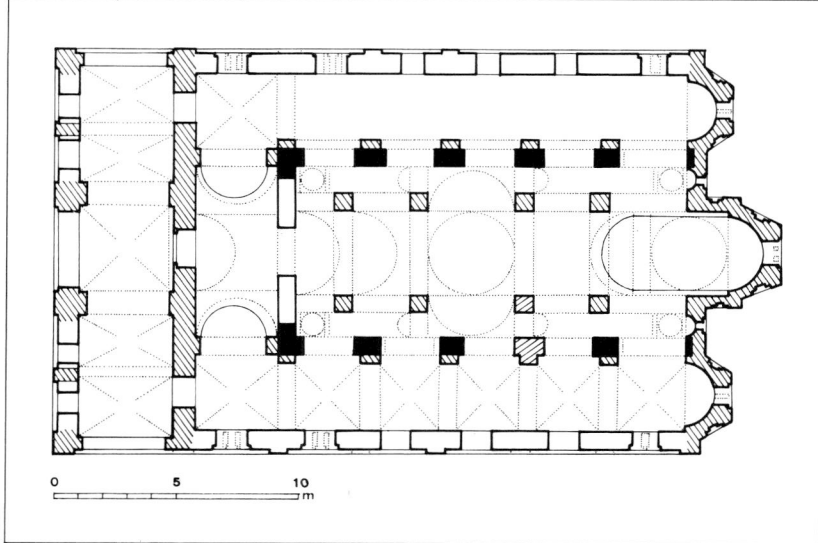

Štip. This exalted match also contributed to a Byzantinization of the Serbian court. Stephen Dušan (1331–55) continued and accelerated the occupation of Byzantine territory. In 1345, after conquering all of Macedonia as far as the Nestos River, he assumed the title of "Emperor of the Serbs and Greeks" and created his own patriarchate, thus repeating the ambitious design of Simeon of Bulgaria more than four centuries earlier. Then he pushed into continental Greece as far as the Gulf of Volos.

Builders and architectural models were naturally taken from the conquered territory. At Ohrid, in particular, important work had been in progress shortly before the Serbian occupation: I have already mentioned St. Clement's, built in 1294–95 by a Byzantine official, Progonos Sgouros; in addition, the outer narthex of St. Sophia, with its elegant portico facade and twin domes, was erected in 1313–14. We happen to know that the gifted painters who decorated St. Clement's, Michael Astrapas and Eutychius, went on to work for the Serbian king and left their signatures in some of the churches we are about to review.

I shall confine myself to four major foundations of Milutin. The church of the Virgin Ljeviška at Prizren, dated 1306–7, was built within the shell of an earlier three-aisled basilica.[20] Eight piers were erected inside the preexisting nave to support a central dome and barrel vaults arranged crosswise, somewhat after the manner of St. Sophia at Ohrid. The four tiny domes placed at the corners are for exterior effect only and do not relate to the system of supports. The most interesting feature of the church is, however, the graceful arcaded porch or outer narthex surmounted by a tall belfry. In this porch is a painted inscription detailing the amounts of flour, salt, and wine that were to be provided to the master builder Nicholas and the master painter Astrapas, presumably the same who had worked ten years earlier at Ohrid.

A similar problem was met in the church of St. George at Staro Nagoričino near Kumanovo (1312–13), which likewise incorporates the walls of an earlier basilica, clearly visible on the outside up to the level of the windows.[21] Here, too, a cruciform system of barrel vaults and five domes (the corner ones being nonfunctional) was superimposed upon the earlier shell, with the difference that the western bay was partitioned off to serve as a narthex. The method of cloisonné masonry and the external decoration of geometric patterns, dentils, and quatrefoil earthenware tubes have more analogies in Greece than in either Thessalonica or Constantinople.

While Prizren and Staro Nagoričino could have been the work of Byzantine builders, this cannot be said of Milutin's last foundation, Gračanica (c. 1318–21), where the Byzantine forms have been put to

346. *Gračanica, monastery church, exterior from the northwest.*

347. *Gračanica, monastery church, ground plan (after G. Bošković, 1930).*
348. *Mount Athos, Chilandar monastery, general view.*

an entirely new use. To obtain a soaring effect, the architect has, so to speak, doubled the formula: instead of placing the central dome directly upon a cruciform structure of barrel vaults, he has made two such structures, a lower one extending to the outer perimeter, and an upper one that is shorter and is set upon the first. Moreover, the upper system of barrel vaults has pointed arches, which create the illusion of an upward thrust. The reduplication of the barrel vaults has necessitated the doubling of the internal piers—eight instead of four. Even the little corner domes have been raised above the roof line on cubic pedestals.

Among Milutin's foundations, one more deserves special mention, namely, the *katholikon* of the Chilandar monastery built in 1303 on Mount Athos. Setting aside the exonarthex, added in the last quarter of the fourteenth century, this as yet imperfectly studied monument appears to be a purely Byzantine work and one of the highest quality. It has the traditional Athonite plan, that of a triconch with four columns placed in the corners of the nave. The spacious proportions and the construction technique suggest that the architect came from either Thessalonica or Constantinople. Avoiding any kind of subsidiary chapels or ambulatory, he built a deep narthex (the present inner narthex), supported on two columns and crowned by two domes. This may not have been an entirely original idea, but it proved to be an influential one. Because of its special association with the royal house of Serbia and the sanctity of Mount Athos, the Chilandar church was to leave a lasting imprint on subsequent Serbian architecture.

The great artistic achievements of Milutin's reign in both architecture and painting were not followed up under his more glorious successor Dušan: this is a paradox that has not yet received ¬ adequate explanation. Dušan's principal foundation, the monastery of the Holy Archangels near Prizren (1343–49), in which he was buried, was, unfortunately, demolished a long time ago, and only its foundations have survived. Its *katholikon* had a conventional cross-in-square plan with four massive piers and was probably crowned by five domes. While the architectural design was Byzantine, the decorative elements in stone, that is, the portal, windows, and corbels, were purely Western—partly Romanesque, partly Gothic. The church was renowned for its inlaid pavement, which included fantastic animals and panels of interlace.[22] Another royal foundation, that of Matejić, near Kumanovo, begun by Dušan and completed by Queen Helena after 1355, is, once again, a spacious but rather conservative five-domed church, more interesting for its extensive fresco decoration than for its architecture. A number of smaller, one-domed monastic churches built by the king's vassals, such as St. Michael's

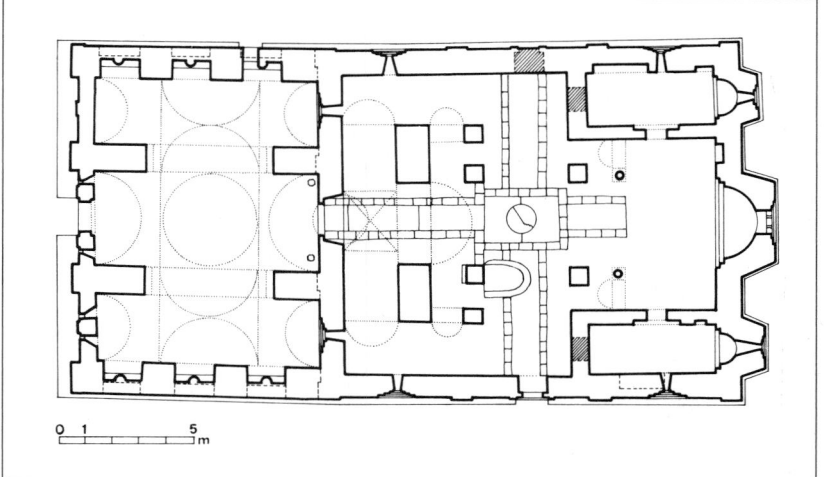

at Štip (c. 1332), Ljuboten (1337), and Lesnovo (1341), illustrate the separatist tendencies which led to the disintegration of the ephemeral "Empire of the Serbs and the Greeks."

After Dušan's death there did not remain in the Balkans a single Christian state powerful enough to withstand the advance of the Turks, who, by about 1365, had established their capital at Adrianople. In 1371, the same year when the Serbian despot of Serres was defeated by the Turks on the Maritsa, the Nemanid dynasty became extinct. The central part of its inheritance, the old land of Rascia, passed to Prince Lazar, who assumed the struggle against the

349. *Monastery of the Holy Archangels, near Prizren, reconstruction of south facade (after S. Nenadović, 1967).*

350. *Matejić, near Kumanovo, Church of the Virgin, exterior from the west.*

351. *Ravanica, Church of the Ascension, exterior from the north.* ▷

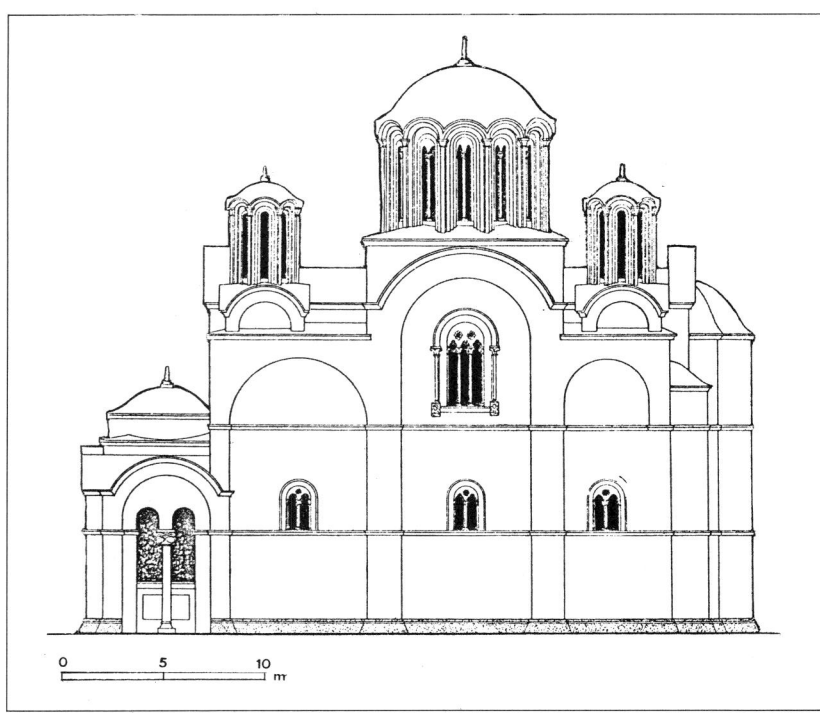

◁ 352. *Kruševac, Lazarica, exterior from the southeast.*

353. *Kalenić, Church of the Virgin, exterior from the southeast.*
354. *Kalenić, Church of the Virgin, detail of a mullioned window.*

Turks until he lost his life on the field of Kosovo in 1389. The Serbs now became vassals of the Turks and would, no doubt, have shared the same fate as the Bulgarians if it were not for Tamerlane's unexpected invasion of Asia Minor, which prolonged for another half-century the life of both Byzantium and Serbia.

The melancholy chronicle of this period should not overshadow the fact that the Serbian principality was still very prosperous and was able to put up a number of sumptuous buildings, at any rate in the reigns of Lazar (1371–89) and Stephen Lazarević (1389–1427). The "school of the Morava"—the rubric under which Millet has grouped the last monuments of medieval Serbian architecture—is an extension of the "Byzantine Serbian school," with the further addition of stone sculpture liberally applied to the exterior.[23] Such was the prestige of Mount Athos, in which the Serbian rulers continued to show a lively interest, that the trefoil plan became, so to speak, obligatory, but the structure itself was reinterpreted along the soaring lines of Gračanica.

A few examples will have to suffice. At Ravanica, the burial place of Prince Lazar, we have a five-domed church (c. 1375) whose central dome rests on freestanding round piers. As at Gračanica the corner domes are raised on square pedestals. The masonry is Byzantine—alternating courses of stone and brick—but to the patterns of tiles and earthenware tubes have been added carved archivolts and window frames, even one perforated rose window on the west facade. At the Lazarica of Kruševac, Prince Lazar's court chapel (c. 1377–78), these decorative tendencies are carried further. A smaller church, it has only one dome and no internal supports, but the narthex is surmounted by a massive belfry. Taller than the belfry, the main dome rests on a square base upon which arches have been applied on the exterior, thus reproducing the scheme of Gračanica. The rose windows have been multiplied and the carving made more exuberant.

We find similar effects at Ljubostinja, built by the princess Milica after 1387, and especially at Kalenić (1413–17), which looks almost like a *bonbonnière*. The origin of the Morava carving, consisting of different kinds of tightly knit interlace, or rinceaux and fabulous animals, and almost totally lacking any sacred character, has not yet been satisfactorily explained: many scholars have traced it to the East, that is, to Russia, even Armenia and Georgia.[24] It has, in any case, little connection with contemporary Western art. Finally, at Resava (Manasija), the principal foundation of Stephen Lazarević, which was built between 1406 and 1418 and still retains its character of a fortress, we return to the structure of Ravanica and to a plain stone facing of the walls, the work, it is said, of masons from Herzegovina. In its simple yet elegant dignity, Resava provides a suitable conclusion to the history of medieval Serbian architecture.

355. *Resava (Manasija), monastery, view from the southwest.*

356. *Kiev, Tithe Church, ground plan of foundations (after M. K. Karger, 1958–61).*

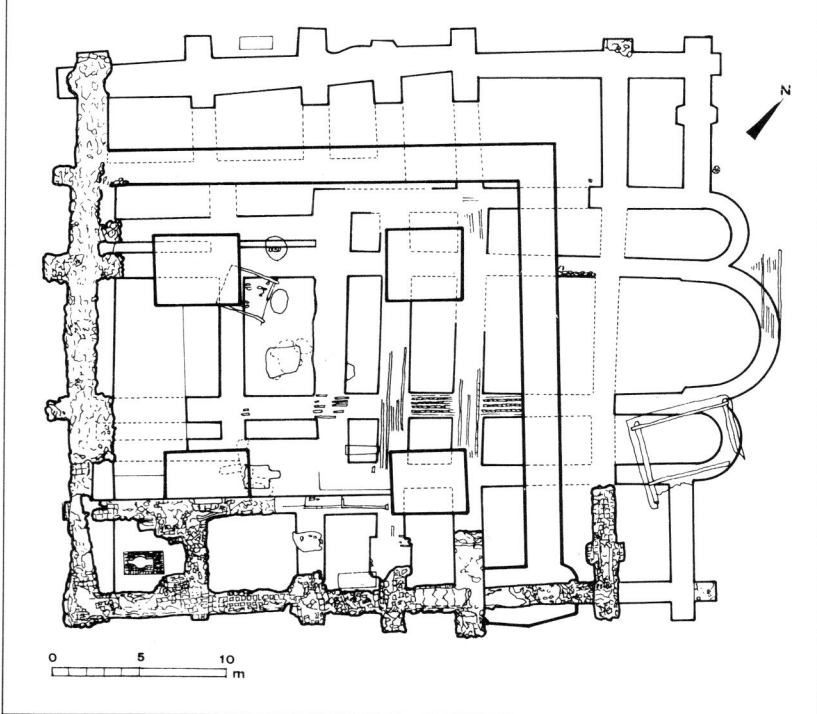

3. *Russia*

Masonry buildings were unknown in Russia until the conversion of Prince Vladimir of Kiev in 989. Dwellings, fortifications, and, presumably, pagan temples were built of timber or timber and earth. The earliest recorded masonry structures were the so-called Tithe Church (Desjatinnaja Cerkov') and the adjoining palace at Kiev. Unfortunately, very little remains of either. The Tithe Church, completed by Greek masters in 996, was destroyed by the Tartars in 1240. After prolonged archaeological investigation, the plan of its foundations has been recovered, but there is still considerable disagreement concerning the form of the superstructure.[25] What can be stated with reasonable assurance is that the church was of the cross-in-square type with a central dome about 20 feet in span and 3 apses to the east; that it had a gallery; and that at a slightly later date a wide ambulatory was added on the north, south, and west sides of the church, so that the total area of the complex, excluding the apses, measured about 110 by 122 feet. It is important to note that the superstructure was built of brick laid in the Constantinopolitan "recessed" technique, which continued to be generally used at Kiev throughout the eleventh century. The interior decoration included carved marble slabs, frescoes, and a pavement of *opus sectile,* composed of different kinds of colored marble.

Remains of palaces have been found on three sides of the Tithe Church. These, along with the church, were probably the only masonry buildings in Vladimir's Kiev, a small town (maximum dimension about 550 yards) situated on a hill overlooking the Dnieper and defended by an earth bank. Vladimir's son Jaroslav the Wise extended the town to about six times its original area, and at the center of it he built the cathedral of St. Sophia to serve as the seat of the metropolitan of Russia. The imitation of Constantinople is evident not only in the name of the cathedral but also in those of other structures of Jaroslav's reign, such as the neighboring monastery of St. Irene and the Golden Gate, which guarded the town on the south side.

St. Sophia, the biggest and most sumptuous building that was put up in Russia until the end of the fifteenth century, was begun in 1037 and completed sometime in the 1040s.[26] It suffered very heavy damage, especially in the seventeenth century, and was then rebuilt in the Baroque style, so that its exterior aspect has been drastically altered. Thanks to prolonged investigation, however, the original form of the church can be visualized with reasonable accuracy. Its core is a regular cross-in-square, but instead of the usual three naves it has five, as well as five apses to the east. The outermost naves as well as the westernmost division of the interior were surmounted by a gallery. The internal supports consisted of twelve cruciform piers, while the gallery was upheld by three pairs of octagonal piers, a pair on each side except for the east. Thirteen domes, arranged in a pyramidal formation, crowned the structure, which was further surrounded by an open single-storied ambulatory. The total area covered by the building was about 99 by 128 feet. Toward the end of the eleventh century a further ambulatory, wider than the first, was added on the north, south, and west sides of the building and provided with two asymmetrically placed staircase towers to give access to the gallery. The interior decoration, in addition to the famous mosaics and frescoes, included a marble chancel screen and a pavement of *opus sectile* of the same general conception as that of Christ Pantocrator at Constantinople.

Various opinions have been expressed with regard to the art-historical character of St. Sophia. Some scholars have considered it as a purely Byzantine work; some have discovered in it traces of Romanesque influence; others have argued that the main inspiration came not from Constantinople but from the Caucasus; and still others have claimed it as a local product, influenced, to be sure, by Byzantium, but expressive of the national spirit, Russian or Ukrainian, as the case may be. For my part, I fail to see any feature of St. Sophia that is not Byzantine: the masonry technique, the plan, the pyramidal arrangement of the domes, the recessed arches, the discreet use of meander patterns on the exterior, and every detail of the interior decoration are not only Byzantine but specifically Constantinopolitan. In saying this I do not wish to imply that Constantinople can provide a carbon copy of the Kievan St. Sophia.

Certain differences do exist between the latter and the very few churches of the eleventh century that have survived at Constantinople, but these differences, far from implying any exotic influence, can best be explained by the practical problems that had to be overcome. The first problem was that of materials. The brick, we know, was manufactured locally, the stone came from local quarries. The marble, on the other hand, had to be imported. This explains the absence of marble columns, a commodity which, as we have seen, was scarce enough at Constantinople; even if they could have been procured, their transportation to Kiev would have posed enormous difficulties. Instead of using columns, the architect built masonry piers, some of which have a "clustered" form: this, too, was known at Constantinople (witness St. George of the Mangana) and does not betoken either Romanesque or Caucasian influence.

The second and greater problem was that of size. St. Sophia was meant to be the metropolitan church of Russia and was commissioned by the ambitious ruler of a rapidly developing state: con-

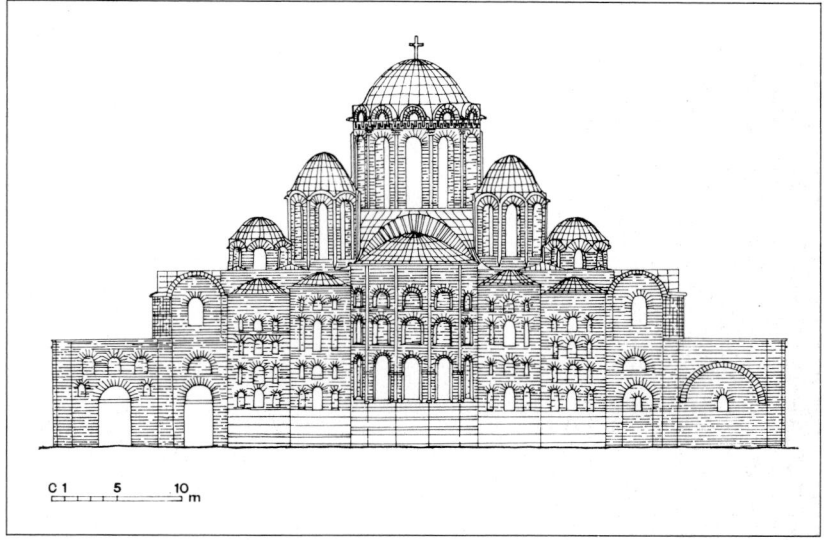

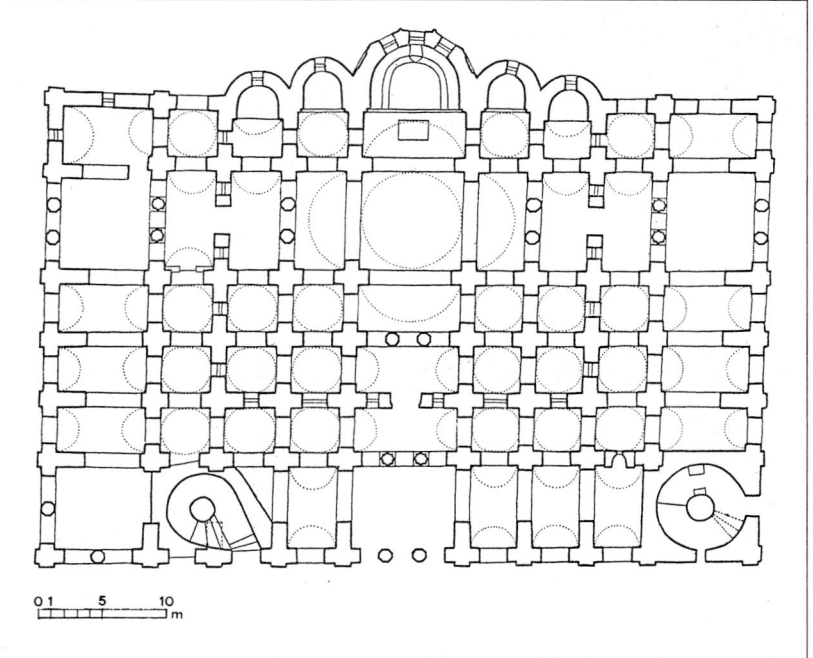

361. *Kiev, Monastery of the Caves, Church of the Dormition, reconstructed ground plan (after M. K. Karger, 1961).*

362. *Černigov, Cathedral of the Transfiguration, exterior view of apses.*

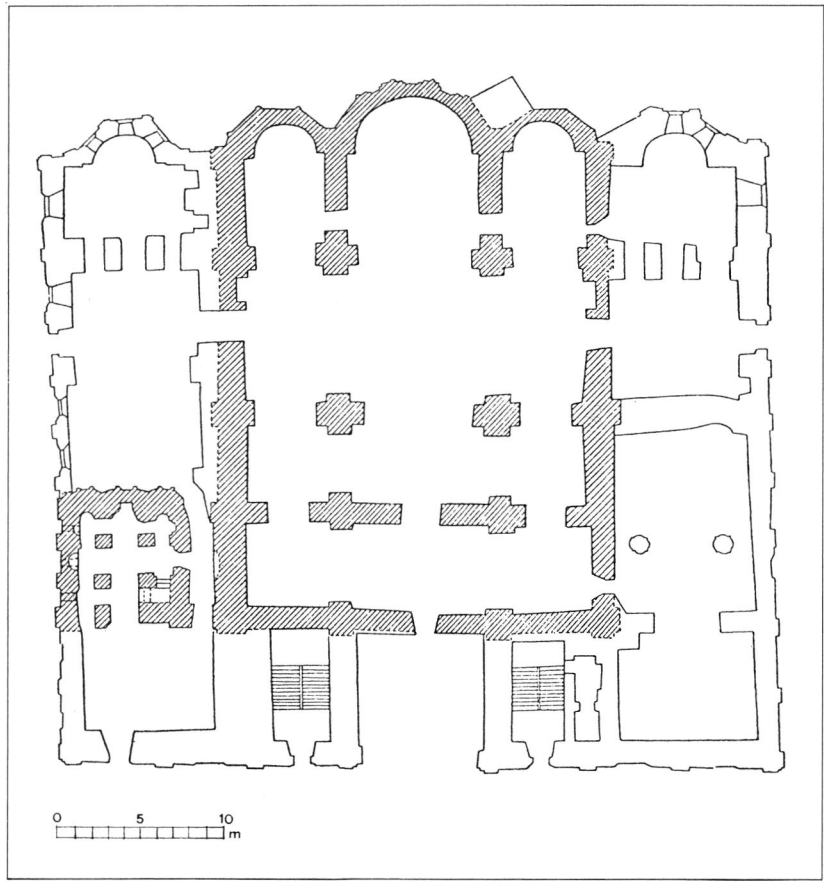

sequently it had to be big. Herein lies the explanation of whatever peculiarities St. Sophia possesses. Not only was its Byzantine architect working in an alien milieu with materials that were either improvised or laboriously imported; he was also required to erect a building much bigger than any he had put up at home.

The solution he adopted was to multiply rather than to enlarge forms that were familiar to him. He built a dome 25 1/4 feet in diameter (exactly double the size of the dome of the north church of Fenari Isa Camii), that is, about as big as he could on the basis of his experience. Given this dimension, a three-aisled, five-domed church of what must have been normal Constantinopolitan type would not have attained the desired size. So he simply added two more aisles and an extra transverse compartment to the west. Having enlarged the width of the building, he had to heighten it in proportion. It is not particularly important for us to know whether the five-aisled plan was current at Constantinople: no example of it has survived, although in the north church of the Fenari Isa Camii we have a five-apsed building.[27] Nor is it very significant whether any church at Constantinople had as many as thirteen domes. What we should like to stress is simply that the form of St. Sophia could have been devised by a Byzantine architect on the basis of dimensions and concepts that were familiar to him, whether or not exactly the same solution had earlier been applied in the capital.

St. Sophia was the biggest but not the only building of its time at Kiev: several others, such as the metropolitan's palace, the Golden Gate, and the churches of St. Irene and St. George (the latter two known from documentary evidence), were put up by Jaroslav. It goes without saying that this vast architectural enterprise—which entailed the manufacture of hundreds of thousands of bricks, the quarrying of enormous quantities of stone, and the preparation of lead sheets for roofing—could not have been carried out without training a local labor force. From this time onward the Russians had, at Kiev, their own construction workers educated in Byzantine methods. Gradually they became capable of working without foreign guidance.

When we glance at the other churches that were built in the Kievan realm in the eleventh century—such as the cathedral of the Savior at Černigov (c. 1036), St. Sophia at Novgorod (1045–50),[28] and several at Kiev, for example, the *katholika* of the Vydubickij monastery, the monastery of St. Michael, and the monastery of the Caves (Pečerskaja Lavra)—we can see that Byzantium gave to Russia basically one, all-purpose form of church, namely, the cross-in-square, which could be used in a number of variants. At its simplest, it had three aisles, four piers, and one dome; by fusing the nave with the narthex, a more oblong, six-pier plan could be obtained; or else the core of the church could be surrounded on three sides by an ambulatory, thus producing the effect of a five-aisled church.

It is interesting to observe that Russia did not borrow from Byzantium either the triconch plan, which was certainly coming into vogue in the tenth century, or the octagon on squinches, which was introduced in the early eleventh. Indeed, one may say that there was only one major infusion of Byzantine architectural concepts into Russia, namely, in the period 990–1070, and that this infusion was confined to the cross-in-square type I have described, a type that remained constant until the Muscovite period. After the eleventh century the Russians did not keep up with Byzantine architectural developments but were content to elaborate on the one traditional form and so produced what may properly be called a national style of architecture. In the realm of painting the situation was quite different: for just as the mosaics of St. Sophia at Kiev embody the contemporary Byzantine style (perhaps not at its best), so the Byzantine style of the twelfth century is reflected, say, in the frescoes of the Mirožskij monastery at Pskov, and the Palaeologan style is expressed in the works of Theophanes the Greek at Novgorod and Moscow. Painting, however, was more readily exportable: one itinerant Greek master could convey the latest Byzantine fashions to the farthest confines of Russia. Architecture, on the other hand, demanded a continuous organization of labor and expertise, and once this had become native, it pursued its own course, clinging faithfully to the initial Byzantine formula, while gradually reinterpreting it so as to produce a result that was unmistakably Russian.

It is, perhaps, rather naive to ask at what precise stage Byzantine architecture gave way to Russian architecture. If my views are correct, St. Sophia at Kiev was designed by a Byzantine. It is also recorded that the Dorimtion church of the monastery of the Caves—the most important monastery of Kievan Russia, built in 1073–77—was the work of Byzantine masters. This, too, was a cross-in-square church, but its stylistic traits remain obscure, since it was drastically remodeled in the seventeenth century and completely destroyed in 1941.[29] It would be reasonable to assume that as a result of the vast architectural activity of Prince Jaroslav the Wise there was formed a sufficient body of qualified local builders who were responsible for the majority of churches erected after the middle of the eleventh century.

We may take as an example St. Michael's at Kiev, founded in 1108, which is sufficiently well recorded, although it was barbarously demolished in 1935–36.[30] Byzantine masters certainly took part in the decoration of this church, as evidenced by the famous mosaic of the

329

Communion of the Apostles that was placed in its apse, but the architecture, though very close to Byzantine models, appears to have been local work. Note the flat surface of the cylindrical drum of the dome, unbroken by engaged pilasters, the clumsy fenestration, and the treatment of the facades, whose arched divisions are nearly of the same height, whereas a Byzantine architect would normally have given greater emphasis to the central one. This last feature was to remain traditional in Russia for a long time to come.

In the course of the twelfth century the principality of Kiev was gradually losing importance because of the fragmentation of its possessions among members of the ruling house and increasing pressure from the peoples of the steppe. Political superiority now passed to northeast Russia, the area between the Volga and Oka rivers, situated astride an important trade route and protected by dense forests from the depredations of the steppe nomads. In addition to the town of Rostov, which is recorded already in the ninth century, a number of other urban centers grew up here—Suzdal', Vladimir, Perejaslavl'-Zalesskij, and Moscow. The principality of Vladimir-Suzdal', as it is called, naturally had a different geographical orientation from that of Kiev—on the one hand, toward Novgorod, on the other, toward the Bulgars of the Volga and the Caucasus. Molded by these factors, there developed in Vladimir-Suzdal' an architecture that may be called specifically Russian.[31]

The continuity with the Kievan tradition is obvious. If we consider one of the earliest monuments of the northeastern group, the church of the Transfiguration at Perejaslavl'-Zalesskij, founded in 1152, we find in it the familiar Kievan ground plan and basic organization of the elevations, although the general effect is very different. The difference (discounting the onion dome, which is not original) is due, in the first place, to the building material: instead of brick it is limestone, carefully squared and laid on very thin mortar joints. The proportions are also different: the elimination of the narthex has produced a cubic mass that tapers very slightly toward the top. The windows are fewer and narrower than in the Kievan churches, almost like slits. The sparseness of the exterior decoration—limited to a corbel table at the top of the apses and a crenellated border at the summit of the drum—contributes to produce an effect at once simple and powerful, despite the small size of the church (50 1/2 by 51 1/2 feet, discounting the apses). It is obvious that this very assured architecture was not of local origin. The limestone was imported from afar (allegedly from the land of the Volga Bulgars), while the craftsmen came almost certainly from Galič, a town that was open to influences from farther west, hence the Romanesque character of the corbel table.

Prince Andrej Bogoljusbkij (1157–74) attempted to raise his

capital, the city of Vladimir, to first rank in Russia and to make it the seat of a metropolitan bishopric. To this end an elaborate legend was invented whereby the Virgin Mary, represented by the miraculous Byzantine icon of Our Lady of Vladimir, assumed the protection of the city, and a new feast, that of the Protective Veil (Pokrov), was instituted. In other words, Andrej was not only trying to emulate Kiev, but he was looking beyond Kiev to Constantinople itself, the city which, above all others, claimed the Virgin Mary as its patron. During Andrej's reign there was great architectural activity in and around Vladimir. The walled area of the city was tripled and provided with monumental gates, one of which, the Golden Gate, has survived in a greatly altered condition. To emphasize his allegiance to the Virgin Mary, he built the great cathedral of the Dormition between 1158 and 1160. This building, which was to assume a symbolic importance in the subsequent development of Russian architecture, has not survived in its original form: burned down in 1185, it was reconstructed on an enlarged, five-aisled plan by Prince Vsevolod III from 1185 to 1189. Andrej also built for himself at a short distance from Vladimir the castle of Bogoljubovo, begun in 1158. Surrounded by a stone wall, this was a remarkable ensemble, containing a palace linked to a church by means of a raised passageway rather like a covered bridge on arches. Part of this passageway, including a staircase tower, still survives, but the church was completely rebuilt in 1751.

To gain a firsthand impression of the architectural achievement of Andrej's reign, we must visit the famous church of the Pokrov on the Nerl' River near Vladimir (c. 1165). Built on an artificial stone platform of pyramidal shape, this small but elegant church strikes us today by its unencumbered cubic shape with accentuated vertical articulations. Its original aspect must have been, however, rather different, since the church was surrounded on three sides by an open ambulatory, probably one story high, that gave access to the gallery. Even without this ambulatory the building has an entirely finished appearance. We may notice certain details that were to gain wide currency in Russian architecture: the deeply recessed Romanesque portals, the division of the facades into two zones by a band of blind arcading supported on ornamental colonettes, and the introduction of exterior sculpture. This sculpture, limited to the lunettes, is here rather restrained and repeats on three sides an identical theme, that of David playing the harp among the animals.

If we compare the church of the Pokrov with that of Perejaslavl'-Zalesskij, which is only ten years earlier, we can see the trend toward greater ornateness that was fostered by Andrej Bogoljubskij. His palace church at Bogoljubovo must have been even more sumptuous, and we know that it was paved with sheets of brass—an

367. *Bogoljubovo, near Vladimir, reconstruction of palace church (after N. N. Voronin, 1961–62).*

368. *Church of the Pokrov on the Nerl' River, near Vladimir, reconstruction of exterior from the southwest (after N. N. Voronin, 1961–62).*

369. *Church of the Pokrov on the Nerl' River, near Vladimir, west facade.*

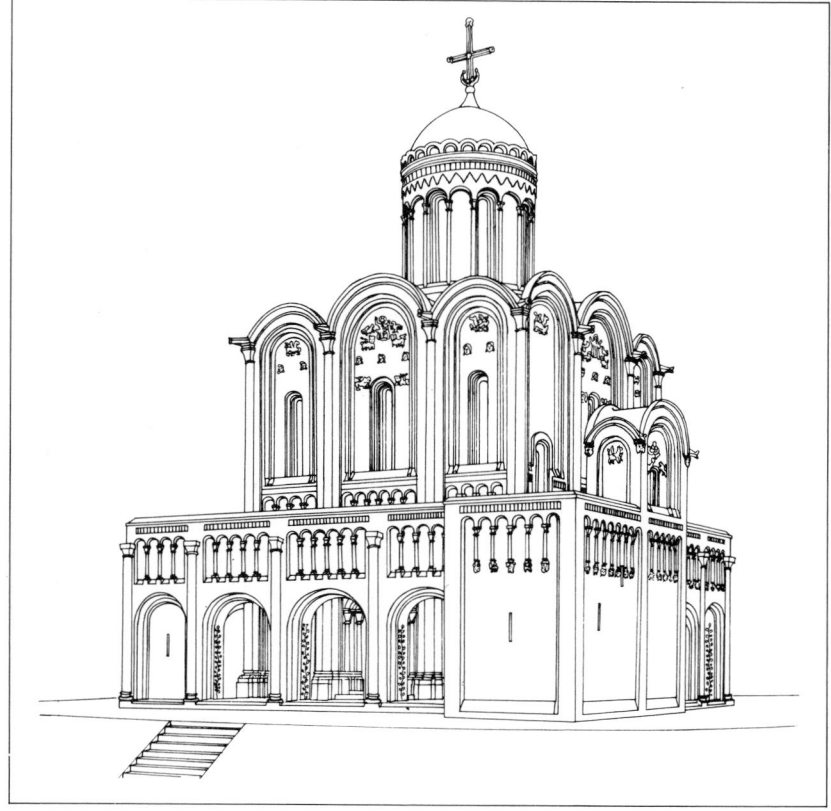

innovation in those days. To realize his ambitious schemes, the prince invited craftsmen from "every land," including Germans. The presence of these foreigners explains the numerous Romanesque elements in the architecture of Vladimir-Suzdal', but it can hardly account for the very characteristic figural sculpture which we find for the first time in the original phase of the Dormition cathedral and which attains an extraordinary richness in the palace church of St. Demetrius, built at Vladimir by Vsevolod III between 1193 and 1197.[32] This is a fairly small building, and in plan it is practically a carbon copy of the Pokrov. On the outside its walls are plain up to the zone of the arcade on colonettes, but from there upward they are covered by a continuous carpet of sculpture whose repertory includes a few Christian subjects but is, for the most part, secular. This is clearly a princely art, and though many analogies may be found with it in mosaics (such as those of the Norman Stanza at Palermo), in metal-work, textiles, and illuminated manuscripts, a similar treatment of facades cannot be found either in western Europe or in the Caucasus.

The last stage in the evolution of the Vladimir-Suzdal' style is provided by the church of St. George at Jur'ev-Pol'skij (1230–34), which is preserved to about half of its original height, the upper half having been rebuilt after its collapse in 1471. This almost square, four-pier church with three outer porches (one cannot help being reminded of St. Sophia at Trebizond) is deservedly famous for its carved decoration, which entirely covered the exterior from the ground up. The decoration was of two kinds: from the arcaded zone upward it was in fairly high relief and included a number of complex Biblical compositions, whereas the lower zone, instead of being left plain, as in the church of St. Demetrius, was carpeted with a continuous rinceau ornament in very low relief which even invaded the engaged columns, setbacks, and archivolts of the portals.

The reconstruction of the upper part of the church is naturally hypothetical, but the view has been expressed[33] that it may have had the towerlike form that is characteristic of several Russian churches of the very end of the twelfth and the beginning of the thirteenth century. This interesting innovation did not pertain to a single region, since it manifested itself almost simultaneously at Černigov (Pjatnica church), at Smolensk (church of St. Michael), Ovruč (church of St. Basil),[34] Polock (Spaso-Efrosin'jev monastery), and as far north as Novgorod (Pjatnica church "in the market"). While the ground plan remained the traditional one, an effort was made to accentuate the verticality of the facades and to raise the dome as high as possible. This was achieved in the Pjatnica church at Černigov (c. 1200) by building the four arches under the dome at a higher level than the barrel vaults of the cross-arms. The dome base, instead of having the normal

372. *Jur'ev-Pol'skij, St. George, exterior.*
373, 374. *Jur'ev-Pol'skij, St. George, north porch.*

cubical shape, was also arched on each side, so that the external effect is that of a pyramid of arches rising in three steps one above the other. The introduction of this new, soaring style is linked by Soviet scholars to the growing importance of towns and of the urban bourgeoisie. However that may be, it was not allowed to develop: the Tartar invasion of Russia in the 1230s put an effective end to almost all architectural activity. Southern and northeastern Russia were the most cruelly devastated: only in the west (Galič-Volyn') and in the extreme north (Novgorod-Pskov), that is, in regions not occupied by the Tartars, could architecture continue, but even in those parts it did so on a reduced scale.

The next significant step came a hundred and fifty years later in the principality of Moscow, which assumed the political and architectural heritage of Vladimir-Suzdal'. Settled sometime in the twelfth century, Moscow was at first a small fort at the confluence of the Moskva and Neglinnaja rivers. From about 1300 on, its territory began to expand rapidly at the expense of surrounding principalities. In 1326 the metropolitan of Russia moved to Moscow and, on this occasion, the first stone church was built—the cathedral of the Dormition, which may have resembled in plan the church of St. George at Jur'ev-Pol'skij. In 1366–67 the older wooden fortifications were replaced by the stone wall of the Kremlin. From the 1390s date the Kremlin churches of the Annunciation (of which only the basement remains) and of the Nativity, a small four-pier structure preserved to about one-third of its original height.

The nature of Muscovite architecture comes into sharper focus from about 1400 on, thanks to a number of churches that are still standing in more or less their original form. These are the Dormition church at Zvenigorod (c. 1400), the church of the Savva (Savvino-Storoženskij) monastery close to the same town (1405), the church of the Sergius (Troice-Sergiev) monastery at Zagorsk (1422) and of the Andronikov monastery in Moscow (1425–27)—the latter two made famous by the painter Andrej Rublev, who took part in their decoration. All of them are nearly square structures with three projecting apses, four internal piers, and one dome. Each side, except the eastern, is pierced by a recessed portal of degenerate Romanesque design, topped by an ogee archivolt. Each church in this group is placed on a podium so that the portals are reached by flights of stairs. Another innovation consists of a band of flat carving that is often set halfway up the facades in the same place as the blind arcading of the Vladimir-Suzdal' school. The roof line has been altered in all of the above monuments: originally it appears to have been fairly complex, with a succession of superimposed ogee arches imitating the same effect that was sought two centuries earlier by the architect of the Pjatnica church at

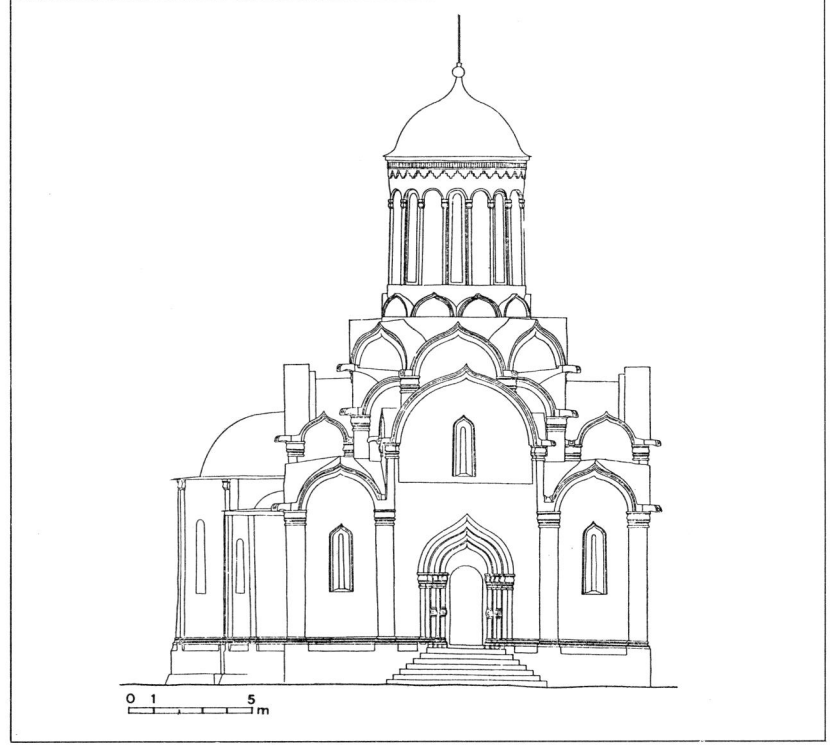

Černigov but without achieving the same bold verticality. Interesting as these churches are in the perspective of the great destiny that was awaiting Moscow, they are in themselves modest, provincial, and frankly retrospective.

Indeed, the insufficiency of this architecture became apparent when, in the second half of the fifteenth century, Muscovy became not only a European power but also, after the fall of Constantinople, the only Orthodox power in the world. In assuming the role of the Third Rome, it needed a new architectural expression. For this it turned not to Byzantium but to its own past and, in so doing, sought, paradoxically, the help of Italian architects. The immediate reason for this new departure was provided by the Dormition cathedral of Moscow. The original building of 1326 being by 1470 in a precarious condition, the czar Ivan III decided to build a larger one after the model of the Dormition cathedral of Vladimir. A local architect was engaged, but in 1474, when the new church was nearly finished, it suddenly collapsed. Convinced of the ineptitude of Muscovite builders, the czar instructed his ambassador in Venice to engage the services of a capable Italian architect. The choice fell on Aristotele Fioravanti of Bologna, who at the time enjoyed a considerable reputation as an engineer and who, it is said, had just declined an invitation from the sultan Mehmed II to build a seraglio at Istanbul.[35]

In the new cathedral of the Dormition, which he built between 1475 and 1479, Fioravanti showed himself to be not only an ingenious technician but also an able artist. He, too, was instructed to imitate the venerable cathedral of Vladimir and this he did, but what he produced was not a slavish replica. He borrowed the basic forms—the five domes, the six internal piers, the arched articulations of the exterior, the belt of blind arcading on colonettes—and subjected them to a regularization that was in the spirit of the Renaissance. All the internal bays were made square and equal, whereas in the original the central bay was, naturally, the largest; the piers of the nave received a round instead of a cruciform shape; the external divisions of the facades were given equal width and equal height; the projection of the apses was minimized to achieve a nearly flat effect; and the zone of blind arcading was integrated with the lower row of windows. By means of these subtle touches Fioravanti was able to fuse the forms of medieval Russian architecture with those of an Italian palazzo.

Fioravanti was not the only Italian architect who was active in Moscow about the year 1500. The Faceted Palace (Granovitaja Palata) was the work of Pietro Antonio Solario and Marco Ruffo; while another major church in the Kremlin, that of St. Michael, which was to serve as the mausoleum of the reigning dynasty, was built in 1505–9 by Alevisio or Aloisio, known as Novyj, that is, "the

378. *Cozia, monastery church, exterior from the southwest.*
379. *Dealu, monastery church, exterior from the north.*

Younger." While borrowing some details from Fioravanti, Alevisio reverted to the traditional division of the interior into a wider nave and narrower aisles, separated by rectangular piers. The most noteworthy feature of his building is, however, its exterior decoration. The vertical facades are treated like those of a two-story Italian palace: the pilasters are provided with Corinthian capitals; the narrow windows are given false rectangular frames to make them look wider; an emphatic horizontal cornice runs at the springing of the arches, while the arches themselves are filled with huge carved scallop shells. The effect is both picturesque and incongruous.

An observer of the year 1500 might well have supposed that Muscovy was about to be drawn into the cultural orbit of western Europe and would adopt Renaissance architecture as one tangible manifestation of this cosmopolitan trend. The Russians, however, were not ready for such an experiment. They turned back to their own traditions in architecture, first, in a bizarre outburst under the czars Basil III and Ivan IV the Terrible, to a presumably native style of spires and tentlike roofs inspired by wooden buildings (of which the cathedral of St. Basil the Blessed on Red Square is the most famous example); then, by way of reaction, they reverted to the traditional five-dome formula, which continued to be repeated until the advent of the Baroque and European Neoclassicism.

4. *Rumania*

The principalities of Wallachia and Moldavia were the last East European countries to fall under the cultural influence of Byzantium. This happened when, after liberating themselves from Hungarian rule—Wallachia in 1330 and Moldavia in 1365—they assumed a political organization and then petitioned the patriarch of Constantinople to appoint their bishops. The metropolitan of Wallachia, who had his seat at the princely capital of Argeş, was installed in 1359; that of Moldavia, whose prince resided at Suceava, in 1401. It is not exactly known by what steps the Rumanian people were won over to the Orthodox faith, but there can be no doubt that they received their religion not directly from Byzantium but from the southern Slavs. Church Slavonic remained their liturgical language until the end of the seventeenth century.

The two Rumanian principalities were not destined to enjoy their independence for a long time. After the failure of the so-called Crusade of Varna in 1444, Wallachia submitted to the conqueror of Constantinople in 1462. Moldavia kept up a brave resistance under its ruler Stephen the Great (1457–1504) but had to surrender upon his death. Though they became vassals of the Ottoman Empire, the two principalities were not brought under direct Turkish rule but were

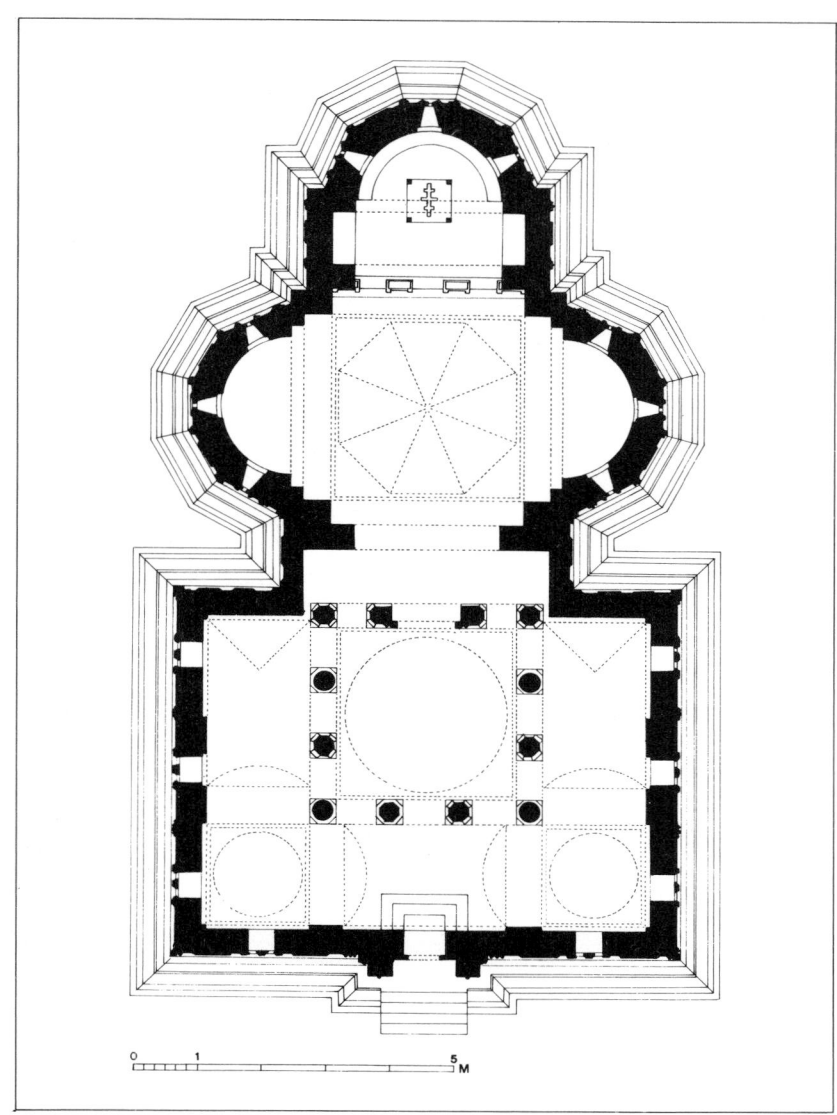

380. *Curtea de Argeş, church of the episcopal monastery, ground plan (after L. Reissenberger, 1867).*

381. *Curtea de Argeş, church of the episcopal monastery, exterior from the northeast, before restoration (after L. Reissenberger, 1867).*

allowed to be governed by their native princes. In fact, it was in the sixteenth and seventeenth centuries that Rumania, thanks to its semi-independent status and its great natural resources, assumed a prominent role in the Orthodox world. The two *hospodars*, as they were called, became the habitual benefactors of the bankrupt patriarchate of Constantinople and of the monasteries of Mount Athos. More and more Greeks, clerics as well as businessmen, migrated to Rumania, where they could count on a better living than they eked out under their Turkish masters. This infiltration continued until the beginning of the eighteenth century, when the native princes were removed from power by the sultan and replaced by Greek governors who exploited the country for the next hundred years. It may be said that until the revolutionary war of 1821 Rumania was the milking cow of the Greek Orthodox Church.

In considering the architectural monuments of Wallachia and Moldavia, which form two quite distinct schools, we must remember that by the second half of the fourteenth century, when the earliest of these monuments was built, the Byzantine capital had ceased to be an architectural center. At that time the only creative school of Orthodox architecture in the Balkans was that of Serbia, but Bulgaria lay closer at hand. It may have been from the latter that builders came to Wallachia to put up the princely church of St. Nicholas at Curtea de Argeş (c. 1350), a fairly large cross-in-square church on square piers.[36] It is marked by the sobriety of its exterior aspect—the walls and even the apses are devoid of plastic effects—and by the unusually small number of windows, which leave a maximum amount of space for the fresco decoration that covers the interior from top to bottom. The influence of Serbia, however, soon made itself manifest. It is said to have been introduced by the monk Nicodemus from Mount Athos, a native of Prilep, who founded a number of monasteries under the protection of the princes of Wallachia. His foundations, which have come down to us in a ruined or highly altered form (Vodiţa near Turnu-Severin, Prislop in Transylvania, and Tismana in Oltenia), are all marked by the trefoil plan, which was to remain dominant in the country. The only reasonably well-preserved foundation in which Nicodemus is said to have taken part is the monastic church of Cozia (1386), which is a pure example of the Morava school not only in its form but also in its carved exterior decoration. Note that here, too, the deep narthex was probably surmounted by a tower.

The fifteenth century is practically a blank in the architectural history of Wallachia. By contrast, the first two decades of the sixteenth were marked by considerable building activity under the princes Radu the Great (1495–1508) and Neagoe Basarab (1512–21) and led to the formation of a curious national style. Two important churches, both

faced with cut stone (an exceptional feature in Wallachia), both, unfortunately, very extensively restored, have come down to us: they are the monastic church of Dealu (1502) and that of the episcopal monastery of Curtea de Argeş, built by Neagoe Basarab. The old metropolitan church of Tîrgovişte of 1517, a vast pile crowned by eight domes, was completely demolished at the end of the last century.

Both Dealu and the episcopal church of Curtea are descendants of the Morava school. It is enough to compare the plans of Cozia and Dealu to see their similarity. The most obvious difference is that, in the latter, two tall domes have been placed over the eastern bay of the narthex. They are very close to the main dome and seem, so to speak, to be huddled together in an unbalanced group. This effect, too, was probably inspired by the close juxtaposition of dome and belfry tower in the churches of the Morava school (for example, Kruševac and Kalenić), a feature which, as we have seen, probably existed at Cozia. Another innovation we find at Dealu is the surface ornament. The facades are divided into two zones by a heavy cornice, and each zone is decorated with blind arcading. In addition, the dome bases and dome drums are covered with a profusion of geometric ornament in flat relief.

These decorative effects are further elaborated in the episcopal church of Curtea de Argeş, "scientifically" restored between 1872 and 1878 by the French architect Lecomte de Nouÿ, who managed to convert it into a Victorian monstrosity.[37] The plan is again a trefoil, but the narthex, placed in a transverse direction, has been enlarged to the point of exceeding the nave in size and has been given an "ambulatory" plan, with a central bay fenced in by twelve columns. The main dome, which is built on squinches, and the dome over the central bay of the narthex are, once again, placed very close together and are nearly of the same height. Two smaller domes, rising over the western corners of the narthex, are spirally fluted in opposite directions and have diagonal slit windows. The organization of the facades is nearly the same as at Dealu, namely, there are two zones divided by a twisted-cord molding. The upper zone is covered with blind arcading, each arch containing a roundel, while the lower zone has been split into rectangular panels.

The profusion of ornament in the episcopal church almost defies classification. It has become customary to see a Caucasian, that is, Armenian and Georgian, influence both in the blind arcades rendered in cut stone and in the panels of carved ornament in low relief.[38] Close as the similarity sometimes is between Caucasian and Wallachian examples, and granted that there was an Armenian colony in Wallachia, it remains to be explained how the decorative scheme of such earlier monuments as the Georgian church of Nikortsminda

(1014) or the church of the Savior at Ani (1036), both of which have been quoted in this connection, could have remained for so many centuries in the consciousness of Caucasian masons. Whatever may be the truth of the matter, much of the ornament of the episcopal church, such as the stalactite cornice under the eaves of the roof and on the base of the main dome, the honeycomb capitals of the narthex, and the spiral fluting of the main domes (often applied to minarets), is clearly Ottoman.

With the episcopal church of Argeş, Wallachian architecture may be said to have attained its own individuality if not its final form. I cannot describe here the scores of churches that were built in the seventeenth and eighteenth centuries, for the most part on the same trefoil plan, and shall instead cast a glance at the churches of Moldavia, which show greater originality and less contact with the Byzantine tradition. This land, at the time when it first appeared on the scene of history—toward the middle of the fourteenth century—was ecclesiastically dependent on Galič and open to Western influences from Poland and Hungary. In fact, the earliest church that has survived in Moldavia, St. Nicholas at Rădăuţi (1359–65), which some authorities ascribe to Bogdan I, is a simple Romanesque basilica adapted to Orthodox usage. It is only after the establishment of the metropolis of Suceava and not earlier than the reign of Stephen the Great that we find the distinctive Moldavian school of architecture which confronts us fully formed, that is, without a preparatory stage during which its peculiarities might have crystallized. It is a great pity that the monastic church of Putna, which was the principal foundation of the reign (1466–81), should have been totally rebuilt in the seventeenth and later centuries.

Among the thirty or so existing monasteries and churches that were built by Stephen,[39] we may choose for consideration that of Voroneţ of 1488. Setting aside the exonarthex, which was added in the sixteenth century, we have before us a plan that is typical of the reign: it consists of a large rectangular narthex or *pronaos* covered by a domical vault, a trefoil nave with a tall dome, and two external buttresses placed between the middle and the lateral apses. There can be no doubt that this is, basically, the Serbian trefoil plan, which, as we have seen, was transmitted to Wallachia in the late fourteenth century. The main difference consists in the vaulting of the nave. In the Byzantine and Serbian systems the arches which support the dome spring from pilasters. In Moldavia the pilasters are suppressed so that the transverse arches go from wall to wall. Having thus increased the lower span of the dome, the Moldavian architect proceeded to diminish it at a higher level. He first made a circular base by means of four pendentives and set a cylindrical drum upon it; then, within

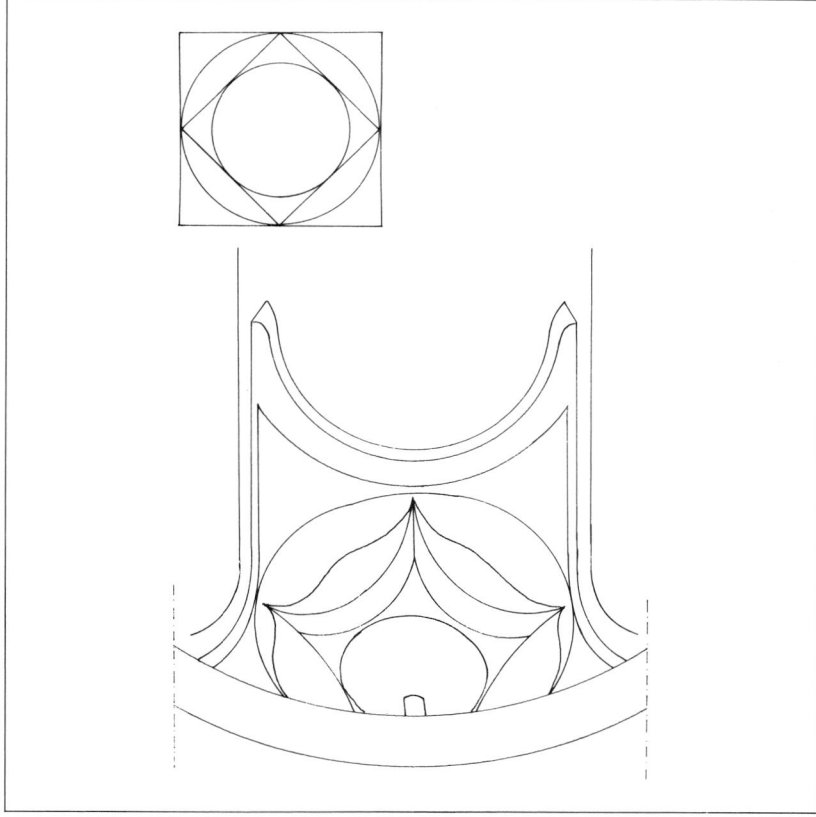

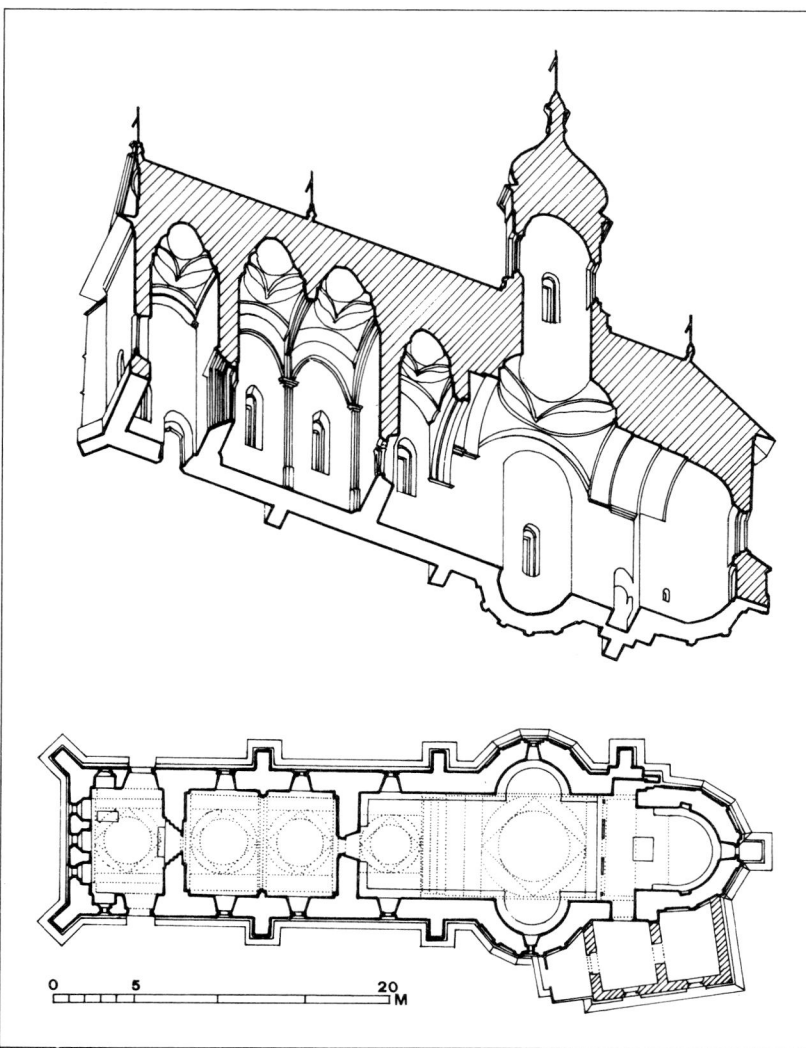

this drum, he made a second set of arches, placed diagonal to the first, so that their springing came directly above the crowns of the lower arches. The upper arches are, once again, joined by pendentives, and upon this diminished base rises a second, very tall cylindrical drum, which is covered by the dome. It is an ingenious, if not a very attractive system which, for an Orthodox church, had the further disadvantage of fragmenting and complicating the surfaces available for internal painted decoration.

The origin of the Moldavian dome has been the subject of much discussion.[40] Since nothing of the kind is found in either Byzantine or Western architecture, scholars have been searching in other directions. The ever-useful Armenians have been pressed into service; so have the Arabs of Spain and even the Assyrians. Yet nothing sufficiently similar has been discovered among those peoples, not to mention a likely means of transmission. The most natural supposition, then, is that the Moldavian dome was devised in Moldavia. The same originality must be claimed for the dome base. In monuments of the true Byzantine tradition this element is cubical, and it encases the internal pendentives; in Moldavia, on the other hand, there are usually two superimposed bases, the lower one square in plan and the upper one star-shaped (sometimes both are star-shaped), and in most cases they are purely ornamental, that is, they do not correspond to anything inside. Even though it is decked out in this fashion, the dome, when seen from the outside, has little organic connection with the rest of the building, which is covered with a steep gabled roof made of timber. The roofs that we see today are relatively modern, and it is admitted that the original ones were more articulated, like the one that has been reconstructed at the cathedral of Suceava; even so, the slender, towerlike domes, which seem to imitate the effect of Gothic spires, must have appeared as an intrusive element. The hybrid character of these churches is further accentuated by their portals, doors, and windows, which are uniformly of Gothic design.

In the largest Moldavian churches, such as that of the monastery of Neamţ (1497) and the cathedral of Suceava (1514–22), the latter being 141 feet long, the ground plan has been considerably elongated both to the east, by the expansion of the bay in front of the apse, and especially to the west: an open exonarthex has been added, the narthex has been divided into two domed bays, and a funerary chamber (which was to become traditional) has been inserted between the narthex and the nave. These several compartments are strung out longitudinally, and each of them is crowned by a little dome that is not apparent on the outside, since they are covered by the steep roof required by the wet climate of the country.

All the distinctive elements of Moldavian architecture were

fully elaborated in the reign of Stephen the Great and continued to be repeated with slight variations for the next century. However, following the transfer of the capital from Suceava to Iaşi (Jassy) in 1564, they began to be modified by a medley of heterogeneous borrowings that were never fused into an organic whole. This decadent trend may be illustrated by the famous church of the Three Hierarchs at Iaşi, built in 1639. Its basic form—that of a triconch preceded by a *pronaos* and an outer narthex—is traditional, but instead of one dome there are two, both of equal height and both raised on clumsy square bases. The entire exterior, which is built of stone, is covered with carved ornament of diverse inspiration: we find here the heavy twisted-cord molding borrowed from Wallachia, the blind arcading on colonettes that must have come from Russia, stylized vases and flowers of an Ottoman flavor, and upward of twenty horizontal bands of geometric ornament—all of this juxtaposed with Gothic doors and windows. It is amusing to note that this piece of "kitsch," made even more vulgar by the ministrations of Lecomte de Nouÿ, was the work of an architect from Constantinople, a certain Ienache Etisi, while the interior was decorated by Russian painters.

It remains to note one feature for which the Moldavian churches are particularly famous, namely, their exterior painted decoration. These are found in a fairly compact group of monuments: the cathedral of Suceava (between 1522 and 1535), Homor (1535), Moldoviţa (1537), Arbore (1541), Voroneţ (c. 1547), Suceviţa (c. 1602–4), and a few more. External paintings were probably more common in Byzantine art than we normally suppose, and it is possible that the idea reached Moldavia via Serbia;[41] in no other Orthodox country, however, do we find exteriors that are entirely carpeted with frescoes, including such enormous and elaborate compositions as the Last Judgment on the west facade of Voroneţ, the Tree of Jesse on the south wall of the cathedral of Suceava, and the Heavenly Ladder on the north wall of Suceviţa. Here we witness the culmination of a trend inherent in the Byzantine tradition: architecture has become subservient to painting; the entire church, inside and out, is merely a framework for exhibiting row of icons.

The foregoing pages have shown that the diffusion of Byzantine architecture in eastern Europe was a complex phenomenon that extended over several centuries and affected, in different ways, the countries in which it took place. Bulgaria, the first of these countries to have fallen under Byzantine influence, never developed a truly distinctive style. Russia received a strong injection of Byzantine architectural forms in the tenth and eleventh centuries and did not ask for a second one—a significant fact to which I shall presently return.

389. Sucevița, monastery, general view.

390. Iași (Jassy), Church of the Three Hierarchs, exterior from the south-west.

391. Homor, monastery church, exterior from the southwest.

Serbia had a brief exposure to Byzantine architecture in the late twelfth century and a more intimate one in the early fourteenth: on the basis of the latter she created her own "school." Finally, Rumania did not come into direct contact with Byzantium but received her Orthodox architectural tradition mostly from the Serbs.

In order to explain the different development of the Byzantine contribution to these countries, we would have, in the first place, to take into account any architectural substratum that may have existed in them. The case of Bulgaria is not altogether clear, for it is recorded that, before the Christianization of the country, the khan Omurtag (814–31) built two palaces for himself, one at Pliska, the other at Silistra.[42] The buildings erected after 864 were not, therefore, the first to have been put up after the barbarian invasions of about A.D. 600; yet in examining the evolution of Bulgarian architecture down to the fourteenth century, it is difficult to detect any trace of a national tradition. In the case of Russia we can confidently say that there was no substratum whatever. In both Serbia and Rumania there was, before the advent of Byzantine influence, some contact with Western architecture—in the former by way of the Dalmatian coast, in the latter by way of Hungary—and this Western element was never completely suppressed.

Byzantine architectural forms were part of a cultural and religious "package," and their adoption was dictated by the king and the ruling class, that is, it was imposed from above. Russia was no more "ready" for Byzantine architecture in 989 than it was for Renaissance architecture in 1500 or for Neoclassicism under Catherine the Great. In the same way Serbia could suddenly switch from the traditions of the Raška school to Byzantine models when the policy of King Milutin made this desirable. In every case, the architecture that was borrowed was contemporary Byzantine architecture, which, evidently, had the value of a "status symbol."

The introduction of Byzantine building methods was normally initiated by Byzantine master builders. After a time native craftsmen acquired enough proficiency to do without their Byzantine mentors, and so local or national schools came into being. We should not imagine, of course, that their subsequent development took place in complete isolation. The institution of itinerant teams of masons was quite widespread in the Middle Ages, both in western and eastern Europe, and provided a means for the dissemination of new ideas. Dalmatian masons worked in Serbia, just as Ruthenian and German masons worked at Vladimir. Their activity can usually be detected by technical and ornamental innovations; it seldom affected the basic design of buildings. Through the agency of both local and external stimuli Byzantine formulas were reinterpreted to produce in Russia, Serbia, and, to a lesser extent, Rumania a series of outstanding monuments that often surpassed the creative potential of the Byzantines themselves. Separate as these developments were, they sometimes showed points of convergence: the same striving for height, achieved by the superimposition of vaulted forms, may be observed at the Pjatnica church of Černigov and a century later at Gračanica.

At the same time we should note that Byzantine architecture did not enjoy in the Middle Ages the same prestige as Byzantine painting. The case of Russia is instructive in this respect. We have seen that after the eleventh century the Russians showed no interest in keeping up with Byzantine architectural developments, and this in spite of the fact that close ties continued to exist between the two countries, that the metropolitans of Russia were usually Greeks, and that Russian pilgrims traveled to Constantinople and a colony of Russian merchants resided there. Yet, when Andrej Bogoljubskij attempted to outdo Kiev and emulate Constantinople, when he claimed for Vladimir the Protective Veil of the Virgin Mary, he did not wish to imitate Byzantine monuments, either contemporary or older. Instead, he had recourse to German masons. "Why," we may ask, "did he not reproduce at Vladimir the basilica of St. Mary of Blachernae (where the miraculous Veil was kept), just as the Venetians had copied, a century earlier, the church of the Holy Apostles? Was it perhaps because Byzantine architecture was no longer considered to be the most impressive in Christendom?"

A final observation. While the Byzantine Church developed a theology of painting, it never developed a theology of architecture. It conferred a symbolic significance on certain features of the church building and especially on items of liturgical furniture: the apse, the bema, the chancel screen, the altar table, and the ciborium. On the other hand, it never prescribed a particular architectural form. It was two centuries after the fall of Constantinople that the zealous patriarch Nikon of Moscow decided that one form of church rather than another was demanded by Orthodox worship. "In conformity with regulative and statutory law," he ordained, "as prescribed by ecclesiastical rules and statutes, churches shall be built with one, three, or five domes, but never in the shape of a tent."

NOTES

CHAPTER ONE

[1]We should note, however, the great folio by W. Salzenberg, *Alt-christliche Baudenk-male von Constantinopel*, published in 1855.

[2]This theme is fully developed in A. Grabar's *Martyrium* (Paris, 1943–46).

[3]J.B. Ward-Perkins, "Memoria, Martyr's Tomb and Church," *JThS*, n.s. 17 (1966), 24 ff.

[4]I. Travlos, "Anaskaphai en tê Bibliothêkê tou Adrianou," *Praktika tês . . . Archaiologikês Hetaireias* (1950), 41 ff.; cf. A. Frantz, "From Paganism to Christianity in Athens," *DOP*, 19 (1965), 196.

[5]For political history, G. Ostrogorsky's *Geschichte des byzantinischen Staates*, 3rd ed. (Munich, 1963), is the best guide. This work has been translated into French and English. For a more comprehensive account, including history, institutions, and culture, see L. Bréhier, *Le Monde byzantin*, 3 vols. (Paris, 1947–50).

CHAPTER TWO

[1]The distinction is developed by G. Millet, *L'École grecque dans l'architecture byzantine* (Paris, 1916), 214 ff.

[2]Cf. J.W. Crowfoot, *Early Churches in Palestine* (London, 1941), 104 ff.

[3]The best available discussion is by J.B. Ward-Perkins, "Notes on the Structure and Building Methods of Early Byzantine Architecture," in *The Great Palace of the Byzantine Emperors, Second Report*, ed. D. Talbot Rice (Edinburgh, 1958), 58 ff. See also F.W. Deichmann, *Studien zur Architektur Konstantinopels* (Baden-Baden, 1956), 19 ff. The pioneer work by A. Choisy, *L'Art de bâtir chez les Byzantins* (Paris, 1883), deserves notice, but has been largely superseded.

[4]See A. Boëthius and J.B. Ward-Perkins, *Etruscan and Roman Architecture*, Pelican History of Art (Harmondsworth, 1970), 246 ff.

[5]This obvious truth is explained by K.A.C. Creswell, *Early Muslim Architecture*, I, pt. 2, 2nd ed. (Oxford, 1969), 470 ff.

[6]G. Anrich, *Hagios Nikolaos*, I (Leipzig-Berlin, 1913), 304 ff.

[7]H. Vincent and F.-M. Abel, *Jérusalem nouvelle*, fasc. I–II (Paris, 1914), 220, 244.

[8]G.H. Forsyth, "The Monastery of St. Catherine at Mount Sinai," *DOP*, 22 (1968), 8–9 and fig. 21.

[9]See J.B. Ward-Perkins, "Tripolitania and the Marble Trade," *JRS*, 41 (1951), 89 ff.

[10]These and many other marbles used in antiquity are discussed and illustrated by R. Gnoli, *Marmora Romana* (Rome, 1971).

[11]See J.B. Ward-Perkins, "Roman Garland Sarcophagi from the Quarries of Proconnesus," *Smithsonian Report for 1957* (Washington, D.C., 1958), 455 ff.; idem, "The Imported Sarcophagi of Roman Tyre," *Bulletin du Musée de Beyrouth*, 22 (1969), 113 ff., 132 ff.

[12]See A.H.M. Jones, *The Later Roman Empire*, II (Oxford, 1964), 1013; G. Downey, "Byzantine Architects: Their Training and Methods," *Byzantion*, 18 (1946–48), 99 ff.

[13]Procopius, *De aedificiis*, II.iii.2, 7 (Dara); II.viii.25 (Zenobia).

[14]I can cite only two: Patrikês, who, about 830, built the palace of Bryas (*Theophanes continuatus* [Bonn, 1838], 98), but he may have been more of a supervisor than a professional builder since he held the rank of patrician; and Nikephoros, who in the early twelfth century erected the monastery of Christ Pantocrator at Constantinople: G. Moravcsik, *Szent László leánya és a Bizánci Pantokrator-Monostor* (Budapest-Constantinople, 1923), 44.

[15]Jones, *Later Roman Empire*, II, 1014.

[16]Ibid., 858 ff.

[17]*Le Livre du préfet*, ed. J. Nicole (Geneva, 1893), ch. XXII; English translation in C. Mango, *The Art of the Byzantine Empire 312–1453: Sources and Documents in the History of Art*, ed. H. W. Janson (Englewood Cliffs, N. J., 1972), 206 ff.

[18]Eusebius, *Vita Constantini*, III.29 ff.; English translation in Mango, *Sources and Documents*, 11 ff.

[19]*Epistula XXV*, ed. F. Pasquali in *Gregorii Nysseni opera*, VIII/2 (Leiden, 1959), 79 ff.; English translation in Mango, *Sources and Documents*, 27 ff.

[20]Mark the Deacon, *Vita Porphyrii*, ed. H. Grégoire and M.-A. Kugener (Paris, 1930), ch. 75 ff.; English translation in Mango, *Sources and Documents*, 30 ff.

[21]See W. Djobadze in *IstMitt*, 15 (1965), 228 ff.

[22]See C. Mango, "Isaurian Builders," in *Polychronion: Festschrift F. Dölger* (Heidelberg, 1966), 358 ff.

[23]The imperial legislation on public buildings is discussed by Y. Janvier, *La Législation du Bas-Empire romain sur les édifices publics* (Aix-en-Provence, 1969).

[24]See A.H.M. Jones, "Church Finance in the Fifth and Sixth Centuries," *JThS*, n.s. 11 (1960), 84 ff.

[25]Agnellus, *Liber Pontificalis ecclesiae Ravennatis*, ed. O. Holder-Egger, "Monumenta Germaniae Historica, Scriptores rerum Longobardicarum et Italicarum" (1878), *De Ecclesio*, ch. 59.

CHAPTER THREE

[1]See *Gerasa, City of the Decapolis*, ed. C.H. Kraeling (New Haven, Conn., 1938).

[2]Ibid., 476 ff.

[3]Ibid., 162 ff., 470 ff.

[4]The excavations, started in 1912, are still in progress. A great number of preliminary reports have been published, but there is no up-to-date synthesis. See the articles by Dj. Mano-Zisi and others in *Starinar*, n.s. 7/8 (1958), 311 ff.; 9/10 (1959), 295 ff.; 12 (1961), 11 ff.; 15/16 (1966), 47 ff.; 17 (1967), 163 ff.; 19 (1969), 111 ff.

[5]See H. Spanner and S. Guyer, *Rusafa* (Berlin, 1926), and the reports by J. Kollwitz in *AA*, 1954, 119 ff.; 1957, 64 ff.; 1963, 328 ff.; idem in *AArchSyr*, 8/9 (1958–59), 21 ff.; 14 (1964), 75 ff.; W. Karnapp in *AA*, 1968, 307 ff.; 1970, 98 ff.

[6]Briefly described by C. Preusser, *Nordmesopotamische Baudenkmäler* (Leipzig, 1911), 44 ff.

[7]See the summary account by J. Lauffray in *AArchSyr*, 1 (1951), 41 ff.

[8]The most comprehensive account of Constantinople is that of R. Janin, *Constantinople byzantine*, 2nd ed. (Paris, 1964), but it hardly does justice to the archaeological remains. Among earlier works see esp. A. van Millingen, *Byzantine Constantinople* (London, 1899). On the early history of the city, see H.-G. Beck, ed., *Studien zur Frühgeschichte Konstantinopels*, "Miscellanea byzantina Monacensia," 14 (1973).

[9]*Codex Theodosianus*, XV.1.47.

[10]See J. Ebersolt, *Le Grand Palais de Constantinople* (Paris, 1910); R. Guilland, *Études de topographie de Constantinople byzantine*, 2 vols. (Berlin, 1969).

[11]See P. Verzone, "I due gruppi in porfido di S. Marco in Venezia . . . ," *Palladio*, n.s. 8 (1958), 8 ff.; R. Naumann, "Der antike Bau beim Myrelaion," *IstMitt*, 16 (1966), 209.

[12]See Van Millingen, *Byzantine Constantinople*; B. Meyer-Plath and A.M. Schneider, *Die Landmauer von Konstantinopel* (Berlin, 1943).

[13]*Notitia urbis Constantinopolitanae*, in *Notitia dignitatum*, ed. O. Seeck (Berlin, 1876), 229 ff.

[14]See F.W. Deichmann, "Frühchristliche Kirchen in antiken Heiligtümern," *JdI*, 54 (1939), 103 ff.; A. Frantz, "From Paganism to Christianity in the Temples of Athens," *DOP*, 19 (1965), 187 ff.

CHAPTER FOUR

[1]*Codex Theodosianus*, XIII. 4.1.

[2]*Historia nova*, II.32, confirmed by the earlier testimony of Themistius, *Oratio*, 3, 47 c–d.

[3]Evagrius, *Historia ecclesiastica*, VIII.1.5.

[4]Ibid., X.4.37 ff.

[5]The literature on the origin of the Christian basilica is immense and, for the most part, sterile. Among more recent contributions, see P. Lemerle, "A propos des origines de l'édifice culturel chrétien," *Académie Royale de Belgique, Bulletin de la Classe des Lettres*, 1948, 306 ff.; J.B. Ward-Perkins, "Constantine and the Origins of the Christian Basilica," *Papers of the British School at Rome*, 22 (1954), 69 ff.; R. Krautheimer, "Constantine's Church Foundations," *Akten des VII. Internationalen Kongresses für Christliche Archäologie, Trier 1965*, 237 ff.; idem, "The Constantinian Basilica," *DOP*, 21 (1967), 117 ff.

[6]See A. van Millingen, *Byzantine Churches in Constantinople: Their History and Architecture* (London, 1912), 35 ff.; J. Ebersolt and A. Thiers, *Les Églises de Constantinople* (Paris, 1913), 3 ff.; T.F. Mathews, *The Early Churches of Constantinople: Architecture and Liturgy* (University Park, Pa., 1971), 19 ff. The accepted date of construction (463) should, I believe, be pushed back by about ten years.

[7]See C. Diehl, Le Tourneau, and Saladin, *Monuments chrétiens de Salonique* (Paris, 1918), 35 ff.; S. Pelekanidis, *Palaiochristianika mnêmeia Thessalonikês* (Thessalonica, 1949), 12 ff.; A. Xyngopoulos, "Peri tên, Acheiropoiêton Thessalonikês," *Makedonika*, 2 (1953), 472 ff.

[8]For the Aegean basin, see the useful synthesis by A.K. Orlandos, *Hê xylostegos palaiochristianikê basilikê*, 2 vols. (Athens, 1950–57).

[9]See D. Pallas in *To ergon tês Archaiologikês Hetaireias* (1961), 141 ff.

[10]The plan published by G.E. Jeffery, "The Basilica of Constantia, Cyprus," *The Antiquaries Journal*, 8 (1928), 345, is in need of considerable revision. Cf. A.H.S. Megaw in *Journal of Hellenic Studies*, 15 (1955), Supplement (Archaeological Reports), 33.

[11]For a partial catalogue of these capitals, see E. Kitzinger, "The Horse and Lion Tapestry at Dumbarton Oaks," *DOP*, 3 (1946), 65 ff.

[12]See J. Lassus, "Les Édifices du culte autour de la basilique," *Atti del VI Congresso Internazionale di Archeologia Cristiana, Ravenna, 1962* (Vatican City, 1965), 581 ff.

[13]See especially A. Grabar, *Martyrium*.

[14]See H. Delehaye, *Les Origines du culte des martyrs* (Brussels, 1933), 50 ff.

[15]Excavation report: W. Harvey and J.H. Harvey, "Recent Discoveries at the Church of the Nativity, Bethlehem," *Archaeologia*, 87 (1938), 7 ff.

[16]See esp. Vincent and Abel, *Jérusalem nouvelle*, fasc. I–II, 154 ff.; E.K.H. Wistrand, *Konstantins Kirche am Heiligen Grab in Jerusalem* (Göteborg, 1952).

[17]See, for example, R. Krautheimer, *Early Christian and Byzantine Architecture*, Pelican History of Art (Harmondsworth, 1965), 39 ff. and fig. 16. The foundations of the Constantinian apse have recently been discovered. See C. Coüasnon, *The Church of the Holy Sepulchre in Jerusalem* (London, 1974), 41 ff. and pls. VIII, XI.

[18]See Vincent and Abel, *Jérusalem nouvelle*, fasc. I–II, 337 ff.; H. Vincent, "L'Eléona, sanctuaire primitif de l'Ascension," *RBibl*, 64 (1957), 48 ff. Half a century later (c. 375), a Roman lady called Poimenia built an octagonal church on the summit of the Mount of Olives, marking the supposed site of the Ascension and enclosing the miraculous traces left by Christ's feet. On the latter see J.T. Milik, *RBibl*, 67 (1960), 557 ff.; A. Ovadiah, *Corpus of the Byzantine Churches in the Holy Land* (Bonn, 1970), no. 74.

[19]G.A. and M.G. Soteriou, *Hê basilikê tou Hagiou Dêmêtriou Thessalonikês*, 2 vols. (Athens, 1952); P. Lemerle, "Saint-Démétrius de Thessalonique . . . ," *BCH*, 77 (1953), 660 ff.

[20]On the saint's life, see H. Delehaye, *Les Saints stylites* (Brussels, 1923), ii–xxxiv. On the monument, D. Krencker, *Die Wallfahrtkirche des Simeon Stylites* (Berlin, 1939); J. Lassus, *Sanctuaires chrétiens de Syrie* (Paris, 1947), 129 ff.; G. Tchalenko, *Villages antiques de la Syrie du nord*, I (Paris, 1953), 223 ff.

[21]As attested by Evagrius, *Hist. eccles.*, I.14.

[22]The argument in favor of Constantine is presented by R. Krautheimer, "Zu Konstantins Apostelkirche in Konstantinopel," *Mullus: Festschrift T. Klauser* (Münster, 1964), 224 ff.; the opposite view by G. Downey, "The Builder of the Original Church of the Apostles," *DOP*, 6 (1951), 53 ff.

[23]See above, ch. 2, n. 19.

[24]See *Antioch-on-the-Orontes*, II (Princeton, 1938), 5 ff.; Lassus, *Sanctuaires chrétiens*, 123 ff.

[25]See J.W. Crowfoot, *Churches at Bosra and Samaria-Sebaste* (London, 1937), 1 ff.; W. E. Kleinbauer, "The Origin and Functions of the Aisled Tetraconch Churches in Syria and Northern Mesopotamia," *DOP*, 27 (1973), 91 ff.

[26]See J. Kollwitz in *AA*, 1957, 100.

[27]See A. Grabar, *L'Empereur dans l'art byzantin* (Paris, 1936).

[28]See I. Lavin, "The House of the Lord," *Art Bulletin*, 44 (1962), 1 ff.; R. Naumann and H. Belting, *Die Euphemia-Kirche am Hippodrom zu Istanbul* (Berlin, 1966), 13 ff.

[29]J. Sauvaget, "Les Ghassanides et Sergiopolis," *Byzantion*, 14 (1939), 115 ff.

CHAPTER FIVE

[1]*De aedificiis*, VI.vii.17.

[2]A. Ovadiah, *Corpus*, table 1.

[3]See the field reports by R. M. Harrison and N. Fıratlı in *DOP*, 19 (1965), 230 ff.; 20 (1966), 222 ff.; 21 (1967), 272 ff.; 22 (1968), 195 ff.

[4]On the original function of the church see C. Mango, "The Church of Sts. Sergius and Bacchus at Constantinople . . . ," *Jahrbuch der Österreichischen Byzantinistik*, 21 (1972), 189 ff. On its architectural features, P. Sanpaolesi, "La Chiesa dei SS. Sergio e Bacco e Constantinopoli," *Rivista dell'Istituto nazionale di Archeologia e Storia dell'Arte*, n. s. 10 (1961), 116 ff.; Mathews, *The Early Churches of Constantinople*, 42 ff.; and the older accounts by Van Millingen, *Churches*, 62 ff.; Ebersolt and Thiers, *Églises*, 21 ff.

[5]See A. M. Schneider, *Die Grabung im Westhof der Sophienkirche*, IstForsch, 12 (Berlin, 1941).

[6]On his contribution to mathematics, see G. L. Huxley, *Anthemius of Tralles* (Cambridge, Mass., 1959).

[7]The excellent account of this church by W. S. George, *The Church of Saint Eirene at Constantinople* (Oxford, 1912), has not yet been superseded, although much more of the structure is apparent today than was the case in the early years of this century.

[8]*De aedificiis*, I.i.68 ff. For a technical discussion of the structural problems of St. Sophia, see R. J. Mainstone, "Justinian's Church of St. Sophia," *Architectural History*, 12 (1969), 39 ff.

[9]See K. J. Conant, "The First Dome of St. Sophia, and Its Rebuilding," *Bulletin of the Byzantine Institute*, I (1946), 71 ff.

[10]See W. Emerson and R. L. Van Nice, "Hagia Sophia, Istanbul . . . ," *American Journal of Archaeology*, 47 (1943), 423 ff.

[11]J. C. Hobhouse, *A Journey through Albania . . . to Constantinople*, 2nd ed., II (London, 1813), 971.

[12]*Constantinople*, new ed. (Paris, 1857), 272.

[13]See the account by E. Unger in E. Mamboury and T. Wiegand, *Die Kaiserpaläste von Konstantinopel* (Berlin-Leipzig, 1934), 54 ff.

[14]P. Forchheimer and J. Strzygowski, *Die byzantinischen Wasserbehälter von Konstantinopel* (Vienna, 1893), 57. K. Wulzinger, *Byzantinische Baudenkmäler zu Konstantinopel* (Hannover, 1925), 94 ff., has tried to show that Binbir Direk was not a cistern.

[15]*Manuel d'art byzantin*, 2nd ed. (Paris, 1925), I, 151.

[16]See K. O. Dalman, *Der Valens-Aquädukt in Konstantinopel*, IstForsch, 3 (Bamberg, 1933), 23 ff.

[17]*Description de l'Asie Mineure*, I (Paris, 1839), 55 ff. and pl. 4.

[18]See R. Farioli, *Ravenna paleocristiana scomparsa* (Ravenna, 1961).

[19]G. Bovini, "La nuova abside di S. Apollinare Nuovo," *FelRav*, 57 (1951), 5 ff.

[20]*Liber Pontificalis eccl. Rav., De Ecclesio*, ch. 59.

[21]F. W. Deichmann, "Giuliano Argentario," *FelRav*, 56 (1951), 5 ff.

[22]Ebersolt, *Le Grand Palais de Constantinople*, 78 ff.

[23]G. Bovini, "L'impiego dei tubi fittili nelle volte degli edifici di culto ravennati," *FelRav*, 81 (1960), 90.

[24]A. Guillou, *Régionalisme et indépendance dans l'empire byzantin au VIIᵉ siècle* (Rome, 1969), 77 ff.

[25]*Architecture and Other Arts*, publication of an American Archaeological Expedition to Syria in 1899–1900, pt. II (New York, 1903), 180.

[26]Tchalenko, *Villages antiques de la Syrie du nord*, I, 344; idem, "Travaux en cours dans la Syrie du nord," *Syria*, 50 (1973), 134 ff.

[27]Lassus, *Sanctuaires chrétiens*, 235 ff.

[28]*Syria*, publication of the Princeton University Archaeological Expedition to Syria in 1904–5 and 1909, div. II, sect. B, by H. C. Butler (Leiden, 1920), 26 ff.

[29]Cf. Creswell, *Early Muslim Architecture*, 614 ff.

[30]G. H. Forsyth, "The Monastery of St. Catherine on Mount Sinai . . . ," *DOP*, 22 (1968), 1 ff.

[31]See *Forschungen in Ephesos*, IV/3. *Die Johanneskirche* (Vienna, 1951).

[32]On Philippi see P. Lemerle, *Philippes et la Macédoine orientale* (Paris, 1945), 415 ff.; on the Katapoliani see H. H. Jewell and F.W. Hasluck, *The Church of Our Lady of the Hundred Gates* (London, 1920); A. K. Orlandos, "La Forme primitive de la cathédrale paléochrétienne de Paros," *Atti del VI Congresso Intern. di Archeol. Crist., Ravenna, 1962*, 159 ff.

[33]A. K. Orlandos, "Neôterai hereunai en Hagiô Titô tês Gortynês," *Ep. Het. Byz. Sp.*, 3 (1926), 301 ff.

CHAPTER SIX

[1]H. A. Thompson, "Athenian Twilight: A. D. 267–600," *JRS*, 49 (1959), 70.

[2]R. L. Scranton, *Mediaeval Architecture*, Corinth, XVI (Princeton, 1957), 27 ff.

[3]See ch. 7, n. 43.

[4]See ch. 7, n. 45.

[5]See Diehl, Le Tourneau, and Saladin, *Monuments chrétiens de Salonique*, 117 ff.; M. Kalligas, *Die Hagia Sophia von Thessalonike* (Würzburg, 1935), argues for a date in the early eighth century.

[6]Krautheimer, *Early Christian and Byzantine Architecture*, 180.

[7]See T. Schmit, *Die Koimesis-Kirche von Nikaia* (Berlin-Leipzig, 1927), based on a survey made in 1912; H. Grégoire, "Encore le monastère d'Hyacinthe à Nicée," *Byzantion*, 5 (1930), 287 ff.; C. Mango, "The Date of the Narthex Mosaics of the Church of the Dormition at Nicaea," *DOP*, 13 (1959), 245 ff.; U. Peschlow, "Neue Beobachtungen zur Architektur und Ausstattung der Koimesiskirche in Iznik," *IstMitt*, 22 (1972), 145 ff.

[8]See H. Rott, *Kleinasiatische Denkmäler* (Leipzig, 1908), 327 ff.; F. Darsy, "Il sepolcro di S. Nicola a Mira," *Mélanges E. Tisserant*, II, Studi e Testi, 232 (Vatican City, 1964), 29 ff.; Y. Demiriz, "Demre'deki Aziz Nikolaos Kilisesi," *Türk arkeoloji dergisi*, 15/1 (1968), 13 ff.

[9]G. de Jerphanion, *Mélanges d'archéologie anatolienne*, Mélanges de l'Université Saint-Joseph, 13 (Beirut, 1928), 113 ff.

[10]"The Byzantine Church at Vize (Bizye)," *ZVI*, 11 (Belgrade, 1968), 9 ff. S. Eyice, "Les Monuments byzantins de la Thrace turque," *Corsi di cultura sull'arte ravennate e bizantina, 1971*, 293 ff., dates this church in the thirteenth or fourteenth century.

[11]J. Morganstern in *DOP*, 22 (1968), 217 ff.; 23/24 (1969–70), 383 ff.

[12]H. Buchwald, *The Church of the Archangels in Sige near Mudania* (Vienna-Köln-Graz, 1969).

[13]Briefly described by F.W. Hasluck in *BSA*, 13 (1906–7), 285 ff. The churches of Pelekete and Megas Agros are discussed by the author and I. Ševčenko in *DOP*, 27 (1973), 235 ff.

[14]J. Strzygowski, *Die Baukunst der Armenier und Europa*, 2 vols. (Vienna, 1918). Among several other monographs on Armenian architecture, I may mention: N. M. Tokarskij, *Architektura Armenii*, 2nd ed. (Erevan, 1961); A. L. Jakobson, *Očerk istorii zodčestva Armenii* (Moscow-Leningrad, 1950). G. N. Čubinašvili, *Razyskanija po armjanskoj architekture* (Tbilisi, 1967), challenges the accepted chronology of several key monuments. A good pictorial guide is provided by *Architettura medievale armena*, published in connection with an exhibition at the Palazzo Venezia (Rome, 1968).

[15]Cf. P. Charanis, *The Armenians in the Byzantine Empire* (Lisbon, 1963).

[16]See A. Khatchatrian, *L'Architecture arménienne du IVᵉ au VIᵉ siècle* (Paris, 1971), 94 ff.

[17]On the Tur 'Abdin see G. L. Bell, *Churches and Monasteries of the Tur 'Abdin and Neighbouring Districts* (Heidelberg, 1933); on Binbirkilise, W. M. Ramsay and G. L. Bell, *The Thousand and One Churches* (London, 1908); S. Eyice, *Karadağ (Binbirkilise) ve Karaman çevresinde arkeolojik incelemeler* (Istanbul, 1971).

[18]See G. N. Čubinašvili, *Pamjatniki tipa Džvari* (Tbilisi, 1948); A. B. Eremjan, *Hram Ripsime* (Erevan, 1955).

[19]See M. and N. Thierry, "La Cathédrale de Mrèn et sa décoration," *CahArch*, 21 (1971), 43 ff.

[20]Bell, *Churches and Monasteries of the Tûr 'Abdin*, 82 ff.

CHAPTER SEVEN

[1]The relevant texts are translated in Mango, *Sources and Documents*, 160 ff., 192 ff.

[2]See S. Eyice, "Bryas Sarayı," *Belleten*, vol. 23, no. 89 (1959), 79 ff.

[3]See J. Lassus, *Sanctuaires chrétiens*, 264 ff.; Tchalenko, *Villages antiques*, I, 145 ff.

[4]See P. Lemerle, "Un aspect du rôle des monastères à Byzance: Les monastères donnés à des laïcs," *CRAI*, 1967, 9 ff.

[5]See A. K. Orlandos, *Monastêriakê architektonikê*, 2nd ed. (Athens, 1958).

[6]See T. Macridy, A. H. S. Megaw, C. Mango, and E. J. W. Hawkins, "The Monastery of Lips (Fenari Isa Camii) at Istanbul," *DOP*, 18 (1964), 249 ff.; C. Mango and E. J. W. Hawkins, "Additional Finds at Fenari Isa Camii, Istanbul," *DOP*, 22 (1968), 177 ff.

[7]Cf. A. Grabar, *Recherches sur les influences orientales dans l'art balkanique* (Paris, 1928), 16 ff.

[8]Van Millingen, *Churches*, 196 ff.; Ebersolt and Thiers, *Églises*, 139 ff.; D. Talbot Rice, "Excavations at Bodrum Camii, 1930," *Byzantion*, 8 (1933), 151 ff.; C. L. Striker, "A New Investigation of the Bodrum Camii and the Problem of the Myrelaion," *Istanbul Arkeoloji Müzeleri Yilliği*, 13/14 (1967), 210 ff. A more detailed investigation of the monument by Mr. Striker is expected.

[9]See Diehl, Le Tourneau, and Saladin, *Les Monuments chrétiens de Salonique*, 153 ff.; D. E. Evangelidis, *Hê Panagia tôn Chalkeôn* (Thessalonica, 1954). The church was drastically restored in 1936.

[10]Michael Psellus, *Chronographia*, Basil II, ch. 20.

[11]A convenient checklist has been compiled by C. and L. Bouras, "Byzantine Churches of Greece," *Architectural Design*, 43 (Jan. 1972), 30 ff.

[12]L. Petit, "Vie et office de S. Euthyme le Jeune," *ROChr*, 8 (1903), 192 ff.

[13]Orlandos, *Archeion*, 7 (1951), 146 ff.

[14]M. G. Soteriou, "Ho naos tês Skripous tês Boiôtias," *Arch. Eph.* (1931), 119 ff. The church appears to have been monastic.

[15]A. Grabar, *Sculptures byzantines de Constantinople* (Paris, 1963), 90 ff.; A. H. S. Megaw, "The Skripou Screen," *BSA*, 61 (1967), 1 ff.

[16]See E. G. Stikas, *To oikodomikon chronikon tês monês Hosiou Louka Phôkidos* (Athens, 1970), 178 ff.

[17]See H. Megaw, "The Chronology of Some Middle-Byzantine Churches," *BSA*, 32 (1931–32), 104 ff.; G. C. Miles, "Byzantium and the Arabs," *DOP*, 18 (1964), 20 ff.

[18]A. K. Orlandos, "To petalomorphon toxon en tê byzantinê Helladi," *Ep. Het. Byz. Sp.*, 11 (1935), 411 ff.

[19]See K. A. C. Creswell, *Early Muslim Architecture,* II (Oxford, 1940), 42 ff., 62, and pl. 14. The view that this form of decoration was descended from Late Roman practice as manifested in the western provinces appears historically most unlikely. See S. Bettini, "Origini romano-ravennati della decorazione ceramoplastica bizantina," *Atti del V Congresso Internazionale di Studi Bizantini,* Rome, 1936, II, 22 ff. On a related problem, see A. H. S. Megaw, "Byzantine Reticulate Revetments," *Charistêrion eis A. K. Orlandon,* III (Athens, 1966), 10 ff.

[20]See the brief sketches by G. Balş, "Notiţă despre arhitectura Sfântului Munte," *Buletinul Comisiunii Monumentelor Istorice,* VI (Bucharest, 1913), 1 ff.; and P. M. Mylonas, "L'Architecture du Mont Athos," in *Le Millénaire du Mont Athos,* II (Chevetogne, 1963), 229 ff. (without illustrations). A comprehensive study is still lacking. On Lavra see G. Millet, "Recherches au Mont-Athos," *BCH,* 29 (1905), 72 ff.

[21]E. Stikas, *L'Église byzantine de Christianou* (Paris, 1951), 38 ff.

[22]See J. Strzygowski, "Nea Moni auf Chios," *Byzantinische Zeitschrift,* 5 (1896), 140 ff.; A.K. Orlandos, *Monuments byzantins de Chios,* II (Athens, 1930)—plates only. The legends concerning the monastery have been collected by Gregorios Photeinos, *Ta Neamonêsia* (Chios, 1865). The date of 1045 was copied from a now lost inscription by the Russian monk Barskij in 1731–32: *Stranstvovanija Vasilja Grigoroviča-Barskago,* ed. N. Barsukov, II (St. Petersburg, 1886), 202.

[23]Its plan was published by G. Jeffery in *Proceedings of the Society of Antiquaries,* 2nd ser., 28 (1915–16), 115.

[24]See R. W. Schultz and S. H. Barnsley, *The Monastery of St. Luke of Stiris, in Phocis* (London, 1901); Stikas, *To oikodomikon chronikon.*

[25]M. Chatzidakis, "A propos de la date et du fondateur de Saint-Luc," *CahArch,* 19 (1969), 127 ff., argues that it was a monastic foundation of 1011, while Stikas, *To oikodomikon chronikon,* 9 ff., 244 ff., believes that it was founded by the emperor Constantine IX Monomachos (1042–55). The problem remains open.

[26]Archimandrite Antonin, *O drevnih hristianskih nadpisjah v Afinah* (St. Petersburg, 1874), 4.

[27]The study by G. Millet, *Le Monastère de Daphni* (Paris, 1899), remains fundamental.

[28]See A. Pasadaios, "Hê en Chalkê Monê Panagias Kamariôtissês," *Arch. Eph.* (1971), 1 ff.; T. F. Mathews, "Observations on the Church of Panagia Kamariotissa on Heybeliada . . . ," *DOP,* 27 (1973), 117 ff.

[29]*Embajada a Tamorlán,* ed. F. López Estrada (Madrid, 1943), 37 ff.; English translation in Mango, *Sources and Documents,* 217 ff.

[30]Psellus, *Chronographia,* Michael IV, ch. 31.

[31]Ibid., Constantine IX, ch. 185 ff. English translation in Mango, *Sources and Documents,* 218 ff.

[32]For the relevant documentation see C. Mango, *The Brazen House* (Copenhagen, 1959), 149 ff. An interesting old engraving of the church was later published by S. Eyice, " 'Aslanhane' ve çevresinin arkeolojisi," *Istanbul Arkeoloji Müzeleri Yıllığı,* 11/12 (1964), pl. VII.

[33]*Descrizione topografica dello stato presente di Constantinopoli* (Bassano, 1794), 28.

[34]Leo Diaconus, *Historia* (Bonn, 1828), 128 ff.

[35]R. Demangel and E. Mamboury, *Le Quartier des Manganes* (Paris, 1939), 19 ff. and pl. V.

[36]S. Der Nersessian, *Aght'amar: Church of the Holy Cross* (Cambridge, Mass., 1965), 7 and figs. 59 ff.

[37]*Histoire universelle par Etienne Asolik de Taron, 2e partie,* trans. F. Macler (Paris, 1917), 132 ff.

[38]Briefly described in the *Life of St. Michael Maleinos,* ed. L. Petit, *ROChr,* 7 (1902), 560.

[39]Cf. G. Ostrogrosky, "Observations on the Aristocracy in Byzantium," *DOP,* 25 (1971), 9 ff.

[40]Zonaras, *Epitome historiarum,* III (Bonn, 1897), 767.

[41]Van Millingen, *Churches,* 212 ff.; Ebersolt and Thiers, *Églises,* 171 ff.

[42]Van Millingen, *Churches,* 219 ff.; Ebersolt and Thiers, *Églises,* 185 ff.; A. H. S. Megaw, "Notes on Recent Work of the Byzantine Institute in Istanbul," *DOP,* 17 (1963), 335 ff.

[43]See D. Oates, "A Summary Report on the Excavations . . . in the Kariye Camii," *DOP,* 14 (1960), 223 ff.; P. A. Underwood, *The Kariye Djami,* I (New York, 1966), 8 ff.

[44]C. Mango, "The Monastery of St. Abercius at Kurşunlu . . . ," *DOP,* 22 (1968), 169 ff.

[45]See C. L. Striker and Y. D. Kuban, "Work at Kalenderhane Camii in Istanbul . . . ," *DOP,* 25 (1971), 251 ff.

[46]See F. Uspenskij, "Konstantinopol'skij Saraljskij Kodeks Vos'miknižija," *IRAIK,* 12 (1907), 24 ff. and pls. 1–6; A. K. Orlandos, "Ta byzantina mnêmeia tês Bêras," *Thrakika,* 4 (1933), 7 ff.

[47]See the stimulating observations of O. Demus, *Byzantine Mosaic Decoration* (London, 1948), 10 ff.

[48]See A. K. Orlandos, *Byzantina mnêmeia tês Kastorias* (Athens, 1939).

[49]For the monuments of Byzantine Athens, see *Heuretêrion tôn mnêmeiôn tês Hellados,* A, 1/2 by A. Xyngopoulos (Athens, 1929); I. N. Travlos, *Poleodomikê exelixis tôn Athênôn* (Athens, 1960), 149 ff., who, I believe, exaggerates the prosperity of medieval Athens.

CHAPTER EIGHT

[1]The case of St. Sophia at Trebizond, discussed in this chapter, is exceptional. Note, however, that in the middle of the twelfth century a hall in Seljuk style, with conical domes, stalactite decoration, and a revetment of glazed, cruciform tiles was built in the Imperial Palace of Constantinople. Description in Mango, *Sources and Documents,* 228 ff.

[2]E. H. Swift, *Hagia Sophia* (New York, 1940), 86 ff., 112 ff., also attributes to the Latins the flying buttresses on the west side of the church as well as the belfry that once existed there.

[3]B. Palazzo, *L'Arap Djami* (Istanbul, 1946).

[4]See K. Andrews, *Castles of the Morea* (Princeton, 1953); A. Bon, "Forteresses médiévales de la Grèce centrale," *BCH,* 61 (1937), 136 ff.; idem, *La Morée franque* (Paris, 1969), 601 ff.

[5]R. Traquair, "Frankish Architecture in Greece," *Journal of the Royal Institute of British Architects,* ser. 3, 31 (1924), 33 ff., 73 ff.; Bon, *La Morée franque,* 537 ff.

[6]Cf. A. Bon, "Monuments d'art byzantin et d'art occidental dans le Pélopennèse au XIIIe siècle," *Charistêrion eis A. K. Orlandon,* III, 86 ff. On ribbed vaults see C. Bouras, *Byzantina staurotholia me neurôseis* (Athens, 1965), who points to the earlier but exceptional existence of such vaults in the Theotokos church of Hosios Loukas and in St. Nicholas in the Fields (twelfth century). On belfries there is the rather uncritical study by C. N. Barla, *Morphê kai exelixis tôn byzantinôn kôdônostasiôn* (Athens, 1959).

[7]Cf. A. Xyngopoulos, "Frankobyzantina glypta en Athênais," *Arch. Eph.,* 1931, 69 ff.

[8]See W. Müller-Wiener, "Mittelalterliche Befestigungen im südlichen Jonien," *IstMitt,* 11 (1961), 5 ff.; idem, "Die Stadtbefestigungen von Izmir, Sığacīk und Çandirli," *IstMitt,* 12 (1962), 59 ff.

[9]S. Eyice, "Iznik' de bir Bizans Kilisesi," *Belleten,* 13 (1949), 37 ff.; I. Papadopoulos, in *Ep. Het. Byz. Sp.,* 22 (1952), 110 ff., has attempted to identify this ruin with the church of St. Tryphon, rebuilt by the emperor Theodore II (1254–58).

[10]E. Freshfield, "The Palace of the Greek Emperors of Nicaea at Nymphio," *Archaeologia,* 49 (1886), 382 ff.; S. Eyice, "İzmir yakınında . . . Laskaris'ler sarayı," *Belleten,* 25 (1961), 1 ff.

[11]A. K. Orlandos, *Archeion,* 2 (1936), 70 ff.

[12]Ibid., 1 (1935), 5 ff.

[13]Ibid., 2 (1936), 3 ff.

14A. K. Orlandos, *Hê Parêgorêtissa tês Artês* (Athens, 1963).

15See T. Macridy et al., "The Monastery of Lips," *DOP*, 18 (1964), 251 ff. A general treatment of Palaeologan architecture at Constantinople has been attempted by S. Eyice, *Son devir Bizans mimarisi* (Istanbul, 1963; in Turkish with German résumé).

16C. Mango and E. J. W. Hawkins, "Report on Field Work in Istanbul and Cyprus," *DOP*, 18 (1964), 322.

17Van Millingen, *Churches*, 152 ff.; Ebersolt and Thiers, *Églises*, 227 ff.; Mango and Hawkins, in *DOP*, 18 (1964), 319 ff.

18On Metochites see I. Ševčenko, "Théodore Métochites, Chora et les courants intellectuels de l'époque," in *Art et société à Byzance sous les Paléologues* (Venice, 1971), 15 ff.; on the reconstruction of the Chora, see P. A. Underwood, *The Kariye Djami*, II (New York, 1966), 14 ff.

19Van Millingen, *Churches*, 243 ff.; Ebersolt and Thiers, *Églises*, 149 ff.; H. Hallensleben, "Zu Annexbauten der Kilise Camii in Istanbul," *IstMitt*, 15 (1965), 280 ff.

20Cf. C. Mango, "Constantinopolitana," *JdI*, 80 (1965), 323 ff.

21See S. Eyice, "Trakya'da Bizans devrine ait eserler," *Belleten*, 33 (1969), 351 ff.; idem, "Les Monuments byzantins de la Thrace turque," *Corsi di cultura sull' arte ravennate e bizantina*, 1971, 303 ff.

22Meyer-Plath and Schneider, *Die Landmauer von Konstantinopel*, 95 ff.; Mango, "Constantinopolitana," 330 ff.

23There is no up-to-date treatment of the major Palaeologan churches of Thessalonica; one still has to consult Diehl, Le Tourneau, and Saladin, *Les Monuments chrétiens de Salonique*. For the minor churches see A. Xyngopoulos, *Tessares mikroi naoi tês Thessalonikês* (Thessalonica, 1952). The church now known as St. Panteleimon may be that of the monastery of the Virgin Peribleptos, built shortly before 1314: see G. I. Theocharides, "Ho Matthaios Blastaris," *Byzantion*, 40 (1970), 437 ff.

24An effort in this direction has been made by S. Ćurčić, "The Twin-domed Narthex in Palaeologan Architecture," *ZVI*, 13 (1791), 333 ff.

25Church of the Prophet Elijah: Diehl, Le Tourneau, and Saladin, *Monuments chrétiens de Salonique*, 203 ff. On the identification with Nea Moni: G. I. Theocharidis, "Dyo nea engrapha aphorônta eis tên Nean Monên Thessalonikês," *Makedonika*, 4 (1960), 343 ff. On the monastery tôn Vlattadôn see A. Xyngopoulos, *Tessares mikroi naoi*, 49 ff.; on the date of foundation (between 1351 and 1380), G. I. Theocharidis, "Hoi hidrytai tês en Thessalonikê Monês tôn Vlattadôn," *Panêgyrikos tomos . . . Grêgoriou tou Palama*, ed. P. K. Chrestou (Thessalonica, 1960), 49 ff.

26There is, unfortunately, no monograph on the architecture of Mistra. Much illustrative material has been collected by G. Millet, *Monuments byzantins de Mistra* (Paris, 1910), an album without a text, to which the same author's *L'École grecque* offers a diffuse commentary. See also the excellent guidebook by M. Chatzidakis, *Mystras*, 2nd ed. (Athens, 1956).

27See H. Hallensleben, "Untersuchungen zur Genesis und Typologie des 'Mistratypus,' " *Marburger Jahrbuch für Kunstwissenschaft*, 18 (1969), 105 ff.

28See C. Delvoye, "Considérations sur l'emploi des tribunes dans l'église de la Vierge Hodigitria de Mistra," in *Actes du XIIe Congrès International des Études Byzantines*, III (Belgrade, 1964), 41 ff. Delvoye assumes that the first permanent governor was appointed in 1308. It seems likely, however, that this happened as early as 1286 and cannot, therefore, be related to the design of the Hodegetria.

29See Orlandos, *Archeion*, 1 (1935), 152 ff.

30Ibid., 11 ff.

31Ibid., 53 ff.; idem, "Les Maisons paléologuiennes de Mistra," in *Art et Société à Byzance sous les Paléologues*, 75 ff.

32See Mango, *Sources and Documents*, 252 ff.

33N. Baklanov, "Deux Monuments byzantins de Trébizonde," *Byzantion*, 4 (1927–28), 377 ff.; S. Ballance, "The Byzantine Churches of Trebizond," *Anatolian Studies*, 10 (1960), 146 ff.

34D. Talbot Rice, ed., *The Church of Haghia Sophia at Trebizond* (Edinburgh, 1968).

35*Byzantine Architecture* (London, 1864), 148.

CHAPTER NINE

1See O. Demus, *The Church of San Marco in Venice: History, Architecture, Sculpture* (Washington, D. C., 1960), 70 ff.

2For a clear account of the historical setting see D. Obolensky, *The Byzantine Commonwealth* (London, 1971).

3See F. Uspenskij and K. Škorpil, "Aboba-Pliska," *IRAIK*, 10 (1905), and, for a more up-to-date account, K. Mijatev, *Architekturata v srednovekovna Bŭlgarija* (Sofia, 1965), 30 ff.

4On the date cf. L. Ognenova, "Les Fouilles de Mésambria," *BCH*, 84 (1960), 224.

5See S. Bojadžiev, *Sofijskata cŭrkva sv. Sofija* (Sofia, 1967), who dates it toward the middle of the fifth century.

6Cf. D. Stričević, "La Rénovation du type basilical dans l'architecture . . . des Balkans aux IXe–XIe siècles," *XIIe Congrès International des Études Byzantines, Ochride, 1961, Rapports*, 165 ff.

7For a succinct account of the site see V. Ivanova-Mavrodinova, *Preslav. Vodač za starinite i Muzeja* (Sofia, 1963).

8See K. Mijatev, *Kruglata cŭrkva v Preslav* (Sofia, 1932),.

9E.g., D. Stričević, "L'Église ronde de Preslav," *XIIe Congrès International des Études Byzantines, Ochride, 1961, Rapports*, 212 ff.

10See G. Millet, "L'Église ronde de Preslav," *CRAI* (1933), 180.

11For the history of the city see Académie Bulgare des Sciences, Institute d'Archéologie, *Nessèbre*, I (Sofia, 1969), 15 ff. For the churches, A. Rašenov, *Mesemvrijski cŭrkvi* (Sofia, 1932).

12See O. Feld, "Noch einmal Alexios Apokaukos und die byzantinische Kirche von Selymbria," *Byzantion*, 37 (1967), 57 ff.

13Cf. G. Bošković, "Note sur les analogies entre l'architecture serbe et l'architecture bulgare au Moyen-Age," *Bulletin de l'Institut Archéologique Bulgare*, 10 (1936), 57 ff.

14*L'Ancien art serbe: Les églises* (Paris, 1919).

15N. L. Okunev, "Stolpy sv. Georgija," in *SemKond*, 1 (Prague, 1927), 225 ff.; A. Derocco, "Les Deux églises des environs de Ras," *L'Art byzantin chez les Slaves. Recueil dédié à . . . T. Uspenskij*, I (Paris, 1930), 130 ff.

16See *Studenica* (Belgrade, 1968).

17See V. J. Djurić, *Sopoćani* (Leipzig, 1967).

18N. Okunev, "Aril'e," *SemKond*, 8 (1936), 221 ff.

19V. Petković and D. Bošković, *Dečani*, 2 vols. and album (Belgrade, 1941).

20S. Nenadović, *Bogorodica Ljeviška* (Belgrade, 1963).

21G. Bošković, "Deux Églises de Milutin: Staro Nagoričino et Gračanica," *L'Art byzantin chez les Slaves*, I, 195 ff.

22S. Nenadović, *Dušanova zadužbna manastir sv. Arhandjela kod Prizrena*, Srpska Akademija Nauka, Spomenik, 116 (Belgrade, 1967).

23See V. Korać, "Les Origines de l'architecture de l'école de la Morava," in *Moravska škola i njeno doba* (Belgrade, 1972), 157 ff.

24J. Maksimović, "Moravska skulptura," in *Moravska škola i njeno doba*, 181 ff.

25M. K. Karger, *Drevnij Kiev*, II (Moscow-Leningrad, 1961), 9 ff.

26Ibid., 98 ff.; H. Logvin, *Kiev's Hagia Sophia* (Kiev, 1971).

27A. H. S. Megaw, "The Original Form of the Theotokos Church of Constantine Lips," *DOP*, 18 (1964), 297 ff.

28See V. N. Lazarev, *Iskusstvo Novgoroda* (Moscow-Leningrad, 1947), 53 ff.

29Karger, *Drevnij Kiev*, II, 337 ff.

30Ibid., 275 ff.; V. N. Lazarev, *Mihajlovskie mozaiki* (Moscow, 1966), 25 ff.

31The most authoritative treatment of the monuments of northeastern Russia, including those of Moscow down to the middle of the fifteenth century, is that of N. N. Voronin, *Zodčestvo severo-vostočnoj Rusi*, 2 vols. (Moscow, 1961–62).

32See G. K. Vagner, *Skul'ptura drevnej Rusi* (Moscow, 1969); A. N. Grabar, "Svetskoe izobrazitel'noe iskusstvo domongol'skoj Rusi," Akademija Nauk SSSR, *Trudy Otdela*

Drevne-russkoj Literatury, 18 (1962), 233 ff. On the sculpture of Jur'ev-Pol'skij see G. K. Vagner, *Skul'ptura Vladimiro-Suzdal'skoj Rusi* (Moscow, 1964).

[33]Voronin, *Zodčestvo severo-vostočnoj Rusi,* II, 104 ff.

[34]P. A. Rappoport, "Cerkov' Vasilija v Ovruče," *Sovetskaja Arheologija,* 1 (1972), 82 ff.

[35]See A. I. Nekrasov, *Vozniknovenie Moskovskogo iskusstva,* I (Moscow, 1929), 44 ff.; V. Snegirev, *Aristotel' Fioravanti* (Moscow, 1935).

[36]The only extensive monograph on this church, that of O. Tafrali, *Monuments byzantins de Curtéa de Arges* (Paris, 1931), is, unfortunately, misleading in many respects.

[37]The state of the church before the restoration is recorded by L. Reissenberger, *L'Église du monastère épiscopal de Kurtea d'Argis en Valachie* (Vienna, 1867).

[38]G. Bals, *Influences arméniennes et géorgiennes sur l'architecture roumaine* (Vălenii de Munte, 1931).

[39]P. Henry, "Le Règne et les constructions d'Etienne le Grand," *Mélanges Charles Diehl,* II (Paris, 1930), 43 ff.; Academia Republicii Populare Romîne, *Repertoriul monumentelor şi obiectelor de arta din timpul lui Ştefan cel Mare* (Bucharest, 1958).

[40]See P. Henry, *Les Églises de la Moldavie du nord* (Paris, 1930), 84 ff.

[41]A. Grabar, "L'Origine des façades peintes des églises moldaves," *Mélanges offerts à N. Iorga* (Paris, 1933), 365 ff.; *Rumania: Painted Churches of Moldavia,* Unesco World Art Series (1962).

[42]V. Beševliev, *Die protobulgarischen Inschriften* (Berlin, 1963), nos. 55, 56.

LIST OF ABBREVIATIONS

AA   *Archäologischer Anzeiger*
AArchSyr   *Annales Archéologiques de Syrie*
Arch. Eph.   *Archaiologikê Eqhêmeris*
BCH   *Bulletin de Correspondance Hellénique*
Belleten   *Belleten (Türk Tarih Kurumu)*
BSA   *Annual of the British School at Athens*
CahArch   *Cahiers Archéologiques*
CRAI   *Comptes-rendus des Séances de l'Académie des Inscriptions et Belles-Lettres*
DOP   *Dumbarton Oaks Papers*
Ep. Het. Byz. Sp.   *Epetêris Hetaireias Byzantinôn Spoudôn*

FelRav   *Felix Ravenna*
IRAIK   *Izvestija Russkago Arheologičeskago Instituta v Konstantinopole*
IstForsch   *Istanbuler Forschungen*
IstMitt   *Istanbuler Mitteilungen*
JdI   *Jahrbuch des Deutschen Archäologischen Instituts*
JRS   *Journal of Roman Studies*
JThS   *Journal of Theological Studies*
RBibl   *Revue Biblique*
ROChr   *Revue de l'Orient Chrétien*
SemKond   *Seminarium Kondakovianum*
ZVI   *Zbornik Radova Vizantološkog Instituta*

CHRONOLOGICAL TABLE

This table includes a number of monuments that are not discussed in the text

CONSTANTINOPLE & VICINITY	ASIA MINOR	SYRIA, PALESTINE, CYPRUS	BALKANS & GREECE	ITALY
			c. 300 *Thessalonica,* rotunda	
		314–17 *Tyre,* cathedral		
324 Constantinople founded				
330 Constantinople inaugurated				
326–37 Palace, hippodrome, forum, etc. St. Irene Holy Apostles St. Acacius		326–35 *Jerusalem,* Holy Sepulcher, Eleona, Mt. of Olives *Mambre,* basilica		
		before 333 *Bethlehem,* Nativity Church		
		327–41 *Antioch,* cathedral		
	mid–4th century *Nazianzus,* church	mid–4th century *Bethany,* St. Lazarus *Ruweha,* south basilica		
360 St. Sophia I dedicated				
		2nd half of 4th century *Gerasa,* cathedral *Jerusalem,* Gethsemane basilica		
		368–403 *Constantia (Cyprus),* St. Epiphanius basilica		
	c. 370 *Nyssa,* martyrium	372 *Fâfertin,* basilica		
		before 378 *Jerusalem,* Mt. of Olives, Ascension octagon	late 4th century *Epidaurus,* basilica	late 4th–early 5th century *Ravenna,* Basilica Ursiana
386–93 Column & arch of Theodosius I		c. 381 *Antioch-Kausiye,* St. Babylas		
c. 390 *Hebdomon,* St John the Baptist				
		395–402 *Brâd,* cathedral		
	c. 400 *Ephesus,* St. Mary	402–7 *Gaza,* cathedral		
404 St. Sophia burned Column of Arcadius erected				

357

CONSTANTINOPLE & VICINITY	ASIA MINOR	SYRIA, PALESTINE, CYPRUS	CAUCASUS	BALKANS & GREECE	ITALY	
413 Land Walls						
415 St. Sophia II dedicated						
late 4th–early 5th century Martyrium of Sts. Carpos & Papylos		418 *Dar Qita*, St. Paul & Moses Church				
early 5th century Palace of Antiochus	early 5th century *Hierapolis*, martyrium			early 5th century *Athens*, Ilissos basilica		
					425 *Ravenna*, Mausoleum of Galla Placidia	
					424–34 *Ravenna*, S. Giovanni Evangelista	
c. 450 St. John of Studius St. Mary Chalkoprateia	c. 450 *Ephesus*, St. John I	mid-5th century *Jerusalem*, St. John the Baptist *Et-Tabgha*, Church of Multiplication of Loaves & Fishes *Salamis (Cyprus)*, Kampanopetra basilica		c. 450 *Thessalonica*, Acheiro-poietos, St. Demetrius,	450 *Ravenna*, Orthodox Baptistery	
450–57 Column of Marcian		454–55 *Gerasa*, Bath of Bishop Placcus		450–60 *Corinth-Lechaion*, St. Leonidas		
		c.460 *Qalbloseh*, church		mid-5th century *Stobi*, Episcopal basilica *Philippi*, Basilica A *Nea-Anchialos*, Basilica A		
		464–65 *Gerasa*, Church of Prophets, Apostles & Martyrs				
	c. 470 *Meriamlik*, St. Thekla *Alahan Manasiri*, east church *Dağ Pazari*, church	479–82 *Khan el-Ahmar*, St. Euthymius monastery	478–93 *Bolnisi*, Sion Church	5th?–6th? century *Sofia*, St. Sophia *Peruštica*, Red Church *Adrianople*, tetraconch		
		c. 480 *Tourmanin*, "cathedral"				
		after 484 *Mt. Garizim*, Church of Virgin				
		last quarter of 5th century *Qal'at Saman*				
		late 5th century *nr. Antioch: Seleucia-Pieria*, martyrium				
		494–96 *Gerasa*, St. Theodore			490 *Ravenna*, S. Apollinare Nuovo	

CONSTANTINOPLE & VICINITY	ASIA MINOR	SYRIA & PALESTINE	CAUCASUS	BALKANS & GREECE	ITALY	
	5th–6th century *Perge*, Basilica A	late 5th–early 6th century *Emmaus*, basilica		c. 500 *Nicopolis*, Basilica B		
		507 *Dara*, city founded				
		512 *Bosra*, cathedral				
518–19 Sts. Peter & Paul		515 *Ezra*, St. George				
		before 520 *Resafa*, Basilica A				
		early 6th century *Bosra*, Episcopal Palace				
524–27 St. Polyeuktos		526 *Gerasa*, Procopius Church		527–65 *Caričin Grad* founded		
527–36 Sts. Sergius & Bacchus	1st half of 6th century *Karabel*, triconch	529 *Gerasa*, St. George	6th century *Ereruyk*, church *Tekor*, church *Urbnisi*, church	6th century *Lesbos*, Aphentelli basilica *Belovo*, basilica *Mesembria*, Old Metropolis		
	6th century *nr. Elazığ*, Karamağara Bridge *Silvan (Martyropolis)*, cross church	after 529 *Bethlehem*, Nativity Church rebuilt				
		c. 530 *Resafa*, City Walls *Dara*, refortified *Zenobia*, enlarged		6th century? *Pliska*, basilica		
532 St. Sophia, St. Irene, Baths of Zeuxippus, Great Palace burned		530–31 *Gerasa*, Synagogue Church				
532–37 St. Sophia III		531 *Gerasa*, St. John the Baptist				
after 532 St. Irene		533 *Gerasa*, Sts. Cosmas & Damian				
c. 532 Cistern of "Philoxenus" Cisterna Basilica		before 536 *Gaza*, St. Sergius		2nd quarter of 6th century *Nicopolis*, Basilica A		
		536–48 *Gaza*, St. Stephen				
c. 540 Chalke		c. 540 *Gerasa*, Sts. Peter & Paul		c. 540 *Philippi*, Basilica B		
543 Column of Justinian		541–65 *nr. Antioch*, Monastery of St. Simeon Stylites the Younger			547 *Ravenna*, S. Vitale	
	before 548 *Ephesus*, St. John II	548–65 *Mt. Sinai*, monastery			549 *Ravenna*, S. Apollinare in Classe	

CONSTANTINOPLE & VICINITY	ASIA MINOR	SYRIA & PALESTINE	CAUCASUS	BALKANS & GREECE	ITALY
550 Holy Apostles dedicated		mid-6th century *Aleppo*, Madrasa Halawiya *Ruweha*, Bizzos church		c. 550 *Paros*, Katapoliani	c. 550 *Parenzo*, Basilica Eufrasiana
		before 553 *Resafa*, quatrefoil			
558–62 St. Sophia: dome falls and is rebuilt			c. 560 *Šio-Mgvime*, monastery		
	c. 560 *Sangarios*, bridge	561 *Qasr ibn-Wardan*, barracks			
564 St. Irene repaired		564 *Qasr ibn-Wardan*, palace		2nd half of 6th century *Konjuh*, Round Church	
		c. 564 *Qasr ibn-Wardan*, church			
565–78 Chrysotriklinos		565? *Gerasa*, Propylaea Church			
		569–81? *Resafa*, Praetorium of al-Mundhir			
late 6th century? *Nicaea*, Dormition Church	late 6th century? *Antalya*, Cumanin Camii *Ankara*, St. Clement *Myra*, St. Nicholas		587–604 *Mtzkheta*, Džvari Church	late 6th century *Gortyna*, St. Titus	
			608–28 *Dvin*, cathedral		
		609–10 *Babiska*, St. Sergius	before 609 *Avan*, church		
		611 *Gerasa*, Church of Bishop Genesius	early 7th century *Sisian*, church *Martvili*, church		
			618 *Vagarshapat*, St. Ripsime		
			624–31 *Bagaran*, church		
			626–34 *Tsromi*, St. Savior		
			630–36 *Vagarshapat*, St. Gayane		
			631–39 *Bagavan*, St. John		
			639–40 *Mren, nr. Kars*, church		

CONSTANTINOPLE & VICINITY	ASIA MINOR	SYRIA & PALESTINE	CAUCASUS	GREECE	BULGARIA	
			1st half of 7th century *Ptgni*, church *Ateni*, Sion Church			
			645–60 *Vagarshapat*, Zvartnotz			
			mid–7th century *Mastara*, church *Bana*, cathedral			
			662–85 *Zoravor, nr. Evgard,* church			
after 740 St. Irene rebuilt Land Walls repaired			667–68 *Aruč (Talyš)*, church			
	764–800? *Trilye*, Monastery of Pelekete		2nd half of 7th century *Upper Talin*, church			
	780? *Sige*, Church of Archangels					
				c. 783 *Thessalonica*, St. Sophia		
end of 8th–9th century *Bizye*, St. Sophia	c. 785? *Kurşunlu*, Megas Agros					
	c. 800? *Trilye*, Fatih Camii					
	812 *Alakilise*, basilica repaired					
829–42 Sea Walls repaired Great Palace, additions					814–31 *Pliska*, palace	
					814–31 *Silistra*, palace	
c. 835 *Bryas*, palace						
867–86 Kainourgion renovations of: St. Sophia, Holy Apostles, St. Mocius, St. Mary Chalkoprateia, etc.				870–71 *Peristerai*, St. Andrew		
				871 *Athens*, St. John Mangoutis 873–74 *Skripou (Boeotia),* Panagia		

CONSTANTINOPLE & VICINITY	ASIA MINOR	CAUCASUS	GREECE	BULGARIA	ITALY
	884–85 *Trebizond*, St. Anne				
	end of 9th century? *Dereağzi*, church				
		895 *Zangezur*, Tatev monastery			
				c. 900 *Preslav*, Round Church *Patleina, nr. Preslav*, monastery	
907 Monastery of Constantine Lips: north church					
920 Myrelaion		915–21 *Aght'amar*, church			
	c. 925 *Mt. Kyminas*, Lavra				
			946–55? *Phocis*, Hosios Loukas, Theotokos		
	10th century *Selcikler (Sebaste)*, church *Göreme*, Tokali Kilise, Kiliçlar Kilise		10th century *Athens*, Petraki Monastery, church *Mt. Athos*, Karyes, Protaton		10th century *Stilo*, Cattolica *Rossano*, S. Marco·
		c. 950–60 *Oški*, church		c. 950 *Vinitsa*, church	
		957–91 *Aghpat*, monastery			
			961 *Mt. Athos*, Lavra founded		
		964 *Kumurdo*, church			
		967–72 *Sanain*, Church of Savior			
c. 972 Church of Savior at Chalkê gate					
			c. 980 *Mt. Athos*, Vatopedi founded, Iviron founded		
989 St. Sophia, reconstruction of part of dome and west arch		988–1000 *Ani*, cathedral			
		end of 10th century *Khakhuli*, monastery			

CONSTAN- TINOPLE & VICINITY	ASIA MINOR	CAUCASUS	GREECE	YUGOSLAVIA	BULGARIA	RUSSIA	ITALY
						996 *Kiev*, Tithe Church	
		1001–10 *Ani*, St. Gregory	c. 1000 *Athens*, Holy Apostles				
		1003 *Kutaisi*, Church of Bagrat					
		1010–29 *Mtzkheta*, Sveti-Tzkhoveli church					
		1014 *Nikortsminda*, church					
1028–34 St. Mary Peribleptos		1st quarter of 11th century *Alaverdi*, cathedral *Katzkhi*, church	1028 *Thessalonica*, Panagia tôn Chalkeôn				
		1029 *Marmašen*, monastery					
1034–41 Sts. Cosmas & Damian		1030 *Samtavisi*, cathedral	1st half of 11th century *Phocis*, Hosios Loukas, katholikon *Kastoria*, Kumbelidiki	mid–11th century *Ohrid*, St. Sophia			
		1032 *Iškhani*, church				c. 1036 *Černigov*, Cathedral of Savior	
1042–54 St. George of Mangana		1036 *Ani*, Church of Savior	before 1044 *Athens*, Panagia Lykodemou			1037–c. 1040 *Kiev*, St. Sophia	
		1st half of 11th century *Mitzkheta*, Samtavro Monastery	1045 *Chios*, Nea Moni, katholikon			1045–50 *Novgorod*, St. Sophia	
	10th or 11th century *Üçayak*, double church		c. 1060–70 *Athens*, Sts. Theodoroi, Kapnikarea				1063 *Venice*, S. Marco
11th century *Chalki*, Panagia Kamariotissa	11th century *Göreme*, Elmali Kilise, Çariklī Kilise, Karanlik Kilise					1070–88 *Kiev*, St. Michael of Vydubickij Monastery	
11th century? Kilise Camii			11th century *Megara*, Hosios Meletios *Kastoria*, Anargyroi, St. Basil		11th century *Mesembria*, St. John the Baptist	1073–77 *Kiev*, Monastery of Caves, Dormition Church	
	Tağar, triconch church			1080 *Veljusa*, nr. *Strumica*, Virgin Eleousa			
	nr. *Niğde*, Eski Gümüş, church				1083 *Bačkovo*, funer- ary chapel		

CONSTANTINOPLE & VICINITY	CAUCASUS	GREECE	YUGOSLAVIA	RUSSIA	CYPRUS
		before 1086 *Triphylia*, Christianou church			1090 *Koutsovendis*, St. Chrysostomos
11th or 12th century Christ of the Chora		last quarter of 11th century *Daphni*, monastery church *Kaisariani*, monastery church		end of 11th century *Kiev*, St. Sophia: N, W, & S ambulatories added	
c. 1100 Christ Pantepoptes				c. 1100 *Kiev*, St. Savior na Berestove	
	1106 *Gelati*, monastery founded			1108 *Kiev*, St. Michael founded	
				1113 *Novgorod*, St. Nicholas	
1118–24 Christ Pantocrator: south church				1117–19 *Novgorod*, Church of St. Anthony's Monastery	
before 1136 Christ Pantocrator: north & central churches				1119–40 *Novgorod*, St. George of Jur'ev Monastery	
12th century St. Mary Pammakaristos Gül Camii *Ainos*, Fatih Camii		12th century? *Monemvasia*, St. Sophia			12th century Antiphonitis Apsinthiotissa
		1149 *nr. Nauplia*, H. Moni			
		1152 *Pherrai*, Virgin Kosmosoteira		1152 *Perejaslavl'-Zalesskij*, Church of Transfiguration	
				1158–60 *Vladimir*, Cathedral of Dormition	
				1158–65 *nr. Vladimir*, Castle of Bogoljubovo	
1162 *Elegmi*, St. Abercius			1164 *Nerezi*, St. Panteleimon	1160 *Vladimir-Volynskij*, Cathedral of Dormition	
				1165 *Vladimir, nr., on Nerl' River*, Church of Pokrov	
			c. 1168 *Kuršumlija*, St. Nicholas *nr. Novi Pazar*, Djurdjevi Stupovi	2nd half of 12th century *Polock*, Spaso-Efrosin'jev Monastery	
	1172 *Ikorta*, church	4th quarter of 12th century *Argolis*, Merbaka church *Elis*, Blachernae *nr. Arta*, Blachernae		1179 *Arkaži, nr. Novgorod*, Church of Annunciation	

CONSTANTI-NOPLE & VICINITY	ASIA MINOR	CAUCASUS	GREECE	YUGOSLAVIA	BULGARIA	RUSSIA
						c. 1180 *Novgorod,* St. George at Staraja Ladoga
end of 12th century Kalenderhane Camii				after 1183 *Studenica,* Church of Virgin		
						1191–94: *Smolensk,* St. Michael
						1193–97 *Vladimir,* St. Demetrius
						1198 *Novgorod,* Spas-Neredica
			1st half of 13th century *nr. Bitsibardi (Peloponnese),* Isova Abbey *Andravida,* St. Sophia *nr. Kionia,* Zaraka Abbey			c.1200 *Černigov,* Pjatnica Church
	after 1204 *Manisa,* fortress *Smyrna,* fortress *Priene,* fortress *Ephesus,* fortress *Nicaea,* church *Nymphaion,* palace *Sardis,* church			1207–9 *Žiča,* Church of Ascension		*Ovruč,* St. Basil
						1207 *Novgorod,* Pjatnica Church
		1213–22 *Pitareti,* church				early 13th century *Galič,* St. Panteleimon
		1215 *Ani,* St. Gregory of Abougamrentz	1220–23 *Chlemoutsi,* castle			
			1231–71 *nr. Arta,* Katô Panagia	1230–37 *Mileševo,* Church of Ascension	1230 *Trnovo,* Church of Forty Martyrs	1230–34 *Jur'ev-Pol'skij,* St. George
	1238–63 *Trebizond,* St. Sophia		1250–1350 *Mistra,* Palace of Despots: stage I	2nd quarter of 13th century *Peč,* Holy Apostles		
				c. 1250 *Sopoćani,* Holy Trinity		
1261–91 Tekfursarayī	13th century *Trebizond,* Panagia Chrysokephalos remodeled		13th century *Arta,* St. Basil *Chalkis,* St. Paraskevi	1252 *Morača,* Church of Dormition	13th century *Asenovgrad,* Church of Virgin	
before 1282 Monastery of Constantine Lips: south church	13th or 14th century *Trebizond,* St. Eugenios *Trilye,* Pantobasilissa		1283 *nr. Trikkala,* Porta Panagia			
			1283–96 *Arta,* Parigoritissa			
			1291–92 *Mistra,* Metropolitan Church			1292 *Novgorod,* St. Nicholas na Lipne
			1290–95 *Mistra,* Sts. Theodoroi	1294–95 *Ohrid,* St. Clement		

CONSTAN-TINOPLE & VICINITY	CAUCASUS	GREECE	YUGOSLAVIA	BULGARIA	RUMANIA	RUSSIA
			c. 1296 *Arilje*, St. Achilleios			
	end of 13th century *Safara*, monastery		end of 13th century *Gradac*, Church of Annunciation			
early 14th century *Galata*, Arap Camii Kilise Camii restored	early 14th century *Zarzma*, monastery	1303 *Mt. Athos*, Chilandar	1306–7 *Prizren*, Church of Virgin Ljeviška			
1310 St. Mary Pam-makaristos, parecclesion		1310 *Mistra*,. Brontochion, katholikon	c. 1307 *Čučer*, St. Niketas			
		1312–15 *Thessalonica*, Holy Apostles	1312–13 *Staro Nagoričino*, St. George			
			1313 *Ohrid*, St. Sophia: narthex added			
			1313–14 *Studenica*, King's Church			
1316–21 Christ of Chora restored			1318–21 *Gračanica*, Church of Annunciation			
c. 1325 *Selymbria*, Apokau-kos Church of St. John the Baptist			1327–35 *Dečani*, monastery church			1326 *Moscow*, Cathedral of Dormition
		14th century *Thessalonica*, St. Catherine St. Panteleimon	1332 *Štip*, St. Michael	14th century *Trnovo*, Sts. Peter & Paul *Mesembria*, Pantocrator, St. John Aleitourgetos, Church of Sts. Michael & Gabriel		
14th century? *Ainos*, Fatih Camii: "portico facade"			1337 *Ljuboten*, St. Nicholas			
			1341 *Lesnovo*, Holy Archangels			1345 *Novgorod*, St. Savior at Kovalevo
1346–53 St. Sophia: part of dome and east semidome rebuilt			1343–49 nr. *Prizren*, Holy Archangels		c. 1350 *Curtea de Argeş*, St. Nicholas	1352 *Novgorod*, Church of Dormition at Volotovo
		c. 1360 *Thessalonica*, Prophet Elijah Vlattadon Monastery	c. 1355 *Matejić*, nr. *Kumanovo*, Church of Virgin		1359–65 *Rădăuţi*, St. Nicholas	1360–61 *Novgorod*, St. Theodore Strate-lates
		1350–1400 *Mistra*, Palace of Despots: stage II				1366–67 *Moscow*, Kremlin Walls
			1375 *Ravanica*, monastery church			1374 *Novgorod*, Church of Transfiguration

CONSTANTI-NOPLE & VICINITY	ASIA MINOR	GREECE	YUGOSLAVIA	RUMANIA	RUSSIA
			1377–78 *Kruševac*, Lazarica	1386 *Cozia*, monastery church	
			after 1387 *Ljubostinja*, Church of Virgin		1390s *Moscow*, Church of Annunciation, Church of Nativity
			1389 *Matka*, St. Andrija		
		1400–1460 *Mistra*, Palace of Despots: stage III			c. 1400 *Zvenigorod*, Dormition Church
					1405 *nr. Zvenigorod*, Savva Monastery Church
			1406–18 *Resava (Manasija)*, monastery church		1406 *Novgorod*, Sts. Peter & Paul at Koževniki
			1413–17 *Kalenić*, monastery church		1422 *Zagorsk*, Sergius Monastery
	1427 *Trebizond*, St. Sophia: belfry	1428 *Mistra*, Pantanassa			1425–27 *Moscow*, Andronikov Monastery
1443–48 Land Walls repaired					1470–74 *Moscow*, Dormition Cathedral: stage II
			1466–81 *Putna*, monastery church		1475–79 *Moscow*, Dormition Cathedral: stage III
			1488 *Voroneţ*, monastery church		
			1497 *Neamţ*, monastery church		
			1502 *Dealu*, monastery church		
			1503–4 *Arbore*, monastery church		1505–9 *Moscow*, St. Michael in Kremlin
			1512–21 *Curtea de Argeş*, episcopal church		
			1514–22 *Suceava*, cathedral		
			1517 *Tîrgovişte*, old metropolitan church		
			1530 *Homor*, monastery church		
			1532 *Moldoviţa*, monastery church		
			c. 1580 *Suceviţa*, monastery church		
			1639 *Iaşi*, Church of Three Hierarchs		

SELECTED BIBLIOGRAPHY

REFERENCE

Dumbarton Oaks Bibliographies. Ser. I. *Literature on Byzantine Art, 1892–1967.* Vol. I, *By Location.* Ed. J. S. Allen. Washington, D.C.: Dumbarton Oaks Research Library and Collection, 1973.

Reallexikon zur byzantinischen Kunst. Ed. K. Wessel and M. Restle. Stuttgart: Anton Hiersemann, 1963–.

SOURCES

MANGO, C. *The Art of the Byzantine Empire 312–1453: Sources and Documents in the History of Art.* Englewood Cliffs, N.J.: Prentice-Hall, 1972.

GENERAL

DALTON, O. M. *East Christian Art.* Oxford: Clarendon Press, 1925.

DELVOYE, C. *L'Art byzantin.* Grenoble: Arthaud, 1967.

DIEHL, C. *Manuel d'art byzantin.* 2nd ed., 2 vols. Paris: A. Picard, 1925.

EBERSOLT, J. *Monuments d'architecture byzantine.* Paris: Les Éditions d'Art et d'Histoire, 1934.

GRABAR, A. *Martyrium.* 2 vols. Paris: Collège de France, 1943–46.

KRAUTHEIMER, R. *Early Christian and Byzantine Architecture.* Pelican History of Art. Harmondsworth: Penguin Books, 1965.

ORLANDOS, A. K. *Hê xylostegos palaiochristianikê basilikê.* 2 vols. Athens: Archaiologikê Hetaireia, 1950–57.

VOLBACH, W. F., and LAFONTAINE-DOSOGNE, J. *Byzanz und das christliche Osten.* Propyläen Kunstgeschichte 3. Berlin: Propyläen Verlag, 1968.

CONSTANTINOPLE

ANTONIADIS, E. M. *Ekphrasis tês Hagias Sophias.* 3 vols. Leipzig-Athens: B. G. Teubner / P. D. Sakellariou, 1907–9.

DEICHMANN, F. W. *Studien zur Architektur Konstantinopels im 5. und 6. Jahrhundert nach Christus.* Baden-Baden: B. Grimm, 1956.

EBERSOLT, J., and THIERS, A. *Les Églises de Constantinople.* 2 vols. Paris: E. Leroux, 1913.

MATHEWS, T. F. *The Early Churches of Constantinople: Architecture and Liturgy.* University Park, Pa.: Penn State University Press, 1971.

MILLINGEN, A. VAN. *Byzantine Churches in Constantinople: Their History and Architecture.* London: Macmillan, 1912.

ASIA MINOR

ROTT, H. *Kleinasiatische Denkmäler aus Pisidien, Pamphylien, Kappodokien und Lykien.* Leipzig: Dieterich, 1908.

STRZYGOWSKI, J. *Kleinasien, ein Neuland der Kunstgeschichte.* Leipzig: J. C. Hinrichs, 1903.

SYRIA AND CYPRUS

BUTLER, H. C. *Architecture and Other Arts.* Publication of an American Archaeological Expedition to Syria in 1899–1900. New York: Century, 1903.

————. *Ancient Architecture in Syria.* Sect. A.: *Southern Syria;* Sect. B: *Northern Syria.* Syria: Publication of the Princeton University Archaeological Expeditions to Syria in 1904–5 and 1909, Div. II. 2 pts. Leiden: E. J. Brill, 1919–20.

————. *Early Churches in Syria.* Princeton, N.J.: Published for the Department of Art and Archaeology of Princeton University, 1929.

LASSUS, J. *Sanctuaires chrétiens de Syrie.* Paris: P. Geuthner, 1947.

SOTERIOU, G. A. *Ta byzantina mnêmeia tês Kyprou.* Athens: Akadêmia Athênôn, 1935.

TCHALENKO, G. *Villages antiques de la Syrie du nord.* 3 vols. Paris: P. Geuthner, 1953–58.

PALESTINE

CROWFOOT, J. W. *Early Churches in Palestine.* London: Oxford University Press, 1941.

OVADIAH, A. *Corpus of the Byzantine Churches in the Holy Land.* Bonn: P. Hanstein, 1970.

CAUCASUS

AMIRANAŠVILI, Š. *Istorija gruzinskogo iskusstva.* Moscow: Iskusstvo, 1963.

ARUTJUNJAN, V. M., and SAFARJAN, S. A. *Pamjatniki armjanskogo zodčestva.* Moscow: Gosudarstvennoe izdatel'stvo po stroitel'stvu i arhitekture, 1951.

BERIDZE, V. *Gruzinskaja arhitektura.* Tbilisi: Helovneba, 1967.

JAKOBSON, A. L. *Ocerk istorii zodčestva Armenii.* Moscow-Leningrad: Gosudarstvennoe izdatel'stvo arhitektury i gradostvoitel'stva, 1950.

KHATCHATRIAN, A. *L'Architecture arménienne du IV au VI siècle.* Paris: Klincksieck, 1971.

STRZYGOWSKI, J. *Die Baukunst der Armenier und Europa.* 2 vols. Vienna: A. Schroll, 1918.

TOKARSKIJ, N. M. *Arhitektura drevnej Armenii.* Erevan: Akad. Nauk ACCP, 1946.

GREECE

DIEHL, C.; LE TOURNEAU, M.; and SALADIN, H. *Les Monuments chrétiens de Salonique.* 2 vols. Paris: E. Leroux, 1918.

MEGAW, H. "The Chronology of Some Middle-Byzantine Churches," *Annual of the British School at Athens,* 32(1931–32), 90 ff.

MILLET, G. *L'École grecque dans l'architecture byzantine.* Paris: E. Leroux, 1916.

ORLANDOS, A. K. *Archeion tôn byzantinôn mnêmeiôn tês Hellados.* Athens: Estia, 1935–.

SOTERIOU, G. A.; XYNGOPOULOS, A.; and ORLANDOS, A. K. *Heuretêrion tôn mesaiônikôn mnêmeiôn tês Hellados.* 3 pts. Athens: Estia, 1927–33.

BULGARIA

FILOV, B. *Geschichte der altbulgarischen Kunst.* Berlin-Leipzig: W. de Gruyter, 1932.

MAVRODINOV, N. *Starobŭlgarskoto izkustvo.* Sofia: Nauka i izkustvo, 1959.

MIJATEV, K. *Arhitekturata v srednovekovna Bŭlgarija.* Sofia: Bŭlgarska Akad. na Naukite, 1965.

RUSSIA

HAMILTON, G. H. *The Art and Architecture of Russia.* Pelican History of Art. Harmondsworth: Penguin Books, 1954.

Istorija russkogo iskusstva. I–III. Moscow: Akademija Nauk SSSR, 1953–55.

KARGER, M. K. *Drevnij Kiev.* 2 vols. Leningrad: Akademija Nauk SSSR, 1958–61.

RAPPOPORT, P. A. *Drevnerusskaja arhitektura.* Moscow: Nauka, 1970.

VORONIN, N. N. *Zodčestvo severo-vostočnoj Rusi.* 2 vols. Moscow: Akademija Nauk SSSR, 1961–62.

YUGOSLAVIA

DEROKO, A. *Monumentalna i dekorativna Arhitektura u srednjevekovnoj Srbiji.* 2nd ed. Belgrade: Naučna Kniga, 1962.

MILLET, G. *L'Ancien art serbe: Les églises.* Paris: E. de Boccard, 1919.

PETKOVIĆ, V. P. *Pregled crkvenih spomenika kroz povesnicu Srpskog naroda.* Belgrade: Naučna Kniga, 1950.

RUMANIA

GHIKA BUDESTI, N. *L'Ancienne architecture religieuse de la Valachie.* Buletinul Comisiunii Monumentelor Istorice, 35, facc. 111–12. Bucharest: Institutul de arte grafice Marvan, 1942.

HENRY, P. *Les Églises de la Moldavie du nord.* Paris: E. Leroux, 1930.

IONESCU, N. *Isotoria arhitecturii in Rominia.* 2 vols. Bucharest: Ed. Acad. R. P. Romîne, 1963–65.

IORGA, N., and BAIL, G. *Histoire de l'art roumain ancien.* Paris: E. de Boccard, 1922.

INDEX

LIST OF PLATES

LIST OF PHOTOGRAPHIC CREDITS

Anderson, R.: 36; 43, 85, 86, 90, 95, 102, 103, 150, 152, 153.

Artamonoff, N. V.: 16, 53, 58, 59, 100, 133, 249, 258, 286, 298, 300.

Bildarchiv Foto Marburg, Marburg/Lahn: 75.

Birelli, Diego, Mestre: 108.

Boyd, S.: 255.

Courtauld Institute of Art, London: 229, 329–31.

Deutsches Archäologisches Institut, Istanbul: 296.

Dumbarton Oaks Byzantine Center, Washington, D.C.: 5, 14, 17, 20, 22, 47, 49, 51, 63, 121, 129, 131, 223, 261, 265, 292, 295.

Ephoreia Byzantinon Mnemeion, Athens: 241.

Faculty of Architecture Polytechnic, Milan: 208.

Fogg Art Museum, Harvard University, Cambridge, Mass.: 180.

Gad, Borel-Boissonas, Geneva: 80, 81.

Harrison, Professor R. M., the University of Newcastle upon Tyne: 104, 105.

Jeremić, M.: 348.

Landesmuseum, Trier: 61.

Mango, Professor Cyril, Oxford: 1, 2, 6, 7, 9, 10, 12, 13, 15, 18, 35, 37–41, 44, 50, 60, 87–89, 96, 97, 149, 151, 155, 157–60, 174, 182, 184, 185, 189–92, 194, 211, 213, 235, 268, 297, 316, 317, 320, 327, 328, 333, 350, 383, 384, 386, 390, 391.

Michigan-Princeton-Alexandria Expedition to Mount Sinai: 21, 162, 163.

Morganstern, J.: 187, 188.

Mundell, M. C.: 355.

Novosti Press, Rome: 256, 275, 277, 359, 360, 362, 364–66, 369–74.

Powell, Josephine, Rome: 197–99, 201–3, 207.

Quiresi, Ezio, Cremona: 378, 379, 382, 388, 389.

Regionalni zavod za zaštitu spomenika kulture, Rijeka: 69.

Ševčenko, Professor I.: 23, 106, 216, 266, 321, 322.

Tasič, Dušan, Belgrade: 215, 248, 276.

Thierry, Nicole, Etampes: 210.

Van Nice, R. L.: 19, 225.

Yale University, New Haven: 29, 32.